Research Resource Management

Valerie Anderson

3rd edition

Valerie Anderson, Chartered MCIPD, is a Reader in Human Resource Development at the University of Portsmouth Business School. She has extensive experience of teaching research methods and supervising research projects, dissertations and management reports. Prior to her career in higher education, she undertook a range of HR roles both in the public and private sectors.

The Chartered Institute of Personnel and Development is the leading publisher of books and reports for personnel and training professionals, students, and all those concerned with the effective management and development of people at work. For details of all our titles, please contact the publishing department:
tel: 020 8612 6204
e-mail: publishing@cipd.co.uk
The catalogue of all CIPD titles can be viewed on the CIPD website:
www.cipd.co.uk/bookstore

Research Methods in Human Resource Management

3rd edition

Valerie Anderson

Chartered Institute of Personnel and Development

Published by the Chartered Institute of Personnel and Development,
151, The Broadway, London, SW19 1JQ
First edition published 2004
Reprinted 2004, 2005
Second edition published 2009
Reprinted 2011
This edition first published 2013
© Chartered Institute of Personnel and Development, 2013

Design by Exeter Premedia, India, London
Printed in Great Britain by Ashford Colour Press
British Library Cataloguing in Publication Data
A catalogue of this publication is available from the British Library
ISBN 978 1 84398 308 8

The views expressed in this publication are the author's own and may not necessarily reflect those of the CIPD.

The CIPD has made every effort to trace and acknowledge copyright holders. If any source has been overlooked, CIPD Enterprises would be pleased to redress this in future editions.

Chartered Institute of Personnel and Development, CIPD House,
151 The Broadway, London, SW19 1JQ
Tel: 020 8612 6200
E-mail: cipd@cipd.co.uk
Website: www.cipd.co.uk
Incorporated by Royal Charter.
Registered Charity No. 1079797

Contents

List of figures and tables

Acknowledgements

The preparation of this 3rd edition would not have been possible without the personal and professional support of many people. I would like to thank my family for their unending patience and tolerance while this, and other projects, have been undertaken. Like many students who have to juggle multiple tasks both in and outside of their work lives, I have found myself working on this book in many different places and environments. I thank the parents and players of Solent Suns Basketball team, of which my daughter is a member, for their many cries of "haven't you finished that book yet?" when I have arrived at training sessions and match days armed with my laptop and notes. Their encouragement has spurred me on when the going got tough and the deadlines seemed impossible to achieve. On the subject of deadlines I would also like to thank those involved with publishing this book and the anonymous reviewers for accepting work later than promised and for their insightful and always constructive feedback and advice.

Teaching research methods is a real pleasure to undertake and I find myself intrigued by the experiences and achievements of the students with whom I come into contact. During the preparation of this book I have worked with colleagues from University of Portsmouth on initiating a University Graduate School and developing a new programme of support and development for research degree students across the University. I have benefited greatly from new insights and perspectives about teaching research methods that have resulted from this project, and I would particularly like to thank Dr Brett Stevens, Dr Kay Peggs and Dr Carl Adams for their friendship and ideas.

I am grateful to the publishers who have given permission to reproduce extracts from copyright material, and these are acknowledged individually in the text itself. For this edition of the book I have increased the number of case illustrations and I thank all those whose experiences feature in this edition. The larger number of illustrations has presented some problems in ensuring anonymity for individuals and their work or placement organisations, and so I have substituted 'real names' for all the case illustrations in this edition.

Valerie Anderson

October 2012

CIPD Students

This book has been written to provide a resource for students studying the CIPD module **Investigating a Business Issue from a Human Resources Perspective.** The following table explains how the learning outcomes of that module map to the chapters of this book.

Number	Learning outcome	Mapped to chapters in *Research Methods in HRM*
1	Identify and justify a business issue that is of strategic relevance to the organisation	**Chapter 1** Investigating and researching HR issues; **Chapter 2** First stages towards an HR project; **Chapter 4** Ethics, professionalism and HR research
2	Critically analyse and discuss existing literature, contemporary HR policy and practice relevant to the chosen issue	**Chapter 3** Finding and reviewing HR literature and information sources; **Chapter 6** Finding and using documents and organisational evidence
3	Compare and contrast the relative merits of different research methods and their relevance to different situations	**Chapter 5** Planning the research process; **Chapter 6** Finding and using documents and organisational evidence
4	Undertake a systematic analysis of quantitative and/or qualitative information and present the results in a clear and consistent format	**Chapter 7** Collecting and recording qualitative data **Chapter 8** Analysing qualitative data **Chapter 9** Collecting and recording quantitative data **Chapter 10** Analysing quantitative data.
5	Draw realistic and appropriate conclusions and make recommendations based on costed options	**Chapter 8** Analysing qualitative data **Chapter 10** Analysing quantitative data; **Chapter 11** Writing up your project and making recommendations
6	Develop and present a persuasive business report	**Chapter 11** Writing up your project and making recommendations;
7	Write a reflective account of what has been learned during the project and how this can be applied in the future	**Chapter 11** Writing up your project and making recommendations; **Chapter 12** Developing effective links between research and practice

Walkthrough of textbook features and online resources

LEARNING OUTCOMES

At the beginning of each chapter a bulleted set of learning outcomes summarises what you can expect to learn from the chapter, helping you to track your progress.

LEARNING OUTCOMES

This chapter should help you to:

- examine how your responsibilities as an HR professional are linked to your ethical choices as a researcher
- identify and address ethical issues arising from your research
- complete any necessary ethical approvals process that may be required at your organisation and study centre.

CASE ILLUSTRATION

A range of case studies from different countries illustrate how key ideas and theories are operating in practice around the globe, with accompanying questions or activities.

CASE ILLUSTRATION 4.8

Ethical assessment and scrutiny – another factor for delay?

Annabel was a full-time student about to embark on a work placement during which she would also be undertaking research for a business research report. The research would be organisationally based; the intention was that the placement company and Annabel would choose a business issue on which her project would be based that would be mutually beneficial. When she arrived at her placement on the first day, her placement manager told her that there were 'engagement problems' in two departments in the organisation

must complete an ethical scrutiny form to assure the institution that appropriate standards would be adhered to. Completion of the form required Annabel to indicate her research objectives; the population from which she would draw her sample; the way that the interviewees were to be selected and recruited; the means by which she would ensure they gave informed consent to participate; her plans for recording and storing the information that she gathered; the extent to which she would be able to

ACTIVITIES

In each chapter, a number of questions and activities will get you to reflect on what you have just read and encourage you to explore important concepts and issues in greater depth.

ACTIVITY 4.1

ETHICAL IMPLICATIONS OF CIPD CODE OF CONDUCT

Find the CIPD 2012 Code of Conduct (http://www.cipd.co.uk/about/code-of-conduct-review/profco.htm)

1. Review this document and identify what elements of conduct it specifically highlights and the ethical requirements on CIPD professionals.

2. What are the implications of these standards for HR practitioner-researchers?

REVIEW AND REFLECT

Questions for reflection

This final part of the chapter enables you to reflect about your professional development and develop your skills and knowledge. This will enable you to build your confidence and credibility, track your learning, see your progress and demonstrate your achievements.

Taking stock

1   To what extent are you so familiar with the organisation that your knowledge of many of its features is 'tacit'? What sources of evidence would justify your understanding through making your knowledge explicit?

2   To what extent might images and photographic evidence help you to answer your research questions or provide a useful context for your analysis?

3   In what ways may data from any HR information system be useful to achieving your research objectives? What would be the most helpful format for the data?

REVIEW AND REFLECT

At the end of each chapter, Review and Reflect questions encourage you to pause and reflect on your learning, tracking progress and highlighting any areas of development.

One way of finding out about the advantages and disadvantages of different methods is to read literature sources about your topic for method as well as for content. Every general textbook on research methods will cover issues of methodology. The following list indicates a selection of them.

Reading

Bauer, M.W. and Gaskell, G. (eds) (2000) *Qualitative research with text, image and sound*. London: Sage.

Bryman, A. and Bell, E. (2007) *Business research methods*. Oxford: Oxford University Press.

Creswell, J. (2009) *Research design: qualitative, quantitative and mixed methods approaches*. London: Sage.

Easterby-Smith, M., Thorpe, R. and Lowe, A. (2003) *Management research: an introduction*. London: Sage.

Gill, J., Johnson, P. and Clark, M. (2010) *Research methods for managers*. London: Sage.

EXPLORE FURTHER

Explore further boxes contain suggestions for further reading and useful websites, encouraging you to delve further into areas of particular interest.

ONLINE RESOURCES FOR STUDENTS

● Annotated web-links – access a wealth of useful sources of information in order to develop your understanding of the issues in the text.

ONLINE RESOURCES FOR TUTORS

● PowerPoint slides – design your programme around these ready-made lectures, including figures and tables from the text.

● Lecturer's guide – provides guidance on how to use the book in your teaching, discussing the context of each chapter and responses to in-text learning features.

For online resources, please visit www.cipd.co.uk/orl

PART 1

INTRODUCTION

CHAPTER 1

Investigating and Researching HR Issues

CHAPTER OUTLINE

- Researching HR issues
- Getting started: the research process and the skills you need
- What is research in HR?
- What kind of a researcher are you?
- Requirements for student projects
- Writing your research proposal
- Working with your supervisor
- Managing the research project
- Working as a practitioner-researcher
- Summary
- Review and reflect
- Explore further

LEARNING OUTCOMES

This chapter should help you to:

- define what is meant by research in HR and how it contributes to effective policy and practice

- identify the different components of an effective research project and the skills needed

- compare different approaches to HR research and the opportunities presented by an investigation of a business issue

- discuss the implications of being a 'practitioner-researcher'.

RESEARCHING HR ISSUES

This book is aimed at people who are undertaking an HR research project as part of a qualification-related course. You may be a part-time student who is investigating a business issue in the role of a 'practitioner-researcher' or a full-time student who will be researching into an HR issue either inside or outside of a particular organisation or group of organisations. You may be studying in your own country or abroad.

The ability to undertake good-quality research which leads to relevant practical outcomes and contributes to the knowledge-base of the HR profession is an important skill. Qualified professionals should be able to research relevant topics and write reports that can persuade key stakeholders in the organisation to change or adopt a particular policy and practice. Most people who make use of this book are likely to be: final-year undergraduate students of management or HRM; students undertaking professional HR courses such as the CIPD Intermediate or Advanced level programmes or students undertaking a taught master's course (usually an MSc or MA in HRM or a related subject).

Making a start with a big piece of work like a research project is a daunting prospect and you may be tempted to put off the moment of making a start. This book is intended to help you make a start and then to see the project through to a successful and rewarding conclusion. The book aims to be practical, accessible and relevant. It should provide you with ideas and resources to apply to your research. I hope that you will use it as a resource to develop knowledge, understanding and the practical skills you need to make best use of the research process you are undertaking and to communicate what you have learned in a convincing and credible way. The book is not a substitute for regular attendance at research methods classes nor does it replace the need to communicate with your supervisor or project tutor.

Research projects are rarely completed quickly and they compete for attention with many other important and urgent matters. Different chapters of the book will be relevant at different stages of your project from initial project idea and research proposal to submission of the final report or dissertation.

When research is done well it can provide a 'win-win' opportunity for you and the organisation or organisations that have participated in some way. Your organisation(s) can learn from the findings and decide whether to implement your recommendations. You can gain valuable personal and professional development in a wide range of areas. Each chapter in this book ends with a self-test so that you can check your understanding and there is an opportunity to review and reflect on your achievements so far. This can inform any continuing professional development (CPD) record that you will maintain if you are a member of a professional organisation, such as the CIPD. Ideas about useful reading are also included at the end of each chapter to enable you to go further or deeper as appropriate.

GETTING STARTED: THE RESEARCH PROCESS AND THE SKILLS YOU NEED

ACTIVITY 1.1

A NICE PROBLEM TO SOLVE

Imagine that a good friend contacts you and invites you to join them for a 'once in a life time' holiday somewhere very special. You are very keen to follow this up but you need to know what would be involved in terms of your time and money and the implications of such a trip for your work and other responsibilities. How will you set about finding out more about the country your friend is keen to visit and the different options that might be appropriate for you?

FEEDBACK NOTES

In order to make decisions about whether to accompany your friend and, if so, how to organise the trip, there are a number of questions that you must find the answers to. These might include:

- What are different parts of the holiday destination country like?
- What climate might you expect at different times of the year? What would be the implications for shopping in advance for clothes and equipment?
- What modes of travel are possible? How much time would be spent on getting there, getting around and getting back?
- What facilities does the country or different accommodation options have to offer?
- What is the opinion about the proposed destination by other travellers who have visited?
- What are the cost implications?
- What health insurance and immunisation requirements are there?
- How safe is the country considered to be?

To answer these questions there are a range of sources of information that you might draw on. These include:

- Internet information sites
- travel brochures/publicity materials
- opinions of others (either given to you face-to-face or through social network media)
- recommendations of experienced travellers
- price comparison sites.

With a situation like this, the more sources of information you can draw on, and the more variety of types of information you can gather (opinions as well as sales brochures; statistics as well as recommendations), the more confident you are likely to feel in your ultimate decision. Merely booking a holiday because it is cheap, it was suggested by an acquaintance you do not know *that* well and it was the first option you stumbled across are less likely to result in a happy time. To enhance the fact-finding process you must first be clear what it is you are really looking for. Then it is necessary to find out what is already known about the destination and the travel process. Next you search for further information, obtaining as many different types of data as possible. Finally, you make sense of all the information and make your decision.

THE RESEARCH PROCESS

Activity 1.1 is, at a basic level, a small and personal research activity. It involves the systematic enquiry into an issue to increase knowledge and underpin effective decision-making. The activities it would involve are, however, indicative of the components of any research process (see Figure 1.1).

Figure 1.1 Components of the research process

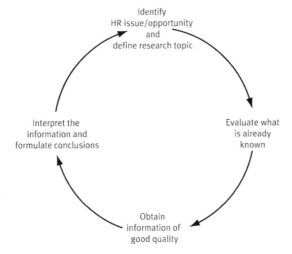

Often research is represented as a series of discrete and linear stages, and this book is structured in a similar sort of way. However, the reality of organisational research is that each stage is often interrelated with the others and experiences in later stages often lead to reconsideration of earlier ones (Saunders et al 2012).

For research undertaken to meet the requirements of the CIPD Advanced level qualifications, the general model in Figure 1.1 is elaborated on by the chief examiner, who emphasises the requirement for CIPD students to:

- diagnose and investigate a live issue of significance to a work organisation
- locate their work within a body of contemporary knowledge
- collect and analyse data
- derive supportable conclusions
- make practical and actionable recommendations
- reflect on implications for professional practice.

Each of these stages is considered in more detail in subsequent chapters of the book, but an indication of the skills you need to carry out these different elements is provided now.

THE EFFECTIVE RESEARCHER

Four interrelated skills underpin any effective research project (see Figure 1.2). You will need:

- **Intellectual and thinking skills:** knowing a lot about your topic is important, but other skills will enable you to undertake a more successful project. When you undertake research you have to act as an independent learner and this involves you being able to ask questions, probe deeply into issues and develop and justify your own thinking about the issues involved.
- **Personal effectiveness skills:** HR professionals are already aware of the importance of good interpersonal effectiveness in people management; the skills you have developed can be put to good effect in your research project, particularly your skills of time and stress management.
- **Organisational skills:** a research project is very like any other work-based endeavour: it has to be project-managed. Knowing how to break down components of a large piece of work, estimating the time requirements for different task areas, undertaking more than one task in parallel when appropriate and keeping track of progress are key skills that you can make use of and develop further.
- **Communication skills:** much of your research project involves you working on your own, but high-level communication skills are also necessary. In particular, you will need to orally articulate your ideas to your colleagues and tutors, listen actively (to get advice and also when gathering your data), share your findings within the organisation through effective presentations and produce a lengthy and well-written research report or dissertation.

Figure 1.2 The skills of an effective researcher

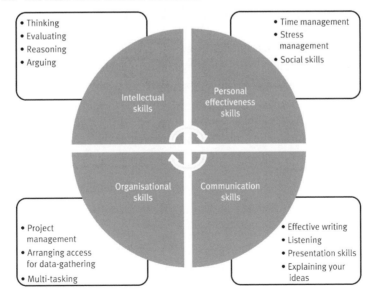

INITIAL FEELINGS ABOUT RESEARCH

It is possible that you are very excited about getting started with your research project. However, most students have mixed feelings at best, or strong doubts at worst, about their ability to complete a research project alongside all the other pragmatic and practical issues and problems facing them in their 'out of study' life.

Table 1.1 Common objections to doing research

Research is:

- just a way of proving what you already know
- best left to academics or to experts
- just a way of justifying what the CEO wants to do anyway
- too difficult
- too time-consuming
- removed from reality
- unable to change anything
- too scientific and statistical
- boring.

(Blaxter et al 2006, Jankowicz 2005)

Table 1.2 shows some recollections by students about their feelings when they were just starting out on a work-based research project required for their CIPD course.

Table 1.2 Feelings about getting started with a research project

I felt overwhelmed; I had never done anything like it before; I was anxious about choosing a 'good' topic. (Lee)
I felt nervous and concerned about how to get going. (Jane)
I was enthusiastic, but found it very daunting; where would I start? (Mike)
I felt daunted; I knew it would be a lot of work; where on earth would I begin? (Lisa)

If these sentiments reflect how you are feeling, read on (Table 1.3) to find out how much more positive the same students were once their projects had been completed.

Table 1.3 Personal benefits from undertaking a research project

I discovered that I can be highly motivated and disciplined. I found that once I feel 'passionate' about a topic I can 'throw myself into it'. (Lee)
How to deal with procrastination! Once I got going I enjoyed the work and found it interesting. I learned different ways to stop putting it off and to deal with the time pressures. (Jane)
I discovered what I was capable of! Self-determination, dogged enthusiasm and perseverance to achieve a significant challenge. (Mike)
I felt relieved and proud to learn that I can be more disciplined in my approach to time management than I ever thought possible (I normally leave things to the last minute!). (Lisa)

It would be foolish to say that doing research in HR is easy; challenges are likely for even the most confident and experienced practitioners and researchers. Personal qualities such as self-motivation, self-confidence and self-centredness will be important for your success (Biggam 2011):

- **Self-motivation:** you will need to maintain your interest and enthusiasm over quite a long period of time. Choose a topic that you are genuinely interested in and try to tackle all the different stages in the process with a positive attitude and curiosity for what you can learn.
- **Self-confidence:** self-doubt is an occupational hazard of all researchers at some point in the research process, so remember that your ideas are just as valuable as those of an established researcher or a chief executive. If you are able to learn from the advice of your tutor and student colleagues, there is no reason why your work should not be more than creditable when the time for assessment comes around.
- **Self-centredness:** the need to undertake your research over a sustained period means that, from time to time, you will have to turn down requests from family members and friends. Wise judgement is required in these circumstances, but it is important to make clear to everyone from the beginning that your project is a priority and you will appreciate their understanding and patience for its duration. Of course, after it is all over you can repay their patience many times over…

BENEFITS FROM RESEARCH

 ACTIVITY 1.2

IDENTIFYING BENEFITS FROM RESEARCH

Imagine that you still have to decide what to do for your project. The chief executive of the organisation for which you work has been to a government-backed seminar on employee engagement, and your manager thinks that 'something to increase engagement' would be a good project for you to undertake.

If you feel it would be helpful to find out more about engagement before tackling this activity, you might:

- listen to (or read the transcript of) the CIPD podcast on employee engagement, where four HR leaders from different types of organisation discuss what employee engagement means for their organisations and the issues raised for engagement when organisations are going through tough times: http://www.cipd.co.uk/podcasts/_articles/_employeeengagement37.htm?view=transcript

- skim-read some of the CIPD resources about employee engagement: http://www.cipd.co.uk/hr-topics/employee-engagement.aspx
- access the MacLeod Report to the UK Government, *Engaging for Success: Enhancing performance through employee engagement*: http://webarchive.nationalarchives.gov.uk/+/http://www.bis.gov.uk/files/file52215.pdf

DISCUSSION QUESTIONS

1   Identify three benefits of tackling a project like this from your own perspective.

2   Identify three benefits from the perspective of your employer.

3   What problems might you foresee if you were to take on this project?

FEEDBACK NOTES

1   There are a number of benefits that may have occurred to you. Undertaking this sort of high-profile project might be good for your career prospects. Engagement is a very 'hot topic' in HRM and may well sound like an area you could get personally interested in. There should be a good level of support for you from both managers and employees as both sets of stakeholders may feel they have something to gain. You know the organisation and can have access to a considerable amount of information. Most of the work could be undertaken in work time rather than at home at weekends.

2   Your organisation also stands to benefit from such a project. Interest in employee engagement by senior managers and HR managers is high. Engagement seems to be right at the top of management's HR agenda. This may also be an opportunity for the HR department to enhance the credibility of its strategic contribution.

3   In spite of some benefits there are also some problems that would probably occur to you in this sort of situation. Practical issues such as your own time constraints may be of concern as well as the extent to which this would be a project that is interesting to you personally. Other questions you might pose include:

- Over what timescale would the employer expect you to work on this project?
- Is it possible to satisfy both your employer and the requirements for your qualification?
- Given that you are (probably) not a senior manager, how would you go about identifying urgent action for senior people in the organisation?
- Is the organisation *really* interested in this project?

Perhaps these concerns might be summed up with four questions:

1   What exactly would this project involve?

2   Is it feasible as a topic for a student project?

3   How would it add value to HR practice in the organisation?

4   How might it add value to the HR community beyond your specific organisation?

The purpose of this chapter is to explore these general questions so that you are in a better position to understand the contribution of research to real organisational situations and consider the role of the practitioner-researcher. This should help you to work out how to use this book to plan and execute your own research project.

WHAT IS RESEARCH IN HR?

There are many different ideas about what 'research' actually is (see, for example, Yin 2009 Silverman 2009). A useful and simple definition to start with is: **finding out things in a systematic way to increase knowledge**. Research is a key function of higher education and informs much of what goes on in work organisations. As a result, universities and colleges as well as professional bodies are increasingly requiring elements of research-based or enquiry-based learning at all levels of study.

HRM involves practical application of up-to-date understanding in the context of 'real world' organisations. Reliable knowledge built on accurate information is needed. To undertake effective HRM, it is important that good-quality information underpins decisions and informs the actions of those involved in the employment relationship, such as trade unions, individual employees, outsourced service providers and professional organisations (Bamber et al 2004, Therborn 2006). The definition of research in HR in this book is: **the systematic enquiry into HR issues to increase knowledge and underpin effective action**.

HR RESEARCH – THE VALUE OF APPLIED RESEARCH

Many writers about research methods distinguish between 'pure' and 'applied' research (see, for example, Van de Ven 2007, Starkey and Madan 2001), although the distinction is not always clear-cut and is best seen as a continuum relating to the purpose and context in which the investigation occurs. The main focus of pure research (sometimes referred to as 'mode 1 research') is on gaining knowledge to describe and explain phenomena, develop and test generalisable theories and make predictions (van Aken 2005, Burgoyne and James 2006). Applied research (sometimes referred to as 'mode 2'), by contrast, is more concerned with developing knowledge that can be used to solve problems, predict effects and develop actions and interventions that are applicable in particular organisational contexts. Although applied research is not always accorded high academic prestige, it may require greater skill across a broader range of areas than pure research demands.

Figure 1.3 Pure and applied research

Applied research	Pure research
Problem-solving	Gaining new knowledge
Predicting effects	Establishing causes
Concern for action	Assessing relationships between variables
Time/cost constraints	'As long as it needs'
'Client' orientated	'Academic' orientation

(Robson 2011, Easterby-Smith et al 2003, Saunders et al 2012)

Most HR research that is undertaken as part of a taught course of study is at the 'applied research' end of the continuum, involving a relatively small-scale investigation in one organisation or using information from a relatively small sample of people or organisations. This book works from the position that, in HR at least, applied research is at least as valuable as pure research. HR research that is carried out in a rigorous way can lead to more effective practice than decisions based mainly on intuition, common sense or personal preferences. Common sense tends to take many features of organisational situations for granted. A systematic process of research, however, makes it possible to challenge 'taken for granted' assumptions and so generate new ways of understanding situations that can form the basis for innovative approaches to solving complex problems. A key capability for effective HR practitioners is the analysis of HR situations and the use of systematic investigative techniques to underpin decision-making and problem-solving.

The basis of this book is that HR research is about advancing knowledge in a way that is relevant to changing organisational priorities, solution of HR problems and the continuous development of organisations involved in the research process itself.

 ACTIVITY 1.3

WEB-BASED ACTIVITY

Visit the website of an HR magazine such as *People Management* (http://www.peoplemanagement.co.uk), *Personnel Today* (http://www.personneltoday.com), *HR Zone* (http://www.hrzone.co.uk) or *Training Zone* (http://www.trainingzone.co.uk) Run a search using the word 'research'. If you can, limit the dates of the search to the most recent one or two calendar months.

FEEDBACK NOTES

An activity such as this demonstrates how important research is to the development of HR practice. Research evidence is used to justify why certain HR practices are beneficial and is also used to evaluate the success (or otherwise) of HR policies and practices. Research contributes to the development of HR at strategic, policy and operational levels.

WHAT KIND OF A RESEARCHER ARE YOU?

Models of the research process and figures showing skill requirements can lead to an assumption that there is 'one right way' to undertake research. This is not the case and every individual HR practitioner or student is likely to undertake research in their own unique way. Indeed, research in the HR and management arena is characterised by diversity and it is important, at an early stage in your project planning process, to clarify for yourself a response to the question: 'what kind of a researcher am I?' This will help you to think more clearly about potential topics that you might investigate and how you might go about it (Brown 2006, Fox et al 2007).

INSIDER OR OUTSIDER?

Are you an insider or an outsider? There are two possible types of insider. One type is the person who will be involved in researching their own area of work in their own place of employment. The second type of insider is the researcher who is keen to find out what is going on *inside* the people that they are researching; their meanings and understandings. Two types of outsider are also possible. Outsiders are those who will be involved in researching in their own organisation but in a different place or part of it, or those who will undertake research into situations and/or organisations where they truly are an outsider. Your position as an insider or an outsider will have implications for your research. Outsiders may find it easier to establish facts and to discuss 'universals' rather than particulars. Insiders, by contrast, may be led to research that contains more 'narrative' than numbers. Examples of the different ways that a topic might be taken forward by people who are insiders or outsiders are shown in Table 1.4. The examples in this table use the illustration of talent management, but the same principles would apply to most HR projects.

Table 1.4 Insiders and outsiders? Examples of different options for research projects

Insider/outsider	Example of research project topic
Insider – who is undertaking research into their own organisation	An evaluation of talent management at XYZ Ltd
Insider – who wants to know about what is *inside* the people that they are researching; their meanings and understandings	An assessment of perceptions and attitudes towards a talent management programme at XYZ Ltd
Outsiders – who will be researching in a different part of their own organisation	An investigation into the implementation of talent management in the information systems division
Outsiders – who will research into situations and/or organisations where they have little or no connection	Research into the application of talent management programmes in retail organisations in the UK

'DETECTIVE', 'DOCTOR' OR 'EXPLORER'?

In addition to the distinction between research as an insider or as an outsider, most HR researchers have different 'mental pictures' of the purpose of their research. Brown (2006) characterises three different ideal types, which are depicted in Table 1.5. Many researchers find that they identify with more than one type. Which of these are you *most* like?

Table 1.5 Researcher similes

Researcher as detective	Researcher as doctor	Researcher as explorer
You have a clear idea about the research **problem**; for example: 'talent management programmes favour younger workers over older employees'. The researcher as detective gathers relevant information to get the clues needed to solve the problem and then marshals the evidence to prove that the solution that they have reached is the correct one.	The researcher as doctor recognises the need to work from the symptoms they are presented with to diagnose the **cause** of the situation before any appropriate 'treatment' can be prescribed. The researcher as doctor looks for the reasons behind the research issue;for example: 'what factors lead employees to be negative about talent management programmes?'	The researcher as explorer loves to enter 'unknown territory' and keep a record about what they find; for example: 'what happens in an organisation that has been acquired and is required to implement the talent management programme of the new parent company?'

(Brown 2006)

Descriptive research

If you see yourself mainly as a detective or perhaps as an explorer, it is likely that you will be interested in carrying out **descriptive** research where you set out to provide an accurate profile of situations, people or events. A descriptive research project focuses on 'what, when, where and who'. Having investigated and described the issue, you can then go further and analyse the data to ask 'why?'

and 'so what?' Both qualitative and quantitative data are useful in descriptive studies.

Explanatory research

If you see your role as a researcher to be like that of a doctor or perhaps as a detective, it is likely that you will undertake **explanatory research** by setting out to explain a situation or problem, usually in the form of causal relationships. Your focus will be on 'why' and 'how', seeking to explain organisational problems and, through assessment of the causes, to recommend changes for improvement. Both qualitative and quantitative data may be useful for achieving these research purposes.

Exploratory research

If you see your role as a researcher as more like that of an explorer, **exploratory research** will appeal to you. The purpose of exploratory research is to seek new insights and find out what is happening. There is an attempt to ask questions and assess phenomena in a new light. A more qualitative approach often (but not always) underpins this sort of research and the focus is on obtaining new insights into new or current situations and issues.

 ACTIVITY 1.4

HOW REAL IS REALITY TV?

Reality TV (as distinct from documentaries or other non-fictional TV programmes such as sports coverage and news) is a form of television programming that has become prevalent in almost every TV network since the beginning of the twenty-first century. Examples from UK channels include talent searches such as: *The Apprentice* and documentary-type programmes such as *The Only Way is Essex* and *Masterchef*. Reality TV shows claim to show ordinary people in unscripted and real situations. Identify and think about three different reality TV shows that you know about. If you do not watch reality TV shows yourself,

you can find out about them from friends or from broadcasters' websites. You might also enjoy reading commentary on *The Apprentice* in John McGurk's (CIPD Adviser for Learning and Talent Development) blog at http://www.cipd.co.uk/blogs/members/j.mcgurk/default.aspx

DISCUSSION QUESTIONS

1   How real is reality TV?

2   In what ways is reality TV *real* and in what ways is reality TV *not real*?

3   To what extent is 'heartbreak' real?

4   In what sense are dreams real?

FEEDBACK NOTES

Discussion about reality TV can evoke strong reactions. Some people watch reality TV programmes with enthusiasm and commitment; they want to decide for themselves about the qualities shown by those involved and may also identify strongly for or against one or more of the participants. Other people might describe reality TV as 'tedious', 'worthless' and 'manipulative'. The extent to which the programme that is broadcast is contrived or the effect of the editing process on what we watch might, however, be seen to make reality TV less real than its name would imply. The discussion about the 'reality' of reality TV makes us wonder how we can *know* about *reality* and this is an important issue for everyone who aims to carry out research in the *real* world.

When discussing the extent to which heartbreak is real, your opinion might be different depending on your current emotional circumstances and relationships. For others their view would not depend on their context or circumstances – they would argue that heartbreak is a feeling rather than a real thing. Others might say that they know what is real when they come across it and are able to distinguish between what *seems* real (dreams and/or heartbreak) and what actually is real as evidenced by the behaviours that they experience. Even those of us who prefer to rely on the evidence of our senses to identify what is real find ourselves challenged by the digital and technological opportunities of the twenty-first century to 're-master' or alter what we see and hear. This can lead us to wonder whether reliance on the evidence provided by our senses or on our experience is a sufficient basis from which to know about the real world (Saunders et al 2012).

WHAT IS YOUR REAL-WORLD VIEW?

Work in HR, and this includes research work in HR, takes place in the real world and is about real world issues (Robson 2011). Most of the time most of us do not trouble ourselves with thinking much about the nature of the real world; we just get on with our lives and our jobs. Before you start with your research, however, you will need to think about your own take on the nature of the real world.

When addressing the question 'what is real?' there are three prominent options (Brown 2006, Fox et al 2007). One answer is that reality is **'out there'** and this corresponds to what is termed an **objective** world-view. If your view is that reality is **'in here'** (that is, a feature of your perceptions and feelings), you may feel more comfortable in what might be called an individually **constructed** world-view. You might think that reality is **'in here'** but influenced by **'out there'**. This would be represented by what is often called a **socially constructed** world-view.

The extent to which you subscribe to an objective, socially constructed or individually constructed world-view may well be influenced by your own personal and professional background. Economists, for example, tend to operate within an objective world-view; social and care workers tend to be most comfortable with a socially constructed world-view. HR researchers are difficult to generalise about: some adopt a socially constructed world-view and others work from an objective world-view. Your assumptions about these issues, therefore, may well be different from other HR practitioners and researchers that you come into contact with. The nature of your thinking in response to these issues, however, is likely to be important for the way that you tackle your project.

If you are most comfortable with an objective world-view, it is likely that you will want to establish objective facts that can be generalised independently of the beliefs, perceptions, culture and language of different individuals and groups. This perspective is often associated with what is termed a **positivist** approach to research, which is outlined in Chapter 2. If you are more comfortable with a socially constructed world-view, it is likely that you will value information from observation or interviews mostly gathered in the form of words and meanings, pictures and other artefacts and value qualitative rather than quantitative data. This world-view is often associated with the **interpretivist** approach, which is also introduced in Chapter 2.

Research into the psychological contract

CASE ILLUSTRATION 1.1

Alex was a part-time student in a retail organisation where performance and the achievement of targets were key features of organisational culture. Anecdotal evidence led her to be concerned about the way sickness absence was managed in her organisation, the extent to which management responses to sickness absence affected levels of employee engagement in her organisation and whether managers' understanding of the 'preventative' effects of their actions with regard to sickness absence was perceived by employees as 'punitive' and the effect this had on engagement. For her research project, Alex decided to measure employees' and managers' perceptions of the absence management process and indicators of engagement, and to compare these with indicators of preventative and punitive approaches to absence which she found in the literature.

From her reading of the literature, Alex identified questionnaire items related with measures of engagement and absence management. These items included such things as: different features of managing absence (which she obtained from CIPD surveys on absence management); factors that maximise attendance at work; perceptions of absence review processes; and engagement measures (which came from her company's regular staff satisfaction survey). Alex

set out to gather and analyse the data from a range of different people who worked in a sample of the retail outlets to make some generalised conclusions about the effects of the organisation's approach to managing sickness absence.

Kingsley was also interested in taking forward research into employee engagement. However, he took a different approach. He focused on finding out about the beliefs, values, expectations and aspirations of employees through a series of in-depth interviews. Kingsley wanted to find out about the different feelings of engagement people might have even if they worked in jobs at the same 'level' and in the same organisation. Through conducting interviews, therefore, Kingsley set out to gather information that was grounded in the experiences and perspectives of those involved to provide an in-depth understanding of the issues from the different participants' perspectives.

Discussion Questions

1   What world-view underpinned the approaches to their research adopted by Alex and Kingsley?

2   To what extent (and why) is it possible to decide which approach is 'superior'?

FEEDBACK NOTES

The approach adopted by Alex was indicative of the objective world-view. She sought to measure features of absence management and engagement as indicated through generalised patterns of questionnaire responses. Kingsley's approach was indicative of the constructed world-view and he was interested in the way in which employee engagement is differently felt by different people on the basis of their unique experiences and contexts.

The different research world-views described here are distinct, but you may also have highlighted that there are overlaps between them. No experience (of employee engagement) is wholly individually and uniquely experienced; some aspects will be shared between individuals and groups. Also, 'socially derived' views (about executive pay, for example) can become so universally accepted that they can be researched as an objective fact.

You may feel that both objectivist and constructivist perspectives are useful ways forward, and research that works from more than one world-view is quite common (although not required or compulsory) within HR. The important thing is to be clear about your world-view – to yourself and to those who will read your work – so that this can be taken into account in making sense of your research and the conclusions that you draw. You may well be reflecting at this point that you can see the benefit of both objectivist and constructivist world-views, and you may be thinking about incorporating both approaches into your research. Within research in HR there is a strong tradition of what is sometimes called a 'mixed methods' approach, characterised by elements of both world-views within a project. Such approaches are discussed in Chapter 2. However, bringing insights from both world-views together can have implications for your research project that can be very time-consuming and difficult to express within a word limit of 7,000 words (which is often applied for CIPD management or business research reports).

 ACTIVITY 1.5

WHAT KIND OF A RESEARCHER ARE YOU?

Think about yourself: your situation, your world-view, your preferences and your interests. Write your comments to the questions on the left in the spaces provided on the right.

About you	Response
Are you likely to undertake research in your own organisation or one where you might be considered an outsider?	

About you	Response
Are you interested in general facts and universal trends or are you more interested in getting *inside* the meanings behind particular issues and experiences?	
To what extent is your preferred research role similar to that of a doctor/ explorer/detective (or a combination)?	
Which world-view do you feel most comfortable with: 'objectivist world-view' or 'constructivist world-view'?	

Your responses to these questions might be useful to share with your tutor or supervisor as you discuss potential research topics and the way you might take your research project forward.

Figure 1.4 Factors affecting the employment relationship

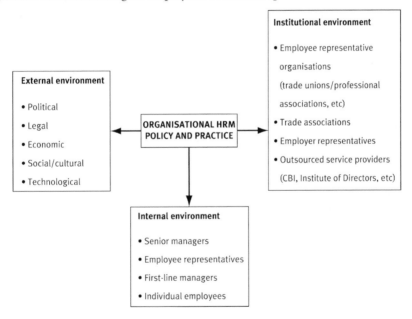

THE AUDIENCES FOR HR RESEARCH

ACTIVITY 1.6

AUDIENCES FOR HR RESEARCH

1 Use Figure 1.4 as a prompt and write down a list of different groups of people who may be interested in the implications of research into HR issues in your organisation (or one you are familiar with).

2 For each group of people that you identify, try to work out how they might find out about relevant research that has been undertaken.

FEEDBACK NOTES

Your list of likely 'audiences' for HR research might include: individual practitioners; individual managers; members of trade unions; people in central government departments; members of your local authority; specialist organisations/pressure groups; professional associations; academics; consultants; employer/trade bodies; trade union members; students; providers of outsourced HR services.

When it comes to finding out about research, there is an equally wide range of publications and opportunities that different groups might use. These include:

- newspapers
- webpages
- specific reports (may be internal or external)
- books
- trade journals
- professional journals
- attending conferences/seminars
- academic journals
- social networking sites
- unpublished research (dissertations, projects, etc).

Each of these different vehicles for communicating knowledge will do so in a different way to meet the needs of its audience. As a result they will engage to different extents with both theory and practice and with the general or the specific.

Figure 1.5 Orientation of different research outputs

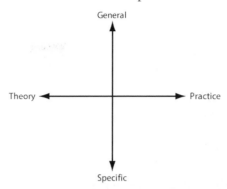

ACTIVITY 1.7

ASSESSING DIFFERENT RESEARCH
PUBLICATIONS

Study one copy of the following types of HR
publication:

- academic peer-reviewed journal (for
  example, *Human Resource Management
  Journal, Human Resource Development
  International* or *International Journal of
  Human Resource Management*)

- professional journal (for example, *People
  Management* or *Personnel Today*)
- practitioner report (for example, IDS Report
  or a CIPD Research Insight report (http://
  www.cipd.co.uk/hr-resources/research/)

Skim-read the publications and try to 'plot'
each of the features of the research articles/
reports guided by the two axes shown in Figure
1.5.

FEEDBACK NOTES

It is likely that different articles from each of the first two types of publication
may need to be plotted differently. Some studies, even within one publication, are
very concerned with one specific situation and others are more general. What is
easier to characterise is the different levels of engagement with theories, models
and concepts. Papers in a peer-reviewed academic journal such as *HRMJ* will be
significantly concerned with evaluating theories as well as with practically
focused investigations. Practitioner reports, by contrast, are more concerned with
describing practice than with explicitly locating it within any conceptual
framework. Feature articles in practitioner journals vary somewhat, although
theory is rarely a major feature.

REQUIREMENTS FOR STUDENT PROJECTS

If you are working towards a professional or educational qualification, the
principal readers of your work will be interested in its academic features as much
as the practical outcomes for the organisation(s) in which your research project is
situated. Therefore it is important that your work corresponds to the
characteristics shown in Figure 1.6.

Figure 1.6 Characteristics of a research project in HR

FOCUS ON A 'LIVE' HR ISSUE

Choosing a topic can be a challenging decision for first-time researchers and this issue is addressed in Chapter 2. A good project will be interesting for you to undertake and will provide the opportunity for added value to those who will read about your results (HR practitioners, student colleagues and academic tutors). Choose something that will be manageable (not too big – your time is short) but something that is challenging enough to merit an academic qualification and will be interesting to those who will find out about your work.

ASSESSMENT OF EXISTING KNOWLEDGE ABOUT THE ISSUE

Most published HR research, particularly reports that are produced for a practitioner audience, do not engage explicitly with theories, models and frameworks. Research written for an academic audience found in academic journals, by contrast, is **explicit** about theory. If your research forms part of a qualification-bearing course, an explicit use of theory is expected. You must take a constructively critical approach to the current state of knowledge in your topic area and work out how your project fits into the wider context. It is worth finding out now about the expectations of your tutors about the balance between theory and practice for your research report or dissertation.

COLLECT AND ANALYSE DATA

All projects undertaken as part of an HR programme of study require the collection and analysis of data. This may be secondary data (which has already been generated for some other purpose) as well as primary data (which you will gather to answer your research questions). If you are undertaking a CIPD course, you must collect and analyse primary data as part of your research. In many cases your data will come from one organisation, but in some circumstances data will be gathered across a range of individuals or organisations. Some HR research involves a new analysis of secondary data sources.

DERIVE SUPPORTABLE CONCLUSIONS

Once you have gathered your data and analysed it to make sense of what you have found, you will need to draw some overall and integrated conclusions. This will require you to reflect in a critical way about the limitations of your data as well as the insights you have achieved. Most HR research projects fall into the category of applied research and so you will also be able to reflect on the implications of your research findings for professional practice.

CREDIBLE PRESENTATION

Your research report or dissertation may be the longest document you have ever written and you will expend a lot of time and energy in producing it. The final product must be persuasive to those who read it; academic and professional credibility are important. The way the report is presented, the quality of your written communication, careful proof-reading, helpful graphics and charts, and the quality of referencing and citation you exhibit will all make a difference to both the persuasiveness of your report *and* to the mark your work achieves.

WRITING YOUR RESEARCH PROPOSAL

Whether you are undertaking a dissertation, business research report or other form of investigative inquiry, it is likely that your study centre will require you to write a research proposal. This is your first opportunity to write down what you plan to do. What is expected of your research proposal will depend on the qualification you are undertaking and the requirements of your study centre. You may find that a short document (one or two sides of A4 paper) is expected and the feedback you receive will be 'formative' (that is, not associated with a mark towards your final qualification). Alternatively, your centre may require a more detailed proposal of 2,000–3,000 words for which a mark will be recorded, which will count towards your final qualification.

Whatever the expected length of the research proposal, most students find this a daunting document to produce. But there are good reasons to overcome any natural tendency to put off the moment of writing. Your research project is an independent piece of work. As you undertake it you will benefit from the advice of your tutor as well as others in your study cohort and work organisation. However, the project is your responsibility and so the research proposal means you can:

- put down your initial ideas in writing
- share your ideas with your tutor/study centre
- get feedback about the strengths and possible difficulties of your idea.

Your tutor will provide you with a suggested format (and indicative word limit) for your proposal. Table 1.6 provides an indication of issues you will need to address.

Table 1.6 Research proposal contents

Topic area; aims and objectives	Provide an overview of the problem or issue you plan to address. Explain why this topic was chosen (what was the catalyst or trigger of the project? what is the value of the project?). Explain what you hope to achieve through the research. You should formulate an initial aim or 'big question' and more-specific objectives or questions (see Chapter 2 for help with this).
Literature review plans or progress	This part of the proposal shows how your research is positioned in the existing literature and where your study fits within existing knowledge about the topic. Requirements of study centres vary. Some require you to indicate the main areas for your literature search and key sources of information you are already aware of. Other centres require an initial review of the most important literature sources and an assessment of where your research would contribute to filling a gap in knowledge.
Research design and methods	This section identifies the way in which you are going to investigate the issue or problem as well as your world-view as a researcher. Your proposal should set out what type of data you intend to collect, your sampling strategy, the research methods you plan to use and your proposed approach to data analysis.
Ethical issues	Indicate here what particular ethical issues or problems you will need to address: in particular, obtaining informed consent of any organisations in which you plan to gather data as well access to individual participants. You will also need to explain the approach you will take to issues of confidentiality and anonymity for your research participants.
Suggested timetable	Present a clear and realistic timetable for the completion of your research and the production of your report. Indicate when important tasks will be carried out. Set achievable targets and time-planning contingencies and build in time for continuous review of different stages by you and your tutor.

WORKING WITH YOUR SUPERVISOR

A dissertation or a business research report is something for which you take personal responsibility. You will find it helpful to discuss your ideas and your progress with colleagues at work and with study 'buddies'. However, the key source of advice, guidance and encouragement will be your project tutor or research supervisor. Different study centres make different supervisory arrangements, and it is important to find out about the practices in your university. Figure 1.7 depicts the main areas that your supervisor will be able to discuss with you.

Figure 1.7 Feedback and discussion with your supervisor

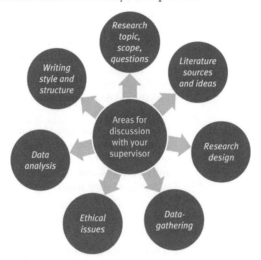

Figure 1.7 shows what a crucial contribution your supervisor can make. Establishing a good working relationship can help you to manage the research process in an effective way. The supervisory relationship is different from other tutorial arrangements as, in most cases, supervisors will work with their students on a one-to-one basis. Different supervisors will have their own backgrounds, experiences and preferred ways of working, just as you will also have your own preferences. If you want to work effectively with your supervisor, consider the list of hints and tips shown in Table 1.7.

Table 1.7 Constructive working with your supervisor

Establish the format, basis and frequency of meetings.	You may agree to meet face-to-face and have a few long meetings or shorter, more frequent meetings. You may prefer to communicate by Skype, telephone, email, and so on, if these media are more appropriate.
Identify times when either of you will not be contactable.	Check out when your supervisor may be away; let them know about your planned absences (holidays, etc). Don't send work to your supervisor just before their planned leave – they won't look at it until they get back.
Identify the key areas you feel you will need support with and discuss these at the beginning of the research process.	Discuss with your supervisor your strengths and skills that are relevant to the research process and the areas that you feel less confident with. Agree an action plan to develop in these areas and seek feedback as appropriate.
Establish project milestones and deadlines by which you will submit draft work for comment.	Your supervisor will be able to advise you about realistic targets. Don't be too ambitious but, once you have established your milestones, make sure you stick to them.

Be honest about your aspirations and priorities for the research project.	Discuss what you hope to achieve with your supervisor. If you are aiming for a distinction, commit to this with your supervisor and discuss what will make this more likely to be achieved. Alternatively, if you will be happy with a 'solid' pass, discuss this. If you are hoping to follow up your dissertation with producing a journal article, you should definitely discuss this in advance with your supervisor.
If you cannot attend a meeting or meet a deadline, make sure you let your tutor know in advance.	Nothing annoys a supervisor more than waiting around for a student who does not arrive or does not submit work at the agreed date. If you anticipate a change in your circumstances, let your supervisor know sooner rather than later.
Don't prevaricate.	Even if you are not fully satisfied with your draft work, try to submit it on time and then learn from the feedback you get.
Don't bluff.	If you do not understand something or have not actually done something, talking about it means you are more likely to get advice on how you can move forward.
Allow time for your supervisor to read your draft work carefully.	Although you will undertake a lot of work at weekends, do not expect your supervisor to do this as well. If they are to read your work carefully, they will need a sensible period of time (they have many other tasks to fulfil in addition to working with you).
Don't ask your supervisor what mark they think your project/dissertation will achieve.	Even if your supervisor will be one of the markers of your report or dissertation, the assessment process is different and separate from the supervision process.

MANAGING THE RESEARCH PROJECT

A research project is like any other project that you undertake: it has a natural progression, following a series of different stages. To undertake any project successfully you will need to undertake the following steps. Remember that this process will not necessarily follow in such a smooth sequence and you will need to continuously evaluate and monitor progress. However, these stages – which are illustrated in Figure 1.8 and also show the logic of the chapter construction of this book – do act as a reasonable 'road map' and none of them should be left out:

Figure 1.8 Stages in your research project

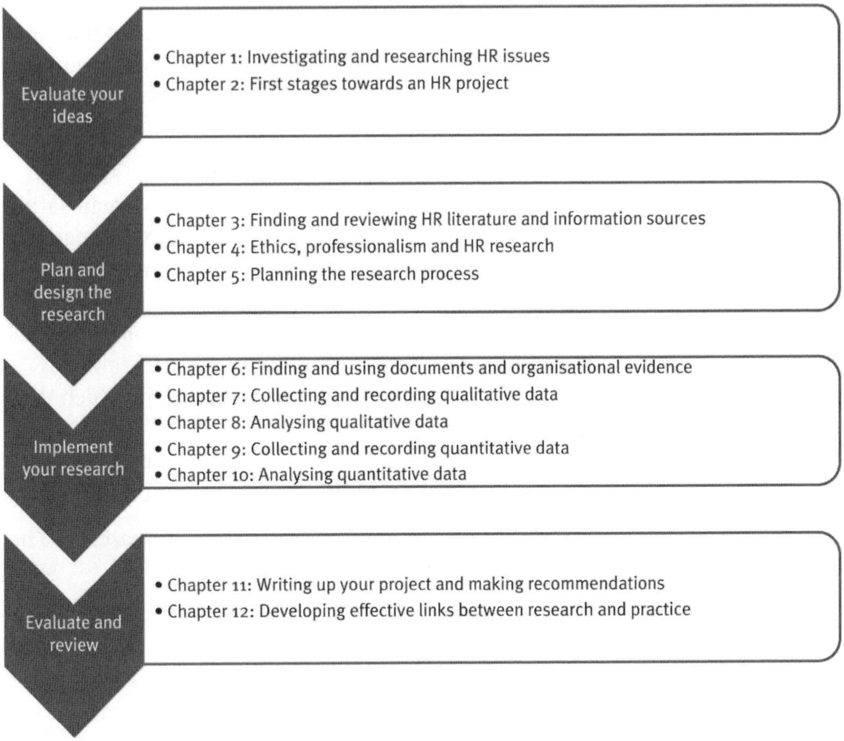

| Evaluate your ideas | • Chapter 1: Investigating and researching HR issues
• Chapter 2: First stages towards an HR project |

| Plan and design the research | • Chapter 3: Finding and reviewing HR literature and information sources
• Chapter 4: Ethics, professionalism and HR research
• Chapter 5: Planning the research process |

| Implement your research | • Chapter 6: Finding and using documents and organisational evidence
• Chapter 7: Collecting and recording qualitative data
• Chapter 8: Analysing qualitative data
• Chapter 9: Collecting and recording quantitative data
• Chapter 10: Analysing quantitative data |

| Evaluate and review | • Chapter 11: Writing up your project and making recommendations
• Chapter 12: Developing effective links between research and practice |

- **Evaluate your ideas** – at this stage you make a research proposal and refine your thinking at an early stage on the basis of feedback you receive. Issues such as the length of time available, any cost implications and achieving necessary permissions to undertake the research need to be considered at this stage.
- **Plan and design the research** – this is where you will think in detail about key activities and tasks within each of your main milestones. Careful planning about access to data and ethics, literature searching and literature review, and plans relating to data-gathering and analysis is required. Research projects without careful planning and design are less likely to be successful.
- **Implement your research** – this stage will involve processes of data-gathering, review and analysis. This stage will involve you finding and using documentary and organisational evidence, collecting and recording your data and then analysing information to make sense of it.
- **Evaluate and review** – this is an important stage of any project, and with research it is important that you undertake a careful review of your analysis and formulate meaningful conclusions. At the same time it is important to reflect on learning points to enable you to develop your practice as both a researcher and an HR professional as your career develops.

It is likely that most research will be undertaken within a specific organisational context and will be focused on the solution of a particular HR problem or issue. In this sense an action orientation is more likely and the implications of this for the practitioner-researcher are now explored.

WORKING AS A PRACTITIONER-RESEARCHER

A practitioner-researcher is someone who is employed in a job and, at the same time, carries out a research project that is of some relevance to their current role as a practitioner. Often the research is undertaken in addition to their normal duties and responsibilities. In the context of this book, this definition embraces three types of people:

- Part-time students undertaking research within their employing organisation: in this case the student may be a 'regular' employee or, alternatively, may be someone who is undertaking some form of consultancy assignment in the organisation. Of course, a practitioner-researcher may also be someone who is undertaking an investigative enquiry within their organisation (or that of a client) for which there is no link with the achievement of a qualification.
- Full-time students who have a part-time job in an organisation in which they undertake their research project.
- Full-time students for whom a work placement forms part of their course and they will be undertaking a research project within the placement organisation.

There are advantages and disadvantages of being a practitioner-researcher. The difficulties that are often encountered relate to:

- **Time:** when the project has to be undertaken in addition to normal workloads, it is difficult to give it the attention it deserves.
- **Preconceptions:** when you are a part of the organisation that you are researching, you may have formed many preconceptions about situations that someone from outside would not be influenced by.
- **Status issues:** often practitioner-researchers are not in senior positions within the organisation. This can make it difficult for their project to be taken seriously. Alternatively, they may have high status within the organisation. This can make it difficult for subjects of the research to express themselves freely.
- **Being critical:** although undertaking a research project involves adopting a critically evaluative approach to both theory and practice, in some organisations taking a critical approach is not encouraged.
- **Being instrumental:** a further danger, from the perspective of the organisation, is that where projects are linked with gaining a qualification, research can become more of a vehicle to achieve the student's purposes than being motivated by the resolution of a problem or issue.

There are also significant advantages to being a practitioner-researcher:

- **Insider opportunities:** if you know the organisation and are a part of it, you have access to a range of knowledge and experience that someone from outside would find difficult to achieve.
- **Practitioner opportunities:** as an experienced practitioner within the organisation it is more likely that actions that you recommend can and will be implemented.
- **Synergy between theory and practice:** as a researcher who engages with theory and also knows the context of the organisation, it is more likely that you will be

able to design and carry out useful studies that contribute to enhancements in both knowledge and practice.

In summary, undertaking research projects in organisational situations provides a number of advantages, but there are also dangers. A key issue for students is avoiding the temptation to merely repeat established organisational 'mantras' and making every effort to ensure that their project leads to new insights. To achieve this, practitioner-researchers must endeavour to:

- explicitly consider the wider context of the problem or issue that is being researched, both within the organisation and with regard to practice and developments outside of the organisation
- critically engage with theories, models and concepts at all stages of the research process
- encourage, where possible, the dissemination of the findings of studies so that they can inform the development of practice and understanding in other organisations and contexts.

Some more ideas about how this can be achieved are shown in Table 1.8.

Table 1.8 Maximising the value of organisational research

- Where possible, negotiate a time-allowance to carry out the research.
- Be prepared to 'sell' the idea of the research within the organisation.
- Try to establish a difference of procedure between activities connected with your research and your normal day-to-day practitioner activities. Be clear to yourself and to others about when you are acting as a researcher and when you are acting as a practitioner.
- Be explicit in your thinking about methods and sources of information. This will allow you to reflect proactively about the strengths and limitations of your research and so improve on it. It will also enable others to make an appropriate assessment of your work.
- Ensure that your research procedures are systematic and can be justified by more than convenience. If you cut corners (and you probably will), you must be explicit about the impact of the shortcuts on your findings and how you have interpreted your information.

SUMMARY

- HR research involves systematically enquiring into HR issues to increase knowledge and underpin effective action.
- Most HR enquiry can be characterised as 'applied research', being concerned with solving problems, considering effects and developing actions and interventions.
- Effective research processes involve: formulating a research topic; evaluating what is already known; obtaining information of good quality; interpreting the information and formulating conclusions.
- Effective HR researchers require a range of skills, including: intellectual and thinking skills; personal effectiveness skills; organisational skills; and

communication skills. Personal qualities such as self-motivation, self-centredness and self-confidence are also required.

- Different research world-views (for example social constructivist and objectivist) can be seen as distinct ways of making sense of the world, but there are overlaps between them.
- Projects undertaken to fulfil the requirements of an academic qualification are expected to make appropriate use of theories, models and concepts as well as primary and secondary data.
- Preparing a research proposal allows you to put down your initial ideas in writing, share them with your tutor and get feedback about the strengths and possible difficulties of your idea.
- Establishing and maintaining a good working relationship with your project supervisor will enable you to benefit from feedback and discussion of your ideas throughout the life-cycle of your project.
- There are advantages and disadvantages to being a practitioner-researcher, but organisational research, properly undertaken, can lead to new insights into HR issues, problems and situations.

 Self-test questions

REVIEW AND REFLECT

1   HR research is:

   a)   gathering data to show the benefits of HR initiatives

   b)   the systematic enquiry into HR issues to increase knowledge and underpin effective action

   c)   describing trends in particular employment issues

   d)   the development of generalised theories about the relationships between different variables

2   Put the following stages of the research process into the most appropriate order:

   a)   Obtain information of good quality.

   b)   Interpret the information and form conclusions.

   c)   Evaluate what is already known.

   d)   Define a research topic.

3   Which of the following statements best describe HR research?

   a)   HR research should ignore theory and concentrate on practical issues.

   b)   HR research should challenge 'taken for granted' assumptions and generate new ways of understanding situations.

   c)   HR research should not get bogged down in trying to solve complex problems.

   d)   HR research should focus exclusively on investigating issues at a strategic level.

4   Put the following CIPD requirements for business research projects into the correct order:

   a)   Diagnose and investigate a live issue of significance to a work organisation.

   b)   Reflect on implications for professional practice.

   c)   Collect and analyse data.

d)   Derive supportable conclusions.

e)   Locate the work within a body of contemporary knowledge.

f)   Make practical and actionable recommendations.

5   The literature search for an academic HR project should rely principally on which types of information?

a)   newspaper and Internet news coverage

b)   professional journals and trade journals

c)   textbooks and management factsheets

d)   academic journals and professional research reports

6   Which of the following would not normally be included in a research proposal?

a)   ethical issues

b)   research design and methods

c)   conclusions and recommendations

d)   suggested timetable

7   Which assumptions about the nature of reality correspond to which research world-views?

a)   Reality is 'out there' corresponds with a constructivist world-view.

b)   Reality is 'in here' corresponds with an objectivist world-view.

c)   Reality is 'in here' but affected by 'out there' corresponds with an interpretivist world-view.

d)   Reality is 'in here' corresponds with a constructivist world-view.

 ## Review questions

REVIEW AND REFLECT

Carefully study the information your centre provides about the requirements for your research project or dissertation. Look closely at the assessment criteria that are provided. Study the indicative structure that may be described. Make sure that you can answer all the questions below. If you cannot, make sure you find out the answers from whoever is responsible for projects in your study centre:

1   What is the submission deadline for the final report?

2   What is the indicative word limit?

3   Over what timescale should the project be undertaken?

4   What level of engagement with theories, concepts, frameworks of best practice, and so on, is expected?

5   How important is it to gather primary data?

6   Does the research have to be based in an organisation?

7   Are recommendations for action a requirement for the project?

8   What support is available to students when undertaking their project and how can that support be accessed?

REVIEW AND REFLECT

Questions for reflection

These questions are designed for two purposes.

1 Project planning

Answering these questions should help you to identify actions and priorities that will be important in undertaking your project. The answers you make to these questions may influence:

- which chapters of this book you need to study particularly closely
- which sources of further reading will be relevant to you
- the extent to which you need to get further advice on features of the research process.

2 Demonstrating reflective practice

If you are a member of a professional body like the CIPD, you will need to undertake continuous professional development (CPD). There are many benefits to a process of reflection about your professional development and a commitment to developing your skills and knowledge. Taking this approach to CPD as part of your research process can help you to be more productive and efficient by reflecting on your learning and highlighting gaps in your knowledge and experience. This will enable you to build confidence and credibility, track your learning, see your progress and demonstrate your achievements.

Taking stock

1   What influence might your professional, organisational or personal background have on the way you approach your research? Do you see your role as a researcher as being like a detective, a doctor or an explorer? Will you be working as an outsider or as an insider? What are the implications of your responses to these questions for your choice of topic and the extent to which your research may set out to achieve a descriptive, explanatory or exploratory purpose?

2   How feasible is it for you to undertake research in one organisation? For how long do you expect to be a part of the organisation in which your research may be based? What other options may be open to you?

3   How clear are you about a topic for your project? Who do you need to discuss your ideas with to decide about the feasibility of the project? (Chapter 2 is particularly relevant to these questions.)

4   What resources or expertise and advice are available to you from your project supervisor? How can you make best use of these resources?

Strengths and weaknesses

5   How confident are you about the process of undertaking a literature search to enable you to critically evaluate what is already known about your topic? What are the skills you will need to search and critically review theories, models and concepts within the literature? (Chapter 4 is particularly relevant to these issues.)

6   How aware are you of sources of secondary data that would be relevant to your project? What skills will you need to obtain and analyse the secondary data you have in mind? (Chapter 7 is particularly relevant to these issues.)

7   What options might you consider to obtain primary data? What are the skill implications of the data-generation options that you are considering?

8   What skills and competences have you already developed that you can use in the process of undertaking your project?

Being a practitioner-researcher

9   What are the status or political issues within your organisation that may affect the process of undertaking your project? How might you be able to manage these effectively?

10 What are the timescales for your project that are required by: a) your study centre; b) your organisation? What are the implications of this for the process of doing your project?

11 What opportunities can you identify to sell your project ideas to: a) your manager and colleagues; b) others in the organisation?

Finally

12 Describe how you will feel when you have completed your project. Hold on to that feeling!

EXPLORE FURTHER

It is very important to carefully read any handbooks or guidance notes relating to project work provided by your study centre. Most students skim through these at the beginning of their project process and only read them carefully at the very end of the process, when it is almost too late.

One of the best ways to learn about research methods is to read and critique good-quality peer-reviewed research-based articles. You can tell if a journal is peer-reviewed by glancing at its notes for contributors, which will indicate that potential contributions will go through a 'blind peer review' process.

Useful Reading

Biggam, J. (2011) *Succeeding with your master's dissertation*. Maidenhead: Open University Press.

Brown, R.B. (2006) *Doing your dissertation in business and management: the reality of researching and writing*. London: Sage.

Coghlan, D. and Brannick, T. (2009) *Doing action research in your own organisation*. London: Sage.

Collis, J. and Hussey, R. (2009) *Business research: a practical guide for undergraduate and postgraduate students*. Basingstoke: Palgrave.

Fox, M., Martin, P. and Green, G. (2007) *Doing practitioner research*. London: Sage.

Gill, J., Johnson, P. and Clark, M. (2010) *Research methods for managers*. London: Sage.

Hart, C. (2010) *Doing your master's dissertation*. London: Sage.

Robson, C. (2011) *Real world research: a resource for social scientists and practitioner-researchers*. Oxford: Wiley.

Saunders, M., Lewis, P. and Thornhill, A. (2012) *Research methods for business students*. Harlow: Pearson Education.

Yin, R.K. (2009) *Case study research: design and methods*. Thousand Oaks, CA: Sage Publications.

PART 2

PLAN AND DESIGN THE RESEARCH

CHAPTER 2

First Stages Towards an HR Project

CHAPTER OUTLINE

- How to use this chapter
- Deciding what to research and developing a credible justification for your project
- Establishing the focus of the project
- Approaches to research methodology
- Research design issues
- Access to data
- Final preparations – project planning
- Summary
- Review and reflect
- Explore further

LEARNING OUTCOMES

This chapter should help you to:

- develop ideas for a research project
- focus your project by developing a research aim and research objectives or questions
- clarify and articulate your research methodology
- evaluate different research strategies
- identify potential sources of information for your project and how you might access them
- develop your skills of project planning.

HOW TO USE THIS CHAPTER

This chapter is concerned with developing a focused and valuable research project in a practical and organisational context. You may have to produce a research proposal as part of your course. If so, this chapter will help you with your research proposal and/or your thinking about what your research project will involve and what it may be about. The CIPD Advanced level research project module requires that students 'identify and justify a business issue that is of strategic relevance to the organisation'. Other students undertaking undergraduate or MSc or MA programmes may also carry out work-based research, although dissertations in a non-work-based context or literature review (theoretical) dissertations are also likely. This chapter addresses all these forms of research into HR issues with the aim of enabling you to develop a project that has practical as well as academic value to you and to those organisations that may well be involved in your project.

 Thinking about research

CASE ILLUSTRATION 2.1

Extracts from: *CIPD launches apprenticeship guidance: Guide aims to ensure employers 'get full benefits' from schemes. People Management* online, 3 February 2012, http://www.peoplemanagement.co.uk/pm/articles/2012/02/cipd-launches-apprenticeship-guidance.htm With the permission of the publisher, the Chartered Institute of Personnel and Development, London [www.cipd.co.uk].

The CIPD has launched an apprenticeship guide for employers to help address perceptions among many businesses that such schemes are not right for them. It will offer advice for employers who may have never run this type of training before or are unsure of the potential benefits. It will encourage employers to take greater ownership of training delivery and ensure that it is relevant to their skills needs.

About a third of employers surveyed by the CIPD currently offer apprenticeships, but of those that don't, most said they believed that apprenticeships weren't appropriate for their organisation. This guide aims to show employers of all sectors and sizes how they can make apprenticeships work for them...

But the CIPD warned that training quality must be as important as quantity for the schemes to be a success. It advised that

apprenticeships should be embedded in workforce planning, the individual's role must be clear, and employers need to secure the support of the existing workforce, senior management as well as line managers and trade unions. The guide also suggests that alternative and more informal recruitment methods should be considered, especially when candidates are very young and have no prior work experience...

John Hayes, minister of state for further education, skills and lifelong learning, comments: 'Evidence shows that apprentices help boost productivity and give businesses a competitive edge, with most recouping their investment in less than three years. This new guide will help employers who haven't previously employed an apprentice take full advantage of all they can offer.'

Dean Royles, chair of the CIPD board, director of NHS Employers and national apprenticeships ambassador, said: 'Apprenticeships are an effective means for employers to develop their own talent. The CIPD's new guide gives practical advice to help employers tailor quality apprenticeship programmes that provide an invaluable first step on the employment ladder for young people and also develop existing employees throughout their careers.'

Katherine, Ahmad and Tosin all needed to find a research topic and were considering the possibilities of 'apprenticeships' as an area they might research. Ahmad and Tosin were international students. Ahmad was studying full-time; his work placement in his course was in a coffee-house chain which was interested in starting up an apprenticeship programme. Tosin was a mature student studying part-time, outside of the UK, on a distance learning basis and had a background and interest in labour market economics. Katherine was a part-time student who worked for a large manufacturing organisation where apprenticeship schemes had been used for many years. All of these students needed to find a research topic that suited them and their circumstances.

Discussion Questions

Listen to or read one or more podcasts on the topic of apprenticeships in the UK (you may find one at http:// publicsectorhrpodcast.co.uk/ category/apprenticeships/ or http://www.cipd.co.uk/podcasts/ _articles/ _thebusinesscaseforemployingyoun gpeople.htm).

Having heard about the topic of apprenticeships from different perspectives and having reflected on the different circumstances of Katherine, Ahmad and Tosin:

1   What factors might influence the way Katherine, Ahmad and Tosin might decide to take forward 'apprenticeships' for their research topic?

2   What opportunities might their different backgrounds present to Katherine, Ahmad and Tosin?

FEEDBACK NOTES

This case illustration highlights the range of factors that can influence not only **what** you research but also how you go about doing research. Your choice of project topic will inevitably be influenced by your personal circumstances, the access to data that you can achieve and your own professional interests and personal research preferences. In this case three different, but equally interesting, projects emerged. Katherine undertook a critical evaluation of the apprenticeship scheme in her organisation and was able to recommend changes to the recruitment, induction and performance management of those undertaking apprenticeship programmes. Ahmad's focus was different; he examined the influence of government policy and the organisation's HR planning and skill-demand priorities and was able to identify the opportunities as well as the potential challenges for his placement organisation in pursuing a strategy involving an apprenticeship scheme. Tosin, meanwhile, undertook a comparative study of government skill supply policies relating to apprenticeships in her own country and the UK. This enabled her to identify important issues associated with vocational training which would have value for organisations operating in both countries.

In any research project there are different sets of stakeholders that have something to contribute as well as something to gain (see Figure 2.1). The choice of a topic and the choice of the research methods will be influenced by all of them. If your research is part of a process of achieving membership of a professional body, such as the CIPD, its requirements must also be taken into account. All of these stakeholders have different (and not necessarily complementary) expectations and this chapter should enable you to articulate the key issues you need to address to move forward with the planning of your research project.

Figure 2.1 Stakeholders in the research project

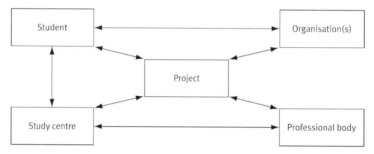

DECIDING WHAT TO RESEARCH AND DEVELOPING A CREDIBLE JUSTIFICATION FOR YOUR PROJECT

For some students, the choice of a topic for a research project is relatively straightforward; for others, it can be a slow and frustrating process. However, finding an appropriate topic is an important first step in developing a worthwhile research process which has the potential to lead to improvements in organisational practice, and enable you to submit a good-quality research report or dissertation.

GENERATING IDEAS FOR PROJECTS

Deciding on a topic to research can be as difficult as writing the first few sentences of an assignment. However, it is possible to structure the process to generate some ideas. Once ideas are generated, it is possible to evaluate them, choose the most appropriate topic and then clarify its focus and objectives.

STARTING WITH THE ORGANISATION

As Figure 2.1 indicates, the organisational context in which you may be working is an important factor in the choice of a broad project topic, and it may be useful for you to 'stand back' from your immediate work context and think about possible issues that would underpin an interesting investigation. Where possible, and where appropriate, part of the topic choice process may involve discussions with relevant managers and colleagues. Many of the suggestions they offer will not be 'right', but listening to them, and considering how you might research into the issues or activities they suggest, will get you thinking.

Key questions that are worth asking in this way are:

- What is currently bothering me/my boss/my department/my organisation?
- What changes may be occurring in the near future?
- What HR developments may impact on the organisation in the next few weeks and months?

In addition, discussions with customers and clients as well as your friends and family may help. They may not work in HR, but the very activity of talking through issues with 'outsiders' can help you to articulate areas of interest and possible research topics.

STARTING FROM JOURNALS

If you still have no idea what you would like to enquire into, the following activity may be helpful.

 ACTIVITY 2.1

GETTING RESEARCH IDEAS FROM WEBSITES AND JOURNALS

Visit the online pages of an HR magazine or organisation, such as www.cipd.co.uk; www.people.management.co.uk; www.shrm.org.

Look at the features and comments; check out the main news; skim through the blogs or discussion threads.

1   As a result of your browsing, make a list of the main issues that are raised. Summarise what each issue is about in no more than one sentence. Generate a list of at least 12 issues.

2   Each of these issues could act as a 'trigger' to the identification of one or more possible topics for your research. Work through the summaries you have made and list the potential topics they highlight. Give each of the topics a rating for the following characteristics if you were to consider them as an idea for an enquiry:

- your level of interest in the topic
- likely value to you
- likely value to your department/future career prospects
- feasibility as a project – could it be achieved 'on time and on budget'?

STARTING FROM PAST ASSIGNMENTS

Another way to generate some research ideas is to look back on work you have already undertaken as part of your course. Perhaps it would be worth re-reading coursework that you have undertaken and recalling which topics you found to be most interesting. Is there a potential topic for a fuller enquiry within your previous assignments? Alternatively, it may be that you have been involved in a particular project at work, or on a work placement, that has excited your sense of curiosity, or about which you realise you and/or your organisation would benefit from knowing more about.

STARTING FROM PAST PROJECT TITLES

If all of these suggestions have so far generated no ideas, you might also review a list of past projects undertaken by students to stimulate your imagination enough to generate some possibilities. Your study centre should be able to provide such a list. An indicative list of project titles is shown as Table 2.1. It is intended as an aid to stimulate your thinking, rather than to suggest that particular topics are more appropriate than others.

Table 2.1 Examples of research topics

Performance management and the use of appraisals at ABC County Council
The effectiveness of XYZ approach to offering apprenticeship opportunities
The effectiveness of flexible working practices at FGH Trust
Factors affecting the success of the performance-related pay scheme at XYZ UK
The talent management implications of devolving recruitment activities to front-line managers
An assessment of the technological interface between line managers and the HR shared service centre in JKL Ltd
The effects of an organisational 'knowledge' culture on continuous employee development and engagement within an HR consultancy
A critical investigation and analysis into the extent to which MNP Ltd offers a total reward package
The recruitment and selection process of overseas staff at QRS University
The methodology and effectiveness of change management and the effect on the psychological contract within two different public sector organisations
A critical evaluation of employee engagement at TUV organisation

DECIDING BETWEEN ALTERNATIVE TOPICS

Having identified two or three possible topics, it is important to select the one that is most likely to lead to a successful research project. Here again the expectations of the different stakeholders must be taken into account: the student; the academic institution; the professional association; and the organisation(s).

Your perspective

- **Personal interest:** choose something that is interesting to you. You will have to work independently on your project for a number of months. If you start on it without much motivation, interest and enthusiasm, there is little chance that you will feel positive about it by the end of the process.
- **Career plan:** you will be more motivated if you can find a topic that has value to you in the medium or long term. Choose a topic that might make you more 'marketable'; increase your knowledge in a specialised area; or improve your skills and experience.
- **Time/resources:** the project must be able to be achieved within the specified time limit and in addition to other work and commitments. Avoid any topic that is so large that it cannot be achieved to a reasonable quality threshold because of time or other resources that are unlikely to be available.
- **Skills:** good research topics are stretching to the researcher, but they must also be within your capabilities. A project studying the difficulties of communication in a multilingual organisation would be difficult to undertake,

for example, if you can read and communicate in only one language. If the thought of quantitative analysis fills you with dread, a project that involves qualitative data analysis might be worth pursuing.

Your study centre's perspective

- **Links to theory/potential for fresh understanding:** to achieve academic credit, projects must be capable of being linked in some way to theories, concepts and frameworks of practice. Which of the topics you are thinking about have the most potential for this?
- **Regulations and expectations:** your study centre will have clear guidelines about what is expected from a research project. Some institutions (and professional bodies) require that primary data are gathered. It is also important to be clear about the expected word count, the relative importance of different features within the project (the marking scheme) as well as the format for presentation. If you are undertaking a course in HR, it will be expected that you will research an issue related with this field (and not principally concerned with marketing or finance, for example). Make sure that you choose a topic that enables you to meet these expectations. The advice of your supervisor is very important as you consider the suitability of your proposed topics.
- **Potential to probe and question:** avoid choosing a topic that merely replicates a certain form of HR practice and does not provide an opportunity to critically evaluate existing assumptions.
- **Wider context:** even if your project is going to be undertaken within one organisation, an appropriate topic will also have some value to one or more of the following 'interest groups': the business sector; the HR profession; other HR managers; academics with an interest in HR.
- **Professional institution:** if the course of study you are taking is linked with a professional body (such as the CIPD), choose a topic that meets the criteria that it has established.

The organisation's perspective

- **Organisational relevance:** a project that has potential value to the 'host' organisation is more likely to receive the support that is needed and to be completed successfully.
- **Access to data:** a topic for research will only be feasible if the information you need exists and can be accessed (politically, logistically and ethically) within your time and budget constraints.
- **Resources required:** although basic IT and other resources are likely to be available, requirements for specialist software or other resources (such as particular training and so on) need to be checked out before a topic is selected.

Having decided on the broad area of your investigation, it is important to establish a focus for the study.

ESTABLISHING THE FOCUS OF THE PROJECT

Focusing a research project involves articulating a clearly stated aim, principal research question or hypothesis. For most students there are two ways of going about this. One is to read around the literature to refine your thinking about which features of your topic you are most interested in. The other is to start from the position of the research project as it is 'situated' in its organisational context. For the purposes of illustrating the two approaches, Case Illustration 2.1 about the study of apprenticeship schemes will be developed further in this section.

READING AROUND THE SUBJECT

Part of the process of refinement from a general idea to a researchable topic is the definition of key concepts, issues and contexts that are relevant for your enquiry. To do this it is necessary to do some initial reading. If you are interested in 'apprenticeship', therefore, you could make an initial assessment of the literature about apprenticeships to work out what the main theories and concepts are in this area and to gain an idea about what is already well researched and where there are some gaps in what is known.

STARTING FROM THE RESEARCH SITUATION

Another way of beginning the process of establishing the focus for your project is to adopt a step-by-step process (Biggam 2011), which is illustrated in Figure 2.2

This approach begins when you articulate the one word that defines your topic, for example 'apprenticeships'. The next step involves identifying other words that are relevant to what you wish to investigate. In the case of this example, the other words might include: government policy; HR planning; youth unemployment; skills supply; demand for skills; employability; recruitment and induction; training; reward; labour market; performance management; employer attitudes. Already this list is too long and the next stage involves distinguishing between 'must-have' words and 'nice-to-have' words. Stick with the must-have words and let the others go. The third step involves bringing the remaining words together to form a meaningful sentence. In our example here, this might be: 'apprenticeship schemes can enable employer skill demands to be met in a cost-effective way'. An alternative sentence, reflecting a different research context, might be: 'apprenticeship schemes require targeted recruitment, effective performance management and effective collaboration between managers and training providers'.

Figure 2.2 Achieving focus for your research project

(Biggam 2011)

The final stage of this process is to convert the sentence into a statement of: the aim of the research, a principal research question or a research hypothesis.

ESTABLISHING THE RESEARCH AIM, PRINCIPAL RESEARCH QUESTION OR HYPOTHESIS

Opinions vary as to whether your research focus is best expressed through an aim, a principal research question or a hypothesis, but the key issue is to express in general terms what your research will address. Remember that an interesting project (one that will be worthy of an academic award) must have the potential to provide fresh understanding for HR practitioners and/or academics. Research that sets out to find 'the best way' of one HR practice or another or to 'prove' the benefits of an organisational initiative are likely to be very limited and will result in an output that will be of little interest to anyone once organisational circumstances change (as they inevitably will). Research that identifies the effect of different contexts on the way HR practices or policies are variously carried out and understood by different participants has the potential to make a valuable contribution.

Research aim

A research aim is a broad statement of the general intention of your research. It indicates what you hope to achieve (not how you plan to do it). For example, 'the aim of this research is to examine the extent to which the outcomes of apprenticeship schemes are affected by labour market factors and employer skills demands'.

Principal research question

Some researchers prefer to articulate their focus through a 'big question' or a principal research question, for example: 'do labour market factors or employer skills demand factors have most influence on the outcomes of apprenticeship schemes?'

Hypothesis

Some supervisors prefer you to articulate the focus of your research through a hypothesis. Opinions vary about the usefulness of hypotheses in action-orientated organisational research (see, for example, Clough and Nutbrown 2007, Creswell 2009, Fisher 2007, Fox et al 2007, Hart 2010, Maylor and Blackmon 2005, Saunders et al 2012). A hypothesis is a specific type of research question based on 'informed speculation' about something (Robson 2011). It is a statement that asserts that a relationship exists between two or more variables or that particular consequences will follow if a hypothesis (or statement) is true. In some areas of HR research, such as in work psychology, the use of a hypothesis to offer tentative propositions as a way of focusing a research project is quite common, although the approach is used less in other forms of HR research.

ACTIVITY 2.2

YOUR RESEARCH AIM AS A 'TWEET'

Twitter is an Internet version of an SMS (texting) service. It is an online social networking and 'microblogging' medium that people use to send and read text-based posts of up to 140 characters, known as 'tweets'. Since its launch in 2006 it has gained worldwide popularity; millions of people send 'tweets', use search queries and 'follow' twitter content online. Twitter forces users to express their thoughts concisely. Concise expression is also very useful when focusing your research.

1   Articulate your research focus as a 'tweet'. This means that you must express your research aim, principal research question or hypothesis in 140 characters or fewer.

2   Once you have a tweet of your research focus, now express, in a further 140 characters, why anyone should care about the outcomes of your research.

FEEDBACK NOTES

Whether or not you are a 'tweeter', this exercise demonstrates how difficult and clumsy it can feel to articulate your research focus. However, being able to communicate what you hope to research and why your research has value will help you to achieve the co-operation and assistance that you will require as your project goes on. It will also ensure that you stay focused on the key features of your research and stop you from getting distracted from the 'need to know' into other 'nice to know' issues that are related to your topic.

Moving forward towards a set of research questions

CASE ILLUSTRATION 2.2

Extracts from: Doherty, N., Dickman, M. and Mill, T. (2010) Mobility attitudes and behaviours among young Europeans. *Career Development International.* Vol 15, No 4. pp378–400. © Emerald Group Publishing Limited all rights reserved.

The paper seeks to explore the career attitudes, motivations and behaviours of young people in initial vocational education and training (IVET) in Europe...

The European Union (EU) provides a context within which mobility and free movement are enshrined in law, where geographical, national, institutional and legal boundaries to working across member states are becoming increasingly permeable. ... Although

there are few reliable statistics on mobility flows in the EU and on the motives underlying them, it appears that rates of mobility, both geographical and occupational, remain low (Eurostat, 2002). ... Many young people who could benefit do not take up the opportunity to have a placement abroad.

Boundary-crossing among young people

There is relatively little attention to the study of young people's boundary-crossing attitudes and behaviours. Selmer and Lam (2003) report that individuals who have lived in a foreign country as adolescents perceive themselves as being international and also show more open-mindedness towards other cultures, more respect and tolerance of others and more flexibility than host and home peers. They show greater international career preferences, a travel and future orientation and a family and language orientation but have lower settling down preferences. This ... significantly differentiates mobile adolescents from their peers, implying that early overseas experiences may nurture a propensity for boundary-crossing behaviour...

Mobility in initial vocational education and training

Research on vocational behaviours among those in IVET is limited. Kristensen (2004) identified potential barriers to IVET placements, including a lack of access, lack of language and cultural skills and lack of financial means. In the literature beyond IVET, Fourage and Ester (2007) found that among Europeans, migration intentions are higher where there are no perceived negative effects on employment and social ties. Youth populations, who can gain foreign experience at a young age and have a longer time over which they may reap the benefits, also have higher mobility intentions. It is suggested that individuals need to have the right resources, to be at the right age, at a particular life course stage and have a

positive mind set to act upon intentions to become mobile...

If large-scale initiatives are to successfully engage young people in boundary-crossing, more data are needed to illuminate not only their mobility attitudes but also how behaviour is impacted. Further exploration of these areas has potential implications for placements supported by European IVET programmes.

Owing to the lack of a previous foundation of research in this field, this study is positioned as exploratory rather than adopting a hypothesis-testing approach. The study aims to explore two research questions:

RQ1. What factors influence the decision of young people to seek work/study placements abroad?

RQ2. Which factors differentiate those who stay at home from those who go abroad?

> **Discussion Questions**
>
> 1   What is the aim of the research described in this extract?
>
> 2   What is likely to be the value of this research?
>
> 3   Why is the formulation of a hypothesis inappropriate in the context of this research?

FEEDBACK NOTES

This extract provides an example of research undertaken outside of one specific organisation but which is concerned with issues of direct relevance to HRM in a global context. The research has an **exploratory** aim, setting out to find out more about the career attitudes, motivations and behaviours of young people involved in initial vocational education and training in different parts of Europe. The research has potential value to a range of different stakeholders, including employing organisations who operate in different European countries and policy-makers at national and EU levels. The research takes place in a context where knowledge of the issues is rather scant – very little research into these specific issues has been undertaken. This makes the formulation of a hypothesis inappropriate as such a statement would need to be grounded in existing knowledge or theory. The different purposes of research (exploratory, descriptive and explanatory) were discussed in Chapter 1. This case illustration illustrates how a hypothesis is most appropriate for **explanatory research**, which sets out to explain a situation or problem, usually in the form of causal relationships. The focus of **descriptive research** or **exploratory research** (represented in this illustration) is likely to be more effectively articulated through a research aim or a principal research question.

FORMULATING RESEARCH QUESTIONS OR RESEARCH OBJECTIVES

Having established a provisional aim for your research, or a possible hypothesis, it is also necessary to achieve further focus for your project (as in Case Illustration 2.2) by formulating some research questions or objectives. Research objectives help you to express what you need to do to realise your research aim and begin with a verb (see Table 2.3) that indicates what sort of activity you will undertake. Research questions articulate what you need to be able to find out to answer your principal research question or to test the propositions that follow from your hypothesis. Most student research projects, which have an appropriately 'scoped' aim or principal research question, will have between two and four meaningful research objectives or questions (see Figure 2.3). If you have more than four objectives, your project may be too big and you will not achieve all your objectives on time or your objectives are too superficial and some further thinking is required.

Figure 2.3 Formulating a research aim and objective

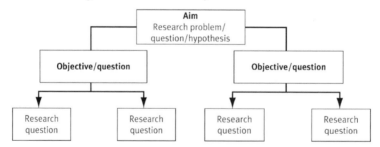

Table 2.2 shows some example research objectives taken from real-life student projects, and Table 2.3 offers some verbs that you may find useful if you are struggling to articulate your research objectives.

Table 2.2 Illustrative research objectives

To investigate the perception of XYZ Ltd sickness absence policy
To evaluate how the sickness absence policy is communicated to employees
To identify whether line managers consider HR information accessible enough via the technology interface
To clarify whether the technology currently in use facilitates the self-service centre and, in turn, the business partner model
To examine the current devolution of HRM strategy for performance management in ABC council
To investigate line managers' perceptions of the effectiveness of devolution of HRM
To investigate the current induction process within the HR resourcing division of LMN organisation
To evaluate the impact of the induction process on employee engagement
To investigate current processes and practices used by PQR Ltd to offer apprenticeships
To identify improvements or modifications to better align apprenticeships with the organisational efficiencies agenda
To evaluate the current performance management function undertaken by line managers
To establish any gap between what line managers currently deliver and what they need to deliver in respect of performance management to meet the organisation's goals

Table 2.3 Useful verbs for research objectives

Analyse	Determine	Explore
Appraise	Diagnose	Formulate
Assess	Discuss	Identify
Classify	Establish	Investigate
Compare	Evaluate	Outline
Construct	Examine	Probe
Derive	Explain	Scrutinise

You may find that you prefer to articulate the focus of your project through research questions. Research topics cover many different issues from a range of perspectives and are undertaken in varied ways. What they have in common is that they resemble a puzzle – something that needs to be 'solved' or 'worked out' using careful thought (Hart 2010). Descriptive research projects tend to set out to solve a 'developmental puzzle' (for example, what factors led to the introduction of apprenticeships in my organisation?). Explanatory research projects tend to set out to solve 'causal puzzles' (for example, what factors influence a young person to apply for an apprenticeship?). Exploratory research projects tend to involve an 'essence puzzle' (for example, how does being an apprentice affect a young person's sense of identity?).

In all cases, to solve the puzzle you need to ask and answer some subsidiary questions, just as you would need to break down any puzzle you attempt to solve into different steps. In research puzzles, the subsidiary questions are referred to as research questions.

RESEARCH QUESTIONS OR RESEARCH OBJECTIVES?

Opinion is divided about whether research objectives are preferable to research questions in expressing the focus of any study. Some study centres (and tutors) may have particular preferences, but many will accept research questions, research objectives, or both.

 ACTIVITY 2.3

RESEARCH QUESTIONS OR OBJECTIVES?

1   Take some of the illustrative research objectives from Table 2.2 and express them as a research question

2   Discuss whether you think research objectives or research questions are preferable.

FEEDBACK NOTES

Research questions that you formulate might be something like:

- How does the devolution of HRM affect performance management processes in ABC council?
- How do managers perceive the devolution of HRM?
- What is the current induction process within the HR resourcing division?
- What effect does induction have on employee engagement?
- How does PQR Ltd recruit to and manage its apprenticeship scheme?
- What modifications would enhance the alignment of the apprenticeship scheme with the organisational efficiencies agenda?
- How do line managers undertake performance management?
- What is the gap between organisational requirements for performance management and line managers' practices?

Careful formulation of either research objectives or research questions forms the basis of any good research. When your work is being assessed, the marker will look carefully at your research questions or objectives to determine both their quality and the extent to which you have addressed them fully by the time they read your conclusions. If you are undertaking research as a practitioner-researcher, it is important to be aware of the danger of formulating research questions that you (or the organisational sponsor of your research project) think you already know the answer to and which will merely serve to reinforce existing personal and/or organisational assumptions or activities. Therefore, as you formulate research objectives or questions, it is worth making explicit what you think the answers may be to your questions **but also** what alternative answers may exist.

In summary, it is important to (Hart 2010):

- **Articulate your aim and objectives as soon as possible** – the earlier you start the better as you will waste time if you do not establish the focus of your project.
- **Start with the general and move to the specific** – identifying the focus of your project is a process of refinement. As you discuss your focus with colleagues, tutors and members of your family, you will find that it gradually becomes easier and less clumsy to articulate what you hope to achieve.
- **Examine your own motivation (personal and political)** – a good mark for a research project is rarely achieved where it seems you want to prove what you already knew all along (however worthy your cause might be). An HR research project forms part of your course to enable you to demonstrate your ability to undertake a systematic and open-minded investigation into an HR issue. If you are more motivated by a desire to provide evidence leading to a predetermined conclusion, you are unlikely to get a good mark and your work will be neither credible nor persuasive.
- **Find the line of least resistance** – choose a topic and develop a focus where you know that data are available and accessible to you and where you are confident that you already have, or could develop in time, the skills you need to analyse the data.

❓ ACTIVITY 2.4

CLARIFYING YOUR TOPIC AND FOCUS

Answer the following questions about your research as a way of clarifying its scope and focus:

What is the central aim, principal research question or hypothesis of your research project?	
What are your research objectives or questions?	1 2 3 4
What do you think the answers will be to your questions?	
What alternative answers might there be?	
Where do you fit into the situation you will be researching?	
What opposition or challenges might you encounter?	

APPROACHES TO RESEARCH METHODOLOGY

Whether or not you decide to dwell on this section of the chapter or to move on to the more practical matters outlined later will depend on: your own personal preference and interests; the requirements of your study centre (expressed in the marking scheme for your research report or dissertation) for a discussion about your methodology. The terms 'method' and 'methodology' refer to different, but interrelated, issues associated with research. All research reports, whether produced at intermediate, advanced, undergraduate, postgraduate, master's levels or beyond, require a description and justification of the **methods** of your research; the forms of data you gathered (qualitative, quantitative or both); from whom you collected your data (your sample); and how you collected and analysed your data. These are important but tactical issues and are different from the more fundamental positional issues associated with **methodology**. If you need to incorporate a discussion of your methodology, read on.

KEY TERMS

The term **methodology** refers to the **theory** and **philosophy** of how research should be undertaken. The assumptions you make about these issues will have important implications for the research method or methods that you choose to adopt.

It is important not to get scared by these terms. The term **theory** refers to the process of explaining things we experience in the 'observable world' to make them intelligible, to suggest why things are the way they are or to describe the way they happen in the way that they do. Theories make use of concepts which help us understand why things are as they are. Concepts are abstract: they do not exist in reality; we can't touch them, but they provide a structure to the way we understand and explain what goes on in the 'observable world'. **Philosophy** is concerned with how, as thinking human beings, we make sense of the observable world. Philosophy is concerned with the fundamental nature of knowledge. As researchers we want to extend knowledge and so we can't avoid philosophy.

Any research philosophy must address two interrelated and fundamental questions (Lee and Lings 2008): **how can we know the world?** and **how do theories, concepts and experiences lead to knowledge?** Figure 2.4 expresses how philosophy plays a role in the way researchers try to 'bridge' the world we observe and experience and the 'intellectual world' of ideas that, as thinking human beings, we also inhabit.

If you are working towards a CIPD qualification, these methodological issues need less attention at this stage. However, a discussion about your methodological stance is likely to be necessary if you are undertaking a dissertation leading to an MSc or MA award. If you plan to move towards a research degree (for example, MRes, MPhil, PhD, Professional Doctorate), you will need to consider these issues in even more depth.

Figure 2.4 Why bother about philosophy?

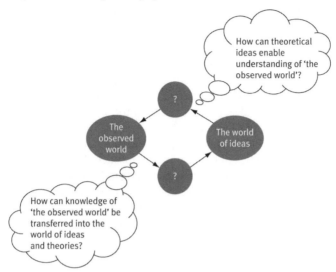

(adapted from Lee and Lings 2008)

Over many centuries researchers have tackled these questions differently and, as a result, different research traditions have emerged. The next section provides a very brief overview of the two most prominent traditions in HR research before highlighting the consequences of these different traditions for your project.

THE SCIENTIFIC RESEARCH TRADITION

Since the sixteenth century the scientific tradition has made a huge contribution to the development of what we know and understand about the natural and social world. Researchers in the scientific tradition are concerned with gaining knowledge by gathering facts and observations about the world to generate and test theory.

Within this tradition there are many strands of thought; the two most prominent are put forward by **empiricists**, who argue that we should rely on the evidence of our senses if we really want to be sure of our facts, and **rationalists**, who argue that our senses may be deceived and so reason and ideas have a crucial role to play in making sense of the apparently random and even contradictory observable experiences that humans try to comprehend. If you want to go further into this, check out the following research traditions: realism; positivism; post-positivism. These are discussed in more detail in some of the useful reading sources at the end of the chapter (see, for example, Lee and Lings 2008, Bryman and Bell 2007, Saunders et al 2012).

What these approaches have in common is an acceptance of a role for both theories and abstract concepts AND a requirement for robust empirical evidence. Those who work within the tradition of a scientific approach, therefore, emphasise (Lee and Lings 2008):

- a focus on the objective world which can be observed and measured
- an acceptance that just because something cannot be seen it might still exist.

THE INTERPRETIVE RESEARCH TRADITION

The scientific research tradition remains a very fruitful and dominant one in research throughout the world. In addition to those working in the 'natural' and 'physical' sciences, the tradition has been continued by many, but not all, of those who research into the social sciences (including those in management and business). However, since the nineteenth century researchers have increasingly debated the extent to which social or organisational research should make use of the scientific method. Critics of the scientific approach draw on a range of earlier philosophical approaches, particularly romantic and humanist world-views that emphasise the importance of collective and community features of social life and emphasise natural and emergent ways of developing knowledge and understanding of the world rather than the mechanical approaches assumed by the traditional scientific method.

An alternative **interpretive** research tradition has developed, therefore, based on the assumptions of **hermeneutics** (the study of the theory and practice of interpretation), which sees human experience as inherently influenced by social context and so less predictable and generalisable than those in the scientific tradition assume it to be. Those working within this interpretive tradition argue that an objective understanding of the world is not possible; instead, they focus on interpreting human experience. Just as the scientific tradition is characterised by different approaches, so the interpretive tradition contains many different variants. Check out 'phenomenology', 'ethnography' and 'critical research' in the useful reading sources listed at the end of this chapter (see, for example, Lee and Lings 2008, Bryman and Bell 2007, Saunders et al 2012) if you would like to find out more about these.

In general terms, researchers operating within the **interpretive tradition** (Lee and Lings 2008) are characterised by:

- a concern for understanding rather than explaining
- interest in the study of experiences bound up with time and context
- seeking understanding without 'reducing' variables to what can be measured
- assumptions that reality is socially constructed in a collaborative and changing way.

You will recognise that this research tradition is based on the constructivist world-views that were highlighted in Chapter 1. The assumptions about the nature of the world, the nature of knowledge and the role of researchers within this tradition are very different from those within the scientific tradition. In particular, interpretive researchers seek to achieve **reflexivity** (where the role of the researcher themselves, as a feature of the research process, forms an explicit part of the analysis).

METHODOLOGICAL IMPLICATIONS FOR HR RESEARCHERS

The term **'positivist'** is often applied to all researchers who work within the traditions and assumptions of an 'objectivist' perspective. This is not strictly accurate but, for the sake of simplicity, the term is used in this book to connote those within the 'scientific tradition'. Positivists emphasise the importance of an objective 'scientific' method (Remenyi et al 1998, Lee and Lings 2008). They see their role as collecting facts and then studying the relationship of one set of facts with another. They analyse quantitative data (data that can be counted) using statistically valid techniques and so produce quantifiable and, if possible, generalisable conclusions. This approach stresses the importance of studying social and organisational realities in a 'scientific' way that mirrors, where possible, the research processes used in the natural sciences.

The term **'interpretivist'** is also used in rather a crude way in this book to connote researchers who are most comfortable with a **'socially constructed world-view'** and see information and facts as 'provisional' and significantly affected by the meanings and experiences of different people in different situations of cultural contexts. From this perspective information from observation or interviews in the form of words and meanings (qualitative rather than quantitative data) is often seen to be more valuable for researchers. Interpretivist researchers are concerned to access and understand individuals' perceptions of the world. This is because they see social phenomena ('facts') as being the product of human interactions that, because they are the product of shared understandings and meanings, are not always predictable or even formally rational (Remenyi et al 1998, Lee and Lings 2008). The less quantifiable and the subjective interpretations, reasoning and feelings of people (qualitative data) are seen as a more relevant line of enquiry to understand and explain the realities of HR situations. The focus of interpretivist research, therefore, is not so much on 'facts' and 'numbers' but on words, observations and meanings (Creswell 2009). The main differences between the two approaches are shown in Table 2.4. Both research approaches have value and are used by HR researchers, as Case Illustration 2.3 shows.

Table 2.4 Positivist and interpretivist principles

Positivist principles	Interpretivist principles
• Work from scientific principles • Analyse phenomena in terms of variables • Start with theory and test/refine theory with data • Data should be collected by 'dispassionate' researchers • A highly structured research process should be used • Theories can be used to predict future relationships and behaviours • Preference for quantitative data • Validity and reliability of data are important for formulating generalisable conclusions	• Knowledge is constructed by human beings as they make sense of their environment • Analyse phenomena in terms of issues • Researchers cannot be wholly dispassionate – they are involved and will influence situations to various degrees (often unintentionally) • Flexibility may be required to allow the emphasis of the research to change as the process unfolds • Preference for qualitative data • Generating 'rich' data is as important (or more important) than ability to generalise

 ## Researching into employer branding

CASE ILLUSTRATION 2.3

Tom was a part-time HR student who worked in a medium-sized, fast-growing, privately owned organisation operating in a high-technology sector. His employing organisation was struggling to recruit the highly skilled and educated people it needed to continue to innovate and grow. His manager asked him to investigate into 'employer brand' issues as a way of tackling this. Tom set about undertaking a literature review and discovered that employer branding ideas draw particularly on principles of marketing; the 'science of branding' is applied to HR activities in relation to current and potential employees who are seen as potential 'brand targets'. When searching for examples of research into the area, he found that very little academic research has been reported, although there was more 'practitioner' literature with suggestions about ways to enhance the employer brand. Within his reading Tom identified two important HR concepts with relevance to the employer brand: organisational identity and the psychological contract. Initially, given the grounding of branding ideas within the 'marketing science' arena, Tom felt that it would be most appropriate to undertake his research with a positivist approach. He began by formulating a hypothesis that: employees who have positive perceptions of organisational identity also have a sense of a strong psychological contract with the organisation.

Discussion Questions

Find out more about employer branding by listening to, or reading the text of, some podcasts on the topic, for example, http://www.cipd.co.uk/podcasts/_articles/episode18.htm and http://www.cipd.co.uk/podcasts/_articles/_buildingauthenticorganisations.htm

1   What variables might be helpful to measure: organisational identity and the psychological contract?

2 What data would Tom need to
   test the hypothesis?

3 How might he obtain the data
   that he needed?

4 What advantages and
   disadvantages would this
   approach provide for Tom?

FEEDBACK NOTES

Within the scientific approach, a commitment to measurement requires you to
operationalise your concepts. In this case, perhaps you might come up with
variables such as:

Organisational identity

> Common sense of shared purpose; clear organisational vision; sense of
> unity in the organisation; shared mission; sense of fairness throughout the
> organisation; consistent approaches to management; engagement levels
> between managers and employees.

Psychological contract

> Trust in managers; job security; career prospects; interesting work;
> involvement in decisions; support for training; fair pay.

As Tom was planning to work in the scientific tradition, he wanted to ensure that
his data-gathering process generated information that was objective, measurable
and could be statistically analysed in a rigorous way. As this was a high-tech
organisation, you may also have suggested that he obtain his data through an
electronic survey to all staff; the larger the sample size, of course, the more
generalisable, and therefore worthwhile, the results of the analysis would be.

If you were to undertake a project in this way, you would be able to analyse your
data and form a conclusion related to the hypotheses. If the evidence supports the
hypothesis, the employer brand links between organisational identity and the
psychological contract are confirmed. If it does not, alternative links or factors
might be examined or the organisation might decide that employer branding is
not something to pursue in the short term.

CRITICISMS OF THE POSITIVIST APPROACH

This case shows that it is possible to undertake research using a positivist
approach. However, having thought through the issues, Tom decided against
working within the scientific tradition and opted instead to work within an
interpretive research approach, which, he felt, would be more appropriate to his
context and would also provide other benefits:

- **Answering the question 'why':** although research undertaken in a positivist
  way might show a relationship between organisational identity and the
  psychological contract, it would be less helpful in trying to explain why this was
  the case. In addition, it would not give Tom much information on the sort of
  employer brand that people would feel most committed to. To address these

questions, he wanted to get an understanding of people's perception of their employment situation and context.

- **Problems of categorisation:** Tom was also aware of problems relating to categories and variables. He was unsure about the extent to which 'shared purpose' and 'shared mission' could be treated as separate variables. The same question might be asked of 'fair pay' and 'sense of fairness in the organisation', which might be seen as elements of BOTH organisational identity and the psychological contract.
- **Issues of the data:** the use of quantitative data can provide for broad generalisations but it only answers questions posed in a fairly short questionnaire. Tom was concerned to avoid the trap of being too superficial; issues of the psychological contract and organisational identity are complex and he, as well as his manager, felt that 'richer' (more qualitative) data were more pertinent.
- **Relevance for applied research:** in Tom's situation he was aware that the purpose of his research was to contribute to the solution of organisational problems. Although the research that Tom originally considered would have been interesting, it did not really relate with the **management** of the employer brand, confining itself only to describing links between variables.
- **Dealing with complexity:** the basis of the positivist approach is to reduce situations and isolate discrete variables for analysis. Most situations in organisations are rather complex and 'messy', and Tom felt that a more flexible and integrative approach to enquiry would be appropriate.

CRITICISMS OF THE INTERPRETATIVE APPROACH

Although Tom opted for an interpretive approach, as he 'wrote up' his research report he discussed a number of limitations that followed from the decision to adopt an interpretivist approach:

- **Loss of direction:** the flexibility of the interpretive approach is attractive, but Tom found he had collected a huge volume of data and, for quite a while, he had no clear idea of what to do with it and he faced a persistent challenge to balance 'flexibility' with 'focus'.
- **Time and resource constraints:** Tom found the time and resource issues associated with data collection and data analysis (arranging interviews, organising focus groups, people cancelling at the last minute and re-arrangements needing to be put in place; unexpected events affecting people's responses) very difficult given the time and resource limitations he was faced with.

MIXED METHODS APPROACH

As indicated already, the research approach that you are drawn to may be influenced by your own background and preferred world-view. However, many people find that they can see the sense in both the 'objectivist' and the 'social constructivist' world-views; equally they wish to benefit from the advantages of research approaches within the positivist and interpretive traditions. The benefits of such a mixed methods approach have been highlighted by a number of authors in the social sciences and business fields who advocate research grounded in both the positivist and interpetivist approaches either 'in parallel' or on a 'one after the other' basis.

Such an approach often, but not always, underpins both action research strategies and the case study approach, in particular the emphasis on the research questions or objectives as being the 'driving force' between the choice of methods and approach to be used in different research projects; the emphasis on diversity of methods; a willingness to appreciate elements of different methodological approaches; and an iterative, cyclical approach to research (Tashakkori and Teddlie 2010).

Those who support this mixed approach (Gill et al 2010, Easterby-Smith et al 2008, Bryman and Bell 2007, Fox et al 2007, Creswell 2009) point out that it:

- reflects the complex and multifaceted nature of work organisations
- provides opportunities to assess whether different data 'converge' (referred to as triangulation)
- enables one approach to facilitate or provide 'ways into' another
- enables different research approaches to complement each other
- offers the potential to investigate both what has happened but also how and why a phenomenon has occurred.

A mixed methods strategy is not for the faint-hearted; it involves trying to forge together two very different sets of assumptions about the nature of knowledge and the social world. Such a project involves achieving a high level of understanding of different research philosophies and approaches (becoming what Tashakkori and Teddlie (2010, p275) refer to as a *methodological connoisseur*). In addition, each research tradition has its own specialised techniques and, within the time limitations of a student project, you would need to be confident that you are competent enough in both quantitative and qualitative data-gathering and analysis. With this in mind, remember that more methods do not always lead to better research – it is better to tackle one project in a very competent way from within one tradition than to undertake it poorly from more than one 'position'.

RESEARCH DESIGN ISSUES

Your research design enables you to move from your initial idea into a competent research process. The terms 'research design' and 'research strategy' are used in different ways by different authors. In this book the terms are used as follows:

- **Research design** – the framework that you devise to guide the collection and analysis of your data. Robson (2011) describes research design as being similar to being an architect in a building project; it is the general plan that will identify how you will achieve your research aim and answer your research questions.
- **Research strategy** – the general approach (similar to the main decisions an architect might take about the nature of materials to be used in a building project) that you will take in your research enquiry. This is one of the key components of your research design, but not the only issue that you will need to consider.

- **Research methods** – the particular choices you will make, having established your overall design and strategy that relate to the specific data-gathering techniques you will use.

RESEARCH STRATEGIES

Books about research methods highlight a range of generic research strategies. Opinion differs about how many strategies there are and what they should be called (see, for example, Saunders et al 2012, Robson 2011, Bryman and Bell 2007). Here, the strategies that are most appropriate to students undertaking an HR project are described.

Figure 2.5 Some generic research strategies

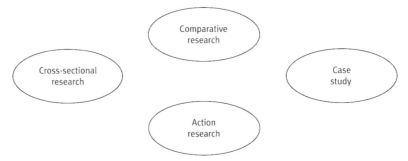

Research strategies that are appropriate for relatively short-term student projects undertaken in organisations are outlined here. These are:

- cross-sectional research
- comparative research
- case study research
- action research.

The choice of strategy for your research will be closely linked to the research objectives/questions of your project. There are advantages and disadvantages with all of these approaches.

Cross-sectional research strategy

If you adopt a cross-sectional research strategy, you will collect data in a fairly standardised form from groups of people at a single point in time. Some people refer to this as a survey strategy. Postal, telephone, web-based/emailed questionnaires or structured interviews may be used to obtain information, but the key approach involves establishing a form of sampling to obtain information from a selection of the wider population. The cross-sectional research strategy will help you to establish patterns and comparisons. However, the data will only be robust and reliable if it can offer an adequate representation of the wider population.

ACTIVITY 2.5

EVALUATING A PIECE OF CROSS-SECTIONAL RESEARCH

Go to the CIPD website, which lists recent survey reports (http://www.cipd.co.uk/hr-resources/survey-reports/default.aspx). Choose a fairly recent survey and skim-read the report to evaluate its strengths and weaknesses.

1   How many people or organisations received the questionnaire (what was the research population?)?

2   What proportion of people or organisations responded to the questionnaire?

3   What are the limitations of the data provided by this survey?

4   What are the useful features of the findings?

FEEDBACK NOTES

You may have found it difficult to find out how many people received the survey. With CIPD surveys you often have to look towards the back of the report to a section titled something like 'Background' where you MAY find out how many people received the survey and what proportion replied. The survey itself may also indicate the extent to which those who replied might be considered to be representative of the overall research population. Survey research offers a range of advantages as it provides a fairly detailed picture 'across the board' about a specific range of issues. However, there are also disadvantages with this strategy.

Table 2.5 Survey-based research

Advantages	Disadvantages
Relatively cheap to organise	'Depth' is sacrificed for 'breadth'
Can achieve a broad coverage for comparisons	Poor questionnaire design leads to poor-quality data
Can be undertaken within a relatively short timeframe	Poor level of responses may make data unrepresentative
Produce a high volume of information	No control over who responds to the questions
Relatively easy to present the data to make comparisons	Will all the questions be interpreted in the same way by all the respondents?
Survey can be repeated again at a different location or at a different time to allow for further comparisons	What are the motivations of those who respond to the questions?
	What do those who do not reply think (and does it matter)?

(Neuman 2011, Bryman and Bell 2007)

Comparative research strategy

This strategy is popular with students who are studying their HR course away from their own country. Comparative research involves examining data from different countries or cultures or organisations to achieve a better understanding through comparing meaningfully contrasting cases or situations. It is then possible to gain a deeper awareness of the topic being researched in different national, cultural or organisational contexts and to consider and explain any similarities and differences that are found (Hantrais 1996, Bryman and Bell 2007).

Comparative research strategies can be based on quantitative or qualitative data (or both). Within HR research there is a strong interest in cross-cultural studies as HR practices are often seen as being significantly influenced by national or societal culture. However, the comparative research strategy may also be appropriate for studies within different parts of organisations or between different organisational sectors. The important issue for the comparative research strategy is the extent to which the distinguishing characteristics of the cases being compared can act as a catalyst for reflection and discussion of theory and practice (Bryman and Bell 2007).

Comparative research may be a particularly attractive research strategy for international students who wish to compare some aspect of HRM practice in their own country with those in their host country. However, a number of difficulties have to be taken into account. First, data access in more than one place is required in a form that will enable an effective comparison. Second, if the research is based on case study data (for example, two or more cases in two or more countries or industry sectors), it is important to ensure that the cases have sufficient in common, but also sufficient distinguishing factors to facilitate a meaningful comparison. Third, where quantitative data are envisaged there are also challenges to be faced in questionnaire design and administration: will the language of the questions be differently interpreted by people of different countries? To what extent will any linguistic translation alter the original intent of any questions asked (McDonald 2000, Stephens 2009)? In spite of these challenges, comparative research in HRM offers a range of advantages. It contributes knowledge about HRM practices and frameworks in a range of situations, taking into account specific 'histories' and contexts. In addition, it encourages practitioners and academics to take a wider perspective of HR issues by reconsidering the extent to which assumptions about HR theory and practice are appropriate in different situations. It can provide HR researchers with an opportunity to probe into questions about the extent to which their learning about HR in their country of study is relevant in their home country.

Case study research strategy

Case study research involves a detailed investigation into a situation in a single case or a small number of related cases. It is the term used for research that investigates a phenomenon in context and in depth, and is particularly useful when the distinction between the phenomenon and its context are unclear or disputed (Yin 2009). The case study strategy is a popular approach for HR students who are in some form of employment, undertaking a project over a limited timescale. Even for full-time students the case study is attractive because it may be easier to obtain access to only one organisation (often where they already have some form of contact) rather than seeking to obtain responses from many companies. This strategy seeks to investigate the interaction of different factors and events that contribute to the focus of the enquiry. A range of types of data (such as observations, interviews, survey data and the analysis of documents) can contribute to the research to provide the basis for a 'rounded' analysis of the issue or problem. 'Historical' research can also be undertaken to find out about the development of the organisation, or a particular problem, as part of the data-gathering process (Farquhar 2012, Yin 2009, Gerring 2007).

Case study research involves achieving access to different forms of data over a period of time. It also involves sharing interim findings with stakeholders and analysing data of different types in a way that develops a robust 'chain of evidence'. Data analysis is an incremental and iterative process making it more 'messy' than other research strategies. For HR students, ease of access to data is also a limitation of the case study strategy, as in such a situation you may already influence and be influenced by the culture and practices of the organisation in which the research is taking place. 'Objective detachment' may be difficult to achieve.

A summary of the main advantages and disadvantages of the case study approach are shown in Table 2.6.

Table 2.6 Case-study-based research – advantages and disadvantages

Advantages	Disadvantages
One issue can be studied in depth	Huge volume of qualitative data may be difficult to analyse
Interaction of factors and events can be taken into account	How can you cross-check information?
Breadth of methods of data collection	Generalisation is not possible
Access to one organisation (or a small number of cases)	Researcher may influence and be influenced by the 'case'
Case study can focus in depth on one department or group	

(Neuman 2011, Yin 2009)

Action research strategy

The action research strategy represents a radical departure from the scientific research tradition. The term 'action research' was first used by Kurt Lewin (1946), a researcher and writer in change management. He argued that, as organisational change processes are continuous and dynamic, so effective organisational research should be seen as an open-ended and continuous process of planning, acting, observing and reflection.

Most HR research, undertaken within an organisation, occurs in the context of change processes, stimulated by external and/or internal factors. It involves investigating HR problems or issues and making recommendations for change and improvement. In turn, any changes that are undertaken will themselves be evaluated and further changes and recommendations are likely to result. This makes the action research strategy very attractive.

Since the 1940s many researchers have developed and modified the concept of action research (see, for example, Eden and Huxham 1996, Coghlan and Brannick 2009, McNiff and Whitehead 2011), but the assumptions on which it was first developed remain central in that:

- researchers are (and should be) involved in the situations they are researching
- researchers are (and should be) part of a cycle of improvement.

ACTIVITY 2.6

ACTION RESEARCH IN PRACTICE

Access an early report of the CIPD Shaping the Future research project. (http://www.cipd.co.uk/binaries/5013%20STF%20interim%20report%20(WEB).pdf)

If you don't have time to read the whole report, go to page 11 and read the parts about: how the research was conducted, why the case study organisations were chosen, and how the data were collected.

1   Why was the action research strategy chosen for this research?

2   In what ways is the process described here different from a case study research strategy?

3   What skills would the researchers require to carry out this action research strategy?

4   Identify three criticisms of the action research strategy.

FEEDBACK NOTES

There are similarities and differences between the case study and action research strategies. Both can use a range of different types of data (both qualitative and quantitative) to inform the research process. Both research strategies are also grounded in the acceptance of the importance of understanding the situational context of what is being researched. The main areas of difference are that action research is firmly grounded in understanding and promoting change where the researcher is part of a continuous cycle of problem diagnosis; taking action and observing the effects of the action that has been instituted (intervention); followed by reflection and theory-building. As such, the researcher is involved in the situations being researched and is part of a cycle of change which may continue indefinitely.

A number of skills are required for effective action researchers (Yin 2009, Coghlan and Brannick 2009, McNiff and Whitehead 2011, Reason and Bradbury 2006), which include the ability to:

- ask probing questions (and be able to interpret the answers)

- be an effective listener – not hearing only what you expect or assume you will hear
- be flexible and responsive to new data-gathering opportunities that may present themselves as the research process goes along
- be alert to, and sensitive to, the likelihood of confusing or contradictory evidence from different stakeholders or places within the situation you are researching.

You may have highlighted some problems with action research. For example, focusing on a discrete 'problem' might lead action researchers to uncritically accept the dominant assumptions, theories and 'ways of thinking' within the organisation(s). A further critique of the problem-solving focus forms the basis for an alternative approach known as appreciative inquiry.

Appreciative inquiry

Appreciative inquiry was first articulated as a research strategy in the 1980s by Cooperrider and Srivastva (1987) as an alternative to traditional action research. They argued that a focus on problem-solving is too limited if significant change is required. They suggested that a more positive 'appreciative' approach is needed to generate more imaginative responses, innovative practice improvement and knowledge-creation processes (Ludema 2001, Hayes 2007, Rogers and Fraser 2003). Appreciative inquiry practitioners argue that their approach is grounded in a range of research 'positions' taking account of insights from a range of research approaches, including scientific, interpretive and pragmatic traditions (Cooperrider et al 2008, Hart et al 2008). The aim of appreciative inquiry is to find out the best of 'what is' in an organisation; to establish ideas of 'what might be'; to enable consent about 'what should be'; and to foster experience of 'what can be'. Instead of identifying problems, appreciative inquiry practitioners examine areas of strength, both those that are already known and those that may be unknown (Watkins and Mhor 2001), through a process that involves application, practice and collaboration.

Opinions about appreciative inquiry differ widely, but the approach has been used in management development, organisation development, adult education and HR settings in a range of sectors, particularly in health and social care. Few systematic evaluations of the approach have been undertaken, however, and it has many critics.

Those within the 'scientific' research tradition are particularly critical of the inclusion of 'positive imagery' and emotive ways of explaining the approach which focus on its potential to: appreciate, initiate, enquire, envision, dialogue, imagine and innovate. Other criticisms are that it is just another 'management fad' more suited to management consultancy than rigorous academic practice (Grant and Humphries 2006, Bushe 2007) because a commitment to work from 'the positive' may lead researchers to overlook tensions and ambiguities inherent in the organisational context for the project. Such an approach might encourage excessive optimism and the avoidance of politically difficult problem areas so that dysfunctional perceptions and behaviours in organisational settings are not examined, leading to descriptive rather than analytical outcomes (Grant and Humphries 2006, Bushe 2007, Fitzgerald et al 2010).

Those who engage with appreciative inquiry, however, have found a number of benefits for both the research process and the organisation. First, the spirit of 'building on the good' encourages more people, particularly those at senior level, to agree to participate as the fear of criticism and negative comment is diminished and higher levels of collaboration are possible, both within and outside of the organisation. In addition, researchers find the approach 'liberating' in its affirmative but also provocative features.

In common with more traditional forms of action research there are also disadvantages with specific consequences for students undertaking a research project or dissertation.

Practical disadvantages of action research

- **Time duration** – the action research methodology requires continuous involvement in planning, taking action, observing the effects and reflecting (often two or three times round the complete cycle) and many student research projects have to be completed in a matter of months.
- **Transparency of research process and outcomes** – a key reason for undertaking research in HR is to expand knowledge and understanding of particular organisational phenomena. If the way that action research is undertaken tends to be limited to the pragmatic and common-sense level, it may be difficult to justify any 'value' in terms of knowledge and understanding outside of the organisation.

PLANNING TO IMPLEMENT YOUR RESEARCH STRATEGY

The brief overview of different research strategies provided here shows how, in any one research project, it may be appropriate to devise a 'hybrid' approach where you use a combination of strategies. The choice you make at this stage will influence what sort of data you decide to gather and where to obtain your information. Before making a final decision about your research topic and strategy, therefore, it is worth thinking through responses to the questions in Table 2.7.

Table 2.7 Initial research design questions

- What will be the main 'level of analysis' in your research: individuals, groups, organisations, societies?
- Will you be able to access the data that you need to implement your strategy?
- To what extent will the data you gather provide a robust basis to achieve your research aim and objectives/questions?
- Do you have the skills (or can you develop them) to collect and analyse the data you need?
- How might your strategy and methods affect the answers you get?
- How will you (your position in the organisation, preconceptions, and so on) affect the research?

ACCESS TO DATA

HR research involves gaining access at three main levels. First, you have to get access to an organisation (or group of organisations). Then you need access to relevant people in the organisation to enable primary data to be gathered. Third, you may require access to sources of secondary data both within host organisation(s) and also from external information sources. Access is a critical aspect of the research design of all projects and the challenges involved are often underestimated. It is important to gain access to participants who are willing to co-operate, rather than those whose initial interest fades away quickly. Access will also present different challenges depending on your position. You may be:

- a part-time HR student in employment in the organisation to be investigated
- a full-time HR student who also works part-time in one or more organisations
- a full-time HR student using a work placement organisation for your research
- an HR student (full- or part-time or 'distance') with no current employing organisation.

ACCESS AS AN 'OUTSIDER'

'Cold-calling'

Although difficult, this is not impossible but access may be time-consuming to achieve and take many weeks to arrange. Most students find that written requests for access go unanswered and that several telephone calls or email messages, once you have established the identity of the appropriate person to contact, are required.

Using your networks

Contacting an organisation with which you already have some form of connection is more likely to be successful. Gaining access to organisations through the employers of colleagues on your course, or members of the local branch of your professional association, for example, is often possible. Sometimes it is necessary to ask your existing contact to introduce you to a more relevant contact within their organisation.

Before attempting contact with an organisation it is important to be clear about the aims and purpose of your project and what sort of data you hope to collect (interviews, surveys, observation and so on). Once contact has been established you should also be prepared to negotiate on issues such as sample size, interview structure and so on. To achieve access you will need to 'sell' the idea of the project in an effective way. Some ideas for achieving this are shown in Table 2.8.

Table 2.8 Gaining access to an organisation for your project

- Communicate clearly about the purpose of your project and the type of access and data that you hope to gather.
- Indicate the time commitment involved (how many interviews? of what duration? who with? how many people to be surveyed? what documents to be analysed?).
- Be aware of organisational sensitivities – if they think you are going to highlight all the weaknesses in the organisation's approach, and none of its strengths, they are unlikely to give permission.
- Be clear about how you propose to ensure confidentiality and anonymity of the organisation and individuals within it.
- Sell the 'benefits' of the research – how will it help the organisation better cope with HR issues in the future? What feedback (copy of your report, production of a summary report and so on) will you provide?
- Use the language of business, rather than the language of academics.
- Be prepared to develop access on an incremental basis. Perhaps get permission for a short questionnaire first. Provide some feedback based on this and then get agreement for some structured interviews of key people. Then indicate how helpful it would be to be able to read the notes of relevant meetings and so on. If you undertake the first stage in a sloppy way, you are unlikely to be allowed to continue. Once your credibility is demonstrated, however, and you are successful in building good relationships within the organisation, there is more chance that you will achieve further access.

ACCESS AS AN 'INSIDER'

Many people will undertake their project in the organisation of which they are already a part, whether on a full- or part-time basis. In this sense, **physical access** is easier, although what is really required for an effective project is **support and acceptance**.

If you are an 'insider' researcher, you have the advantage of knowledge of the politics of the organisation and who best to approach for different types of data. Hopefully you will also have some organisational credibility. There are a number of difficulties, however, that you will have to take into account:

- separating your role as a researcher from your role as a practitioner
- the dynamics of interviewing colleagues who know you and are known by you
- handling confidential disclosures that may affect your future working relationships
- living with the consequences of any mistakes that you make.

Planning and preparing for research in your own organisation requires just as much thought as for one with which you have limited contact. Important features of the access process are shown in Table 2.9.

Table 2.9 Negotiating access in your own organisation

- Establish appropriate points of contact (not just your manager).
- Produce an outline of your proposed project and get it cleared at all necessary levels in the organisation (you don't want your questionnaire blocked by the CEO just days before you plan to issue it).
- Be honest with yourself and others about the purpose of the study and the data you need to achieve your objectives.
- Discuss your project with 'gatekeepers' (heads of department, manager, union representatives and so on) and attempt to anticipate possible sensitive issues and areas.
- Discuss your study with participants. They will be more likely to co-operate if you inform them what is to be done with the information they provide.
- Be aware of the needs of those in the organisation with regard to politics, confidentiality and sensitivity. Decide what level of anonymity and confidentiality will be possible and acceptable.

Many of the issues raised with negotiating access also relate to issues of ethics in research, and these issues are discussed in Chapter 3. Figure 2.6 highlights how the different factors that have been introduced here might influence your approach to your research.

Figure 2.6 Influences on research design

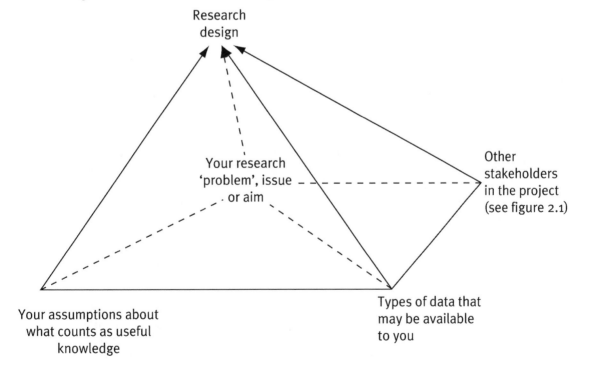

Figure 2.6 highlights the importance of:

- your assumptions about what counts as useful knowledge; factors that are linked with your world-view about research and the tradition within which you decide to work. This in turn will influence the purpose of your research
- other stakeholders in your research, which will also influence the design of your study, in particular the expectations of your employing or sponsoring organisation, your study centre (and in particular your supervisor) and your professional association
- practical issues such as access to data, which will also influence your research design.

These issues are represented in the form of a 'decision chart' in Figure 2.7.

Figure 2.7 Research design decision path

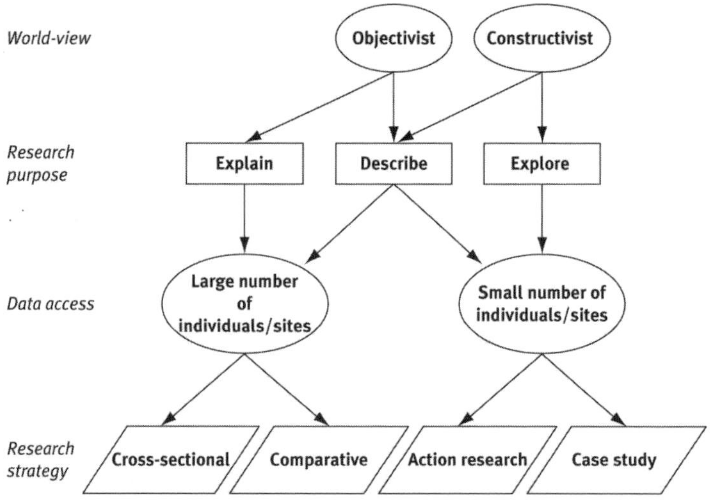

FINAL PREPARATIONS – PROJECT PLANNING

Unlike many other features of taught courses in HR, the research project or business research report is a piece of **independent** work, undertaken with the benefit of the guidance and advice of a supervisor or tutor. Responsibility for planning your project so that you can be sure to submit work of appropriate quality, on or before the submission date, remains with you. There is more chance that this will be achieved if an effective project management approach is adopted (Marchington and Wilkinson 2008).

As indicated in Chapter 1, important project management skills are: identifying the component tasks and milestones you will need to achieve and then planning a sequence in which to undertake them; and identifying which can be carried out 'in parallel' and which must be achieved before other tasks can be started. In addition, you need the skill of accurate estimating so that your schedule of tasks is both honest and reasonable. Experience of writing up a coursework assignment might be used to estimate the time required for writing up one section of your final report, for example.

A typical list of tasks that comprise the 'journey' to a completed research project is shown as Figure 2.8.

Figure 2.8 The research project 'journey'

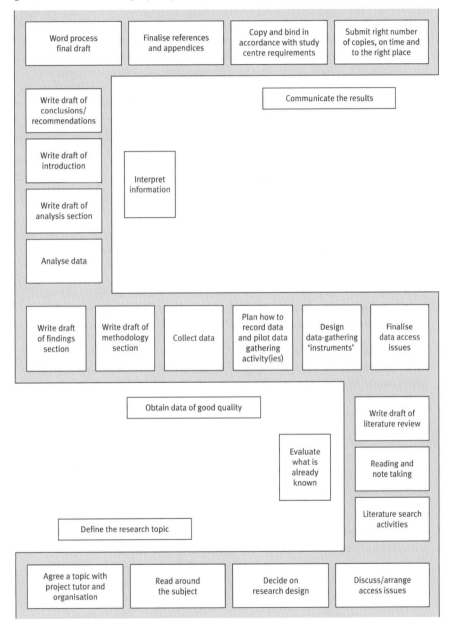

Having identified the various tasks it is important to allocate appropriate time to achieve them. At this stage it may become clear that other activities, both at home and at work, may be affected, and you will need to discuss this with those involved to overcome any potential difficulties. Some tasks can be undertaken in parallel (such as the initial drafting of the literature review and drafting a questionnaire or carrying out some initial interviews) and this is a good opportunity to work out how you wish to proceed.

Many students find that producing a Gantt chart helps them plan and implement their research project in an effective way. A Gantt chart is a type of bar chart used to illustrate the start and finish dates of the different elements of a project. It is a useful tool for analysing and planning your work, it gives you a basis for scheduling when you will carry out the different tasks and to plan ahead for particular resourcing demands (help with software, access to the HR information system and so on) and you can also work out the critical path (what tasks you must complete by a particular date). Once your project is under way, a Gantt chart can help you to assess whether you are staying on schedule and, if you fall behind, you can identify what you will need to do to put it back on schedule.

There are many different ways of producing a Gantt chart (using Microsoft Project, Microsoft Excel and so on), but it is also possible to produce one using graph paper without the need for a software package by following these steps:

Step 1: List all the tasks you need to complete in your research project. For each of them, estimate how long they will take and whether they can be undertaken in parallel with others or 'in sequence'.

Step 2: Head up your graph paper with the time (in weeks) from the start of your project through to the date the research report or dissertation must be completed (these represent the headers for your 'columns').

Step 3: Draw up a rough draft of the Gantt chart. Allocate each task a 'row' on the vertical axis of your graph paper. Plot each task on the graph paper, showing it starting on the earliest possible date. Draw it as a bar, with the length of the bar being the length of the task expressed in weeks. Above the task bars, mark the estimate of time needed to complete each of them.

Schedule your tasks in such a way that sequential actions are carried out in the required order. Ensure that dependent activities do not start until the activities they depend on have been completed.

Step 4: Review and redraw. The last stage in this process is to prepare a final (and probably tidier) version of the Gantt chart to show how sets of sequential activities link together and where critical points occur. You can do this manually on graph paper or, without the need for specific software, you can produce one using Excel, as in the example shown as Figure 2.9.

ACTIVITY 2.7

PROJECT PLANNING

Critically review the Gantt chart shown in Figure 2.9, which shows a project duration of 16 weeks. What tasks would you consider to have been allocated too much or too little time? Which times of the 16-week period look overcrowded and what might be done to 'smooth out' the tasks?

FEEDBACK NOTES

It may be that you have longer than 16 weeks to undertake your project and this will give more space. If you have a short period of time, however, the Gantt chart shows how important the early weeks are. There is no time to lose. You may feel that some tasks require more time; where this is the case, make sure that you identify where time can also be saved. A further issue not factored into this illustrative example is the requirement to find out how long your tutor will need to give feedback on different sections or chapters of your project. Another issue you may have identified is that there is no scope in this Gantt chart for holidays or time off. If your project plan extends over a public holiday you may need to factor this in (as well as arrangements for other family celebrations).

Figure 2.9 Example Gantt chart

	1	2	3	4	5	6	7	8	9	10	11	12	13	14	15	16
Agree aims + research questions	▓															
Draft introduction and get feedback	▓	▓														
Literature search		▓	▓	▓												
Literature review					▓	▓	░	░	░	░	░	░	░	░		
Draft literature review and get feedback							▓	▓								
Read methodology literature			▓													
Discuss research strategy																
Design data-gathering tools																
Ethical scrutiny process																
Agree access arrangements			▓													
Collect data			▓													
Draft methodology chapter and feedback				▓	▓											
Analyse data																
Draft findings chapter and get feedback							▓									
Draft analysis chapter and get feedback								▓								
Draft conclusions and recommendations								▓								
Full draft to tutor for comment									▓							
Finalise references and appendices													▓	▓		
Review and revise whole document													▓			
Proof-read															▓	
Print and bind															▓	
Submit																▓

MONITORING PROGRESS

As with all projects, it is important to 'go public' with the project plan so that any significant errors of estimation can be discussed, any logistical oversights can be incorporated and those around you – at your study centre, your workplace (where appropriate) and your family and friends – are aware of your commitments. Progress meetings with your manager (where the project is organisationally based) and your project tutor or supervisor will also be an important way to gauge whether you need to revise the plan.

SUMMARY

- An appropriate research topic will meet the different expectations of: the student; the employing organisation(s) involved; the study centre; and, where appropriate, relevant professional associations.
- Research projects need to be focused such that the aim and purpose of the project are clear and appropriate research questions or research objectives have been formulated.
- The choices you make about what to research and how you plan to undertake your research may be influenced by: your situation at work; your personal and

professional interests and background; and your world-view about what counts as useful knowledge.

- Methodology refers to the philosophical framework and foundation upon which research is conducted; the choices you make about these issues will have important implications for the research method or methods that you adopt.

- The positivist research tradition emphasises the importance of a 'scientific' approach to gathering facts and analysing them to formulate generalisable conclusions.

- The interpretivist research tradition emphasises the subjective nature of human interactions and focus on the meanings and understandings of those involved in organisational processes.

- There are advantages and disadvantages to both positivist and interpretivist research traditions, and some form of 'methodological pluralism' may be appropriate. Some organisationally based HR projects adopt a 'mixed methods' approach.

- Research design is the general plan that will identify how your research aim will be achieved and how your research questions or objectives will be addressed.

- Research tactics are the particular choices you will make about specific data-gathering techniques you plan to employ.

- Four research strategies are popular with student HR researchers: cross-sectional research; case study research; action research; and comparative research (or a combination).

- Implementing an HR research design involves gaining access at three levels to organisation(s), people and documents. In addition to physical access, support and acceptance is important for effective research to be undertaken.

- Effective project planning and management involves breaking the research process down into stages and tasks, scheduling those tasks, identifying dependencies and critical tasks and dates, and monitoring progress on a regular basis.

 **Self-test questions**

REVIEW AND REFLECT

1 Research design is:

   a) a matter of choosing between qualitative and quantitative methods

   b) the way you structure your research report or dissertation

   c) the general plan that identifies how your principal research question will be answered

   d) the basis for your conclusions and recommendations

2 Which of the following statements represents the positivist research position?

   a) Research should be value-free, use a scientific method and be based on empirical observations.

   b) Unexpected events and contextual differences prevent researchers from generalising about their research findings.

c)   There is no substitute for an in-depth, reflexive understanding of the social world.

d)   It is important to find something positive from research, even when it does not go according to plan.

3   An interpretivist perspective about organisational culture suggests that:

a)   features of 'desired' organisational culture can be measured

b)   culture can be managed from the top

c)   culture is a construct that is used to make sense of organisational experiences

d)   a strong culture will result in consistent behaviours regardless of context

4   The cross-sectional research strategy is:

a)   the study of a particular phenomenon across a range of cases at a particular time

b)   best suited to proving what the CEO already thinks about important issues

c)   a comparison of two or more variables over a long period of time

d)   one that focuses on the negative expressions of disgruntled employees

5   Cross-cultural studies make use of:

a)   a case study research strategy

b)   a comparative research strategy

c)   an appreciative inquiry approach

d)   a longitudinal research strategy

6   Which of the following is a research strategy?

a)   the interview

b)   positivism

c)   SWOT analysis

d)   action research

7   Methodological pluralism is:

a)   research designed to be read by the participating organisation and the academic supervisor

b)   a research method for cross-cultural research

c)   the use of interviews as well as focus groups

d)   a flexible approach to the selection of research methods and tolerance towards different research traditions

Review questions

REVIEW AND REFLECT

Take the time to review two or three recently submitted research reports at your study centre (those that got good marks) and then consider these review questions:

1   What topics have other people chosen to research?

2   How clearly have research questions or objectives been articulated? Does there seem to be a preference for a hypothesis, a research aim or a principal research question in your study centre?

3   How long (and extensive) are the methodology or methods sections/chapters and what are the implications of this for what will be expected of you?

4   What research strategy or strategies were used? What research methods were used? What hints and tips can you glean for arranging access to data for your project?

Questions for reflection

REVIEW AND REFLECT

As with Chapter 1, this part of the chapter enables you to reflect about your professional development and develop your skills and knowledge. This will enable you to build your confidence and credibility, track your learning, see your progress and demonstrate your achievements.

Taking stock

1   How much time is left until your project must be completed and submitted? What are likely to be the main stages of your project? How long will you have to complete each of them? How, and with whom, will you monitor your progress?

2   If you have not yet determined your project, identify three possible research ideas. For each of them, write down three advantages/disadvantages. Make sure you take account of the perspective of: yourself, your study centre and (where appropriate) your employing

organisation in the advantages and disadvantages that you identify. Who might you also consult in the process of identifying a research idea?

3   Write a summary (no more than three sentences for each) of the four research strategies (cross-sectional research; case study; action research; comparative research). Which strategy is most attractive to you and why?

Strengths and weaknesses

4   How clear are you about the aims of your potential project? What do you need to read to identify key concepts, issues and contexts? Who might you discuss your research ideas with?

5   What will be the main challenges for you with regard to access to organisation(s), people and documents? What skills and behaviours will you need to develop to overcome those challenges? What opportunities

does your current situation afford for access to people and data?

Being a practitioner-researcher

6   How might your position in the organisation affect, and be affected by, the research project you plan to conduct? What are the implications of your role for the research strategy that you are considering?

7   How might you be able to link your practitioner research with your professional development? To what extent will your position within your professional area or within your organisation affect the extent to which you can probe into

and challenge your own (and others') assumptions about HR practices and processes?

Moving forward

Following your reflection, it is important to develop an action plan to take your development forward:

● What are the key things you need to learn more about?
● How will you achieve this?
● What resources or support do you need?
● When does this need to be achieved and who can provide feedback for you on what you have learned?

EXPLORE FURTHER

Biggam, J. (2011) *Succeeding with your master's dissertation*. Maidenhead: Open University Press.

Bryman, A. (ed.) (1988) *Doing research in organisations*. London: Routledge.

Bryman, A. and Bell, E. (2007) *Business research methods*. Oxford: Oxford University Press.

Coghlan, D. and Brannick, T. (2009) *Doing action research in your own organisation*. London: Sage.

Cooperrider, D.I., Whitney, D., Stavros, J. and Fry, R. (2008) *Appreciative inquiry handbook: for leaders of change*. Brunswick, OH: Crown Custom Publishing.

Gill, J., Johnson, P. and Clark, M. (2010) *Research methods for managers*. London: Sage.

Hart, C. (2010) *Doing your master's dissertation*. London: Sage.

Lee, N. and Lings, L. (2008) *Doing business research: a guide to theory and practice*. London: Sage.

McNiff, J. and Whitehead, J. (2011) *All you need to know about action research*. London: Sage.

Neuman, W. (2011) *Basics of social research: qualitative and quantitative approaches*. International edition. Harlow: Pearson Education.

Robson, C. (2011). *Real world research: a resource for social scientists and practitioner-researchers*. Oxford: Wiley.

Saunders, M., Lewis, P. and Thornhill, A. (2012) *Research methods for business students*. Harlow: Pearson Education.

Yin, R.K. (2009) *Case study research: design and methods*. Thousand Oaks, CA: Sage Publications.

CHAPTER 3

Finding and Reviewing HR Literature and Information Sources

CHAPTER OUTLINE

- How to use this chapter
- Why read, when to read and what to read
- Different types of literature
- Searching for and finding appropriate literature and information sources
- Evaluating your sources
- Reading the literature and making notes
- Evaluation and analysis
- The structure of the literature review
- Referencing and citations
- Summary
- Review and reflect
- Explore further

LEARNING OUTCOMES

This chapter should help you to:

- identify what you need to read and where to find it
- establish an effective note-taking and recording system
- read in a critically evaluative way
- plan and structure your literature review
- reference your work in a credible way.

HOW TO USE THIS CHAPTER

A literature review is exactly what the name implies: it is a 're-view' of what has been written about your topic (Lee and Lings 2008). Students undertaking research at any advanced level are expected to discuss existing literature and contemporary HR policy and practice relevant to the topic of their research. Many students struggle to find the time to keep up with their 'normal' coursework, let alone undertake the additional reading required for a research project. However, a good review of relevant information sources can add value to your research. This chapter focuses on helping you to work in a 'time effective' way to find and read appropriate materials and to construct a literature review section or chapter for your research report.

Different parts of this chapter will be relevant at different stages of the research process. The early sections of the chapter introduce the main purposes and benefits of a good literature review. Next, different strategies for literature searching are discussed. If feedback on previous assignments has suggested that your work is too descriptive, the ideas about reading and writing in a critical, analytical and evaluative way will also be helpful. The final parts of the chapter focus on how to structure the literature review and how to ensure that your work is appropriately referenced. This may well be a section that you skim through at the beginning of your research process but come back to as you begin to draft your literature review chapter or section.

 From topic to literature review

CASE ILLUSTRATION 3.1

Mona was an international student who decided that the topic for her research would be the training and development implications of quality assurance and certification processes currently being introduced by the healthcare organisation in Saudi Arabia in which she worked.

Discussion Questions

1   What topics would Mona need to 'read up on' to make progress with this project?

2   What difficulties might she face?

FEEDBACK NOTES

The first challenge for Mona was to identify an appropriate focus for her literature search and review. As a result of her previous employment she had collected quite a lot of information about quality management and accreditation processes and 'kitemarks', as well as a range of articles and case studies from practitioner journals related with healthcare organisations. However, these lacked sufficient depth and were written from either a tactical or over-generalised perspective and were too limited for a project linked to an academic qualification. To make progress with her literature review, Mona had to search for literature relating to three relevant areas: quality management; learning, training and development; and the healthcare system in Saudi Arabia.

Other challenges facing Mona were:

- Although she had already undertaken some reading about quality management and accreditation, new material was being published all the time although very little was apparent in 'academic' journals. There were plenty of sources from a practitioner perspective but Mona found it hard to identify what was most useful.
- The library of the UK business school where she was based was well resourced with regard to materials related to training and development, but there were almost no sources relating to HRM or HRD in Saudi Arabia.
- The sources that Mona accessed about training and development contained a range of different frameworks and models, but it was harder to find any theories associated with quality management and accreditation.

Many practitioners are worried by the requirement to review the literature. The amount of written material around seems to be limitless and assessing its relevance for a potential project seems difficult. The range of different types of material is also extensive and you may feel unsure about what the 'best' types are. This chapter addresses some of these issues.

WHY READ, WHEN TO READ AND WHAT TO READ

WHY READ?

A key feature of any project is to demonstrate an awareness of how your investigation fits into the wider context of theory, policy and practice in HR. The length and extent of the literature review varies depending on the nature of the qualification (intermediate or advanced level; undergraduate, postgraduate and so on) as well as the assessment criteria used by the people who will mark your work. However, for all projects an initial evaluation of what has been published about your topic and where there are areas of uncertainty or a 'gap' in knowledge as well as an assessment of how your findings 'fit' within the general realm of what has been published are all vital components.

You may feel apprehensive about undertaking a literature review, perhaps because of anxious memories about previous assignments which have not been as successful as you would have liked, but there are a range of benefits that you will discover once you start the reading process (Brown 2006):

- **Getting ideas for your project:** you can gather background information on your topic and get a feel for the sort of perspectives on the subject that are relevant, particularly views that might not be expressed in an everyday work or managerial environment. In this way you can generate 'fresher' or more interesting ideas and you should be able to clarify your initial thoughts about the way forward with your research.
- **Expand your understanding of your topic area:** if you have an idea about your research topic, your reading about the topic will provide you with useful information about the issues that will need to be considered in your research.
- **Find out how others have addressed and 'solved' similar research problems to the one you are taking forward:** as you read you can find out not just 'what

is known' but also find out how others have researched a similar area or tackled a similar problem. This will help you as you come to think about the research methods that you might use.

- **Identify a way of making sense of your data:** later in the project, when you have gathered some information, you will have to interpret and analyse it. To do this effectively you will need to know what the key issues, concepts and questions are and how they relate to each other.
- **Sources of secondary data:** reading around the subject might also reveal relevant secondary data. This might include examples of other organisations in a similar position to yours or numerical data that are useful for comparative or benchmarking purposes.

WHEN TO READ

The reading process underpins the planning of your project so it is important not to delay. Start the reading process as soon as you have some ideas about your project topic. This will help you to establish the scope and decide what particular aspects are relevant for your project. Once you have come up with some initial research questions and/or objectives, further reading will help you to clarify the main issues and concepts. Use this knowledge to make sure you gather primary data that cover all the important aspects.

New sources of information are always becoming available and research into HR operates in a context of development and change, and so the literature scanning and reading process will underpin the whole lifecycle of your project. Brown (2006) points out that, where the literature is concerned, researchers have to be like jugglers, keeping a number of items in the air at the same time, including:

- searching for relevant literature
- reading the literature that you have found
- starting to write the literature review section or chapter
- defining and refining the research objectives or questions
- planning how to undertake the research.

WHAT TO READ

'The literature' is made up of published and unpublished materials often in the form of books, reports, 'papers' and statistics (Hart 2010). Although you will find yourself reading a range of materials from different sources, it is important to ensure that what you read is 'credible' and that you do not waste time and effort reading unattributed sources from Internet sites where there is no information about the author and their credentials. Broadly speaking, you can divide the sources of information about 'what is already known' (the literature) into three types:

- **Primary literature sources:** most of these come from within the organisation(s) you are studying. They will mostly be 'unpublished', for example, internal reports and email correspondence.
- **Grey literature:** documents that are more widely available in the public domain but are not controlled by commercial publishers. Grey literature

includes company reports, government publications, technical reports, newsletters, bulletins, white papers, position papers, factsheets, conference proceedings, dissertations or research reports. Such sources are often produced by the Government, academics (and students), professional associations, business and industry. Often, but not always, this has been generated with practitioners in mind.

- **Published literature sources:** what is already known at a more general level about your topic will be found in more widely available published sources such as books, newspaper articles or reports, features and articles in journals. Some of these sources will be written with academic readers in mind and some might be categorised as 'teaching literature', which comprises both textbooks and published case studies (Lee and Lings 2008).

Although the distinction between these three types of source is not always clear cut (items from many of them may be available through the Internet, for example), this chapter focuses mostly on the issues involved in making effective use of published sources and 'grey literature'. Obtaining and using primary sources are covered in Chapter 6.

DIFFERENT TYPES OF LITERATURE

Different types of literature

CASE ILLUSTRATION 3.2

Jo was a part-time student who worked in an outsource provider of telephone and Internet support for a range of client organisations in the UK. She was aware that many organisations were considering the option to take their outsourced business 'offshore' and Jo's employer had already established a small organisation in India. Jo decided to undertake a work-based study into the influence of different approaches to motivation in India and the UK on levels of customer service. Jo knew that she needed to 'read around' to expand her understanding of the topic and identify a set of questions that would help her develop a framework by which to decide on a research design and, ultimately, to guide her analysis of her data.

Discussion Questions

1   In addition to the study of documents available within her organisation, what other sources would be useful to Jo in finding out more about motivational strategies and levels of customer service in call centres in the UK and India?

2   For each of the sources that you identify, list at least one advantage and one limitation of it as a basis for establishing what has been written about these issues.

3   Jo was a student with very limited discretionary time. How might she access the relevant parts of each source without having to read everything?

FEEDBACK NOTES

You can probably identify a range of different sources that would help Jo to find out more about this broad topic. From time to time, **newspapers** publish articles and news reports about call centre work, particularly in relation to offshored services. In addition, you might suggest Jo consults relevant **trade or professional journals** relating to the areas of business her organisation is involved with as well as those concerned with HRM, such as *People Management*. There is also likely to be some helpful material in a range of **books**. General HR textbooks will contain materials on motivation-related topics and some international HRM texts now discuss patterns of offshore outsourcing. Specialist **factsheets or resources or specialist websites** are also available.

Another important source of information is relevant articles in **academic journals**, such as the *Human Resource Management Journal*, the *International Journal of Human Resource Management*, the *International Journal of Service Industry Management* and the *British Journal of Management*. They provide information that is the result of careful research and academic consideration and usually incorporate a thorough review of the literature. As a result these articles are useful, not only for their content, but also for the list of references they provide, some of which Jo could follow up for her project. Finally, it is possible that another student based in the same study centre or workplace has undertaken a research project for their qualification and the **dissertation, thesis or project report** that they have produced may also be a useful source of information.

An overview of different types of sources (primary and secondary) is shown in Figure 3.1.

Figure 3.1 Different types of literature

ASSESSING THE VALUE OF DIFFERENT SOURCES

When evaluating different sources of information, it is important to identify the main audience that they would have been written for and the style of communication that is appropriate for that readership (see Figure 3.2). Newspaper articles, online news items or blog postings, for example, are written to be of interest to a cross-section of the general population and will often have been produced in line with an editorial policy or perspective. As a result issues will be covered very generally and the item may not explore all the possible interpretations of what is being described. Materials from trade or professional journals, while accessible in reading terms, also tend to reflect particular editorial beliefs and priorities. Articles in refereed journal articles, by contrast, while providing a good framework of analysis and critique, may seem more 'remote' from your particular interest, and reading them may be hard work as a result of the careful and evaluative style of writing that is necessary if a full consideration of a range of factors is to be included in the discussion. While harder work to read, however, they can provide a useful basis for critical and evaluative thinking to enable you to carry out research that probes and analyses the underlying causes and issues relevant to HR problems or opportunities.

Figure 3.2 Different approaches underpinning different types of literature

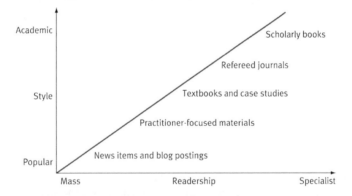

SEARCHING FOR AND FINDING APPROPRIATE LITERATURE AND INFORMATION SOURCES

When searching the literature there are some basic questions that need to be addressed when you start on the literature review. These include (Hart 2010):

- What research and theory is there on my topic?
- What are the main theories and who are the main researchers in this area?
- What is the 'history' or chronological development of the issue or topic?

Once you have had a chance to answer these questions, it is important to address other questions, which include:

- How has the topic or issue been defined?
- What are the key concepts, variables or factors?

- Where do authors and researchers agree and disagree about the topic – what are the debates?
- What are the areas where not much is known in this area or where evidence is lacking?

The volume of available information made possible with the development of digital systems can make the identification of relevant material seem overwhelmingly difficult, and an effective literature **search and selection** process is essential. Students in different parts of the world tend to vary in the approach they prefer to use when looking for literature. In some countries or cultures students strongly favour and value information from books and are prepared to invest considerable time and money in libraries or online bookshops looking for as many books on the topic area as possible. A problem here is that the books themselves can vary in quality and may not provide sufficient depth in what they cover. Students from other countries, cultures or educational backgrounds head straight for a general Internet search engine to try to find papers and articles, as well as webpages, which deal with their topic. Their difficulty is that they are often quickly overwhelmed with the volume of material that they find and they do not know how to select what will be most useful.

Although the temptation(s) to rush either to dedicated books or to Internet search engines can be powerful, a more productive, focused and systematic way to start a literature search for an academic research project is to assess the range of resources of your academic library, either by a personal 'physical visit' or through an electronic 'virtual' visit. For student projects the academic library is a more focused place to start. A keyword search of the library catalogue will indicate readily available sources, such as: print books and journals; e-books and electronic journals; student dissertations and PhD or MPhil theses. Once you have found the location of some useful-looking materials, you can identify the main sources that they refer to and see if they are readily available (or can be accessed through the inter-library loan process that your library will be part of). For physical (print) resources, all libraries use the same 'classmarking' and cataloguing system. Table 3.1 indicates some of the main HRM-related classmarks. If you follow the numbering system shown on the shelves of the library and on the spines of the books, you will find what you are looking for.

Table 3.1 Library classmarks for HRM subject areas

Subject area	Classmark	Subject area	Classmark
Organisation behaviour	302.35 658.402	HRM (General)	658.3
Industrial relations / labour economics	331	Recruitment	658.311
Flexible working	331.257	HR development / training	658.3124
UK employment / labour law	344.4101	Performance appraisal	658.3125
Employee relations	658.315	Motivation	658.314
Cross-cultural management	658.049	Reward management	658.32

LITERATURE SEARCHING: STARTING FROM BOOKS AND OTHER PROJECTS

 ACTIVITY 3.1

FIRST STEPS IN FINDING LITERATURE

Imagine that you have decided to undertake research into the general area of 'executive coaching'. Undertake a keyword search of your library's catalogue and identify three–four books that are relevant to this subject. Study the 'Further Reading', 'Bibliography' or 'References' sections of those books (or the most relevant chapters) and identify some of the main authors or sources of information that they have used.

1 Produce a list of five–six possibly relevant sources of information.

2 Explain why it might be necessary to read some of these articles and books, rather than relying on the coverage about them in the books where they were cited.

FEEDBACK NOTES

If you have undertaken this activity (which you could do for any topic) and undertaken a first-level 'browse' of the catalogue, you might have come across sources such as these:

- Bluckert, P. (2006) *Psychological dimensions of executive coaching*. Maidenhead: Open University Press.
- Chapman, T., Best, B. and Van Casteren, P. (2003) *Executive coaching: exploding the myths*. Basingstoke: Palgrave Macmillan.
- Chartered Institute of Personnel and Development. (2008) *Real-world coaching evaluation: a guide for practitioners[online]*. London: CIPD. Available at: http://www.cipd.co.uk/hr-resources/guides/real-world-coaching-evaluation.aspx
- Chartered Institute of Personnel and Development. (2008) *Coaching and buying coaching services*[online]. London: CIPD. Available at: http://www.cipd.co.uk/hr-resources/guides/coaching-buying-coaching-services.aspx

- Gladis, S.D. (2008) *The executive coach in the corporate forest: a business fable*. Amherst, MA: HRD Press.
- Lloyd, C. (2010) *Integrated experiential coaching: becoming an executive coach*. London: Karnac.
- Peltier, B. (2009) *The psychology of executive coaching: theory and application*. New York: Routledge.

A review of the sources that these authors have made use of will enable you to take the next step towards identifying relevant literature, and it is likely that they will make reference to a variety of articles, books and websites that reflect the different preferences of those authors. For this topic these might include:

- Brunning, H. (2006) *Executive coaching: systems-psychodynamic perspective*. London: Karnac.
- Coutu, D. and Kauffman, C. (2009) The realities of executive coaching. *Harvard Business Review*. January
- Gray, D.E. (2006) Executive coaching: towards a dynamic alliance of psychotherapy and transformative learning processes. *Management Learning*, 37(4): 475–97.
- Jarvis, J., Lane, D.E. and Fillery-Travis, A. (2006) *The case for coaching: making evidence-based decisions*. London: Chartered Institute of Personnel and Development.
- Parker-Wilkins, V. (2006) Business impact of executive coaching: demonstrating monetary value. *Industrial and Commercial Training*, 38(3): 122–7.
- Passmore, J. and Gibbes, C. (2007) The state of executive coaching research: What does the current literature tell us and what's next for coaching research? *International Coaching Psychology Review*, 2(2): 116–29.

These initial sources will provide you with an initial overview of the main issues in the topic you will need to think about. When you are short of time there is a big temptation not to bother with this process and to 'just' read the information in a few textbooks on the topic you are interested in. However, there are potential dangers with this 'short cut'. Textbook authors and business report writers have to briefly summarise and describe a wide range of material in a generalised way. As a result there is limited scope for a deeper level of examination. You may be tempted to refer to the sources that the textbook authors have used without reading them for yourself, but you will potentially miss many important features and perspectives on your topic. In addition, too many 'derivative sources' will lead to a disappointing mark for the literature review section or chapter of your research report.

FINDING OTHER SOURCES OF INFORMATION: CLARIFYING WHAT RESOURCES ARE AVAILABLE

As you continue with your literature search, find out where information might be most easily available. The main options are listed below:

- **University or college library:** the benefits of using the library have already been indicated. You have paid for the facilities as part of your course fee so it makes sense to use them. Find out what types of books, journals and other collections are held in the main library and what electronic resources are available to you (ask about database facilities, e-books and reference tools). Prepare to be pleasantly surprised. Clarify what usernames and passwords you will need to access material off-site. Make sure you know how to reserve copies of books, should they not be immediately available.

- **Other libraries and inter-library loan facilities:** find out if your study centre has any reciprocal arrangements that enable you to use the resources of libraries of other campuses or institutions. Most libraries operate an inter-library loan (ILL) system for students undertaking projects so that the institution can obtain a copy of a book or article from elsewhere for a short period of time (and at a price). Find out in advance what your entitlement might be to the inter-library loan facility (often students have a fixed allocation of ILLs).

- **Access to professional libraries:** many HR practitioners, when surveying the literature, will want to make use of a specialised library collection such as that provided for members by the CIPD or the Chartered Management Institute.

- **Remote access to electronic resources:** all libraries now have facilities enabling registered users to gain electronic access to the full text of materials or to abstracts, summaries or other listings. Once you know how to do this it is easily achieved from within the library itself. It is also possible to access the resources from a PC outside of the institution provided that you can prove you are an academic user from a study centre that is registered with the provider. Universities in the UK purchase their electronic resources from a number of different publishers who link to an international access management system called 'Shibboleth', although often the publishers use other names, such as: Athens/Institution Login, Institutional Login/Access, Federated Login, or Academic Sign-in. When you come to a point where you are asked for a password it is important to look for the (often small) link to the institutional login page and do not be tempted with other (often more prominent) username and password boxes, which will usually charge you a fee for access to materials.

- **Electronic searching:** electronic search engines are vital ways of finding further sources of information for projects. There are a range of options, from general searches on the Internet as a whole to more specialised searches using academic 'information gateways'. The temptation to start 'broad' and then narrow down the focus of a search is high, but this can be very time-consuming and if time is precious it is better to start with the more specialised search processes and then broaden the search only if you feel you need further information.

SYSTEMATIC LITERATURE SEARCH

A systematic and transparent literature search provides the basis for a good literature review and enables your supervisor or tutor to provide effective advice and guidance. Achieving a transparent process requires you to think ahead about how you will record what you find and to 'cross-reference' items as appropriate (Smallbone and Quinton 2011). The seven-step model shown in Figure 3.3 should provide a basis for a systematic search process.

Figure 3.3 Seven steps to an electronic literature search

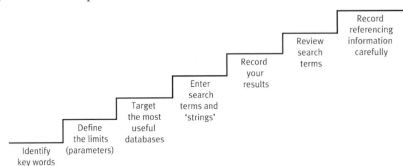

1   **Identify/generate keywords.** This part of the process is where you think about the topic and those areas in the literature that might be useful. It is worth consulting dictionaries and encyclopaedias at this stage to develop a list of key words that you can use to inform your search. Aim for 6–10 keywords that you can enter in different combinations or 'strings'.

2   **Define the limits (parameters).** A search with the keyword 'performance' is likely to bring a multitude of extracts relating to financial performance and accountancy rather than anything to do with HR. It is important to include the terms 'personnel' or 'human resources' within your combination of keywords. Also establish whether you wish to limit your search to sources that are from the UK and also to sources published in the most recent five years and, if you are a multilingual student, you can also specify the language(s) of the papers you may wish to read.

3   **Target the most useful databases.** Find out which electronic databases and electronic journal collections are available to you. Get advice from your tutor on the best databases for your topic. Your library will have information on how to operate these and will also tell you what passwords are required. If you can start the search process on the library premises, you can get help from a librarian if you experience any initial problems. Once you know what to do, you may prefer to work 'remotely'. Table 3.2 shows a selection of useful databases for HR research purposes.

Table 3.2 Some useful databases for HR research

Full-text databases	Comments
EBSCO	In the UK the EBSCO database is often branded as 'Business Source Premier, Business Source Complete and Business Source Elite'. It is a good all-round database. It holds thousands of online resources, including academic journals, periodicals, trade publications, as well as industry and company profiles. As it is so extensive, it is important to use 'search limiters' to avoid being overwhelmed with inappropriate 'hits'.

Full-text databases	Comments
ABI/INFORM	This database includes full-text journals as well as business press and trade publications, dissertations, conference proceedings and market reports. The focus is on general business and management areas.
Emerald Full Text	This includes all the journals provided by MCB Press. Abstracts and/or full-text articles (depending on the level of subscription) are available and MCB publications contain a fair range of HR-related journals.
XPertHR	This is a source of practitioner-focused HR information, articles and reports drawn from journals and online services published by Reed Elsevier.
ISI Web of Knowledge for UK Education	This database provides a route to all the Thomson Scientific products subscribed to by an institution. In addition, a range of conference proceedings and papers are held on the database.
Ingenta Connect	This is a general database of papers from a number of publishers, including both academic and practitioner-focused publications.
Sage Journals Online	This provides a link to SAGE products, which publish some good-quality journals in business, humanities and social sciences as well as science, technology and medicine. SAGE is a particularly good place to look for resources about research methods.
Science Direct	This database, containing articles and e-books published by Elsevier, focuses mostly on the physical sciences but also contains an extensive range of social science (including business and management) titles and sources.
Google Scholar	As part of the 'Google' service Google Scholar aims to provide an avenue for a broad search for scholarly literature. The database contains a wide range of disciplines and sources including peer-reviewed papers, theses, books, abstracts and articles, from academic publishers, professional societies, preprint repositories, universities and other scholarly organisations. For those students who are 'addicted to Google', Google Scholar may feel like a more familiar way forward.

4 Enter search terms and strings. This is where you use your keywords and 'search strings' to combine your keywords making use of terms such as 'AND', 'OR' and 'NOT'. Also make use of the * (truncation) tool to use word stems to help you find different, but relevant words. *Develop**, for example, should help you select material with 'development', 'developing' and 'developmental'. In addition the **?** wildcard term will enable the search to include different forms of the same word, for example *human resourc** should result in a selection of articles with *human resource* and *human resources* in the text and *organi?ation* will select *organization* and *organisation*. Different levels of subscription, resulting in different levels of access to materials, are taken by different libraries. Therefore, to avoid frustration, make sure you only choose to know about 'subscribed titles' or 'subscribed content'.

5 Record your results. This stage involves making a note of the sources that meet your search criteria. Potential criteria that you may wish to apply include:

- must be published after (say) 2006
- must be focused on (say) SMEs
- must be written in English
- must be full-text.

It is a good policy to keep a record of the searches you have undertaken and the results so that you can discuss it with your supervisor, who may be able to provide guidance on alternative search strings you may want to try. In addition, you can use the results to provide a brief outline of your search process in an early part of your literature review chapter or section. Table 3.3 shows the results of a journal paper search undertaken from two well-known databases. The criteria for the search were:

- **EBSCO** – full-text available; references available; published between 2006 and 2013.
- **Emerald** – journal article; published between 2006 and 2013.

Table 3.3 Example of search results from two databases

Keywords / string	EBSCO Number found	Emerald Number found
Coaching	159	2,233
Coaching and SME	2	97
Coaching and small firm	0	448
Learning and SME	28	676
Learning and coaching and small firm	0	37
Learning and coaching and SME	1	87

ACTIVITY 3.2

REFINING YOUR SELECTION CRITERIA

Imagine that you wish to conduct research into coaching in small firms and you have undertaken this initial search.

1 What issues are raised by the different pattern of 'returns' to your search terms?

2 How might your search be further refined?

FEEDBACK NOTES

You may have highlighted the difference in 'return numbers' for these two databases, and you probably noted the difference it makes to search for 'full-text available' – it is possible that your university might not have access to the full text of all the papers in the Emerald database. If you investigate the Emerald database, you will also notice that you can specify different types of article (case study;

conceptual paper; general review; literature review; research paper; technical paper; viewpoint). Depending on the focus of your search, you may choose to select one or other of these. As you scan the abstracts generated by the EBSCO search, you might notice that some of them are concerned with research or practice in different regions of the world (Spain is well represented in the papers in this search), so you might also decide to apply regional selection criteria.

A systematic process such as this will enable you to reduce the volume of sources to a level that you can manage and which represents information of appropriate quality.

6 Review search terms. Before you end your initial search process, it is worth reviewing your search terms. Have you missed out any relevant words that might generate important literature sources or are your result rates still too high? This is an area to discuss with your supervisor.

7 Record referencing information carefully. Effective electronic record-keeping is essential for student researchers who do not have time to waste towards the end of the project when they have to compile their list of references and discover they have mislaid some of the information they need. A number of software applications can help you store and organise the information you gather from your literature search and, once you start writing your review, to integrate your references into your Word documents and create a list of references. Commonly used software (check if you can access these for no charge through your study centre) include: EndNote, Reference Manager and RefWorks, and there are also free reference management tools on the Web, such as **Zotero** and **Mendeley**.

If your search generates a number of articles which you wish to print, it might be more effective either to save them to a disc or to email them to a more suitable address from which you can print them at a more convenient time.

If your search generates articles for which the full text is not available electronically, it is likely that you can obtain a hard copy, either through your own library or from another library.

OTHER INTERNET SOURCES

Having searched the journals you may feel that there may be other resources that would be useful. There are many millions of documents about a variety of subjects which can be found on the Internet. Every medium in digital form can be stored on the Internet: text, sound, photographs, cartoons, video images and so on. It is possible that the most relevant sources of electronically stored information can be accessed through specialist HR gateways, such as those shown in Table 3.4.

Table 3.4 Some useful HR websites and electronic gateways

Gateway	URL
Chartered Institute of Personnel and Development	http://www.cipd.co.uk
HRM: The Journal	http://www.hrmthejournal.com/
biz/ed – Human Resources Management	http://www.bized.co.uk/learn/business/hrm/index.htm
HRM Guide Network – Human Resources	http://www.hrmguide.net/buscon4.htm
Work Foundation – part of Lancaster University	http://www.theworkfoundation.com
Human Resource Links – Strathclyde University	http://www.lib.strath.ac.uk/busweb/hrmnet.htm
Society for Human Resource Management (US organisation)	http://www.shrm.org/Pages/default.aspx
UK Work Organisation Network	http://www.ukwon.net/
Institute for Employment Studies	http://www.employment-studies.co.uk/main/index.php

Sources of information derived from official publications can be found from websites such as those in Table 3.5, and sources of information about companies are indicated in Table 3.6. If you are an international student wishing to obtain specific country information, the sites in Table 3.7 may be helpful, and some websites relevant to international HRM are included as Table 3.8.

Table 3.5 Some websites for sources of information from official publications

Name	URL
GOV.UK	http://www.gov.uk
UK Legislation Service	http://www.legislation.gov.uk/
UK National Archives	http://www.nationalarchives.gov.uk/information-management/
The Official Documents	http://www.official-documents.gov.uk/
Acas (Advisory, Conciliation and Arbitration Service)	http://www.acas.org.uk/index.aspx?articleid=1461

Table 3.6 Sources of information about companies

Name	Notes	URL
CAROL	Corporate online service with annual reports covering the UK, Europe and Asia	http://www.carol.co.uk/
Companies House	Basic information available via Free Company Information link	http:// www.companieshouse.gov.uk/
Corporate Information	Over 3 million company profiles, research links, searches through search engines	http:// www.corporateinformation.com/ Country-Industry-Research-Links.aspx
Financial Times (pay for access)	Key financial data for 20,000 limited companies worldwide	http://www.ft.com
Fortune 500	Information on companies in the 'Big 500'	http://money.cnn.com/ magazines/fortune/rankings/
FTSE International	Provides access to 'headline' information on FTSE indices and member companies	http://www.ftse.com/ Research_and_Publications/ index.jsp

If your enquiry requires information about more than one country, you can get country information from websites such as those in Table 3.7.

Table 3.7 Websites providing country information

Name	Notes	URL
CIA World Factbook	Country profiles which provide geographical and government information as well as key economic indicators	https://www.cia.gov/library/ publications/the-world-factbook/ index.html
IMF country reports	Full-text access to country reports	https://www.imf.org/external/ country/index.htm
International Monetary Fund	IMF statistics and articles, including exchange rates and economic indicators for countries of the world	http://www.imf.org/external/ country/index.htm
Mondaq Business Briefing	Access to world business news pages	http://www.mondaq.com
Natlex	US Department of Labor resources	http://www.dol.gov/dol/topic/ index.htm

Table 3.8 International HRM websites

World Federation of Personnel Management Associations	http://www.wfpma.com
American Society for Training and Development	http://www.astd.org
International Federation of Training and Development Organisations	http://www.iftdo.net/
Eurofound, The European Foundation for the Improvement of Living and Working Conditions	http://www.eurofound.europa.eu/

This brief overview of potential sources of information indicates that a wide range of material is available. To obtain a suitable breadth of knowledge in an applied discipline area such as HRM, your literature search and review may extend across a range of information types (Quinton and Smallbone 2006):

- media sources – newspapers and news-pages; general periodicals (for example, *The Economist*)
- practitioner sources – HRM practitioner journals (for example, *People Management*); trade journals for your business sector
- government sources – for example, national statistics; labour market figures and so on
- commercial sources – for example, commercially published market or labour market reports
- company sources – for example, publicly available reports, statements, press releases, webpages and so on
- academic sources – books and articles written by academics in the higher education sector.

DETECTIVE WORK – CITED REFERENCE SEARCHING

With so many sources available it is possible to feel overwhelmed with the volume of material and selecting the most appropriate sources is important. A good strategy is to try to identify two or three of the most important authors in your chosen topic area. The chances are that subsequent researchers will have made use of their work, and so you can follow the development of knowledge over time by reading the articles that have cited them. In this way you will be able to assess how the 'big ideas' in your topic area have been used by other authors and researchers. A useful tool by which you can do this is a 'cited reference search'.

Searching for a focus

CASE ILLUSTRATION 3.3

Kajal was a distance learning student who wished to undertake research into talent management, but her supervisor was concerned that this topic was too broad and that her research would lack focus. During the course of her initial literature search Kajal used Google Scholar and found an edited collection of articles about global talent management (Scullion and Collings 2011). She decided to follow the cited sources link to see which further resources had cited this book. As she scrolled down the list she reviewed the titles of the various papers and books, and her attention was caught by a paper: Whelan, E. and Carcary, M. (2011) Integrating talent and knowledge management: where are the benefits? This gave her an idea. Her interest was attracted to the extent to which knowledge management and talent management processes influenced each other. However, a subsequent search of databases using the search string 'talent management' and 'knowledge management' revealed that this area had not been researched – she drew a blank.

Discussion Questions

1   If you were Kajal's supervisor, what advice would you give her at this point?

2   What are the advantages and disadvantages of citation searching undertaken in this way?

FEEDBACK NOTES

In this instance Kajal's supervisor was tempted to advise that she find a different topic with a stronger basis in the published literature. However, Kajal and her supervisor soon realised that the gap in the literature might be a positive advantage as this might be an area where Kajal could make a contribution. In addition, Kajal was able to follow up the references in the paper she had found and she also undertook literature searches relating to talent management and knowledge management (as separate issues), which provided a robust way forward for her research.

The advantage of the Google Scholar cited reference facility is that it can provide you with an indication of how influential a source or an author may be. Items with a high number of other citations may well be worth following up. The academic database 'Web of Knowledge', which your study centre may also subscribe to, has a similar facility whereby you can see how many subsequent authors have cited the publication and you can follow the links to read their items. Remember that newly published items will not have had the chance to be cited much, so don't discount them. Also, the number of citations does not necessarily reflect the quality of the source.

EVALUATING YOUR SOURCES

Once you have explored a few search engines, gateways and academic databases you may feel that you have amassed so many sources that there is no time to read them all properly. A great benefit of Internet-based sources is their volume and variety. However, there is also no quality assurance built into the World-Wide Web, and there are as many out-of-date and poor-quality documents as there are useful and appropriate sources of information. Key questions to ask when you are evaluating web-based documents (Dochartaigh 2007, Quinton and Smallbone 2006) are:

- Is there any indication of the date when the document/webpage was written? How current is the information?
- When was the information last updated or revised?
- Is the author, publisher or organisation responsible for the source clearly identifiable? If so, what are their credentials? What are their affiliations or biases?
- Are the sources used in the document clearly listed?
- Has the source been through an editorial process? If so, by whom?
- How closely related is advertising or marketing with the information that is presented?

Careful selection and evaluation of your sources is required, and Table 3.9 provides some tips on the potential value of different forms of web-based documents.

Table 3.9 A hierarchy of web-based resources for research students

Relevance	Document / webpage type	Purpose	Comments
Low	Entertainment sites	Marketing or download purposes	Hard to see any value for HR research
	Personal webpages / blogs / wikis	Various	Find out the background of the originator – may provide an insight into a feature of HR that you had not thought of before. Sites such as Wikipedia and Businessballs.com fall into this category. Before you go ahead and accept all their content, you must validate the information you find there using other sources where you know the credentials of the originator of the materials.
	Business and marketing pages	Promote a company or a product	Will present a biased view and selected information but may be useful if you also supplement with information from other sources.
	Advocacy sites	To promote a particular view on an issue	Published by pressure groups, political parties, NGOs, action groups and so on. May reflect the opinion of only a small minority. Information needs to be assessed against data from other sources.
	Trade press pages	Specialise in information about one business sector or trade	Potentially helpful information but reliant on company briefings and press releases for much of the content. Unlikely to be critical or controversial. Supplement with other sources of information.
	News pages	Purpose is to 'sell' news	Will be subject to editorial control which may well be one-sided. Each news organisation will take its own 'slant'. Ensure you look in several different sites to assess how 'your' issue is covered.
	Official documents / pages	To provide a news management service and overview data that will attract visitors (investors, tourists and so on)	Can be a rich source of information but may well be one-sided. It may be worth looking in less prominent parts of websites to find the basis for the data. Try to get back to the 'raw data' behind the announcements in government department pages.

Relevance	Document / webpage type	Purpose	Comments
High	Academic documents	To 'share knowledge' with other academics and to achieve 'research output' points in academic esteem processes	Quality can vary. Find out the basis for publication if you can: a 'double-blind reviewed' journal article will be of higher quality than a 'working paper', for example. Domain names such as .ac or .edu indicate an academic background for the source.

(Dochartaigh 2007, Quinton and Smallbone 2006)

READING THE LITERATURE AND MAKING NOTES

Finding the literature is just the start and you may, like many other HR students, begin to feel overwhelmed by the prospect of reading and making notes on all your sources. For this reason it is important to develop effective reading and note-taking processes.

'JUST IN TIME' READING AND NOTE-TAKING

Time is your most precious resource when you are undertaking a research project; there is never enough of it and it is important that the reading and note-taking process is undertaken speedily, but effectively. When you are reading material for your research project, there are different approaches you can take to suit different requirements (Brown 2006):

- **Skim-read** – look quickly through the list of contents, headings, introduction and conclusions. If you are looking at a journal article, start with the abstract. Skimming is a good way to get familiar with something on a superficial level. You can do this to check whether the publication is relevant or has the information that you need.
- **Scan** – this involves a quick search for something specific – a title or keyword. Scanning involves ignoring everything except what you are looking for. This is easier using electronic copies than the printed versions.
- **Reading to understand** – studying the material in detail to absorb the major facts and ideas that are expressed. You may need to read the section(s) more than once and make notes to summarise what you have learned.

Table 3.10 indicates some ideas that may help you to undertake 'just in time' reading. Your aim is to be able to undertake an initial reading of any source in just 5–10 minutes to identify those sources that will need more careful attention.

Table 3.10 Undertaking 'just-in-time' reading

Strategy	Notes
Decide on your note-taking and filing system in advance.	Options include (and preferences vary) systems such as: ● card index system ● word-processed notes ● A4 paper ● collection of photocopies.
Make an accurate note of the author, title and other details about the source.	See Tables 3.13 and 3.14 for information on how to reference your work. If you are going to make use of bibliographic referencing software, now is the time to start.
If a book – 'speed-read' the introduction and concluding chapter and note down the main points.	Read from the author's perspective – don't reject it because it is not the approach you instinctively prefer.
If an article – look for the abstract or executive summary as well as for the conclusion. Read them quickly and note down the main points.	As above.
If a book or report – look for the contents page and index.	Each chapter or section should have an introduction or conclusion, so start there each time and note down the main points made.
Speed-read the text, summarising the main text and highlighting any ideas that might be useful to you.	Well-written material will highlight key points in the first and/or last paragraphs of each section. The first or last sentences of each paragraph are likely to be the most useful. Use this to speed up your reading.
Make notes on the method as well as the subject.	As well as the findings from other research, record the methods used (for example, interviews, observation, telephone survey) and where the data came from (the sample).
Make a clear note of useful quotations.	Copy out the quote (or highlight if it is a photocopy) but note down the page number it is on. You will need this to reference the quote when you submit your work.
Note down any other sources that you need to follow up.	Make full notes of the author, title, publisher and date. Also, prioritise follow-up sources – you may not have time to find all of them.
Be prepared to read important sources more thoroughly.	Make a clear note of the details of all your sources so that you can find and retrieve the ones you need to read more thoroughly without wasting precious time.

EVALUATION AND ANALYSIS

As you undertake your reading, it is helpful to keep in mind the main purposes of the literature review (Gill et al 2010, Oliver 2012), which your notes will help you with. These are shown as Figure 3.4:

- **Examining the context:** if you are undertaking a project in an organisation that you know well, it is important to understand the influences on the topic you are investigating beyond its immediate priorities. The literature review will help you understand and explain why your project is worthwhile within HR more generally.
- **Identify relevant concepts, issues and methods:** this provides a basis from which to know what data to look for in relation to your investigation.
- **Devise a framework for the analysis of your data:** obtaining data is the easy part. Knowing how to analyse and interpret it is much harder. Reviewing the literature will help you to devise a framework for the interpretation of the facts that you gather.
- **Position the investigation:** the literature review can demonstrate how your research can add value in a practical way, in terms of the organisation or business sector, as well as in an academic way, through considering important issues in a different way.

Figure 3.4 **Main purposes of the literature review**

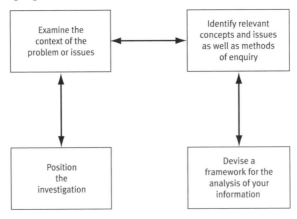

Once you start reading and making notes, therefore, you have to consider the information you have found in an analytical way. One way to start this process is to **filter and categorise** the material that you have read. Figure 3.5 provides some ideas about how to go about this.

Figure 3.5 Filtering and categorising what you have read

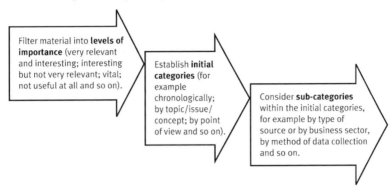

Filter material into **levels of importance** (very relevant and interesting; interesting but not very relevant; vital; not useful at all and so on).

Establish **initial categories** (for example chronologically; by topic/issue/concept; by point of view and so on).

Consider **sub-categories** within the initial categories, for example by type of source or by business sector, by method of data collection and so on.

(Quinton and Smallbone 2006)

Reading for a research project involves going further than 'soaking up' and recording facts; the aim is to become an analyst, an evaluator and a constructive critic. Filtering and categorising your literature sources is the first step to becoming an analyst. Maybe you can draw a chart of your categories onto a flipchart or sheet at the front of your folder. It is likely that you will rethink some of these as you carry on with the project and you can make amendments as you go. A further benefit of the process is that, once you come to start writing your literature review, you can tackle one category at a time and the task will not seem too daunting.

You will also avoid the accusation of writing too descriptively if, when you are making notes on what you read, you try to be active in assessing the value of the ideas presented to you; evaluate their strengths as well as their weaknesses. This issue is addressed in Activity 3.3.

 ACTIVITY 3.3

READING IN AN EVALUATIVE WAY

Read the following passages, which are extracts from longer articles relating to mental health and well-being in the workplace. For both passages, use some of the tips for 'just in time reading', but in addition try to answer the following questions:

● How have key concepts been defined?

● What are the limitations of the scope of the enquiries?

● What assumptions about the issue do the authors seem to work with?

● What data have been used?

● How were the data generated?

Extract 1 – Extracts from: Chynoweth, C. (2012) Mental health: irrational fear [online]. http://www.peoplemanagement.co.uk/pm/articles/2012/02/mental-health-irrational-fear.htm With permission of the publisher, the Chartered Institute of Personnel and Development, London (www.cipd.co.uk).

Talking about mental health is still a major workplace taboo, with line managers often lacking the confidence to discuss it one-to-one. But what should really scare employers is the cost – in both human and financial terms – of ignoring this issue.

Robbie Williams and Carrie Fisher have done it, Alastair Campbell is refreshingly honest about it, Stephen Fry even made a BBC documentary about it. But it seems that, despite the lead taken by these high-profile people, admitting to mental health problems is still stigmatised in British workplaces.

According to CIPD research, 26 per cent of all employees report they have experienced mental health problems while in employment, yet just 41 per cent of all workers would feel confident telling their employer if they had a problem. In addition, only a quarter of the 2,000 workers surveyed for *Employee Outlook: Focus on mental health in the workplace* said their organisation would encourage such a disclosure, and just 37 per cent believe their employer does a good job of supporting people with mental health problems.

Despite such disappointing statistics, society's attitude is 'getting better all the time', says Susannah Robertson, who leads Remploy's Access to Work mental health service, although she adds that, while there is less of a taboo, 'there is still some way to go'. 'We are moving away from this idea that mental health is associated with individuals who will commit crimes and harm people towards understanding how it affects people day to day,' she says. This includes the realisation that it need not affect workers' performance or capacity. 'Perhaps stress is a bit easier to talk about in the current climate because everyone is under so much pressure that there is an acceptance – an understanding that it could happen to anyone,' she says.

A broadening awareness of well-being and the fact that it includes mental as well as physical health has also helped. Even so, as Dame Carol Black, National Director for Health and Work, told PM earlier this year, there still needs to be a major cultural shift in the way we respond to mental illness at work. 'If you returned to work today having had your knee replaced, we'd all be very comfortable in welcoming you back. But what we have not been so good about is welcoming people back to work after they've been away for a while with a mental health problem,' said Black, co-author of a government-backed review into sickness absence. It's an issue that is relevant to all workplaces, says Emma Mamo, policy and campaigns manager at mental health charity

Mind, which has worked with the CIPD to produce a guide for employers: *Managing and Supporting Mental Health at Work: Disclosure tools for managers*. 'Everyone has mental health,' she says. 'It's not just when you have an employee with a diagnosed condition.'

Extract 2 – Extracts from: Zwetsloot, G.I.J.M., van Scheppingen, A.R. and Dijkman, A.J. (2010) The organizational benefits of investing in workplace health. *International Journal of Workplace Health Management*, 3(2): 143–59. © Emerald Group Publishing Limited all rights reserved.

A healthy and vital workforce is a strategic asset to any organization. Workplace health management and health promotion are therefore increasingly relevant for organizations. This paper seeks to identify the organizational benefits companies strive for, and analyzes the ways companies use and manage data in order to monitor, evaluate and improve the achievement of organizational benefits through workplace health management. This is key to understanding the decision-making process organizations use as it relates to occupational health and safety. In particular, it helps us to understand the barriers to investments in health and safety that would appear to have positive payoffs but are not made...

In our research ... health is not regarded from a medical perspective or a health protection perspective, but is seen as a factor that codetermines the functioning of people (human and social capital) and may contribute to an organization's value: a production factor to be developed and promoted. In fact we regard health in its broadest sense as a resource. For instance positive mental health is likely to be a primary resource for creativity, which is increasingly relevant with a view on the emerging knowledge society. ... By contrast, mental health problems are closely associated with productivity losses (due to sickness absence or to presenteeism...). Our perspective on health is consistent with the World Health Organization's definition of health as a complete state of physical, mental and social wellbeing, not merely the absence of disease or infirmity...

This study was carried out as a case study of four organizations regarded as frontrunners in health management in The Netherlands. ... Information about the companies and their strategic business aims was gathered from company documents and web sites. Company contacts (and associated company documents) provided overviews of the companies' health activities and the strategic aims of the companies' health investments; these were sometimes complemented with interviews or workshops. Relevant company databases, as well as databases controlled by external service providers, were made available to the researchers. We were especially interested in those activities that were supposed to contribute to business benefits (both cost reductions and value creation), and in data that were used to steer or evaluate health activities, especially with a view to business benefits. In

this way we collected monitoring data from our company partners about relevant activities and their potential impacts. No new data were generated for this research. We made use of monitoring data that became available via the health and HRM company contacts. Our prime interest concerned longitudinal data at the individual and organizational level...

Our research provided insights into several implicit assumptions used by key company personnel who make decisions on health programs. It will be interesting to test such tacit knowledge in future empirical research. Three examples of such implicit assumptions are:

1   positive attention to mental health helps to develop an innovative corporate culture;

2   engagement is a predictor of good mental health; and

3   synergy between programs promoting physical and mental health can be achieved.

FEEDBACK NOTES

These two extracts show how literature sources about similar activities can tackle the issues in different ways and with very different stylistic approaches. Both extracts start from the premise that there are many benefits to be gained from workplace health management. One considers issues from the perspective of people in the UK who advocate greater support from those suffering from mental health difficulties. One paper begins with comments from a survey about which there is very little information provided; the other is based on a case study research strategy making use of a range of sources provided by the four case study organisations involved.

Being critical does not mean being 'negative', but it does involve you in responding to what you have read in a way that is objective and that examines its component parts and assesses the value of the ideas and the evidence. The way that you do this may vary slightly depending on the type of source you are reading. Fisher (2007) and Quinton and Smallbone (2006) highlight a number of ways of doing this. Table 3.11 is adapted from their approaches.

Table 3.11 Questions to ask when reading critically

Questions	For sources that use primary data	For sources that are based on theory or opinion
Date / currency	When was the research carried out? How current are the results?	When was it written, revised, published? How current is the discussion?
Credentials	What are the author's credentials?	What are the author's credentials? What is the author's perspective? Where is he or she 'coming from'?
Data collection methods	What did the author(s) do to collect their evidence?	
Provenance	Does the work build on previous research? Are the references clearly cited in the text and at the end? What is the ratio of books to articles in the references? What types of sources have been used?	Does the work build on previous research? Are the references clearly cited in the text and at the end? What is the ratio of books to articles in the references? What types of sources have been used?
Position	In what ways is this material similar to or different from others that you have read?	In what ways is this material similar to or different from others you might have read?
Style	Is the structure clear? Can you follow the argument through a logical progression? Does the use of tables, diagrams and charts add value to the conclusions or the explanations?	Is the structure clear? Can you follow the argument through a logical progression? Does the use of tables, diagrams and charts add value to the conclusions or the explanations?

Questions	For sources that use primary data	For sources that are based on theory or opinion
Analysis	What is the central issue? Is there a particular cultural bias? What assumptions have been made, for example about the generalisability of the results? What is the evidence supporting these conclusions?	What is the central issue? What assumptions have been made? Are they explicit? If so, what are they? Are they implicit? If so, what are they? Are the sources drawn from a variety of areas? Are the sources drawn from a wide range of different authors? Is there an apparent cultural bias?
Reflection / evaluation	How do you respond to what the author is saying? How do you rate this article (and why)? How does it relate to other concepts / ideas you have come across? How can you verify the results? Does it point to further research in a particular direction? Is it relevant to your current work?	How do you respond to what the author is saying? How do you rate this article? If this article is purely theoretical, how do you assess its academic quality? How does it relate to other concepts / ideas you have come across? Does it point to further research in a particular direction? Is it relevant to your current work?

EFFECTIVE READING AND WRITING – THE ALT MODEL

The questions in Table 3.11 provide a detailed way forward for evaluating what you read in a constructive way. A more general (and memorable) way of evaluating what you read is the ALT framework (you will have an ALT key on the keyboard of your personal computer), which is illustrated in Figure 3.6 and which is derived from the following key issues:

Argument

Logic

Trustworthiness

You can use the ALT framework to help you evaluate the sources that you read but you should also remember that your tutors will be using a similar framework to assess your research report when it is submitted. Get used to reading other people's work with these issues in mind, therefore, but also be prepared to write in such a way that your work can be seen to adopt the ALT principles.

Figure 3.6 The ALT principles

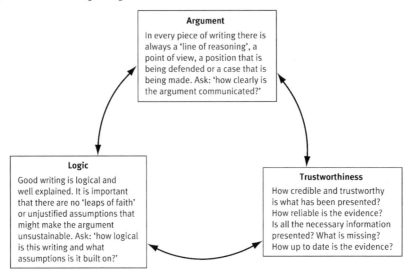

Follow the tips shown below to ensure that you produce a literature review that meets the criteria of being evaluative, critical and analytical (Hart 2010, Brown 2006). What not to do is shown in Table 3.12:

- Include work that supports your ideas but also consider approaches that oppose them.
- Identify and discuss the key sources for your subject.
- Define the key concepts and terms you are writing about.
- Include as much up-to-date material as possible.
- Make explicit the values and theories that lie beneath what you are reading about and then consider how successfully the component parts fit together.
- Make clear distinctions between facts and opinions.
- Discuss what you are reading in the light of existing critiques of theories and concepts.
- Relate different readings with each other – look for similarities but also for contradictions or tensions between the opinions and approaches of different authors.
- Support your arguments and judgements about the value of different approaches with reasoned explanations.
- Adopt a writing style that is objective and impersonal. Avoid terms such as 'should', 'must', 'this is obviously wrong' and so on. Use terms such as '[authors] argue that', '[author] asserts that', 'another perspective is offered by…'.

- Structure your material effectively. While the reading that underpins any project will involve the collection of facts, the project can only really add value if those facts are organised and classified in an effective way. You will need to reorganise what you have read, therefore, and select what is important in each of the sources before putting it together in a way that is relevant to the concerns of your investigation.

Table 3.12 What not to do for your literature review

Do not...	Check that you have not...
leave out any important publications that relate to your topic	discussed ideas without citing or referencing the source of ideas
be boring, tedious or descriptive	believed everything you have read and reproduced it uncritically
use 'pretentious' language, informal language or jargon	relied on long quotations by other authors

(Brown 2006, Hart 2010)

THE STRUCTURE OF THE LITERATURE REVIEW

A key skill in producing an effective review of the literature is to identify what sources to include and how to make sure that you achieve all the purposes of the review. It is also important to ensure that the literature review 'feeds into' the subsequent sections of the project report, rather than being a stand-alone exercise done to 'keep the markers happy'.

You must include key academic theories that are relevant to your research and you must also demonstrate that you are up to date in your knowledge of the topic. Another important aspect of any literature review is a critical assessment of previously published work on the topic. This involves identifying its strengths and weaknesses as well as any areas that may have been left out or handled in a biased way.

Having undertaken a lot of reading you may find it helpful to generate a 'mind-map' to start the planning process for the construction of your literature review. A related approach is to generate a concept map: a diagram that illustrates the relationships between the different ideas or concepts that are important for your topic where you 'plot' features of your topic that the literature suggest 'cause' other features or what practices the literature suggests may well 'result from', are 'required by' or 'contribute to' particular outcomes (Alias and Suradi 2008).

Whatever method you use to get started, the general structure indicated in Figure 3.7 will enable you to write in an effective way to communicate what is already known about the topic.

Figure 3.7 Indicative structure for a literature review

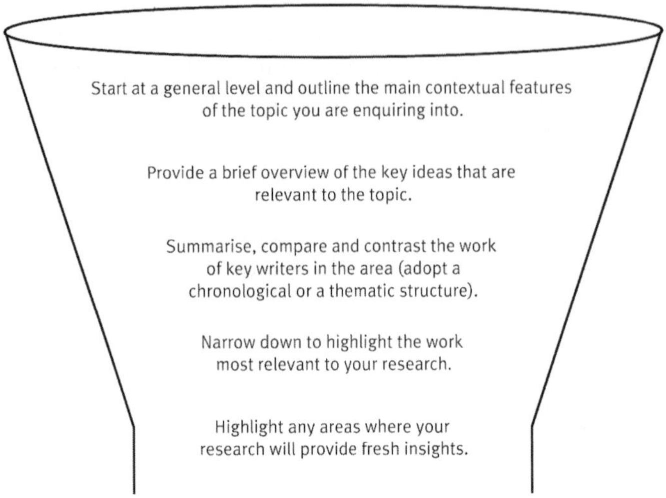

Start at a general level and outline the main contextual features
of the topic you are enquiring into.

Provide a brief overview of the key ideas that are
relevant to the topic.

Summarise, compare and contrast the work
of key writers in the area (adopt a
chronological or a thematic structure).

Narrow down to highlight the work
most relevant to your research.

Highlight any areas where your
research will provide fresh insights.

 Writing in an analytical way

CASE ILLUSTRATION 3.4

Dana was undertaking a business research report into diversity in the workplace. When she undertook her literature search she found a huge volume of sources, both specialist books as well as journal articles. She took careful notes and set about drafting her literature review. She then sent the draft work to her supervisor for comment and feedback. When her tutor got back to her Dana was somewhat disheartened. Her tutor indicated that she was pleased with the range of sources that Dana had made use of, but she commented that the review was 'descriptive' rather than analytical and

she suggested that Dana move away from writing about 'one author at a time' and adopted a more thematic approach to her review.

Discussion Questions

1   How might Dana go about revising her literature review to make it more analytical and less descriptive?

2   What structure would help Dana to achieve a more effective literature review?

FEEDBACK NOTES

Rather than merely describing some theories or initiatives relating to diversity in the workplace, it was important for Dana to demonstrate her critical thinking abilities by indicating the different approaches and also the difficulties that are associated with each of them. It is also important to probe beneath the surface and identify some of the underlying assumptions of different authors relating to these issues.

Many students find it hard to understand how to achieve this within a fairly restricted word count. If you feel that this applies to you, have a go at Activity 3.4.

ACTIVITY 3.4

ESTABLISHING COHERENT CATEGORIES AND CRITERIA

(adapted from Smallbone and Quinton 2011)

This task is unrelated with HRM. Imagine that you have just obtained a new MP3 player (either on your new phone or another tablet or gadget) and you need to organise your extensive music collection. You have a mixture of individual tracks that you have downloaded over the years as well as complete albums; some of your tracks are duplicates and there is a bewildering array of file names and so on. You start off by establishing a consistent file structure along the lines of: *Artist; Album; Track Number; Title*.

1   Now that you have consistent labels you must decide how to organise your collection into discrete folders so that you have something more suited to your likely listening preferences. What folder structure will you establish and why?

2   Your MP3 player allows you to build a range of different folder structures and to set up links between them, and so your next task is to reorganise your collection into different folders to suit different circumstances. What folders might you set up?

FEEDBACK NOTES

This exercise acts as a metaphor: reviewing the contents and organisation of your music collection is quite similar to the process of sorting and reinterpreting the literature. You might, for example, have undertaken an initial sort of your music by genre (dance music; rock and pop; classical; rhythm and blues and so on). However, you could reorganise your collection to fit with listening occasions, such as 'driving music', 'music to chill to', 'party tracks' and so on. Another way of organising things might be to separate live recordings from studio tracks, albums from singles, music from the 1950, '60s, '70s and so on.

You can adopt a similar approach with your literature where you sort elements of the literature into categories or themes. However, unlike the example of music collections, the themes and categories that you generate to help you make sense of the literature collection must relate to your research objectives, and it is likely that you will then develop one or two alternative approaches to structuring the main body of the literature review (Lee and Lings 2008): a chronological structure or a thematic structure. A **chronological structure** is helpful if you need to explore how ideas about your topic have evolved over time. This might be appropriate, for example, for discussing how ideas about the psychological contract have developed over time or the development of ideas about leadership or motivation. Alternatively, you might decide to use a **thematic structure** where you organise your review around the concepts that you have found in the literature. This might be appropriate for reviews of the literature relating, for example, to talent management.

Figure 3.8 Chronological structure

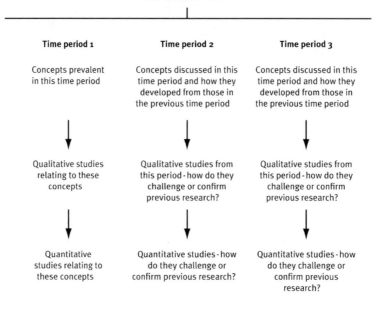

Introduction

Outline of the main contextual features of your topic and a brief overview of the key ideas that are relevant

Time period 1	**Time period 2**	**Time period 3**
Concepts prevalent in this time period	Concepts discussed in this time period and how they developed from those in the previous time period	Concepts discussed in this time period and how they developed from those in the previous time period
Qualitative studies relating to these concepts	Qualitative studies from this period - how do they challenge or confirm previous research?	Qualitative studies from this period - how do they challenge or confirm previous research?
Quantitative studies relating to these concepts	Quantitative studies - how do they challenge or confirm previous research?	Quantitative studies - how do they challenge or confirm previous research?

Conclusion

What important concepts are relevant to your research objectives?

What concepts will your research examine? How does your review indicate you should make sense of the data you will gather?

Figure 3.9 Thematic structure

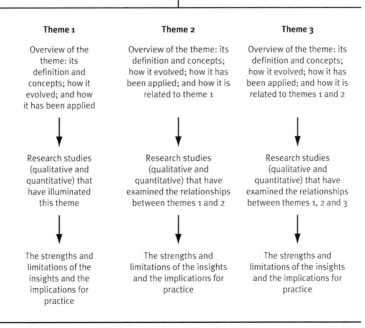

Introduction

Outline of the main contextual features of your topic and a brief overview of the key ideas that are relevant

Theme 1	**Theme 2**	**Theme 3**
Overview of the theme: its definition and concepts; how it evolved; and how it has been applied	Overview of the theme: its definition and concepts; how it evolved; how it has been applied; and how it is related to theme 1	Overview of the theme: its definition and concepts; how it evolved; how it has been applied; and how it is related to themes 1 and 2
Research studies (qualitative and quantitative) that have illuminated this theme	Research studies (qualitative and quantitative) that have examined the relationships between themes 1 and 2	Research studies (qualitative and quantitative) that have examined the relationships between themes 1, 2 and 3
The strengths and limitations of the insights and the implications for practice	The strengths and limitations of the insights and the implications for practice	The strengths and limitations of the insights and the implications for practice

Conclusion

What important concepts are relevant to your research objectives?

What concepts will your research examine? How does your review indicate you should make sense of the data you will gather?

REFERENCING AND CITATIONS

There have been a number of occasions in this chapter already where the importance of appropriate referencing has been highlighted. You may think that your tutors' requirements for effective referencing are unnecessarily picky. However, referencing and citation allows you to get credit for showing what you have read, and how and where you have used what you have read in your project report.

KEEPING A RECORD OF WHAT YOU HAVE READ (REFERENCE MANAGEMENT)

Maintaining an accurate record of everything that you read is important as you will need to include the references when you come to finalise your research report. Failure to keep accurate records has led many students to tears of frustration and days lost in 'hunting down' reference information that was not recorded accurately earlier on. You may wish to keep a manual record of what you read. Alternatively, most word-processing software systems have a referencing function that can automatically generate a bibliography based on the source information provided in your document, and formatted in an appropriate style. If you think you may conduct more research in the future, a more specialised reference management (or bibliographic) software such as EndNote or Reference Manager would be worthwhile. Most study centres have a licence for at least one form of bibliographic software and you can use it as you find references to articles, books and other literature. This software enables you to import references from online databases, sort them in various ways, retrieve them efficiently, and it automatically generates a bibliography when you have completed the research report.

Important points for referencing are:

- You acknowledge the work by other people that have influenced your thinking and research.
- There should be enough information to allow readers of your work to follow up your reference and access it for themselves – if it cannot be found again, do not try to reference it.
- You take a consistent approach to layout and punctuation.
- There are many different sources of information that you may wish to reference (media clips, blog posts, email correspondence and so on). There will not be guidance or a 'style' for every type of source, so use the nearest format you can to fit the source.
- If in doubt, do what your tutor says (not what your librarian or this book says) – only tutors give and take away marks!

In HRM publications the most commonly used format for referencing is the Harvard APA system, which is based on the surname of authors and date of publication, rather than on any system of footnoting or numbering. This system is briefly outlined below.

Citing references in the text itself (citation)

You can demonstrate how you have used sources through appropriate referencing in the text itself. The Harvard system uses the author's surname and year of publication as the main way to identify documents within the text. Preferred practice varies in different publications as to how to punctuate references and the order of various pieces of information, but the practical illustrations of referencing within the text shown in Table 3.13 may be helpful.

Table 3.13 Citing your sources in the text

Occasion	Format	Example
For a single author	Family name, year	It has been shown that … (Jones, 2009) or Jones (2009) shows that…
For something written by two people	Family name & Family name, year	The main features of … have been identified as … (Jones & Brown, 2009) or Jones & Brown (2009) have highlighted…
For something written by more than two authors: **For three to five authors name all authors the first time, then use *et al* (and others)** **For six of more authors go straight for the first named author *et al***	Family name, Family name & Family name, year	First time – Smith, Jones & Brown (2009) indicate that … or Key features of … are important within this concept (Smith, Jones & Brown, 2009). Subsequent citations – Smith *et al* (2009) indicate that … Key features of … are important within this concept (Smith *et al*, 2009).
When the author you are referring to is themselves referred to by another author and you have not read the original work (this is a derivative reference)	Family name, year, cited in family name, year, page numbers	Another view of the issue is … (Brown, 1999, cited by Smith, 2009, p. 27) or Brown (1999), cited by Smith (2009, p. 27), found …
For corporate authors, for example an organisationally generated document (and the organisation is commonly referred to by an abbreviation)	Corporate name, [Abbreviation] year	Ethical issues to take into account include … (Chartered Institute of Personnel and Development [CIPD], 2012). Then the next time you wish to cite this organisation – Diversity challenges are reported to be increasing (CIPD, 2009).
For a source that has no author and does not fit into any other clearly defined category	First two or three words of the title, year	Alcohol Concern ('Call to stop', 2011) have proposed…

Quotations

When you quote directly from a source you should place the quotation in 'quotation marks' and the page number should be given in the reference after the year of publication, for example 'Russ-Eft and Preskill (2005, p.71) comment that evaluation "seems to be stuck in an intellectual quagmire … because of an over-reliance on a conceptually simple approach to evaluation, namely the four-level taxonomy introduced and promoted by Kirkpatrick".'

Referencing in the bibliography or references section

Having provided some information about your sources in the text, it is important to provide full details in the section that follows the end of the main text of the report (but comes before the appendices). Strictly speaking, a reference list is a list of all sources that you have cited within your text, whereas a bibliography is a list of everything you have read or drawn upon while researching your piece of work, whether you have actually cited them in your text or not. In reality, the distinction between the two is often not recognised and the terms are used interchangeably. If you have been careful to acknowledge all your sources within the report, the list of references will differ only slightly, if at all, from the list of sources you have drawn upon in your research. It is worth checking with your study centre whether a bibliography is required or a reference list is what is expected.

Whether you produce a bibliography or a references section, the aim is to list the publications in full and in alphabetical order. The following information should be provided to allow anyone to follow up your reference and access it accurately:

- author's surname and initial(s)
- year of publication
- title of book/article
- publisher of the book/name of journal in which the article was found
- if a book, place of publication (for example, London, New York, Paris).

It is not difficult to find the information you need for accurate referencing. For books, the information will be on the front and back of the title page. Take care to record the name of the publisher and not the name of the printer or typesetter. Ignore any reprint dates and be sure to note down the date when the edition of the book you are referring to was published. The information you need for referencing journal articles should also be easy to find from the contents list of the issue of the journal you have referred to or at some place in the article itself; different publishers position this information in different places.

Some examples of appropriate referencing in the bibliography/references section are shown in Table 3.14.

Table 3.14 Referencing in the bibliography or references section

Occasion	Format	Example
Print book	Name, Initial & Name, Initial. (year). *Title*. Place of publication: Publisher	Robinson, S. & Dowson, P. (2012). *Business Ethics in Practice*. London: CIPD.

Occasion	Format	Example
Electronic book	Name, Initial. (year). *Title*. Retrieved from …	Kirkpatrick, D.L. & Kirkpatrick, J.D. (2007). *Implementing the Four Levels: A Practical Guide for Effective Evaluation of Training Programs.* Retrieved from http://site.ebrary.com/lib/portsmouth/docDetail.action?docID=10205948
Edited book	Name, Initial. (Ed.). (year). *Title*. Place of Publication: Publisher.	Gilmore, S. & Williams, S. (Eds). (2009). *Human Resource Management.* Oxford: Oxford University Press.
Reference to the work of someone cited in a different source (such as a textbook)	Family name, Initial (year). Cited in Family name, initial. (year). *Title*. Place of publication: Publisher, page numbers of section being referred to.	McGregor, M. (1960). cited in Marchington, M. & Wilkinson, A. (1996). *Core Personnel and Development.* London: CIPD, pp296–7.
Reference to a particular chapter in an edited book	Family name, Initial. (year). 'Title', in Initial, Family name (eds), *Title*. (ppx–x). Place of publication: Publisher.	Iles, P. (1996). International HRD, in J. Stewart and J. McGoldrick (Eds). *Human Resource Development: Perspectives, Strategies and Practice* (pp12–22). London: Pitman.
Reference to a journal article (use this format if you retrieved the article from the Internet as a PDF file and is also published in hard copy)	Family name, initial. (year). Title of article. *Journal name, volume number* (part or issue number), start and end page numbers of article.	Wang, G.G. and Swanson, R.A. (2008). The idea of national HRD: an analysis based on economics and theory development methodology. *Human Resource Development Review, 7*(1), 79–106.
Reference to a paper or report found on the Internet that is not also available as a print version	Family name, initial. (year). *Title of paper*. Retrieved from … (Internet address).	Chartered Institute of Personnel and Development [CIPD]. (2012). *Strategic Human Resource Management.* Retrieved from http://www.cipd.co.uk/hr-resources/factsheets/strategic-human-resource-management.aspx
Podcast	Last name, Initial (Year, Month Day). *Title* [Podcast]. Retrieved from …	Chartered Institute of Personnel and Development. (2012, March 6). *Pathways back to work: HR's role* [Podcast]. Retrieved from http://www.cipd.co.uk/podcasts/_articles/_pathways-back-to-work.htm?link=title

Occasion	Format	Example
Blog post – if the author adopts a nickname or screen name, you can use this at the beginning of your reference	Name. (Year, Month Day). *Title* [Web blog message]. Retrieved from …	Nor Franco. (2011, Oct. 26). *Doing your best with a desperate workforce* [Web log message]. Retrieved from http://www.hrmbusiness.com/ 2011/10/desperate-workforce.html
Intranet document – use this approach for an intranet document (which cannot be accessed by anyone outside the institution)	Author, Initials. or Organisation if no named author. (year, month day if given). *Document title* (policy/report/ circular number if given). Unpublished intranet document, Organisation (if not listed first).	Brook, P. (2009). *Human Resources Strategy 2009–2012.* Unpublished intranet document, University of Portsmouth.
Interviews and email messages	Interviews and email messages are not 'recoverable data' so you cannot give details in your reference list. You can cite such material within your text as a 'personal communication'.	…and this point was strongly reiterated (F. Smith, personal communication, 28 February 2011).

As indicated already, some publications will show their references in different formats. The final format that you use will depend on the preference of your tutor or study centre. The main thing is to reference your work in a consistent format and in an accurate way. If you do not reference appropriately and you use material originated by someone else without showing a citation, you may be accused of plagiarism, which is a form of cheating (passing off the work of someone else as your own).

SUMMARY

- A critical review of the literature, focused on the issues relevant to your research aim, principal research question or hypothesis, is an important feature of any research project.
- 'Reading around' a topic can help to provide ideas for a project, provide a framework to interpret data and help to identify worthwhile sources of secondary data.

- A wide range of different types of literature should be included in the literature review, incorporating both 'practitioner', 'teaching literature' and 'academic' perspectives.
- Effective literature search processes will include both 'manual' and electronic methods.
- Finding literature and then not reading it is a waste of your time. Effective reading and note-taking are key skills for effective researchers.
- A good literature review will examine the context of the research problem; identify relevant concepts, issues and methods; develop a framework for the analysis of data; and position the study.
- A literature review that is both analytical and critical will include work that supports and opposes your ideas, refers to key ideas within the topic area and uses up-to-date sources. It will distinguish between facts and opinions, establish relationships between different readings and be explicit about the values and theories that underpin them. It will use an objective and impersonal writing style and provide reasoned explanations for arguments and judgements.
- In critically reviewing the literature it is best to start by establishing the broad context, issues, theories and concepts before 'funnelling down' to discuss work that is particularly relevant to the research.
- A good literature review will demonstrate a clear line of argument that links discussion of important concepts in a logical structure and will make use of evidence and sources to establish its trustworthiness or credibility.
- Referencing and citation skills are important parts of any literature review in academic work. Failure to reference properly is evidence of poor scholarship. Plagiarism (passing off someone else's work as your own) is treated as a serious offence in academic institutions.

 Self-test questions

REVIEW AND REFLECT

1   Why is a literature review important for your research project?

   a)   to establish what is already known about your topic

   b)   to ensure you achieve the word count

   c)   to impress your tutor with a long list of references

   d)   to set the organisational and local context for your research

2   Being critically evaluative involves:

   a)   being negative about what you read

   b)   adopting the opposite view to the conclusions reached in what you have read

   c)   skim-reading to ensure you cover a lot of sources

   d)   assessing the strengths and weaknesses of what you read in the light of your research aim or questions

3   A systematic literature search:

   a)   begins in a public library before going to Internet search engines

   b)   gives equal attention to all authors who write about the topic

c) takes a methodical approach involving clear record-keeping

d) generates a project plan and involves effective time-management

4 The literature review should examine:

a) every fact written about the topic

b) all relevant aspects of a topic

c) the grammatical correctness of the sources

d) the sources that represent one perspective about your topic

5 Internet sources need to be assessed with some care because:

a) they are too recent to be trustworthy

b) they represent 'second-hand' knowledge

c) the quality is unknown

d) the author's name is never known

6 Which of the following is a 'peer-reviewed' journal?

a) *The Economist*

b) *People Management*

c) *Financial Times*

d) *Human Resource Management Journal*

7 When you read about important research in a textbook you should:

a) try to find the original source, read it and refer to the original text

b) not refer to the research you have read about

c) refer to the research and copy its reference from the textbook

d) refer to the research and cite the textbook as the basis for what you are claiming

8 Why is it important to keep an accurate record of the references for your sources as you read them?

a) because it puts off the moment when you have to start reading

b) it makes you feel good about a growing list of sources

c) effective referencing is vital for effective citation within the literature review

d) your tutor will be checking up on you

9 Plagiarism is:

a) having your own opinion about the ideas you read about

b) the crime of the century

c) inevitable given the prevalence of Internet sources about every topic

d) when someone 'passes off' the work of someone else as their own

Review questions

Take the time to find out about the requirements of your study centre for the literature review.

1   What sort of word length is expected? To what extent are 'academic' articles and books expected?

2   What literature and information sources are available to you (physically and electronically) from:

- your study centre
- your place of work
- any professional institutions of which you or your organisation is a member?

3   What username and passwords do you need and where can you get them?

Questions for reflection

This final part of the chapter enables you to reflect about your professional development and develop your skills and knowledge. This will enable you to build your confidence and credibility, track your learning, see your progress and demonstrate your achievements.

Taking stock

1   How familiar are you with HR-related Internet 'gateways' and other search engines?

2   Who is the best source of help to explore opportunities of finding out 'what is already known' through the Internet?

Strengths and weaknesses

3   Reflect critically on your use of literature in previous assignments. To what extent have you relied on ideas 'derived' from other places (usually textbooks)?

4   Revisit assignments you have produced previously for your course. What feedback have tutors made about your referencing technique? How confident do you feel about referencing?

5   How effective are your reading and note-taking 'habits' and strategies? In previous assignments how easy has it been to write an overview of what you have read about a topic? How organised is your note-taking system? To what extent do you note down readings that you agree with and tend to skip over those that oppose your viewpoint?

6   To what extent do you adopt a questioning and an evaluative approach when you are reading? How successful are you at making explicit the underlying theories and assumptions in what you read?

7   In your writing are you able to distinguish between facts and opinions? To what extent is your writing style 'objective and impersonal'?

Being an investigative practitioner

8   To what extent is your thinking determined by features such as the organisational culture of your employing organisation, your national cultural background, your

political preferences and so on? What steps do you need to take to ensure you consider the issues from a range of perspectives when you are reviewing the literature?

2   What strategies might you adopt to manage the time pressures of organisational and academic deadlines and produce a literature review of good quality?

EXPLORE FURTHER

The best way to learn how to write an effective literature review is to read journal articles about your topic. Similarly, the best way to learn how to make notes and to read in an evaluative way is by doing it and learning through practice. The following sources also provide useful tips and hints.

Useful Reading

Alias, M. and Suradi, Z. (2008) Concept mapping: a tool for creating a literature review, in A.J. Cañas, P. Reiska, M. Åhlberg and J.D. Novak (eds), *Third International Conference on Concept Mapping*. Tallinn, Estonia and Helsinki, Finland [online]. Available at: http://cmc.ihmc.us/cmc2008papers/cmc2008-p048.pdf

Blaxter, L., Hughes, C. and Tight, M. (2006) *How to research*. Buckingham: Open University Press.

Cottrell, S. (2008) *The study skills handbook.* Basingstoke: Palgrave Macmillan.

Dochartaigh, N.O. (2007) *Internet research skills.* London: Sage.

Fisher, C. (2007) *Researching and writing a dissertation: a guidebook for business students*. Harlow: Pearson Education.

Gill, J., Johnson, P. and Clark, M. (2010) *Research methods for managers*. London: Sage.

Hart, C. (2010) *Doing your master's dissertation.* London: Sage.

Oliver, P. (2012) *Succeeding with your literature review: a handbook for students*. Maidenhead: Open University Press.

Quinton, S. and Smallbone, T. (2006) *Postgraduate research in business: a critical guide*. London: Sage.

CHAPTER 4

Ethics, Professionalism and HR Research

CHAPTER OUTLINE

- How to use this chapter
- HR professionalism and ethical conduct
- HR research and research ethics
- Ethics in a digitised society
- Research ethics at different stages of your project
- The positive features of ethical assessment processes
- Summary
- Review and reflect
- Explore further

LEARNING OUTCOMES

This chapter should help you to:

- examine how your responsibilities as an HR professional are linked to your ethical choices as a researcher
- identify and address ethical issues arising from your research
- complete any necessary ethical approvals process that may be required at your organisation and study centre.

HOW TO USE THIS CHAPTER

This chapter is relevant to everyone involved with HR research. Whether you are undertaking a business research report at intermediate or advanced levels, an undergraduate or postgraduate dissertation or thinking about a proposal for a postgraduate research degree, you will need to consider the way in which your project might affect others who participate in it as individuals or as organisations. Your study centre, and any organisations in which you hope to conduct your research, may well have an ethical policy or codes and you must comply with them. All universities have a university-wide ethics committee that is responsible for ensuring that appropriate consideration is given to ethical issues and this includes regulating and approving research projects. In many institutions the process of ethical scrutiny is devolved to schools or faculties and, for taught courses, a 'light touch' approach to ethical scrutiny may be applied such that your supervisor or tutor is given responsibility, on behalf of the institution, to ensure appropriate ethical standards are built into your research design. The ethics of HR research cannot be considered in isolation of wider business and personal ethical matters, something that is illustrated in many of the case illustrations in this chapter.

CASE ILLUSTRATION 4.1

Extract from: Stevens, M. (2011) News review 2011: Phone hacking, *People Management Online*, 22 December [online]: http://www.peoplemanagement.co.uk/pm/articles/2011/12/news-review-2011-phone-hacking.htm
With the permission of the publisher, the Chartered Institute of Personnel and Development, London (www.cipd.co.uk).

This year saw the long-running phone hacking scandal that engulfed the *News of the World* and parent company News International finally culminate in the closure of the UK's best-selling weekend paper. As more shocking details emerged and the police inquiry progressed, a string of senior executives – including Rupert and James Murdoch – were forced before MPs to answer questions about whether the practice was widespread and who was culpable. The actions of HR within the organisation and its part in the affair also came under the spotlight.

In July, the role of former NOTW group HR director Daniel Cloke was called into question. It emerged that he was one of only a handful of directors who were privy to thousands of emails contained in the original internal investigation into phone hacking in 2007. The review – which followed the jailing of former royal editor Clive Goodman and private investigator Glen Mulcaire – had concluded that their criminal activity had been an isolated incident. But Cloke was called before a parliamentary select committee in September and forced to defend his conduct. He insisted that senior executives were 'surprised' when Clive Goodman claimed that phone hacking was widely discussed at the Sunday tabloid. MPs also heard that Goodman had received payments totalling more than £200,000 following his dismissal in order to avoid an employment tribunal.

One of *People Management*'s most commented on stories of the year was our interview with Professor Roger Stear, who insisted that the scandal highlighted the need for HR professionals to take responsibility for behavioural standards and company culture. His view that 'HR are delinquents when it comes to ethics' prompted much debate among readers.

PM blogger Graham White also agreed that HR needed to do more to avoid impropriety within organisations. Fellow commentator Susan Jacobs questioned at what point internal organisational behaviour went from being acceptable to outside the moral code, while PM's editor Rob MacLachlan said that the NOTW debacle had highlighted the difficulties HR can face when it comes to influencing business culture.

Discussion Questions

1   What issues relating to 'right and wrong' were raised by the news story referred to in this extract?

2   Do you agree with the assertion in this extract that 'HR are delinquents when it comes to ethics'? What challenges do HR professionals face when trying to deal with issues of conduct and ethical behaviour at the level of individuals and the organisation as a whole?

FEEDBACK NOTES

These questions raise a number of difficult but important issues that are relevant to both HR generally and to HR researchers. On the one hand, it is possible to argue that actions taken by the HR department to limit the exposure of their organisation to bad publicity (and further investigation) as a result of an employment tribunal is morally inappropriate, particularly given the benefit of hindsight with this issue during 2011–12. On the other hand, you might wish to argue that there are occasions when 'the ends justify the means'. Discussions in this area tend to revolve around why activities are necessary as well as their intended and unintended consequences.

Most people like to think that there are some ethical or moral principles that are intrinsically good and should be adhered to whatever the situation (for example, 'justice' and 'truthfulness'). Frequently, however, we are faced with actions and behaviours that do not accord with these principles but may be justifiable if they lead to good (or less bad) outcomes. These issues are rarely consensual and are always situation-specific.

Within any business organisation there are difficult ethical dilemmas to be faced. General principles which most people support include values such as respect, honesty, openness and responsibility. However, **business** values focus more on profit, growth and efficiency where there is the potential for conflict with more generally accepted moral values. Dealing with tensions like these is an important part of HR work. The ability to consider and justify ethical choices becomes particularly necessary in research activity, particularly if it involves gathering information that individuals might not otherwise have volunteered to provide.. This chapter provides a framework to help you identify the ethical implications of your research and then manage the process in such a way that will achieve a good-quality research outcome that takes account of important ethical considerations.

HR PROFESSIONALISM AND ETHICAL CONDUCT

In day-to-day language the terms 'ethical' and 'moral' are often used interchangeably. The term 'moral' is mostly associated with the extent to which specific actions are seen to be consistent with accepted ideas of right and wrong. The term 'ethics' refers to general principles as to what people 'ought' or 'ought not' to do. Both terms are closely related and Remenyi et al (2011, p1) define ethics as 'a branch of philosophy which addresses issues of human conduct related to a sense of what is right and what is wrong'.

 ## Ethics and employment

Extracts from: Roma'n, S. and Munuera, L. (2005) Determinants and consequences of ethical behaviour: an empirical study of salespeople. *European Journal of Marketing*, 39(5/6): 473–95. © Emerald Group Publishing Limited all rights reserved.

Sales professionals have been frequent targets of ethical criticism (Abratt and Penman 2002). ... There are several reasons for focusing specific attention on salespeople's ethical behaviour. Salespeople are exposed to greater ethical pressures than individuals in many other jobs. They work in relatively unsupervised settings; they are primarily responsible for generating the firm's revenues, which at times can be very stressful and they are often evaluated on the basis of short-term objectives (Dubinsky et al 1986, Bellizzi and Hite 1989, Wotruba 1990). In addition, research suggests that a salesperson's ethical behaviour can play a critical role in the formation and maintenance of long-term buyer–seller relationships (Gundlach and Murphy 1993). In contrast, unethical behaviour can even generate liability problems for salespeople's organizations through both intentional and inadvertent statements (Boedecker et al 1991).

... Since ethical sales behaviour is situation specific (Lagace et al 1991), we first reviewed financial services literature looking for relevant unethical practices in the industry that take place during the salesperson–customer interaction (Mitchell et al 1992, Dunfee and Gunther 1999, Cooper and Frank 2002, Roma'n 2003). We selected the scale developed by Roma'n (2003),

because it measures ethical sales behaviour from the customers' perspective in the Spanish financial services industry. Next, we pre-tested this scale during in-depth interviews carried out with salespeople. Based on the results of these interviews a three-item scale adapted from Roma'n (2003) was used to measure the salesperson's ethical behaviour (ESB).

... Questionnaires were administered during regularly scheduled meetings to a total of 280 financial services salespeople. The salespeople questioned were mainly specializing in selling high-involvement financial products (e.g. mortgages, life insurance) to final consumers.

... Results suggest that method of compensation and control system (CS) are important determinants of ethical behaviour. Age (AGE) also proves to be a significant antecedent of ethical behaviour. However, education (EDU) [training] is not significantly related to ethical behaviour. Additionally, a salesperson's ethical behaviour leads to lower levels of role conflict ... and higher levels of job satisfaction, but not higher performance.

Discussion Questions

1   What ethical pressures are referred to in this extract that affect the way that salespeople conduct their work?

2   What are the implications for HR practitioners of the findings outlined here?

CASE ILLUSTRATION 4.2

FEEDBACK NOTES

You probably highlighted the short-term pressures and relatively independent approach to work that may affect the behaviour and the ethical choices made by salespeople. However, you may also have discussed how long-term business success and customer relationship can be negatively affected by behaviour that is perceived to be unethical. In addition, the findings highlight the important role of HR in contributing to a pay and performance management system that enhances the chance of ethical practice, and it is interesting that the findings suggest that training programmes (referred to as 'education' in this extract) are less effective. In addition, the paper suggests (although you may not feel you are convinced by this finding) that ethical choices may change with the age of those involved.

What is clear is that, at an individual level, ethics involves choices affecting our actions as well as our motives and objectives, and in recent years a range of professional organisations have developed codes of practice and ethics that professionals within their remit are expected to subscribe to.

Examples of codes of ethics and professional conduct that are published from a range of HR-related professional organisations are shown in Table 4.1.

Table 4.1 Professional institutes – codes of conduct and ethical policies

Chartered Institute of Personnel and Development	http://www.cipd.co.uk/about/code-of-conduct-review/profco.htm
Institute of Training and Occupational Learning	http://issuu.com/drstevebyrd/docs/itol_code_of_professional_conduct_1_
BCS Chartered Institute for IT	http://www.bcs.org/category/6030
European Mentoring and Coaching Council (EMCC)	http://www.emccouncil.org/src/ultimo/models/Download/4.pdf
Society for Human Resource Management (SHRM)	http://www.shrm.org/about/Pages/code-of-ethics.aspx
American Society for Training and Development (ASTD)	http://www.sewi-astd.org/pdfs/Code_of_Ethics.pdf

Recognising the increasing importance of ethical issues in business and society, the CIPD published a revised code of professional conduct in 2012 which sets out the standards expected at all stages of an HR professional's career, regardless of their place of employment and the nature of their role.

ACTIVITY 4.1

ETHICAL IMPLICATIONS OF CIPD CODE OF CONDUCT

Find the CIPD 2012 Code of Conduct (http://www.cipd.co.uk/about/code-of-conduct-review/profco.htm)

1   Review this document and identify what elements of conduct it specifically highlights and the ethical requirements on CIPD professionals.

2   What are the implications of these standards for HR practitioner-researchers?

FEEDBACK NOTES

You will have noticed four key areas highlighted by the CIPD as important standards: professional competence and behaviour; representative of the profession; stewardship; and ethical standards and integrity.

Key principles required by the code of conduct that specifically relate to ethics are:

- the maintenance of relationships based on trust, confidence and respect
- professional and personal standards of integrity and honesty
- sensitivity for customs, practices, culture and beliefs of others
- advancement of business practices that are inclusive and support human rights and dignity
- safeguarding of confidential and personal or commercially sensitive information
- challenging others if unlawful or unethical behaviour or conduct is suspected.

HR RESEARCH AND RESEARCH ETHICS

All research, whatever discipline it is based in (marketing or medicine and so on), has to work within general principles of acceptable behaviour and practice. Research ethics is about adherence to a 'code of behaviour in relation to the rights of those who become the subject of your work or are affected by it' (Wells 1994, p284). We take for granted that researchers in many scientific fields (for example, medicine) have an explicit concern about the ethical consequences of their activities. Research in HR, like business and management research more generally, however, is a 'younger' field and the consideration of ethical issues related with the research process is something that has emerged more recently. As you consider the ethical foundation for your research, it is important to think about:

- the purpose and intent of your research
- the way in which you intend to answer your research questions
- your own safety and well-being as well as the safety and well-being of those with whom you come into contact (your research participants)
- issues associated with honesty and openness with those involved in your research

- what your research outcomes will lead to (how your findings will be applied and to what end).

These issues all translate directly into the way research projects are managed. A key principle of research ethics is that the interests of participants should be protected. People from whom you gather data should be no worse off at the end of your research than when you started. This sounds easy, but closer examination of what may be involved for them highlights three important issues.

Changing circumstances

CASE ILLUSTRATION 4.3

Emma was a part-time student who worked as an HR manager in a public sector organisation. She was interested in the way HR practitioners perceive change when it affects them, and she decided to focus her research on the changes brought about in the HR department in which she worked as a result of the Equality Act 2010. This new legislation required a review of a range of HR policies and procedures affecting issues such as: the management of employees with disabilities; protection for employees at risk of harassment from a third party (such as service users or other clients); and the potential introduction of gender pay reporting mechanisms. In a context where her HR colleagues were having to manage a range of organisational change processes associated with cuts in public sector spending and organisational restructuring, Emma was keen to assess the perceptions of HR staff about the additional demands being placed on them as a result of the Equality Act. She planned to carry out interviews with 12 HR practitioners over a period of four weeks. However, when she had completed 2 of her planned 12 interviews, her organisation instituted consultations about possible redundancies which were likely to have a direct effect on both Emma and members of her staff.

Discussion Questions

In this situation, what ethical concerns might Emma need to take into account? Consider the issues from the perspective of a) her employing organisation and b) the individuals within the organisation from whom she would be seeking to gather data.

FEEDBACK NOTES

When she commenced her project Emma did not feel that her research would raise any particular ethical issues but, as her situation changed, more ethical issues became apparent. From her managers' perspective there was the concern that people who were already 'unsettled' by the consultation about possible redundancies might be further distracted by the need to reflect on change management processes and the way they fulfilled their current role requirements. A second concern is that her interviewees might feel inhibited from speaking 'from the heart' about their frustrations in their role in a context where they were aware that the organisation might be selecting people for a redundancy process. Emma had to ensure that both individuals and the organisation would not be 'worse off' as a result of her research project: would it be fair to them to ask her staff to discuss issues they might regard as sensitive in such circumstances? In this context Emma's project went ahead, but she had to revisit the issue of checking the 'informed consent' of all her intended interviewees and reassuring them that there would be no disadvantage (or special advantage) to them whether or not they participated in the research. She also spelled out very clearly that she would not be 'passing on' any comments that people made to anyone in the organisation so that a strict protocol of confidentiality could be maintained. In addition, it is possible that some people may choose not to participate and it is important to acknowledge their right to privacy (the right not to participate).

ISSUES OF CONFIDENTIALITY

Even the most uncontroversial-looking projects might become more sensitive as a result of factors outside the control of the researcher. There are a range of possible issues that have ethical implications in almost all research projects that involve 'human subjects' either directly or indirectly. In many cases (as in Case Illustration 4.3), participants and/or organisations that feature in a piece of research may want their participation in the research be 'hidden'.

If your research is to meet the standards set by the CIPD relating to the maintenance of relationships based on trust, confidence and respect, it is important that you respect people's rights to know whether you will achieve **anonymity** (the extent to which their identity as a participant cannot be known) when you undertake your research. If your research involves a small number of interviews with high-profile people in one organisation, it might be impossible to achieve anonymity as identities could be 'deduced' by those who know the organisation even if they have not been formally named. Some participants may be happy to accept this situation and some may not see anonymity as something that must be achieved in their case (the individual or organisation may be willing to be named in your research), particularly where they are sponsoring your project in some way. However, this is something that should be established at the planning stage and before information collection begins.

A second important issue in relating to the professional standard of maintaining relationships of trust is **confidentiality** (the guarantee that data will not be shared with unauthorised people). Here it is important that those who participate in your research are aware of and agree to arrangements you will make relating to any communication of information that you gather. They need to know, before they participate, who will be able to read and scrutinise the information that they have provided.

A further expectation of the CIPD professional code is the safeguarding of confidential and personal or commercially sensitive information, and so **data storage** arrangements that you make are also important. Individuals and organisations have become increasingly aware of the potential dangers of the loss or theft of confidential information. A further ethical principle is that arrangements for the secure storage of any data you gather are made and communicated to potential participants before the information is gathered. At some point the data will also need to be disposed of, and so your plans (and timescales) for this should be clearly communicated to those who participate in your research.

DIGNITY AND WELL-BEING OF RESEARCH PARTICIPANTS

A third general ethical principle is that research should not cause distress, embarrassment or harm to anyone involved with it. However small your group of respondents, it is likely that there will be differences between them (and you) relating to gender, employment experience, ethnicity, language and educational background. Any research process that makes someone feel 'stupid', for example, is inconsistent with the principle of not causing distress or embarrassment. Where research across international boundaries is being undertaken, it is important to be sensitive to different values, attitudes, social customs and religious beliefs. There is an ethical duty of care to take account of the culture of your research participants. Careful determination of the location for data-gathering might be necessary, for example, to avoid causing offence or embarrassment in cultures where females and males would not normally be alone and 'unsupervised'. Where an interview has been agreed with someone from another country or region of the world, it is important to ensure that the 'dress code' of the interviewer is not likely to cause offence or embarrassment.

POTENTIAL FOR CONFLICTS OF INTEREST

Although many student HR research projects are undertaken without any form of direct or indirect sponsorship, a significant number are 'sponsored' by an organisation or by a particular manager within an organisation. Where your employing organisation is supporting your studies, or where your employer has given you permission to carry out a specific piece of research into a specific topic, they will have some 'interest' in what you do, how you do it and the eventual outcome. If you are a full-time student who is undertaking research in an organisation, the person who arranged the access for you (the 'gatekeeper') may also assume that their interests should be taken into account. Ethical issues here revolve around potential **conflicts of interest** and these should be discussed before the project commences. Issues to resolve are: the extent to which you can expect to conduct your research in an 'objective' and 'independent' way; the support that the organisation will offer to you for data-gathering processes; the extent to which your sponsor needs to 'authorise and approve' any interview or questionnaire questions; the obligations of your sponsor to allow you to formulate your research conclusions in a format that is appropriate for your study centre; the expectations your sponsor may have of a copy of your final research report (or, more usually, an abridged summary). Other issues for discussion relate to your plans for any dissemination of your findings after the project has been completed. Some organisations and sponsors might be very comfortable with the idea of an article or paper being published in a professional, practitioner or academic publication that draws on the research data, but these matters should be established early on (at least in principle) so that both parties are clear about their rights and responsibilities.

ETHICAL ISSUES FROM DIFFERENT STAKEHOLDER PERSPECTIVES

A number of different stakeholders will have an interest in your research project and each of these may have a different perspective about ethical issues. In addition, the rights of those involved as research subjects, participants or respondents are very important. Table 4.2 offers a brief summary of the issues from the different perspectives, which are then discussed more fully later in the chapter.

Table 4.2 Ethical perspectives of different stakeholders

Stakeholder group	Ethical issues to consider
Individual respondents; 'research subjects'; participants	<ul><li>To what extent might the research process affect their well-being? Is there any risk of distress, embarrassment or inconvenience? How disruptive will the research process be to their work or home life? What time commitment would be involved? Is this their 'own time' or 'work time'?</li><li>Confidentiality and anonymity – to what extent will any information given to you be treated as confidential and to what extent will they be assured of anonymity?</li><li>Privacy and consent – to what extent will they know and understand what is involved and feel that they can freely choose to take part or not to take part?</li></ul>
Organisation(s) in which research is undertaken	<ul><li>To what extent might the research process affect the reputation of the organisation? Is there any risk of disruption to working patterns as a result of the data-gathering processes?</li><li>Does the organisation have its own ethical policy or framework which must be taken into account in any research process?</li><li>Would the research process comply with wider organisational policies (for example, data protection, health and safety and so on)?</li><li>Consent – has someone with appropriate authority been informed about the research and given permission in advance for the information to be gathered?</li><li>Anonymity and confidentiality – is the organisation willing to be named and what information must be treated as confidential?</li></ul>
Study centre	<ul><li>To what extent might this research affect the reputation of the study centre?</li><li>Does the research comply with wider study centre policies (for example, data protection, equal opportunities and diversity, ethics)?</li><li>Would the data-gathering process pose any risk to the researcher (for example, travel at night in a remote area to interview employees on a night-shift)?</li></ul>

HR researchers who are undertaking organisationally based research in their own employing organisation also have particular tensions to take into account. In addition to being a 'researcher', they may also be closely involved with individuals in a range of other organisational 'real life' situations. This involves a careful consideration of power relationships within the organisation. While the research process may be a 'project' for you, those who have been 'researched' will have to live with the consequences of it in the longer term. Throughout the research process it is important to recognise that being a researcher is quite different from being a practitioner. It may be difficult for you, and those around you, to distinguish between the two roles. Practitioner-researchers need to be aware that the involvement of colleagues in any research project may impact on the work relationships that they have. Particular issues can arise where an HR researcher wishes to invite someone that they line-manage to be included in their research. To what extent might the person feel that they could decline the invitation? To what extent will the person feel that they can provide truthful information? Key principles that may be helpful in this context are:

- make sure that all relevant permissions have been gained before commencing the project
- involve participants – encourage them to shape the form of your enquiry
- be prepared to negotiate access with individuals, don't assume it will be given
- be open about your progress so that any concerns can be taken into account
- never undertake 'observation' without the explicit permission of 'the observed'
- get permission before you examine or copy files, correspondence or other organisational documents
- report back to participants your accounts of interviews and observations of them and allow them to suggest amendments which enhance fairness, accuracy and relevance
- take responsibility for maintaining confidentiality.

ETHICS IN A DIGITISED SOCIETY

DATA PROTECTION

The Data Protection Act 1988 (DPA) provides for the protection of the privacy for individuals in the UK in relation to the data about them that is collected by employers and other organisations. The law provides protection against the inappropriate storage and use of data relating to people's names, addresses, contact information, employment history, medical conditions, convictions and credit history. Many (but not all) countries have enacted laws to regulate how data concerning people may be collected, transferred, stored and processed. Although legal regulation varies in different countries, the main concerns are:

- Who could access information?
- How accurate is the information?
- What precautions are there to prevent data copying?
- What information is stored about a person without their knowledge or permission?

The Data Protection Act applies to data which refers to living and identifiable people; anonymised and aggregated data (statistical data) do not fall within its regulatory remit. Nonetheless, there are a number of implications affecting HR researchers. Relevant principles underpinning the Act which may have direct implications for the approach you take in your research project are that:

- Data may only be used for the purpose for which they were collected.
- Data may not be disclosed to other parties who are not connected to the original purpose for which the data were collected.
- Data should only be held for the time required to achieve the stated purpose.
- Data must be stored in a secure way.
- Data transfer outside of Europe where no appropriate data protection legislation is in place is prohibited.
- People have a right of access to any data held about them.
- People have a right to have incorrect data about them corrected by the information-holder.

 ACTIVITY 4.2

IMPLICATIONS OF THE DPA

Imagine that you are planning to undertake research using a case study research strategy that will involve using secondary data from the organisation as well as primary data (interviews and a questionnaire-based survey).

1   What are the DPA implications for the way you undertake your research?

FEEDBACK NOTES

Points you may identify from this activity include: if you plan to gather data that cannot be fully anonymised (qualitative data often cannot be fully anonymised), it is important that you communicate clearly to those who will be participating the use to which the data will be put. If you say it is just for your dissertation or research report, you are not entitled to use the data for other forms of communication (organisational newsletter items, journal article, conference paper and so on). If you think you may wish to use the data after the end of your project, you must make this clear when the data are gathered. A second issue concerns the length of time you hold on to the data. Even if you think you may want to use the data after the end of your project, you should define the length of time you intend to hold the data set (five years is often the norm), and you should have secure methods to destroy the data at the end of that period. A third implication relates to data security: you have an obligation under the DPA that data should be stored securely, password-protected and somewhere where your laptop is not likely to be stolen or mislaid. A fourth implication relates to an individual's right to see what data you hold about them: if you are creating a transcript of your interview, the interviewee has a right to request a copy of the transcript and to request that any inaccuracies are changed.

FREEDOM OF INFORMATION

Freedom of information (FoI) legislation has been incrementally developed in the UK and fully enacted since 2005, and access to information (ATI) mechanisms exist in a number of other countries (Walby and Larsen 2011). The legislation provides for public access to information held by public authorities in the UK such as government departments, local authorities, the NHS, state schools and police forces. One feature of the Act is that public authorities are obliged to publish information about some of their activities. Another is that members of the public are entitled to request information from public authorities. Within the FoI legislation, access requests are 'motive-blind', which means that anyone can request information and, once they have received information under the legislation, the information is considered to be in the 'public domain' (Birkinshaw 2010).

Within the research community, FoI legislation is seen as a potential 'double-edged sword', although the impact on student projects is likely to be minimal. One potential benefit of the legislation is that the appropriate use of FoI enquiries, made to an organisational FoI officer in a constructive way, can be a useful tool for obtaining information from a public authority that is pertinent to a research project. However, well-publicised cases surrounding the disclosure of data and other information, such as FoI requests and subsequent publicity about research into climate change at the University of East Anglia and Queen's University Belfast, have highlighted other implications of the legislation (Walby and Larsen 2011). As most student projects are undertaken through affiliation with a publicly funded organisation (the university), there may, in some circumstances, be a case when a FoI request for research data may be made, although this is a most unlikely scenario.

INTERNET RESEARCH

Internet research provides a range of opportunities and challenges for HR researchers. In addition to personal research on a particular subject (for example, something mentioned on the news, making shopping decisions and so on), many student researchers are increasingly considering the Internet as a basis for recruiting research participants and gathering data. However, there are a number of ethical issues to be considered (Denscombe 2010).

 ACTIVITY 4.3

USING INTERNET SOURCES FOR RESEARCH

Imagine that you have decided to undertake research into the problems as well as the opportunities of performance management. You have undertaken some interviews to explore the issues, and you notice that HR professionals can only see the advantages of performance management, whereas some of

the line managers that you interview are rather cynical about the process. You are concerned that your HR respondents may not be speaking 'freely' in their interviews as they feel they 'ought' to support the process. You wonder if HR professionals may be able to express their views more freely on less formal social networking sites.

Visit an Internet online community such as the CIPD Shaping the Future Community at: http://www.cipd.co.uk/community/subjects/subject.aspx?ForumID=83&PageIndex=4&sb=0&d=1&df=11&uf=0&hrp=0&lf=0 and see if you can find any discussions that would be pertinent to your research.

DISCUSSION QUESTIONS

1   To what extent would the issues of informed consent and confidentiality relating to this form of data be different from those for the interviews that you have undertaken?

2   What ethical issues would be raised by researchers who made use of contributions of people who participate in chat rooms and post items on to bulletin boards or blogs?

FEEDBACK NOTES

The developing use of Web 2.0 applications (such as blogs, social networking sites, wikis, podcasts and so on) mean that an increasing amount of data are available that could contribute to research projects (Association of Internet Researchers 2002), but ethical issues arise where data from such applications which have been placed there for one (possibly private) purpose may be used, without prior knowledge, to achieve different (research) purposes. In such situations, ethical and legal issues may arise relating to copyright, data protection and deception. Although Internet-based research involves the same research ethics principles, Activity 4.3 highlights some of the issues that may warrant particular attention. Contributions to discussion threads are made on a 'named basis' and so issues of anonymity may be raised. Anonymity cannot be achieved in such circumstances and confidentiality issues may also arise if the data gathered in this way is then used in some form of 'public' dissemination. The names might be removed in your project report, for example, but views expressed in a 'discussion thread situation' would be reproduced in a different context and it would be possible for a reader to access the discussion thread itself and find out the identity of the participants.

There may be an argument that indicating to people that you might use their contributions for your research would mean that they would decide not to make any postings or contributions, but such instances would be rare within the scope of student HR research projects.

RESEARCH ETHICS AT DIFFERENT STAGES OF YOUR PROJECT

Three stages of the research process have ethical implications (Saunders et al 2012, Oliver 2010). These are shown in Figure 4.1 and considered in more detail in the following sections:

- research design and planning
- during the data-gathering process
- after data-gathering.

Figure 4.1 Ethical issues through the research process

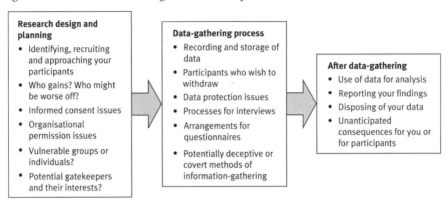

Research design and planning
- Identifying, recruiting and approaching your participants
- Who gains? Who might be worse off?
- Informed consent issues
- Organisational permission issues
- Vulnerable groups or individuals?
- Potential gatekeepers and their interests?

Data-gathering process
- Recording and storage of data
- Participants who wish to withdraw
- Data protection issues
- Processes for interviews
- Arrangements for questionnaires
- Potentially deceptive or covert methods of information-gathering

After data-gathering
- Use of data for analysis
- Reporting your findings
- Disposing of your data
- Unanticipated consequences for you or for participants

DURING THE PLANNING STAGE

CASE ILLUSTRATION 4.4

Research into employee share ownership schemes

Rachael was a distance-learning student who was out of work but who hoped to specialise in 'pay and benefits' in her career. She became intrigued by issues associated with bonus schemes that had become prominent in debates about executive pay. She 'read around' the subject of bonuses and identified four different types of scheme targeted at incentivising and rewarding: individuals; teams; people at specific work locations; across entire organisations. Rachael wanted to understand more clearly the expectations of those in receipt of bonuses and the intentions of those responsible for agreeing them. With this in mind she felt that a case study research design would be appropriate and she set about contacting a range of large organisations that she hoped would allow her to conduct research in their organisation.

Discussion Questions

Write down a list of about five concerns that an employer might have about giving Rachael permission to carry out this research in their organisation.

FEEDBACK NOTES

It is possible that you could list far more than five concerns that you might have in this situation. These might include:

- What would this project involve? Who would be required to provide what sort of information?
- Why has the organisation been chosen? Is there a problem that the organisation should be aware of? Would you have to release sensitive data?
- How much 'poking around' would this person want to undertake?
- How 'open' would those who receive the highest bonuses want to be about their rewards?

- Could some employees be 'unsettled' or demand higher bonuses if the subject was 'out in the open' in this way?
- What difficult public relations issues would be likely?
- How confidential would the information be?
- How competent is the person to undertake such a project?
- Who would get to read the findings of the research?

Concerns such as these represent some of the ethical issues that have to be considered as part of the planning of any research project. Key issues are related to the ethical themes of privacy (individual and organisational) and consent. All of the subjects of your research have the right to know how and why you identified them for inclusion in the research. For organisationally based research, managers will be able to give or withhold permission for your project. Privacy and data protection issues are also relevant if you plan to make use of secondary data held within the organisation.

It is important, right from the planning stage of your enquiry, to ensure that potential participants are able to give **informed** (rather than implied) consent to be involved. In any HR project it would be difficult to make an ethical justification of a situation where there was a lack of consent, that is, the participant did not know that data about them was being gathered. It is also insufficient to assume that consent has been implied just because an interview, focus group or some other intervention has taken place. An important principle is that people have the right to give or withhold consent on the basis of full information about what the data they provide is for and how it will be stored, used and ultimately disposed of. Informed consent involves clearly communicating the scope and intention of the project to potential participants so that they are clear about:

- the nature of the research – its purpose; who is undertaking it; who should be contacted if they have any further questions
- what participants can expect – the type(s) of information to be collected and methods of collection; the time commitment involved; their right to withdraw without repercussions
- arrangements with regard to anonymity and confidentiality
- subsequent use of data – who will have access to it; how results will be communicated; what will happen after the project has been completed
- compatibility with organisational or other relevant professional codes or policies.

To achieve these standards it may be necessary to develop an information sheet or briefing note for potential participants that clearly sets out, in the language of the participant (rather than in academic jargon), what is involved.

ACTIVITY 4.4

INFORMED CONSENT

Imagine that you plan to collect data from within one organisation about training and development processes. You anticipate gathering data through some form of questionnaire to be completed by a sample of the organisation's employees (all types of staff)

and also through semi-structured interviews with a selection of line managers. Complete the relevant sections of the information sheet below to ensure that any individuals would be able to give informed consent to their participation.

Research into Training and Development processes at XYZ Ltd

Please read the following information. You should feel able to ask any further questions you may have about the project. Contact details are provided as part of this information sheet.

Who will undertake this project?	Your name(s) and contact details
Which study centre is supervising the research project?	Your affiliation
What is the title of the research project?	
What is the purpose of the project?	If your research aim and objectives are rather 'technical', make sure that this explanation of your research purpose can be easily understood by the people whose participation you are requesting.
What contribution am I requesting from you?	What sort(s) of data? What time commitment? How many times? Over what time period?
Why have you been asked to participate?	
How will I gather information?	Be clear about the methods you will use.
How will the information be recorded?	
When will the information be gathered?	Be clear about whether this is the participant's 'own time' or 'work time'.
What arrangements will be made regarding confidentiality of information?	
What arrangements will be made regarding anonymity of participants?	
What if you do not want to participate?	
What will happen to all the data when they have been gathered?	Be clear about data storage and data disposal.

How will the findings be reported?	Explain your procedures relating to confidentiality and anonymity in what you report.
	Explain your plans for your business research report / dissertation.
	Indicate if you plan to provide other reports / accounts of your findings in any other format.
What are the possible disadvantages?	You may foresee no negative consequences, so don't be afraid to say so.
In what way will the project be beneficial and to whom?	Indicate who can benefit and in what ways.
Who has reviewed the research study to ensure that it complies with appropriate ethical standards?	Say here who has reviewed the study at the university/study centre and, if the organisation has its own ethical scrutiny processes, explain how this has been undertaken.
Can permission be withdrawn having previously been granted?	Indicate how and when a contributor can withdraw from the study, but also indicate if there is a point in time when the data cannot physically be disaggregated from the overall data set.
Can you refuse to answer a question?	

To be completed by the research participant

I confirm that I have read and understood the information on this sheet relating to this research and I confirm that I consent to take part:

Name (please write clearly): ………………………………………….

Signature: …………………………………………..

Date: ………………………………………………

FEEDBACK NOTES

As a result of completing this activity you may be feeling that ethical issues make the research process rather restrictive and the planning process particularly time-consuming. Many students get impatient with the requirement for thinking and planning in ethical terms at the beginning of their research process. However, by tackling questions early on about how and when you will gather data and from whom, clarifying who might benefit as well as what disadvantages there may be for your proposed participants, and by making commitments about data storage and your plans for communicating your findings, you will find that you have a stronger and more robust research design and you are putting yourself in the position of being able to undertake a better piece of research with the potential to get a good mark.

The spectrum of consent

Ethical research will meet the full criteria of 'informed consent' (Saunders et al 2012) whereby all participants, regardless of the way data are gathered, give their consent freely, having received full information about their participation and the use to which the data will be put. Implied consent, where you infer consent as a result of participation or completion of a survey instrument, is not sufficient. A lack of consent, where deception may have been used or where participants have no knowledge about the project, is rarely if ever justifiable in HR research projects.

Cross-cultural research

When research is carried out within different ethnic groups there may be ethical implications relating to the extent to which cultural and language differences are taken into account in the research process. People with different cultural backgrounds and assumptions are likely to be encountered in most research projects that take place where there is a diverse population, but the issues are more direct when research is carried out 'abroad'.

CASE ILLUSTRATION 4.5

Going abroad: how relevant is ethics?

Salman was a full-time international student studying in the UK. For his dissertation he wanted to undertake a study situated in a private hospital in his own country. Salman had become interested in the work of West et al (2006) into the extent to which human resource management practices can result in patient outcomes such as lower mortality in hospitals. Salman knew that he could obtain access to undertake research in a large hospital in his own country and he wished to undertake a study involving questionnaires and interviews with people delivering healthcare in the hospital but, in addition, he wanted to gather data from patients and their families to assess their levels of satisfaction with the service they were receiving.

When he first discussed this idea with his supervisor he discovered that research involving patients and their families (who may be considered to be 'vulnerable adults') in health organisations in the UK requires an extensive process of ethical scrutiny (http://www.nres.nhs.uk/applications/is-your-project-research/) and that, given the sensitive issues faced by many people within the healthcare system, he would be unlikely to find the research – as he envisaged it – would be approved by his institution. Salman felt aggrieved: he was more than happy to respect the ethical protocols in the UK but, he pointed out, these did not apply in his country and so they should not be regarded as a hindrance for his research.

Discussion Questions

1 What are the merits and problems of Salman's views?

2 If you were Salman's supervisor, would you be prepared to agree to this research being undertaken?

FEEDBACK NOTES

You may feel some sympathy with Salman in this context. After all, the research is not taking place in the UK. In addition, you may have found out that even in the UK the full ethical scrutiny process of the NHS applies to research projects rather than 'service audits' and you may wish to try to make the case that Salman's research constitutes a service audit rather than a full 'research project'. Such a perspective would be difficult to take forward, however (see http://www.nres.nhs.uk/applications/is-your-project-research/ for the distinction between 'research' and 'service audit' within the NHS in England and Wales). An alternative perspective is that the CIPD professional code of conduct advocates the advancement of business practices that are inclusive and support human rights and dignity. In the UK children, as well as those who are elderly, ill, in prison or are refugees, are considered to be 'vulnerable'. Undertaking research which requires the time and attention of those who are already unwell or are related to people in extreme poor health is equally problematic, regardless of the country in which it is carried out.

In this instance Salman's study centre would not approve his research plans, taking the view that, as his qualification would be awarded by an English institution, the research should be undertaken in accordance with the same ethical standards as would apply in England and Wales. All was not lost, however, as Salman was able to revise his research question and research design. He revised his proposal to cover data-gathering from employees but not patients and made extensive use of already existent secondary data about patient outcomes, and so he was able to submit a dissertation which fully met the assessment criteria.

Other ethical principles associated with sensitivity for customs, practices, culture and beliefs of others apply when undertaking research in other countries, particularly when a researcher of one nationality decides to gather data in another country. In these circumstances it is often necessary to access research participants through a 'gatekeeper' (an intermediary person or organisation) and it is important to consider the influence this may have on the research project. Additional care is also required when seeking informed consent (Remenyi et al 2011): is the language translation of any information sheets accurate? Do the words used have 'resonance' with the proposed respondents? Will they know what is being talked about?

As in any research, a key ethical principle is that researchers should guard against possible harmful consequences for participants. Risk factors may be physical or psychological, and processes that may be seen to coerce people to participate in research must be avoided.

THE DATA-GATHERING PHASE

Once your research project is under way, it is important to keep basic ethical principles in mind, such as:

- participants' (and organisations') right to withdraw at any time

- the importance of scoping out (and then sticking to) the purpose of the project and the data-gathering methods you plan
- collecting and recording data accurately and fully
- ensuring that you keep to any promises made about data confidentiality and participant (and organisational) anonymity
- fair treatment – making sure that you do not put participants in a position where they feel undue pressure or which might diminish their self-esteem.

CASE ILLUSTRATION 4.6

Research into the nature of the HR function

Extracts from: Harris, L. (2007) The changing nature of the HR function in UK local government and its role as 'employee champion'. *Employee Relations*, (1): 34–47. © Emerald Group Publishing Limited all rights reserved.

Introduction

The role of the HR function in UK local authorities has undergone significant changes. ... In recent years the modernisation of public services agenda has meant that the HR function in local government has not only been required to continuously review working practices (White 2000) but is also facing unprecedented changes in how its own services are provided. This paper examines the challenges and dilemmas facing the HR function in UK local government if it is to effectively support the organisation in maximising levels of employee commitment crucial to the high performance workplace (Boxall and Purcell 2003). It focuses on how changes in the role and services provided by the HR function may impact on its role as 'employee champion': one of the four proactive roles Ulrich (1997) argues are essential to it making a valuable strategic organisational contribution. This theme will be addressed though findings drawn from case studies of three large local authorities, and the discussion will particularly consider:

- the changing nature of the role of the HR function in UK local government; and

- the implications of these changes for its role as an employee champion.

Research design

The case study authorities, based in the Midlands, were a large city unitary authority and two county councils. ... All three had long established HR functions, a Head of HR with Chief Officer status and reported similar constraints, challenges and changes in the provision of HR services. As a result it is not the intention of this paper to compare and contrast provision at the three authorities but rather to identify the common emergent themes. Perceptions of the role of the specialist HR function was explored through an independent assessment of HR services undertaken by the author at the three authorities during 2002 to 2005 and there is continuing involvement with two of the authorities. The role of an independent third party engaged to provide a critical perspective on the service created significant opportunity for 'participant observation' and had the advantage of legitimising the 'freedom to be critical' by allowing for a level of challenging questions that might be unacceptable in research roles which offer a lesser degree of involvement (Watson 2000). The role of the HR function and its perceived responsibilities as an employee champion were explored through the perspectives of specialist HR staff, senior, middle and supervisory managers, individual employees and trade union representatives...

Discussion Questions

1   What ethical issues might be raised by the use of 'participant observation' as a way of gathering data?

2   To what extent would 'covert' (secret) observation be justifiable in HR research?

FEEDBACK NOTES

The use of observation as a way of gathering information raises a large number of ethical issues. The principles of informed consent suggest that if you are observing anyone for your research, they have a right to know in advance about your plans and can withhold consent if they wish. Whenever observation is used as a data-gathering strategy, however, it is important to enact another ethical principle: that of the objectivity of the observation process. This addresses an important question: to what extent might one observer 'see' a behaviour and describe it in one way and another observer 'see' the same behaviour and describe it differently?

In the research situation described in this paper, those who participated would have known they were being observed and would have consented to it. However, it might be argued that their behaviour might be different as they knew they were being watched. In some situations researchers might argue that 'truer' or 'fuller' data would be available through covert observation. However, it is unlikely that this would accord with the ethical policies of your study centre and would need a detailed justification in advance to ensure the ethical legitimacy of your plans. The issue of covert observation is also relevant where HR practitioners are undertaking research into their own organisations and have particular opportunities to observe interactions in (say) meetings or on training courses but without declaring the 'real' purpose of their interest. The ethical questions below would need to be addressed whether any planned observation was 'overt' or 'covert' (Saunders et al 2012, Zikmund 2009):

- Can you justify the use of covert rather than overt observation?
- Why is informed consent not appropriate?
- Are the processes for data-recording objective and accurate?
- Will there be a detrimental effect on your relationships with those who you will be treating as 'research subjects'?
- How might the process of observation 'fit' with the organisational culture in which it will take place?
- What time and opportunity is required through which to establish the co-operation of those who will be observed?
- Would it be appropriate to undertake a debriefing with the participant(s) after any observations?

When thinking through these issues, it is important to consider the level of trust and confidence that your intended participants will have of you. This will be affected by the nature of the power relationship you have at present with them as well as the organisational culture and management style of the organisation in which your research is to be conducted.

ETHICAL ISSUES AFTER THE DATA HAS BEEN GATHERED

Once data have been collected you will be involved in interpreting it, formulating conclusions and then communicating your findings by writing and submitting a research report or dissertation. It is attractive to imagine that the main research ethics 'challenges' have been dealt with once your data have been collected. However, in addition to continuing concern about participants' anonymity and data confidentiality (which span all parts of the research project lifecycle), the time that you spend after the data have been collected also raises more ethical issues.

First, the ethical responsibility of collecting data in an objective and accurate way 'carries forward' to the phase of the research where you are interpreting the information you have gathered and formulating conclusions (Zikmund 2009). Here again it is important that your analysis honestly represents the data and that you **report fairly and accurately** on the information (rather than editing out the parts that are inconvenient).

Second, it is possible that some of your research participants (a line manager or the HR director, for example) are sufficiently interested in your research that they request some of the results. Perhaps an **interim report** is sought to gain some idea of the conclusions that might be drawn. Here the type of research project with which you are engaged and the relationship with any project sponsor or manager involved will influence the extent to which such requests could be met. For organisationally based projects where organisational sponsorship and support has been provided, it is reasonable to provide a summary of the findings. However, if you hurry to meet an organisational deadline, it is important that you do not fall into the trap of presenting partial results that may be misinterpreted as the **final** conclusions of your analysis (Kane 1995).

A third issue with the reporting of findings revolves around **permission to identify** any organisation(s) that participates in your research. If you have entered into a commitment to maintain organisational anonymity, you must abide by this unless the organisation agrees to a change. Where the organisation (or any individual) agrees to be named, it is possible that this will depend on them being able to read relevant parts of your report to assess the context within which their name will appear. They may also insist on some revisions.

Disposal of data is another issue that has ethical implications. Where data have been gathered for a student project, there are few occasions when it will be needed after the successful assessment of the dissertation or research report. Disposal in such circumstances should be undertaken thoroughly and carefully: shredding paper rather than leaving in your organisation's waste paper bin and ensuring that files are deleted or 'wiped' from the storage devices on which they were held. However, there may be circumstances where the data you gathered is to be used for further purposes. You may, for example, have devised an attitude survey for the organisation as part of your project and follow-up surveys are to be undertaken in subsequent years. Alternatively, in addition to your research report, you may be hoping to disseminate your findings in other ways (presentation at a conference or in journal article). This may involve subsequent reference to your data set. Another circumstance might be that your data might be donated to a data repository, which may then be accessed by subsequent researchers so that they can undertake some comparative research. Where there is a case for data retention, it is important that the principles of data privacy are maintained and all references to names or other forms of identification are removed. It is also important that such issues are anticipated well in advance and that the permission of those who provided the data in the first place (the participants) is obtained.

 Unintended consequences of research participation

CASE ILLUSTRATION 4.7

Brocket, J. (2011) Stress tops list of long-term absence causes, *PM Online*, 5 October [online] http:// www.peoplemanagement.co.uk/pm/ sections/misc/search/all-of-people-management.htm?q=Stress%20tops %20list%20of%20long-term %20absence%20causes

With the permission of the publisher, the Chartered Institute of Personnel and Development, London (www.cipd.co.uk).

Stress is now the number one cause of long-term sickness absence as employees struggle with heavy workloads and job loss worries, research from the CIPD and Simplyhealth has shown. This year's *Absence Management* survey reveals that stress has taken over from musculoskeletal problems as the top cause of absence for both manual and non-manual workers. Nearly four in ten (39 per cent) of employers say that absence due to mental health problems has gone up in the last year, while only 12 per cent say that it has decreased. There is a clear link between the rise in mental health problems and job security, with employers who are planning redundancies significantly more likely to report an increase in

stress-related absence (51 per cent) than other employers (32 per cent)...

... Overall, employee absence levels have remained relatively stable, with an average of 7.7 days lost per employee. Public sector absence stood at 9.1 days, a slight improvement on last year, while private sector absence was 7.1 days, slightly worse. ... The survey also revealed some evidence of an increase in 'presenteeism' with 28 per cent of employers saying that employees were now more likely to come to work despite being ill. Organisations where presenteeism was noted were more likely to have also experienced an upturn in stress.

Discussion Question

Imagine you wanted to undertake research into the underlying causes of absence in your organisation (or one in which you have been granted research access). This news item indicates that one of the variables you will need to investigate is 'mental health issues'. What unintended consequences might result from participation in the research? Consider the question for (a) your organisation and (b) individual employees.

FEEDBACK NOTES

This case illustration concerns research undertaken into prevalent issues in times of economic challenges. It is possible that raising the issue of mental health might lead some participants in your research to have to face up to issues they would rather not discuss or articulate. As a consequence of the research and the actions taken after its publication, employees might be more likely to believe their levels of stress demand more management support; managers might feel inhibited from asking their people to work extra hours or 'go the extra mile' for fear of being accused of causing higher levels of stress. However, the positive outcome from the research is the identification of stress-related issues and the importance of employment strategies to support employees in difficult circumstances which the organisation will be better placed to tackle. In this instance, you may well argue that the benefits of awareness about stress and its consequences and associated policy changes over the long term would outweigh the 'losses' and an ethical justification can be made on that basis.

THE POSITIVE FEATURES OF ETHICAL ASSESSMENT PROCESSES

CASE ILLUSTRATION 4.8

Ethical assessment and scrutiny – another factor for delay?

Annabel was a full-time student about to embark on a work placement during which she would also be undertaking research for a business research report. The research would be organisationally based; the intention was that the placement company and Annabel would choose a business issue on which her project would be based that would be mutually beneficial. When she arrived at her placement on the first day, her placement manager told her that there were 'engagement problems' in two departments in the organisation and her project would involve examining the nature of the problems and recommending solutions. He also told her that he had arranged a series of interviews for her to undertake and that she should begin gathering her data in one week's time. In addition he indicated that he would expect to read a full copy of her business research report.

Annabel's university supervisor indicated to her, however, that she must complete an ethical scrutiny form to assure the institution that appropriate standards would be adhered to. Completion of the form required Annabel to indicate her research objectives; the population from which she would draw her sample; the way that the interviewees were to be selected and recruited; the means by which she would ensure they gave informed consent to participate; her plans for recording and storing the information that she gathered; the extent to which she would be able to achieve confidentiality and anonymity; her plans for when and how she might dispose of any of the data she had gathered. Annabel was in a hurry; she did not want to upset the placement manager. She had a vague idea of what she might to do to examine engagement but had not yet formulated firm plans for her data collection, storage and analysis processes.

FEEDBACK NOTES

At the beginning of her placement Annabel was very resistant to the requirements for the completion of an extensive ethical assessment form. Her 'objections' were somewhat similar to some of those expressed (usually in private) by other students. One objection that you might have identified was that the requirement for an ethical approval process would be an unnecessary delay in an already tight schedule. A further objection that might be raised was that 'it's only a student project'. While ethical assessment is often seen to be important for large-scale and significant pieces of research, there might be the view that such a process is too extensive for a small-scale investigative enquiry. The interviewees for Annabel's project had already been selected by the placement manager and he was dismissive of any concerns about the requirement for her to get 'proof' that they knew about her research plans and consented to being interviewed.

However, once she had invested the time in the ethical assessment process (which her study centre was able to help her complete within the week that she had been allocated by her placement manager), Annabel recognised its benefits. First, it enabled her to go forward with her research process with confidence that she was acting in a way that would not adversely affect any of the research participants with whom she came into contact. In addition, the process encouraged her to discuss with the placement manager the sampling strategy and methods for recording data, which meant that she was better able to plan a good-quality research enquiry and avoid mistakes that she might have otherwise made.

Many student researchers (not just in HR) are tempted to want to move ahead quickly without undue delay with their data-gathering processes. The requirement for ethical scrutiny in the planning and execution of research is becoming more prevalent in many higher education institutions. Managed appropriately, this can lead to better research being undertaken.

 ACTIVITY 4.5

ETHICAL ASSESSMENT PROCESSES

1   Find out the ethical assessment requirements for your study centre and obtain a copy of any forms that you must complete. Identify (a) the main issues behind the questions that are asked and

(b) the level of 'permission' you will require for your planned research. If your study centre does not have an ethical assessment form or checklist, you can enter the search words: 'ethical assessment form' into any Internet search engine and you will find many examples of different forms and procedures from which you could undertake this activity.

2   If you are a student researcher planning to undertake your research in your own organisation, find out if your organisation has any ethical policies or forms of assessment and identify how you should go about obtaining ethical approval to enact your plans.

FEEDBACK NOTES

Ethical assessment forms and processes are all structured and organised in different ways, but the principles that lie beneath them are those outlined in this chapter. They relate to individuals and organisations and concern privacy, anonymity and confidentiality, the dignity and well-being of research participants and the management of any issues involved in the relationship with organisations, sponsors or 'gatekeepers'. Even with small-scale research, it is becoming increasingly likely that your research plans will be scrutinised by someone (perhaps your supervisor or an ethics 'champion' within your study centre). Many educational institutions are developing different levels of scrutiny to reflect the different scope of research activities, perhaps distinguishing between undergraduate or postgraduate-level studies, staff and research degree projects. In some institutions the research tutor or course leader may be responsible for ethical scrutiny of your proposals. In other instances, however, you may be required to submit your plans to the scrutiny of an ethics committee and this can be a slow process.

There are both advantages and disadvantages to the increased level of ethical scrutiny that has been developed in research in HR (and business and management more generally) over recent years. Timescales for research projects are increasingly difficult for students to achieve and so you may feel that this is yet another burden. However, there are important benefits to be achieved. If you take the time to address all the ethical issues in the planning stage of a project, it is likely that your project will achieve better-quality outcomes. You will also find that you are better prepared to write the 'methodology' or 'methods' section or chapter in your dissertation or business research report (see Chapter 5) and it may well achieve more marks than it might have if the ethical issues had not been considered early on. Explicit concern with ethics is no longer an 'optional extra' in HR investigative enquiries; rather, it is now seen as a fundamental feature of 'good research'.

SUMMARY

- Research ethics is about adherence to a 'code of behaviour in relation to the rights of those who become the subject of your work or are affected by it' (Wells 1994, p284). Explicit concern with ethical issues is a fundamental feature of good research in HR.
- Key ethical principles that are relevant to any research involving 'human subjects' at both individual and organisational levels are: privacy, confidentiality and anonymity; the dignity and well-being of research

participants; and potential conflicts of interest with sponsors and/or organisations.

- HR practitioners operate within a professional code of ethics and conduct. HR research should be undertaken in a way that is professional, honest and characterised by integrity and sensitivity for customs, practices, culture and beliefs of others and which safeguards confidential, personal and commercially sensitive information.
- Ethical issues arise throughout the research process and need to be taken into account at the project planning stage, during the data-gathering processes and after data-gathering has been completed.
- There are a number of ethical issues to be considered where Internet-based research or use of personal data held in a digital form may comprise part of a data-gathering strategy, particularly relating to compliance with legislation, informed consent and the potential for deception.
- Ethical scrutiny is increasingly required for student research projects. Although this can be time-consuming, it can lead to a better investigation than might otherwise have been the case.

 Self-test questions

REVIEW AND REFLECT

1   Why are ethical considerations an imperative in HR research?

   a) because the ends justify the means

   b) because research, like HR, is an inherently bureaucratic process

   c) because adherence to a professional code of conduct and ethics is important for the development of relationships of trust and integrity

   d) because it is a requirement to get a good mark in any qualification

2   HR researchers have a duty of care to minimise any risk to research participants of:

   a) physical discomfort or injury

   b) stress or anxiety

   c) coercion to participate

   d) all of the above

3   Why is it important that research data are stored in a secure way?

   a) so that you can track down your respondents at a later date if you want to get more data from them

   b) so that people will not know what you have written about them

   c) so that the external examiner can see the data if they want to

   d) to prevent research participants from potential harm through identification or disclosure of confidential information

4   Which method of data-gathering is associated with a lack of informed consent?

   a) structured interviewing

   b) questionnaire survey

   c) covert observation

   d) focus groups

5   Which of the following approaches to organisational data-gathering

goes against the principles of organisational informed consent?

a)   taking internal organisational documents without permission

b)   the researcher pretending to be a job applicant to find out how the process works from an 'applicant's perspective'

c)   telling the organisation you wish to research one thing when, in reality, you are interested in something else

d)   failing to ask permission to interview someone

6   A gatekeeper is:

a)   a pathway to continuing access to a group of people or organisation

b)   gaining acceptance for your research from someone who

can arrange access to research participants and other forms of data

c)   someone who requires money to 'let you through' into an organisation

d)   the person in charge of ethical approval for student research projects

7   Which of the following are **not** part of the principles underpinning the Data Protection Act?

a)   data may only be used for the purpose for which they were collected

b)   data must be stored in a secure way

c)   data must be kept for five years

d)   people have a right of access to any data held about them

---

Review questions

REVIEW AND REFLECT

Take the time to find out what the requirements are for the ethical scrutiny and assessment of your research.

1   What are the ethical scrutiny requirements of your centre?

2   If you are undertaking your research in one organisation, does it have any ethical policies or procedures you must adhere to?

3   What is the ethical or code of conduct of your professional organisation?

4   Are there questions on any of the ethical forms you need to complete that you do not understand? Is it possible to access guidance for the completion of the forms?

Questions for reflection

REVIEW AND REFLECT

This final part of the chapter enables you to reflect about your professional development and develop your skills and knowledge. This will enable you to build your confidence and credibility, track your learning, see your progress and demonstrate your achievements.

Taking stock

1   In the research context in which you will be working, who has an interest in the findings, conclusions and outcomes of your project? Might there be a potential conflict of interest between your role as an 'objective investigator' and the expectations of your line manager? a 'gatekeeper'? a project sponsor? What actions might you consider to clarify your role as investigator and as colleague / employee / supervisor / internal consultant, and so on?

2   To what extent is your research idea a 'sensitive issue' for any organisation(s) and for any individuals who participate? What influence might this have on your ethical choices about informed consent and respect for dignity and well-being?

Strengths and weaknesses

3   How clear are you about the type of data you propose to gather? Can you articulate the sampling strategy that you propose and explain how you would recruit and select your research participants? Who might help you to clarify these issues?

4   How clear are you about what information to provide on an information or briefing document that would ensure informed consent has been achieved? Who might help you to clarify these issues?

5   What plans do you have for the secure storage of data? Think about (a) paper-based data and (b) electronically stored data. Can you access locked storage in the workplace? Would you be permitted to remove data gathered at work and store it at home? Do you know how to add password protection to any electronic files that you keep?

6   What expectations might your sponsor or organisation have about the retention of any data for subsequent use after your research project has been completed? Who do you need to discuss this with and what steps would be required to ensure data confidentiality and organisational anonymity?

Being a practitioner-researcher

7   To what extent will it be possible for you and those with whom you work to be able to distinguish between your role as a researcher and your 'usual' work role? What steps might you take to maintain this distinction during the research process?

8   What organisational sensitivities will you need to take into account in your research to ensure the dignity and well-being of all those who are involved and in relation to any potential unintended consequences?

EXPLORE FURTHER

Web Links

Applied Ethics Resources on WWW [online] http://www.ethicsweb.ca/resources/research/index.html

Association of Internet Researchers. (2002) *Ethical decision making and internet research* [online] http://aoir.org/reports/ethics.pdf

Chartered Institute of Personnel and Development. (2012) *Code of conduct* [online] http://www.cipd.co.uk/about/code-of-conduct-review/profco.htm

Institute of Business Ethics. *Codes of ethics: introduction to ethics policies, and programmes and codes* [online] http://www.ibe.org.uk/index.asp?upid=57&msid=11

Useful Reading

Birkinshaw, P. (2010) *Freedom of information: the law, the practice and the ideal.* Cambridge: Cambridge University Press.

Oliver, P. (2010) *The student's guide to research ethics.* Maidenhead: McGraw-Hill.

Remenyi, D., Swan, N. and Van Den Assem, B. (2011) *Ethics protocols and research ethics committees.* Reading: Academic Publishing International Ltd.

Saunders, M., Lewis, P. and Thornhill, A. (2012) *Research methods for business students.* Harlow: Pearson Education.

CHAPTER 5

Planning the Research Process

CHAPTER OUTLINE

- How to use this chapter
- Qualitative, quantitative and mixed methods research
- Research, theory and practice
- Data quality issues
- Planning to gather data
- Writing up the methodology
- Summary
- Review and reflect
- Explore further

LEARNING OUTCOMES

This chapter should help you to:

- decide what data to gather and when
- highlight key differences between qualitative and quantitative data
- examine the implications of using a mix of qualitative and quantitative methods
- clarify the relationship between research, theory and practice
- evaluate the quality of your data
- write about your research methods.

HOW TO USE THIS CHAPTER

This chapter draws together some of the themes and issues that have been introduced in Chapters 1–4 to help you to clarify the overall approach and the different types of data that will be most appropriate for your research. By the time you read this chapter you should have a fairly firm idea about the focus of your topic and some ideas about the overall research strategy that you will adopt. Now you need to make further decisions about how you will put your ideas into action and take the project forward in a coherent and justifiable way.

An explanation and justification of your research methods is required for projects at all levels, whether you are undertaking a small-scale research project for an intermediate-level qualification, a dissertation for an undergraduate course, a CIPD advanced-level investigation into a business issue or someone who is undertaking a dissertation for a taught master's-level qualification in HRM. This chapter will help you to develop that justification. If you are in a hurry to get on with your project, you may be tempted to skip this stage and launch straight into some form of data-gathering. However, the investment of a small amount of time and thought now will reap significant rewards in the quality of the research that you carry out and prevent costly mistakes which you may come to regret when you begin your data analysis.

 From research idea to research plan

CASE ILLUSTRATION 5.1

Vivienne was a student undertaking a distance learning course in her home country in Central Europe. She worked at an HR service centre which provided HR advice, support and processes for all of her organisation's many European operations. For her research project Vivienne gained permission to study communications and knowledge management in one of the divisions in her organisation where some problems about miscommunication had recently arisen. When she read her course materials Vivienne noticed that before she undertook any research she had to produce a research proposal for her supervisor to scrutinise and also complete a fairly detailed form about issues associated with research ethics. However, the manager of the division where Vivienne was due to be

undertaking her project was impatient: he wanted the data NOW and some recommendations for action VERY SOON. He told Vivienne he had already decided which staff she could interview and had set up some of the appointments for her. The first appointment was scheduled for the following week.

Discussion Questions

1   What are the opportunities and the dangers of proceeding quickly into a data-collection process as described in this case illustration?

2   What advice would you give to a student in this circumstance?

FEEDBACK NOTES

You may have guessed that, in the circumstance in which she found herself, Vivienne felt confused. On the one hand, she was lucky to be given the opportunity outside of her normal service centre work role to undertake a piece of research with the support of a divisional manager. The risk of losing the support of the manager and permission to undertake the research was a big worry. This made her inclined to proceed gratefully in the way the divisional manager had arranged. However, his concern for haste could lead to a range of problems. First, Vivienne was anxious that the manager seemed to have already decided her research method (interviews) and her sample respondents. Vivienne did not know the basis on which they had been chosen but felt it was unlikely that they would be a representative sample of people in the division. Second, in her course materials Vivienne had been reading about the importance of informed consent, anonymity and confidentiality for those involved in her research, and she had no idea about whether such issues had been taken into account when the manager arranged the interviews for her. Third, Vivienne was not even sure that interviews would be the most appropriate way to gather data. She was very nervous about his request for recommendations within a month; as a distance learning student working part-time, Vivienne was conscious that she could not work full-time on this project and that a full analysis of the data and completion of her research report would not occur for three–four months. Her distance learning course workbooks were very clear about the importance of thinking through methods to formulate an approach capable of generating meaningful and valuable conclusions. She knew that, whatever methods she used, they must be clearly explained and justified.

After an email exchange with her tutor, Vivienne arranged an urgent meeting with the divisional manager. At this meeting she reassured him that she acknowledged the urgency of the issue he had asked her to investigate but also explained the requirements of her course. In this context, Vivienne proposed that she undertake some initial interviews (as planned by the divisional manager) to take the form of a 'pilot study'. This would help identify any other issues that were pertinent and allow for some initial thoughts to be fed back to the management team in an aggregated and generalised form and for the development of a fuller research strategy to take forward a study. The manager accepted these proposals and the study centre was also in agreement, so Vivienne had a good basis on which to proceed.

The aim of this chapter is to help you develop and articulate a credible rationale for the method or methods that you decide to use to answer your research question. This is a focal chapter of the book; many of the issues about approaches to research that were introduced in earlier chapters are brought together in this one. Many of the issues about types of data that are introduced in this chapter will also be considered in more detail in the chapters that follow.

QUALITATIVE, QUANTITATIVE AND MIXED METHODS RESEARCH

Hart (2010) points out that all research needs data. In HR research data can be found in a variety of places, for example from: focus groups or interviews; video or audio recordings; survey responses; photographs; diaries, drawings and test results, for example psychometrics. The type of data that researchers gather to answer their research questions tends to vary depending on the research tradition they are working within. Chapters 1 and 2 considered the different approaches to thinking about knowledge that affect how researchers undertake their investigations. The traditional scientific world-view underpins an objectivist research approach grounded in a 'scientific' method of collecting facts and testing for relationships between them to make generalisable conclusions. The constructivist world-view underpins the interpretivist research approach, which examines the meanings and experiences of people in different situations or cultural contexts to understand and explain their unique situations. As indicated already, researchers within these traditions tend to find different forms of data more meaningful. Those within a positivist tradition tend to value **quantitative data** (the term given to data that can be quantified and counted). Interpretivist researchers value **qualitative data** (the term given to data based on meanings which are observable and expressed through words and language).

 Deciding about research methods

CASE ILLUSTRATION 5.2

Carly was a mature student who had been very involved in running apprenticeship schemes in her organisation. She was passionately committed to the ideals of vocational education and training and apprenticeship processes but became increasingly aware that HR practitioners and those who applied to join apprenticeship schemes seemed to lack a common view of the purpose and benefits of work-based apprenticeships. She decided to compare different understandings of apprenticeships for her business research report and had to decide what data to collect and how to do it. She contacted a number of local organisations that she knew employed apprenticeships and eight of them agreed to participate in the research. She offered them a summary of her findings in return for their help. Having achieved the involvement of these

organisations, Carly had to decide how to gather data and which groups of the workforce within each organisation she needed to access. She considered using focus groups, interviews and a questionnaire.

Discussion Questions

1   What are the advantages of a questionnaire survey method for measuring expectations of apprenticeship schemes?

2   What value might interviews or focus groups add to the research?

3   Which method of gathering data is best, and why?

4   If Carly were to opt for gathering both qualitative and quantitative data, what challenges would she face?

FEEDBACK NOTES

There were a range of methods that Carly could use to find out what people think about apprenticeship schemes. It would be possible to interview those responsible for recruiting apprentices and also to interview a sample of the apprentices themselves. Alternatively, a series of focus groups could be organised or, perhaps, people could be encouraged to keep a diary for a period of time, in which their understanding of the apprenticeship scheme could be recorded in their own words and over an extended period of time.

Carly also felt that an attitude survey might be a useful way of collecting data from the apprentices. She was keen on this idea because a questionnaire is very structured and is easily replicable. Therefore she felt that it would be possible to compare the results from surveys at each of her eight participating organisations. The anonymity afforded by a questionnaire would also mean that apprentices could respond in a more honest way. As a result of both of these factors (structure and detachment), Carly felt that data generated in this way could be analysed to identify relationships between different variables such as different educational backgrounds, different employment sectors and so on.

On the other hand it might be possible that the questions in the questionnaire might be interpreted differently by people with different backgrounds (cultural and organisational). While people filling in a questionnaire will tick boxes, their responses may not really reflect what they know and feel about the apprenticeship process. Similarly, surveys can be undertaken by a large number of people, but the depth of their replies is very limited. Where the researcher is more involved in interviews it would be possible to probe for meanings and interpretations and to ask why the respondent feels the way that they do in relation to a question.

Consideration of these issues might lead you to suggest that a mixture of methods would be appropriate to generate data to help Carly answer her research questions. You might suggest that she undertake some quantitative research first to establish the 'broad trends' and then use qualitative data to probe into the underlying reasons and meanings behind these trends. Mixed methods research can also bring difficulties, however, and Carly was very conscious that her time was limited. Undertaking one form of data-gathering and analysis in a systematic and competent way is time-consuming enough. Using more than one method, particularly when the skills required in collection and analysing data are so different, would present major challenges to her in terms of a lack of time and expertise.

The main differences between qualitative and quantitative approaches to research are shown in Table 5.1.

Table 5.1 Qualitative and quantitative approaches to research

Quantitative data	Qualitative data
Based on a familiarisation of current research rather than specific situations	Based on a familiarisation with a real-life context or situation
Analysis of a limited number of variables	Analysis of significant themes that are suggested by a range of sources
Concern to establish significant and separate relationships between a limited number of variables	Concern to understand the interrelationships between different factors
Variables are expressed in the language of the investigation	The preconceptions of the researcher are suspended and the language of informants is valued and used
Seeks to achieve abstraction from repeated observations	Seeks to find out how people understand a situation and how their understanding influences their actions

(Neuman 2011, Jankowicz 2005)

Figure 5.1 provides an overview of the different methods in relation to the extent to which they are structured/unstructured and the level of involvement that the researcher has with the process of gathering data.

Figure 5.1 Different methods of gathering data

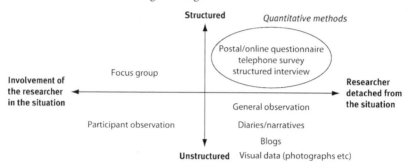

MIXED METHODS RESEARCH

As indicated in Case Illustration 5.2 many HR researchers, particularly those who are undertaking case study research, find that they can see the value of both qualitative and quantitative data. The term 'mixed methods' research is often used to describe research that makes use of both data types in a way that enables the insights to be mutually illuminating (Hammersley 2005, Bryman 2006, Bryman and Bell 2007, Saunders et al 2012). Mixed methods research provides a number of advantages to HR researchers:

- **Triangulation:** this term is used to describe the process whereby data from different sources are used to 'cross-check' the findings. In this way you can add credibility to your conclusions (Hammersley 2005, Saunders et al 2012).
- **Facilitation of alternative methods:** in some cases qualitative data might generate an interpretation about a number of important variables, and a quantitative approach might then enable you to examine the extent to which the relationships between these variables apply across a wider research population.
- **Interpreting the relationship between different variables:** in other cases quantitative analysis may have established that relationships between variables are significant and did not occur 'by chance', and qualitative data may then help you to establish 'why' such relationships are occurring.
- **Researching into different 'levels' of an HR issue:** quantitative approaches to research are often used to consider the issues at a 'macro' level in organisations, whereas qualitative data is useful to understand the 'micro' issues that are also relevant. This has significant benefits for practitioner-researchers where HR research is focused on addressing organisational issues and problems and it is important to achieve a 'rounded' view of the situation.
- **Moving between different stages of a project:** some researchers start with a broad research question. Once they have made use of data from a quantitative survey, they find they are better able to refine the focus of their research for the next stage. Other researchers invite people who have participated in a survey to

provide access information so that they can participate in a second, more qualitative, phase of research.

Although there is no consensus on these issues, mixed methods research is advocated by an increasing number of business and HR researchers (see, for example, Gill et al 2010, Bryman and Bell 2007, Fox et al 2007, Creswell 2009). In some cases qualitative and quantitative data are gathered and analysed 'in parallel' and in others the data are gathered on a 'one after the other' basis. However, mixed methods research should not be confused with 'messy methods' research. A systematic and rigorous approach is required, regardless of the range of the different data types that are gathered and analysed. Key issues for the quality of mixed methods research are (Bryman and Bell 2007):

- To ensure a competent and justified research design and execution. Poorly designed and implemented research will generate dubious and unreliable findings, even if more than one method is used.
- 'More is better' is not an appropriate justification for mixed methods research. The rationale for choice of method(s) must follow from your research questions or objectives.
- To ensure that you have the time to engage in different data-gathering and analysis methods within the constraints you are under for your student project.
- To ensure that you have the expertise to gather and analyse different types of data. Mixed methods data-gathering followed by poor-quality analysis will not lead to a valid outcome.

In organisational research, particularly when it is part of a qualification process, there are also other practical issues that influence decisions about methods. Operational issues, time pressures and the preferences and imperatives of others who will be involved in the project, such as the employees, line managers and the project sponsor, will all have to be taken into account. Part of the planning process of any project, therefore, will require discussion and negotiation about the methods to be used, the participants that will be available and the timescale over which the research must be undertaken.

A number of different factors will influence the choice of methods that you make and these are briefly outlined below:

- **Nature of the topic:** the nature of your research objectives and questions are a fundamental starting point for deciding on appropriate methods. Key things to ask are: what are my research questions? What data will enable me to answer those questions? What is the most appropriate way to obtain the data? If you find that your initial data-gathering plans have changed for some reason, it is a good idea to review (and consider amending) your research questions or objectives if the changes may have resulted in a lack of alignment between your research aim and questions and the type of data you will be analysing.
- **Extent of literature:** if you know that there is a lot of literature already about your topic, it is likely that you will choose methods that enable you to build on what is already known. If, however, your area is relatively new and 'unexplored', this will also influence your choice of method(s).

- **Timescale:** another issue to take into account is the time available to you. Some methods might be able to be undertaken over a shorter time-span than others.
- **Resources:** some methods require specialist resources (perhaps facilities to generate transcripts of unstructured interviews or the availability of quantitative data analysis software), and it is important that you find out if these are available and if you have time to learn how to use them.
- **Issues of access and permission:** some project sponsors, in organisational research, have clear preferences for different methods, and these must be taken into account in deciding which methods to adopt and whether the nature of the research questions/objectives might need to be reviewed.

RESEARCH, THEORY AND PRACTICE

In Chapters 1 and 2 the different purposes of research (do you see yourself as an 'explorer', a 'detective', a 'doctor'?) were discussed. Regardless of the way in which you see your role, while you are undertaking your research and whether you intend to undertake descriptive, exploratory or explanatory research, you will need to position your work within a broad body of theory. The way you use theory will affect your reasoning process and the way that you take your research forward. This affects decisions about: what data to gather, where to look for the data and how you will make sense of the data. This section considers the issues about theory and practice-based research in 'plain English' so that you can: work out an appropriate reasoning process; be clear about your own use of theory; and work out your data-gathering and data analysis intentions in a justifiable way.

 ACTIVITY 5.1

WEB-BASED ACTIVITY

Go to a general search engine (such as google.co.uk or yahoo.co.uk) and type in the search word 'theory'. (Choose to search on UK sites only to limit the list.) Glance through the first 10–20 sites that are given as a result of your search. You do not need to open them unless you become intrigued. What impression does the list of sites you have seen give you of 'theory'?

FEEDBACK NOTES

Common sites generated on a search such as this include:

- set theory (a branch of mathematics)
- number theory
- political theory
- media theory
- legal theory
- learning theory
- feminist theory.

An activity such as this makes us think that 'theory' must be very complex and difficult. Many HR students, particularly practitioners with very little time to spare for thinking 'great thoughts', associate the word 'theory' with ideas that are complex, incomprehensible, specialised and divorced from their immediate HR practice. Like many practitioner-researchers, you may have developed an interest in your topic as a result of HR practice issues that have arisen in your organisation. HR practitioners who are busy undertaking a 'business partner' role in their organisations are also aware that many operational managers have little time for 'theory' and insist on a more pragmatic approach to people and management, the outcomes of which (they may believe) are operationally relevant and more valuable.

However, this perception of theory is mistaken. Theory is the foundation on which almost all HR practice and research is based, and your research project needs to be 'grounded' in a theoretical perspective; it needs a theoretical 'home'. Even if the term is a difficult one for you, theory is useful in all credible research processes. Theory provides ideas about how different HR relevant phenomena are related to each other and why these things are related. People make use of theories (often in an implicit way) to 'make sense of' what is happening. Maslow's theory of motivation (Maslow 1943), for example, still provides something of a basis for a range of career or personal development processes undertaken within organisations. One of the important outcomes of research is to find out which theory is better at explaining what is happening 'in practice' and help people make sense of data to refine and develop professional practice.

As theory plays an important (if implicit) part of effective HR practice, it is important that professionals working in HR are able to evaluate different theories, models and frameworks to provide a clearer understanding of what is going on in organisational situations. From there it is possible to plan and implement HR interventions that have more chance of achieving their objectives.

WHAT IS THEORY? WHAT ARE MODELS? WHAT ARE FRAMEWORKS?

In everyday conversation people tend to use the word 'theory' to mean 'opinion' or 'conjecture' (Lee and Lings 2008), and it is true that many HR practitioners often seem to base what they do on intuitive opinions or propositions. HR research, however, involves making use of, and refining, explicit theory, defined as: **a logical model or framework of concepts (abstract ideas) that describes and explains how phenomena are related with each other and which would apply in a variety of circumstances.**

Theory is particularly useful for HR practitioners for three reasons:

- **Theory helps us understand what is happening.** In HR departments or functions, people come from all over the organisation to find out what is known about people-related situations and problems. However, to contribute to the solution of those people-related problems or issues, HR professionals cannot just rely on **'know about'** knowledge; they need to have an equivalent body of **'know why'** knowledge. Theory provides that 'know why' knowledge.
- **Theory helps us to understand issues from more than one perspective.** Anyone who works, or aspires to work, in HR comes to realise that people issues are never simple; they always invoke the need to see things differently

and through more than one 'lens'. Knowledge of theory equips us to do this as HR practice draws on a wide range of different and often overlapping areas of theory such as: systems theory, complexity theory, psychology, sociology, economics and anthropology. Therefore, theory helps us to diagnose what is going on and evaluate credible approaches to address HR situations and opportunities.

- **Theory provides a basis for models and frameworks of practice.** Much of day-to-day HR practice is dominated by models and frameworks. **Models** are derived from theories; they make use of theoretical concepts (abstract ideas) to represent and describe what is (or could be) going on in organisational situations. Performance-related pay is an example of an HR model of reward that is guided by concepts about performance and behaviour derived from economic theory. However, an understanding of some of the potentially dysfunctional consequences of performance-related pay might come from theories of human action and development grounded in other areas of the social sciences. **Frameworks** are also linked to both models and theories. They describe the underlying structure of the way that work-based practices are carried out. Kirkpatrick's (1959) four levels of training evaluation are a good example of a framework (or structure) through which the value of training interventions can be assessed. Although Kirkpatrick has never made this explicit, his approach is grounded in systems theory.

WHERE DO THEORIES COME FROM?

Having established that everyday life for HR practitioners, at both individual and organisational levels, would be difficult to sustain without the use of theory, it is interesting to ask where theories come from in the first place. Gill et al (2010) use Kolb's Learning Cycle (Kolb et al 1979) to illustrate the point that theory and practice are like 'two sides of a coin' and that it is possible to understand the relationship between theory and data in terms of how people learn to make sense of the world.

Kolb suggests that learning involves a number of different stages. Each stage feeds into the others, and Kolb suggests that the learning process can begin at any part of the cycle. This can be illustrated by referring to the learning experience that many HR practitioners go through when they develop their skills in recruitment interviewing. Some HR professionals, in the early stages of their careers, are asked to carry out interviews with no formal training. They undertake their first interviews in a state of nervous tension, armed only with the company's forms and procedures which they have, hopefully, read in advance. They undertake the interview(s) and, afterwards, they reflect on 'how it went'. There will be some features of their practice that they are pleased with and some that they will want to improve. They will devise for themselves some general guidelines (the dos and don'ts of interviewing) and they will try them out the next time that they interview. In this way their learning process involves **HR practice** (doing the interviews), **reflection/evaluation** (what went well and not so well), **generalisation** (personal/organisational dos and don'ts) and **implementation** (applying the dos and don'ts the next time that they interview). This cycle will, of course, repeat itself many times and, over time, the HR practitioner may be able to go on a course or read some books on effective interviewing to enhance the quality of their practice.

This example illustrates how, at an individual level, generalised concepts and principles (theories) form part of the normal process of developing practice in HR and there is a link between theory and research based on our experience and practice. It also shows how 'theory-building' can occur as a result of different reasoning processes which researchers refer to as: 'deduction' and 'induction'.

Figure 5.2 Inductive and deductive reasoning

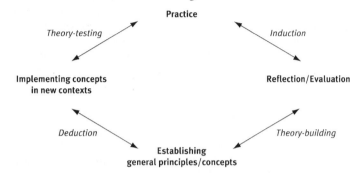

DEDUCTION AND INDUCTION

A key point to make is that any theory is always provisional (Lee and Lings 2008). No theory can ever be '100% proved'. **Deductive** reasoning involves refining and reconsidering theories through a process of testing out their propositions (what they suggest should happen) in different contexts or situations. Research is needed to generate the evidence about what happens in these conditions, and on the basis of the evidence the theory can be provisionally confirmed or amended (and in extreme cases it may be discarded altogether).

Inductive reasoning starts at the level of practice. Through a process of gathering data through research the inductive researcher will develop some general propositions about what is happening and start to 'theory-build'. In many cases theory that has been developed from an inductive approach will go on to be further developed through empirical testing in a deductive way. Therefore, both inductive and deductive approaches to research are rooted in practice and in theory. It would be unrealistic to think that your research (or mine!) will ever develop a 'new' theory; most HR research, particularly that which is carried out by practitioner-researchers, works at the 'margins' of theory. Nonetheless, it is important to be clear about the theoretical 'anchor' or starting point for a project so that it is possible to add new ideas to it, expand its power to explain what is happening or highlight areas of weakness within it.

Choosing a research approach

Pavlin was a part-time HR student who worked in an education ministry in his government outside of the UK. A key issue for all government departments in Pavlin's country was to try to develop a more performance-orientated and less bureaucratic style of management. In addition, government policy was to base HR decisions on employee competence rather than relying on employees' family connections and other networks associated with traditional 'patronage' processes. Pavlin was given responsibility for finding an objective and reliable selection process that would help managers recruit appropriate people for appropriate job roles. He decided to make this the focus of his dissertation research.

Pavlin did some reading around the topic of recruitment and selection and found very little reference to 'theory', although he found many lists of different methods of selection and noticed that most authors recommended a mix of methods to increase reliability. When reading about selection mechanisms, he came across a lot of literature about 'scientific' selection methods such as psychometric testing and assessment centres. Pavlin decided to focus his research on an evaluation of psychometric methods of selection as a basis for future practice within the education ministry.

Discussion Questions

1   To what extent would a deductive or an inductive approach be most appropriate for this research?

2   To what extent is it possible for a dissertation like this to be grounded in theory?

FEEDBACK NOTES

You may have noticed that it is not possible to rule out either the inductive or the deductive approach in this sort of situation. Pavlin considered using a deductive approach. His idea was to take a sample of existing staff comprising a mix of those considered to be very effective in their roles as well as those whose performance was less good. He thought that he would then give them a number of different psychometric tests and assess which tests were associated with results that offered the best prediction for work performance. If he had undertaken his research this way, Pavlin's research would involve gathering data to 'test' the propositions around the predictive ability of different psychometric tests.

On the other hand, Pavlin also considered using a more inductive approach. His reading had alerted him to the way in which a number of different factors, such as employee expectations, management style, clarity of expectations, initial training and employee reward, make a difference to employee performance. Therefore, he wondered about exploring these issues by asking newly appointed staff and their managers to describe their experiences and the factors that both inhibited and encouraged performance to make a more rounded set of recommendations about selection and induction processes to enhance performance.

Pavlin also had to think hard about the extent to which he could use a theoretical perspective in his dissertation as so much of the literature in this feature of HR involves descriptions of models and frameworks with very little reference to theory. In this instance, Pavlin had to make a choice. If he decided to pursue the approach of testing out different psychometric tests, he would need to position his work within psychological theories about personality traits, attributes and work performance. On the other hand, if he decided to explore the different organisational factors influencing employment performance, he would need to ground his work in systems theory by examining the way these different features related with each other.

The main features of the inductive and deductive approaches to research are shown in Figure 5.3. This indicates the different relationship with 'theory' of the two approaches. It also indicates how an inductive approach is sometimes associated with the constructivist and interpretivist understanding of the research process and the deductive approach can be informed by an objectivist/positivist approach. Both deductive and inductive approaches have value in HR research. The points summarised below (Robson 2011, Saunders et al 2012) represent ends of a continuum rather than a hard and fast distinction. Where a mixed methods approach is being adopted, there is also likely to be an interaction and overlap between them.

Figure 5.3 Inductive and deductive approaches

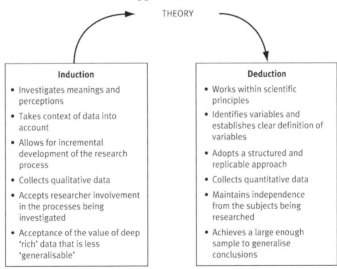

Deduction (theory-building through testing propositions):

- involves the formulation of **propositions to be tested** which are derived from theory
- concepts are **operationalised** such that the variables involved can be identified and measured in an objective way and this measurement process could also be repeated by others in different situations.

Data-gathering takes place to test the evidence against the propositions. As a result of the analysis process, it is possible to identify weaknesses in the theory or to show ways in which the theory may be slightly modified.

Induction (theory-building through exploring different patterns of data):

- involves observation and investigation into the relationship between different variables in complex situations
- occurs without prior assumptions about propositions, categories and measurement
- incorporates the context of the situation into the analysis process
- develops an analysis process to build a credible explanation of the phenomena that have been observed
- is less concerned with the need to generalise although further avenues for research may be identified.

DATA QUALITY ISSUES

Regardless of whether you take a broadly inductive or deductive approach to your research, it will lack credibility if you are not able to ensure that your data are relevant and trustworthy. Key concepts in the traditional scientific research tradition are **reliability and validity**. In general terms, valid research uses research strategies and data collection processes that are appropriate to your research question and are implemented properly; validity means that your research is sufficiently robust to allow confidence in your conclusions. It involves a judgement about whether the data really provide evidence about what they are supposed to be about. Reliable research is research that is accepted as trustworthy, fair and objectively undertaken (Biggam 2011); it involves an assessment of the extent to which similar results would be obtained by researchers on similar occasions. This section of the chapter addresses these issues.

 How trustworthy is the research?

CASE ILLUSTRATION 5.4

Abigail was a full-time student who was passionate about issues associated with violence in the workplace. She had worked for many years in 'front line' public sector occupations and had been threatened on more than one occasion by angry members of the public. In her HR course she was determined to undertake research to show without doubt the level of violence faced by casual employees on low wages in many public-facing occupations. However, she was running short of time and she was unable to get any work organisations in her area to give her permission to approach their staff with a questionnaire designed to measure their exposure to violence as a result of their work roles. However, Abigail was active on social network sites and had been involved with one or two networks that focused on supporting people who had suffered from aggressive behaviour and she had some friends with similar interests.

To take her research forward and to meet the fast-approaching deadline, Abigail devised a very short web-enabled questionnaire using a free online survey provider. Money was short, so she limited herself to a few questions in her survey about the extent to which people worried about violence at work. There was no space to ask biographical or demographic questions. In addition, she reproduced the questionnaire in a paper format. Then she set up a specific email address that could not be traced to her personally and posted invitations on various websites and forums inviting people to contact the email address to get a link to the online questionnaire.

Next she and her friends set off and stood outside public places, such as the library, the job centre, the train station, the citizens' advice centre and the bus station. They approached people who were passing and conducted short 'structured interviews' based on the online survey questions. Abigail was disappointed with the number of responses that she got although, one way and another, she

and her friends managed to get the number up to 50. When she looked at the questionnaire responses she felt able to show that workplace violence was a prevalent issue for many people and employers were not doing enough to deal with it.

However, when Abigail paid a fleeting visit to her supervisor to reassure her that the somewhat delayed data collection had been completed, she was upset to find that her supervisor did not praise her for her quick work but instead asked her to discuss the validity and reliability of her data.

Discussion Questions

1   Why do you think Abigail's supervisor may have had concerns?

2   What issues of reliability and validity should Abigail address in her response?

FEEDBACK NOTES

You may feel that the basis for the concerns about Abigail's approach to data-gathering related to the rather ad hoc basis on which she collected her data. The survey instrument that she devised was very short, and her supervisor was anxious about whether the questions were measuring levels of anxiety about violence at work or the extent to which respondents had actually suffered from violence. Another issue connected with validity was the way in which 'violence' was defined and whether all of the survey respondents would have understood it in the same way. It is possible that, without a careful explanation by those who were administering the survey about the definition of the term 'violence at work' (physical harm and contact; psychological abuse; shouting?) people may have responded in different ways, making it hard to know whether the research really was measuring what it set out to measure. You may have also noticed that Abigail recruited her friends to try to help with the data collection, and her supervisor was certainly concerned about the extent to which they were all briefed to behave in the same way (not to 'put answers in people's mouths', for example). Here the issue is one of reliability: did the different ways that the data were gathered and by different people make the study unrepeatable? In addition, you might be wondering how representative her sample was and how reliable in their responses people might be who had been recruited at train and bus stations and through special interest sites set up to support those who are concerned about violence at work. The lack of any demographic data also made it hard to assess the extent to which the 50 responses Abigail managed to achieve were spread across different demographic groups and different employment sectors. Important questions about data quality to ask in relation to any research project are (Easterby-Smith et al 2003, Robson 2011):

Questions relevant to assessing reliability

- Would similar observations be reached by different observers?
- Is it easy to understand how raw data have been collated and analysed?
- Would the methods used generate the same results on other similar occasions (are the results generalisable?)?

Not all research sets out to produce conclusions that are generalisable (Hart 2010); indeed, statistical generalisation is rarely possible in HR research and is very difficult even in randomised 'scientific' experiments. However, it is possible to consider the extent to which 'comparative generalisation' between two or more different types of 'case' is possible. You might also consider the extent to which an analysis of concepts important to explaining an HR phenomenon in one context might also be helpful to understanding what is going on in other situations (this is known as concept generalisation).

Questions relevant to considering validity

- What difference might the context of the investigation make to data that have been collected?
- To what extent has the enquiry process itself influenced the possible answers?
- How easy is it to separate cause from effect in the data (the chicken and the egg scenario)?
- How sure can you be that other factors (intervening variables) have not affected your data?

The concepts of validity and reliability are most frequently used by researchers who make use of quantitative data, and they are less easy to apply in a direct sense to mixed methods studies or research making use of qualitative data. It is equally important (some researchers argue that it is **more** important) to undertake a careful assessment of data quality if your approach does not make use of a 'traditional' randomised sampling approach and if your pursuit of 'rich' data makes generalisation less possible. If your research is based around a qualitative approach, other assessments of data quality and trustworthiness may be more appropriate (Lincoln and Guba 1985) and you should consider the following issues:

- **Credibility:** have your respondents had a chance to validate that you have made an accurate record of their data? Can you cross-verify from more than two sources?
- **Transferability:** have you offered a rounded picture (often called a 'thick description') that draws on a range of perspectives incorporated into your data to make a judgement possible about the transferability of your findings to another context?

- **Dependability:** have you provided enough information about the research procedures you have used to enable an 'audit' of the process?
- **Confirmability:** have you reflected on the extent to which your own personal bias or that of some of your respondents has been discussed or acknowledged?
- **Authenticity:** can your research outcomes be judged to be genuine through the inclusion of a range of data sources?

Activity 5.2 provides an opportunity to consider how these questions would apply in a practical situation.

ACTIVITY 5.2

ASSESSING DATA QUALITY

Imagine that you are undertaking a project to investigate the effectiveness of performance management processes in an organisation. You will be obtaining information through interviews from a range of people in different departments and at different levels within the organisation. Using the criteria for data quality (credibility; transferability; dependability; authenticity; confirmability), try to identify what the main practical issues might be with regard to data quality.

FEEDBACK NOTES

Important questions you would need to consider in a project such as this might include:

Reliability/data credibility – how replicable is the research process?

- Would interviews about performance management that took place just **prior** to the annual pay review process generate different findings if they were undertaken just **after** the pay awards had been announced?
- Would interviews carried out by someone from the HR function within the organisation generate the same data as interviews that were carried out by an external researcher?
- To what extent might two different people make sense differently of the same raw data generated by the interviews?

Validity/trustworthiness – do the data give evidence about what you are trying to examine?

- To what extent does data generated in interviews just after the pay review process actually reflect opinion about performance management or might it really provide opinions about pay awards by interviewees?
- To what extent will interviewees give you the answers they think you want?
- If an interviewee has recently been subject to a disciplinary procedure and they are negative about performance management in the organisation, can you be sure whether the process leads to negative perceptions of performance management, or have problems with managing performance then led to the employee performing their role in an unacceptable way?

- How confident can you be that what you have found out about performance management would also be applicable in different types and sizes of organisation?

No one project is going to be able to produce findings that are 100% reliable, trustworthy, valid and credible. It is, however, necessary that you address these issues so that you are able to determine an approach to data-gathering that indicates you have attempted to take an open-minded approach to gathering data and that you have taken steps to minimise the limitations of your study and maximise its credibility. This means taking a planned approach to gathering data and being able to justify the decisions that you make. This will be done in the **methodology** section of the report that you write.

PLANNING TO GATHER DATA

Preparation is very important in any research project and your data-gathering procedure needs to be thought out in advance. Many students find that their tutor's advice about the feasibility of their plans is invaluable in achieving a process that generates good-quality data. HR professionals often have to remind managers of the saying: 'recruit in haste and repent at your leisure'. This might be differently expressed for students undertaking projects as: 'gather data in haste and repent at your leisure'. As you plan your data collection process, therefore, it is important to be clear about **what** data you plan to collect and **why**. Make sure you are clear about how your proposed data will help you to answer your research questions and have reasons to justify the particular methods you propose to use and the sample of respondents you plan to invite to participate. Planning also extends to the data-gathering instruments you develop (your questionnaire or interview questions), and it is important to plan to run a small 'pilot process' for your methods so that you can find out if any of your questions are ambiguous; how long the interview really does take; whether your questions are likely to generate data that you can analyse in a relevant way.

Important points for planning a research project likely to enable persuasive conclusions to be drawn are (Hart 2010, Bauer and Gaskell 2000):

- Ensure that the methods you use are transparent, ethical and justifiable.
- Make sure that your own 'position', in relation to both the topic and those from whom you will gather data, is clear and open.
- Fully inform anyone who participates in your research about what you are setting out to learn and the implications for them of their participation.
- Take into account alternative theories and interpretations of the data you gather.
- In addition to reflecting on the data, develop your ability to reflect about your role in the research and the implications of this.

The methodology chapter is where you address these issues and explain: the basis for your research design; your specific methods of data-gathering; and the piloting process that you undertook. This is the chapter that will help your tutor assess the quality of the data you have gathered and is crucial to the mark you will get. Poor-quality data always leads to conclusions that lack credibility.

The term 'methodology' is used differently by various authors, but in this book it is taken to mean the philosophical framework or orientation within which your research is based (for example, positivist or interpretivist). Methodology is important as it provides the rationale for your particular method or methods of data-gathering. The methodology section of your report, therefore, should address what world-view underpinned the approach you adopted to gathering and making sense of the data. Although some study centres, for some qualifications, do not require a discussion of these features in your project report, they are still worth thinking through as they will form the basis from which you can take consistent action and gather and analyse data of good quality. If your study centre requires you to consider these issues in a methodology section or chapter, three, interrelated issues require explanation, as indicated in Figure 5.4.

Figure 5.4 Key issues to establish in your methodology

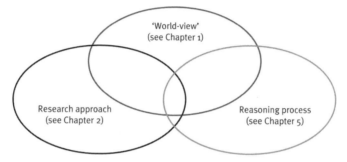

Having established your initial 'position' with regard to your own world-view, your research approach and whether your reasoning is inductive or deductive, it is also necessary to explain and justify the way you have designed and executed your research. Although some study centres (increasingly few) may not require a full explanation of the more philosophical features of your research approach, every study centre will require a full justification of the methods of data collection and analysis that you have used as well as your approach to accessing a sample and your sampling strategy. Key points that are helpful in determining these features are indicated below and further illustrated in Figure 5.5.

Figure 5.5 Factors influencing research methods

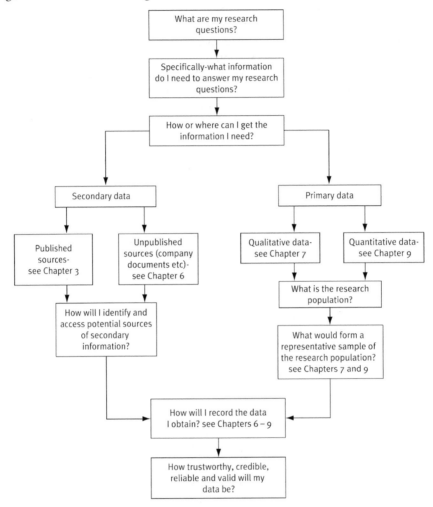

To make sure that your methodology is as credible as possible, it is important to:

- **Clarify the research questions/objectives and research approach first.**
  Planning the methods for any study is a logical sequence of judgements taking
  into account what is reasonably possible. Your first decisions relate to the
  research questions or objectives. These decisions will involve discussion with
  other stakeholders in the project (the organisation(s) and your supervisor,
  tutor or advisor, and so on). It is also necessary to be clear about what
  approach will be adopted (inductive or deductive) as this will affect the way
  you organise your reading and the data-gathering methods that you choose.
- **Carefully consider what information you need to answer your questions and
  achieve your objectives.** Many students obtain information that is easy to find
  but it is not always sufficient to answer their research questions. Work out
  what data you need and where to find the information. Then decide the extent

to which this is feasible. Again, discussions with the project sponsor in the organisation(s) and your supervisor are likely to be important.

- **Consider what different sources of information and data are available to you and make use of as wide a range of sources as possible.** Many students rush to collect some form of primary data (for example, from a questionnaire or from a focus group) and they do not use other available information such as documentary evidence that already exists within the organisation or secondary data from a range of published sources. Ideas about this are given in Chapter 6.

- **Clearly identify and justify the research population and your sample selection.** The research population is all the units of analysis (people, organisations, and so on) within the scope of your research. Is your study to be concerned with all employees in the organisation, one particular business unit or department or one specific staff grouping? It is unlikely that you will be able to gather data from the whole population (unless it is very small), so some form of sampling will be required and you will need to consider, and justify, how you will choose the people who will form your sample. This may also need to be discussed with the project sponsor at organisational level and with your supervisor. Issues of sampling are considered in more detail in Chapter 7 (qualitative data) and Chapter 9 (quantitative data).

- **Decide on the type(s) of primary data that you will gather and allow time to devise and pilot effective data-gathering 'instruments'.** Many people choose to use a questionnaire method, because they think it will be quick, or the interview method, because they think it will be easy. Many then find that their questionnaire was misinterpreted by many respondents or that their interviews did not provide sufficient information to answer their research questions. All forms of data-gathering require considerable thought in the design process, and it is also important to allow time to pilot the instrument (and then amend it in the light of the pilot) prior to launching into the full-scale data-gathering process. See Chapters 7 and 9 for more on this.

- **Decide in advance how you will record the data that you gather and then how you will perform the analysis.** As part of the planning and design process for any primary data-gathering 'instrument', it is important to be clear about how you will record and analyse the data. These issues are discussed in Chapters 7–11.

- **Consider issues related with data quality.** If you can, get someone to act as a 'devil's advocate' and try to expose areas where the validity, trustworthiness, reliability and credibility of the approach you are planning to adopt could be questioned. As noted already, no study can ever be wholly valid and reliable, but being critically evaluative at this stage will enable you to address any issues that you can resolve. You will also be better placed to discuss the advantages and limitations of your study within the report that you produce.

WRITING UP THE METHODOLOGY

Study centres tend to have different expectations about the methodology section, and the level of the qualification you are undertaking also has implications for what you should explain and justify about your research methods. Therefore, it is very important to find out in advance how long your methodology section should be and the issues you are expected to explain and discuss. All project reports must explain and justify how data (primary and secondary) were gathered and analysed. The points below indicate the key issues to address, as a minimum, for **any** HR research project:

- **Appropriateness of the methods:** what was the context for the research? For research in one organisation – what was the organisational context? What was the nature of the relationship of the researcher with the organisation(s)? What were the research questions? What approach to data-gathering (qualitative, quantitative, both?) was adopted and why?
- **Quality and quantity of data collected and analysed:** how were secondary sources identified (literature search as well as any organisational documents, and so on)? What primary data were gathered? How was the sample of respondents selected? How were data-gathering instruments (questionnaires, interview questions, and so on) developed? What were the response rates and what are the implications of the response rates? How were the data analysed?
- **Management of access and co-operation:** in what way did the context of the study influence the research process as it actually occurred? What ethical issues were raised by the project and how were they handled? How were non-returned questionnaires or other refusals to provide data taken into account?
- **Evaluation of methods:** what issues of data quality were there? What were the advantages and limitations of the methods and research process used?

SUMMARY

- There are many different ways of tackling research projects in HR, and it is important to formulate an approach that is contextually appropriate and will generate data and conclusions that are meaningful and valuable.
- Quantitative data (data that can be quantified) and qualitative data (data based on meanings and expressed through language) are both relevant to HR research. Both approaches can form part of research projects that generate useful knowledge. Mixed methods approaches may also be used effectively within HR research.
- Triangulation is the process of using data from different sources to analyse a phenomenon from different perspectives and to cross-verify data from more than one source.
- Organisational research and decisions about methods of gathering data will be influenced by contextual factors such as operational issues, time pressures and the preferences of organisational stakeholders.
- Theory and practice are not separate things. People use theories in everyday life to generate expectations about the world and to make sense of things. Theories are refined through practice so that everyday experience informs the generalisation process.
- Theories can be evaluated by testing them empirically (in practice) or by analysing their component parts to establish the extent to which they make sense.
- Theories are developed through the processes of induction and deduction. Induction (theory-building) involves observing facts, behaviours and meanings to form a generalised interpretation of what is occurring and why. Deduction

(theory development through testing) involves identifying propositions from existing theories and testing them in different situations and contexts to refine and amend them where appropriate.

- The value and credibility of an investigative enquiry can be assessed by considering the quality of the data on which the conclusions are based. Reliability is the extent to which similar results would be obtained in all similar occasions, and validity is a judgement about whether the data really provide evidence of what the researcher claims they are about. Qualitative researchers will also need to consider issues of data credibility and trustworthiness.
- All project reports require a section that explains and justifies the method or methods that were used. Different study centres have different requirements for this section.
- The methodology section of any report should evaluate the appropriateness of the method for the particular enquiry; the quality and quantity of data collected; the appropriateness of the analysis processes; and the management of access and co-operation.

 Self-test questions

REVIEW AND REFLECT

1   Which of the following is a data collection method?

   a)   case study

   b)   positivism

   c)   focus group

   d)   social constructivism

2   Which of the following is associated with quantitative data?

   a)   analysis begins as data are collected

   b)   emphasis is on measurement of constructs

   c)   research process takes full account of the research context

   d)   the emphasis is on 'thick description'

3   Which of the following is associated with qualitative data?

   a)   meanings and words

   b)   pie charts

   c)   randomised sampling strategy

   d)   positivism

4   A study based on 12 in-depth interviews with people from different departments in an organisation is:

   a)   a longitudinal study

   b)   a structured study

   c)   a quantitative study

   d)   a qualitative study

5   Issues of data credibility and transferability are particularly relevant to:

   a)   experiments

   b)   cross-sectional research

   c)   case study research

   d)   positivism

6   Inductive reasoning involves:

   a)   refining and reconsidering theories through testing propositions in different conditions

   b)   maintaining independence from the subjects being researched

c) incrementally developing the research process

d) adopting a structured and replicable approach

7   One of the advantages of mixed methods research is:

a) facilitation of different methods to answer a research question

b) focus in depth using open interviews

c) theoretical purity

d) eliminating different perspectives

8   Theory is important for HR research because:

a) tutors give a bad mark if there is no theory

b) theory relates to 'know-about' knowledge

c) there is a general theory of HR

d) theories provide a basis for understanding issues from different perspectives

9   Which of the following approaches to data enable a consideration of change over time?

a) cross-sectional 'one moment in time' survey

b) secondary data analysis

c) longitudinal data

d) literature review

10 Data quality issues involve thinking about:

a) the sampling strategy

b) the data-gathering instrument

c) data-recording processes

d) all of the above

 Review questions

REVIEW AND REFLECT

1   Find out about the requirements of your study centre for the methodology section of your report. What word length is expected? What headings or key issues should be discussed?

2   What are the expectations of the organisation(s) with which your research will be concerned? What organisational issues or priorities might affect the methods by which you gather data or the timing of your data-gathering activities?

3   What secondary data sources (organisational documents and so on) are available to you? What level of permission will you need to obtain company information? Who are the 'gatekeepers' of such information?

Questions for reflection

REVIEW AND REFLECT

This final part of the chapter enables you to reflect about your professional development and develop your skills and knowledge. This will enable you to build your confidence and credibility, track your learning, see your progress and demonstrate your achievements.

Taking stock

1   How clearly articulated are your research questions/objectives? To what extent have your research questions informed your decisions about the research design and data-gathering process?

2   How has your review of the literature informed your thinking about methods of data-gathering? How satisfied are you with your review of the existing literature?

Strengths and weaknesses

3   What is your level of expertise in designing 'instruments' of data collection (questionnaire design, interview design, facilitating focus groups, and so on)? What development might be helpful in

this area and how might you undertake it?

4   What knowledge and understanding do you have of sample selection processes? Where might you obtain effective advice about this?

5   What experience and level of expertise do you have in recording and analysing quantitative and/or qualitative data? Where can you learn more about these activities?

Being a practitioner-researcher

6   What skills will you need to enable you to obtain access to organisational information (primary and secondary) and to achieve the co-operation of participants in your research?

7   To what extent have organisational stakeholders got firm ideas about the methods you should use? What skills will you need to manage these expectations and ensure the validity and reliability of the data that you gather?

EXPLORE FURTHER

One way of finding out about the advantages and disadvantages of different methods is to read literature sources about your topic for method as well as for content. Every general textbook on research methods will cover issues of methodology. The following list indicates a selection of them.

Reading

Bauer, M.W. and Gaskell, G. (eds) (2000) *Qualitative research with text, image and sound*. London: Sage.

Bryman, A. and Bell, E. (2007) *Business research methods*. Oxford: Oxford University Press.

Creswell, J. (2009) *Research design: qualitative, quantitative and mixed methods approaches*. London: Sage.

Easterby-Smith, M., Thorpe, R. and Lowe, A. (2003) *Management research: an introduction*. London: Sage.

Gill, J., Johnson, P. and Clark, M. (2010) *Research methods for managers*. London: Sage.

Hart, C. (2010) *Doing your master's dissertation*. London: Sage.

Jankowicz, A.D. (2005) *Business research projects for students*. London: Thomson Learning.

Lee, N. and Lings, L. (2008) *Doing business research: a guide to theory and practice*. London: Sage.

Neuman, W. (2008) *Basics of social research: qualitative and quantitative approaches*. International edition. Harlow: Pearson Education.

Robson, C. (2011) *Real world research: a resource for social scientists and practitioner-researchers*. Oxford: Wiley.

Saunders, M., Lewis, P. and Thornhill, A.(2012) *Research methods for business students*. Harlow: Pearson Education.

IMPLEMENT YOUR RESEARCH

CHAPTER 6

Finding and Using Documents and Organisational Evidence

CHAPTER OUTLINE

- How to use this chapter
- Different forms of documentary evidence
- Using data from organisational management information systems
- Finding and selecting appropriate secondary data sources
- Analysing documentary and organisational information
- Summary
- Review and reflect
- Explore further

LEARNING OUTCOMES

This chapter should help you to:

- identify documents or organisational evidence that will help to answer your research questions
- evaluate the use of different types of evidence (written and visual) in designing and implementing a research project
- determine how to make use of data from management information systems
- identify the most appropriate and relevant forms of organisational evidence for your research
- think about different ways of analysing documentary and organisational information.

HOW TO USE THIS CHAPTER

If you are planning to carry out an organisationally based piece of research, there is likely to be a range of information that already exists in or about the organisation that can help you to answer your research questions. Many people invest considerable time generating new data and overlook sources of valuable information that already exist within the organisation or are to be found in both physical and electronic formats.

Researching the cultural consequences of an organisational relocation

Poppy was a distance learning student who had recently joined the head office of a large retail organisation and was responsible for the HR provision for the head office staff. The staff at the head office had recently moved into new purpose-built premises where 'open plan' working had featured strongly in the design. The idea was to facilitate a culture change at the headquarters of the organisation from functionally separated sub-cultures to an approach characterised by flexibility and cross-functional communication. Poppy decided to focus her research project on the leadership style consequences and challenges of the new environment. Poppy thought that a questionnaire to staff would be a good way of finding out the extent to which they thought leaders' behaviours had

changed as a result of the move to new premises. Her supervisor was also very keen that she find and make use of organisational data that might also provide relevant and useful information.

Discussion Questions

1   In addition to the data from the questionnaire that Poppy planned for her research, what other forms of organisational evidence might be relevant for this study? Try to list about four sources of evidence.

2   What difficulties might Poppy have in trying to locate and use the information you have identified?

FEEDBACK NOTES

Poppy found that internal documents such as management handbooks and policies had not been updated since the move and so were not particularly helpful. However, she did find records of management meetings and documents issued to staff to keep them updated about the progress of the move and the opportunities that the new 'architecture' presented. In addition, Poppy made use of visual information: she took photographs of the old building and some of the offices prior to the move and also took photographs of the new office layouts immediately prior to the move as well as at a point three months after it had taken place once things had become more 'embedded'. These enabled her to show how offices 'worked' in reality as well as in the vision of the architects and planners.

There is a huge range of potential sources of information that can add value to any organisationally based research project. Much of this information is 'unobtrusive' and easy to overlook. Sometimes students opt for time-consuming data-generation methods that merely serve to duplicate data that are already available within the organisation. However, there are some difficulties with the effective use of organisational documents and sources of evidence. It might be the case, for example, that organisational policy documents give a view of things that are not implemented in practice. In addition, detailed reports from computerised information systems might not add much value to the findings of the project, although the researcher may have invested many hours in obtaining access and getting the report in an understandable format.

This chapter, therefore, seeks to highlight different forms of organisational evidence that are likely to be relevant. It discusses different approaches that can be taken to finding documents about organisations, selecting what is most relevant and useful, and then making sense of the information they provide.

DIFFERENT FORMS OF DOCUMENTARY EVIDENCE

 ACTIVITY 6.1

SOURCES OF INFORMATION ABOUT AN ORGANISATION

Imagine that you know absolutely nothing about an organisation. It is not possible for you to contact any of the people (either verbally or in writing) who are involved with the organisation, although you can access

documents within the company. Produce a list of all the sources of information that might help you to know something about the organisation: its purpose, culture, business operations and so on. Include different kinds of evidence in your list, not just written forms of information.

FEEDBACK NOTES

There are a wide variety of sources of information that can help you to learn about any organisation (see Table 6.1). Your list of evidence might include external marketing information, such as company website information as well as internal documents such as hard copies of emails, agendas, minutes of meetings, reports submitted to working groups, proposals for business projects and also progress reports. In addition, it is possible that there may be information about the organisation to be found in newspaper clippings, online news items or articles about the organisation in trade journals or business-related books. It would be possible to get more knowledge of the type of organisation and its type of business if you could access generalised information about its client or customer base and about its market share. Information about employee numbers, skills, length of service, turnover and so on would also be useful as well as financial information through its published annual accounts.

In addition, you may be able to find out about the organisation by accessing publicly available documents. For example, CIPD members and students whose library subscribes to the Business Source Premier database can access Datamonitor Company Profiles. It is also possible to find case-study-based articles from electronic database collections such as Emerald Full-text and Web of Knowledge.

Other non-written sources would be valuable in helping you to understand about the organisation. This might include maps (also available electronically) showing the sites of different parts of the organisation, architectural plans of some of the buildings, diagrams showing the production or work flow processes and so on.

Table 6.1 Different types of organisational evidence

Examples of evidence produced internally for internal use	Examples of evidence produced internally for external use	Examples of evidence produced externally using internal sources of evidence
Administrative sources • HRM records • safety records • production / service records	**Organisational website(s)**	**Newspaper cuttings**
Business records • agendas • notes from meetings • progress reports • project proposals	**Corporate brochure(s)** (for clients / potential investors and so on)	**TV / radio transcripts / recordings**
Operational records • letters • memos • emails • handwritten notes	**Corporate video streaming** (for PR purposes)	**Books and journal articles featuring the organisation**
Policy documents and procedures • HR • procurement and supply • finance and accounting • marketing	**Marketing information**	**Internet hosted 'postings' about the organisation, 'blogs' and so on**
Other internal 'artefacts' • briefing notes • induction presentations • maps, plans and drawings • process diagrams	**Published diaries / memoirs of key people**	**Company profile about the organisation**

 ACTIVITY 6.2

MAKING USE OF PUBLISHED DIARIES, AUTOBIOGRAPHIES AND MEMOIRS

Imagine that you are undertaking some research into HR issues in entrepreneurship. As part of the background research you are reading diaries and autobiographies of prominent 'self-made' figures in business. There are a huge range of these and you are not sure how useful such sources will be. If you have the time (and the interest), skim-read one such book. You may already be a 'consumer' of biographies of business leaders, but if not, and you are not close to a bookshop or library, you can read limited previews of books from any e-book collection that your study centre may subscribe to or through the Google-book search engine (use a search term such as 'business autobiography'). You will need to choose 'full or limited preview' to ensure you choose a book that you can actually browse inside the cover and you will need to scroll down the list of titles that are presented to find one that really is an entrepreneur's autobiography.

DISCUSSION QUESTIONS

1 Why do business leaders (and others) publish their diaries and autobiographies?

2 What are the advantages and disadvantages of evidence from sources such as these?

FEEDBACK NOTES

Sources such as these, produced by the people involved, are helpful to researchers in finding out about the background of issues they are interested in. An advantage of this sort of account is that they have come into existence within a close proximity to the people or the events you are interested in and have been produced by or authorised by those who were involved. However, the motivation to write such documents must be taken into account. This will include the commercial incentive for well-known and influential figures to publish their autobiographies or some form(s) of memoir. They are also likely to have been motivated by the desire to ensure that the most flattering side of their story is available. In some ways, therefore, such forms of evidence have been produced for the attention of future readers and must be read with this in mind. In addition, none of them will have been produced for the purposes of your research, and so it is important to remember that they are 'inadvertent sources' (Bryman and Bell 2007) and are the result of someone else's interpretation.

Nonetheless, this sort of information and these documents can be very useful. Although those who already work within an organisation in which their research is based will feel that much of the evidence they may have to hand merely replicates their existing 'tacit' knowledge, this will not be the case for the people who will read and mark your research report. They will be less knowledgeable about the organisation, and reference to this sort of evidence enables you to justify the context and the particular characteristics that you highlight in your report. In addition, data generated within the organisation may also enable you to challenge 'taken for granted assumptions' about 'the way things are around here'.

There are also more reasons for the use of documentary evidence in HR research. First, documentary evidence can provide specific details about particularly relevant events (Yin 2009). Interviews with those involved in a culture change process, for example, might suggest that those involved felt that the need for a major change was triggered by significant factors (such as loss of key accounts, acquisition of a new business, financial and budgetary difficulties within the organisation and so on). However, people make sense of events in different ways and their interview data may not fully reflect the actual chain of events. Study of relevant documents from the time of the decisions might enable you to pinpoint whether the factors that are cited by those involved really did occur prior to the change process.

Second, documentary evidence can corroborate and augment evidence from other sources. For example, research into appraisal interviews may indicate that those being appraised feel their objectives are unachievable and unrealistic. Analysis of a sample of the appraisal forms themselves might yield further evidence about the quality of objective-setting by managers and provide a further justification (or otherwise) for this conclusion.

Third, documentary evidence can provide 'inferences'. Research into the management of a redundancy process, for example, would be enhanced by analysis of news cuttings, blog entries and other public documents relating to the months before any formal announcements were made as well as the process itself once the redundancies were communicated and then enacted.

What is referred to here as documentary evidence can take many forms, including films, photographic images and other artefacts as well as collective, electronic 'administrative' data (such as that held by an HR information system). This sort of information is often overlooked in research projects, although it requires as much thought and planning as other forms of primary data so that you do not end up wasting time dealing with organisational evidence that is inappropriate. Organisational sources such as these will usually be supplementary to other forms of primary and secondary data, but for some research projects they will form an important part of the data that are analysed. In some cases the data for a research project may come entirely from documentary evidence about one or more organisations.

This chapter will consider the use of data generated by routine administrative processes first and will go on to discuss sources of organisational evidence that can add value to your research.

USING DATA FROM ORGANISATIONAL MANAGEMENT INFORMATION SYSTEMS

All organisations collect information relating to the people that they employ. These records can form a valuable source of information, and it is important at the planning stage to determine how information from this type of source can help you to answer your research questions. Prior to electronic data sets most of this information existed in the form of card index systems or collections of paper records in filing cabinets. Perhaps it will be possible to compare data over different time periods or for different parts of the organisation, as a way of identifying priorities for further probing in your research. However, such administrative records are unlikely to provide direct answers to your research questions, and it is important not to waste time with pages of descriptive statistics that carry little meaning in their own right.

ACTIVITY 6.3

RESEARCH ISSUES WITH MANAGEMENT INFORMATION SYSTEMS

Imagine that you are undertaking a project into the employment of disabled people in your organisation. The organisation has an HR information system which contains details about disabilities that employees have declared as well as historical data on pay, grading and disability for the last ten years. Five years ago the HR information system was linked with the organisation's payroll system to ensure consistency of data. Subject to a range of security and confidentiality safeguards, the organisation has agreed that you can have access to the system, but only for the purposes of obtaining quantitative reports and not for the study of the records of any individual employee.

DISCUSSION QUESTIONS

1   What reports from the HR information system would help you to evaluate the employment experiences of disabled people in the organisation?

2   What challenges will you face in obtaining this information?

3   What issues should you bear in mind, assuming that you are able to generate the reports that you need?

FEEDBACK NOTES

The development and use of HR information systems has enabled research to be undertaken that would have been almost impossible 10 or 20 years ago, and research into employees reporting disability is one such area. Reports that you might decide to generate could include:

- number of male and female staff on each grade who have declared a disability
- bonus payments or other discretionary awards achieved by employees with disabilities over the last ten years
- average pay for disabled employee (per year; per month or week; and per hour) in the organisation
- proportion of disabled employees working on a part-time basis
- a comparison of average pay for disabled and non-disabled employees
- length of service for disabled employees.

One of the challenges you would face in obtaining this sort of data relates to the functionality of the system – that is, the extent to which the system itself is capable of generating these reports. Many HR information systems are very good at taking in information, but generating reports in the form required by those who use them is more difficult. Establishing whether the system could generate these reports may well require liaison with local 'system experts'. Assuming that the system is able to generate the reports that you require, a further challenge may be the development of your own skills with the system to obtain and interpret the reports. Here again it would be necessary to allow sufficient time for you to develop such an expertise.

You may also have highlighted a further range of issues that you would need to take into account and these are outlined below:

- **Access:** irrespective of whether the information is in paper or electronic form, if it shows people's names or other means of identification there are data protection implications which will affect what data you can access and how you use the information.

- **Quality and reliability of the data:** how thoroughly and regularly have records been updated? Have some data been re-coded when system upgrades have been implemented, making time comparisons difficult? System experts should have access to code books or data dictionaries that can clarify these issues. Are there areas of ambiguity in the way the system is set up that might allow for different responses to reflect the same situation? Is the recent data more reliable than the information that is five years old? To what extent have all relevant employees declared a disability?
- **Focusing on research questions:** the range of information included in digital databases can encourage a rather addictive process of devising and running queries, but valuable time can be lost scrutinising information that is 'nice to have' but not really 'need to have'.

In spite of these issues, many practitioner-researchers find that data from the HR information system of the organisation in which their research is based can help them to answer (and in some cases to formulate) meaningful research questions. This sort of data can also help you to judge how representative information from survey data you subsequently obtain may be.

FINDING AND SELECTING APPROPRIATE SECONDARY DATA SOURCES

 ### ACTIVITY 6.4

USING ONLINE COMMUNITY CONTRIBUTIONS AS A FORM OF DATA

Imagine that you are a full-time student interested in researching into the HR implications of stress at work and mental health. You want to find out about the key issues surrounding stress from the perspective of HR practitioners. You want to probe further into questions that you might address in your research. Visit a discussion thread section of any HR practitioner Internet site, for example: http://www.cipd.co.uk/community or http://www.hrzone.co.uk/discussion-groups Navigate your way to relevant opinions or discussions. Select what looks like a promising discussion thread (make sure you assess this on the basis of the number of postings rather than the number of 'hits'). Open the site and skim-read the contributions.

DISCUSSION QUESTIONS

1   Identify the ways in which this sort of information would assist your research.

2   What problems might arise from study of these postings 'in isolation'? What do these postings **not** tell you?

FEEDBACK NOTES

There are many ways in which these postings might be helpful to your study. They will provide an overall indication of the immediate concerns of the practitioners who made contributions. From this basis you could devise a study or formulate meaningful research objectives or questions that build on this starting position. Such sources can be valuable, although a study that was based only on these contributions would be very partial as you do not know about the background or context of the contributors whose words you are reading. Also, they might not consider the issues in much depth. The postings that you have seen are unlikely to be representative of all HR practitioners, being confined to those who engage with these and other Web 2.0 applications (such as blogs, wikis and social networking sites).

It is always necessary to take a critically evaluative approach to the use of evidence generated in this way. It would be naive to believe that something that has been recorded in written form provides evidence that is not biased in any way. All organisational documentary sources of evidence are partial, and they need to be critically assessed and compared with other forms of evidence generated in different ways. An overview of the strengths and weaknesses of documentary sources is shown in Table 6.2.

Table 6.2 Advantages and disadvantages of documentary and other organisational evidence

Advantages	Disadvantages
Not time-constrained – repeated study of the documents is possible.	Identifying and accessing all relevant sources of evidence can be difficult.
Unobtrusive – those in the organisation are not inconvenienced and their work is not disrupted. Also, you can 'observe' without being observed.	Partiality – incomplete information may lead to exaggerated bias in the information the sources provide.
Level of detail – sources can provide exact details of names and details of particular events or initiatives as well as quantitative data about organisational processes.	The bias or perspective of the author/ producer of the document is not known.
Coverage – documents can show trends over time, incorporate many events and include many locations.	Access – the organisation may not be willing to allow access to some forms of evidence for confidentiality reasons.
Time – there are opportunities for an element of longitudinal analysis when the time span available to undertake other forms of data-gathering is very limited.	Analysis – it may be difficult to say whether the documents you are studying 'caused' the phenomenon you are interested in or resulted from it.

(Robson 2011, Yin 2009)

To maximise the advantages of organisational sources of evidence and minimise the difficulties, it is necessary to think systematically about how to locate and select appropriate information and it is also important to take data quality issues into account.

The first stage in an effective process to make use of appropriate organisational evidence is to **identify and categorise** the types of evidence that would be helpful to your research. Having done that, it is necessary to **locate** where such sources might be and then to **select** the material that will be most relevant to the aims and research questions underpinning your project. In particular, it is important not to choose sources that will merely reinforce the conclusions you expect to draw, but to look for evidence that might develop your thinking, and therefore the value of your study.

Once you have obtained the evidence you have selected, it is also necessary to evaluate it against the following criteria (Saunders et al 2012, Scott 1990):

- **Authenticity and credibility:** the accuracy of what is described in one source of information would need to be assessed by comparison with other sources of data about the same issue.
- **Representativeness:** to what extent are the views expressed in sources from one part of an organisation (say the HR function) also reflected in the views of other functions (such as marketing or finance)? Alternatively, if you are studying sources related to the activities of a trades union, to what extent does the information you are reading about reflect all members of the union, or is it more reflective of the union activists?
- **Meaning and significance:** this may be the most challenging area, particularly if you are unfamiliar with the culture and language (jargon) used within the organisation that you are studying. This difficulty is most apparent where sources may have been generated in a different country with a different cultural context. Words used in HR in the UK, for example, may mean different things when used by the HR function based in Germany. Titles of different jobs are also expressed and understood differently in different countries. Organisational cultures also can lead to different interpretations of the same language. The term 'strategy', for example, is understood in somewhat different ways in different organisations.

To make best use of organisational evidence it is necessary to undertake a deliberate evaluation of it. This will involve asking questions such as:

- What kind of 'source' is it?
- What does it actually 'say'?
- Who produced it and for what purpose?
- What was the context of its production?
- Is it typical or exceptional for its time?
- Is it complete – has it been altered or edited?
- What is known about the background and experience of the people who generated this source?

 ACTIVITY 6.5

SOCIAL MEDIA POLICY

Imagine that you came across this document on the website of a large university as part of your research into social networking and social media issues in employment in the UK.

Introduction and scope

The university recognises that the Internet provides unique opportunities to participate in interactive discussions and share information on various topics using a wide variety of media such as Facebook, Twitter, blogs and wikis. The use of such online media sites has become a significant part of life for many people as a way of keeping in touch with friends and associates and can be used to exchange ideas and thoughts on common interests, both from a personal and employment perspective.

However, the use of social media by students and employees of the university can pose risks to the university's confidential information, reputation and overall compliance within the law. To minimise such risks the university expects its students and employees to comply with this policy in relation to the use of social media.

This policy is intended to apply to personal use of social media by students and employees of the university. If such personal use does not make any reference to the university and the university cannot be identified, the content is not likely to be of concern to the university. If students are encouraged to use social media as part of their study, in the absence of a formal policy being put in place, such use should be conducted in line with the spirit and intent of this policy.

Guidelines for students relating to use of social media

If you wish to have a social media presence, or already have a presence in place, which refers to the university or from which the university can be identified, please make sure it is clear that you are speaking on your own behalf, for example by writing in the first person and using a personal email address. You are personally responsible for what you communicate in social media.

Remember that what you publish may be readily available to the public (including the university, prospective future employers, the media and social acquaintances) for a long time. Keep this in mind when posting content. Inappropriate posting of content can damage your career potential, since potential (and current) employers often screen social media sites when considering applications.

Social media should not be used to verbally abuse or intimidate staff or students. Respect should be had at all times for other people's privacy and feelings. Care should be taken to avoid language which may be deemed as offensive to others. For example, you should not:

- say defamatory things about people or organisations
- say anything that is or could be construed as discriminatory
- engage in any criminal activity
- tell lies or mislead people, or
- post inappropriate pictures or videos.

Before posting pictures or details of another person, you should obtain their consent.

Any member of staff or student is free to talk about the university on social media sites. However, please be aware that disparaging or untrue remarks which may bring the university, its staff or students into disrepute may constitute misconduct and disciplinary action may be applied. You should avoid posting any communications which might be misconstrued in a way that could damage the university's goodwill and academic reputation, even indirectly.

If you are approached by a media contact about content on a site relating to the university, you should contact the Director of Communications before taking any action. If you wish to complain about any inappropriate posting of content, which identifies the university, you should contact the Head of Registry, who will investigate the matter on behalf of the university to ascertain what action, if any, may be appropriate.

Social media should not be used for accessing or sharing illegal content.

Compliance with related policies and agreements

All of the university's other policies which might apply to the use of social media remain in full force and effect. Social media should never be used in a way that violates any other university policies or obligations relating to employees or students. If your post would violate any of the university's policies in another forum, it will also violate them in an online forum. If there is any conflict between this policy and any of the other relevant university policies, the more restrictive policy shall take precedence.

DISCUSSION QUESTIONS

1   Evaluate this document using the questions shown below:

- What kind of 'document' is it? Is it authentic and credible?
- Who produced it and for what purpose? What is known about the author(s)' background and experience?
- What was the context of its production?
- Is it typical and representative of such documents or exceptional for its time?
- To what extent is its meaning clear?

● Is it complete – has it been altered or edited?

if you were researching into social networking and social media issues in employment in the UK?

2   In what ways is this a useful document and what other information would you require

FEEDBACK NOTES

Your evaluation of this document would probably highlight the following issues. There seems to be very little doubt about the authenticity of the policy statement because it 'reads' like the policy of a large university and it was accessed on the website of a large, reputable organisation. In this sense its 'espoused' meaning is clear, but what is not known is the extent to which those in the organisation know about and comply with its statements and intentions. It is also not clear who 'authored' the statement and the extent to which other stakeholders had an opportunity to contribute to it. Further information is required, therefore, on these points and it is also necessary to access other organisational evidence.

In addition, this source relates to a university and may not be typical of policies in other employing organisations, particularly those in the private sector.

ANALYSING DOCUMENTARY AND ORGANISATIONAL INFORMATION

 ACTIVITY 6.6

COMPARING SOURCES

Researching harassment and bullying

Go to a general web-based search engine (such as Google or Yahoo) and enter the search terms 'harassment' and 'bullying'.

1   From the 'hits' for this sort of search you are likely to be able to access the harassment and bullying policies of a range of different public sector bodies. If

you were interested in researching into harassment and bullying, as part of your topic, what steps would you take to make sense of the information contained within these documents?

2   Navigate to the 'images' part of the site and select two or three images that represent harassment and bullying. How might you include an analysis of these images as part of your research?

FEEDBACK NOTES

Making sense of the documents is at the heart of the analysis process, and you need to do this in a systematic way. You may wish to assess the similarities and differences between the different sources you have found. You might also try to find out how harassment is defined in different organisations and the different routes open to a victim of bullying in different situations. In this way, therefore, you will need to engage in a categorisation and comparative process.

Information from policy documents alone, however, is a very partial and unrepresentative selection of how harassment and bullying is managed in practice in different organisations. Much of the significance of the information is only apparent when considered in relation to other documents and evidence from within the organisation(s). Analysis of documents, therefore, tends to be comparative and involves abstracting elements of relevant information, grouping these elements and comparing them with other relevant evidence.

Analysing images presents different challenges. Images can capture different aspects of issues or situations; these can also be categorised and analysed. This process can supplement other evidence you are analysing or, if you ask research participants to describe their reactions to images that you show them, it can help you to explore meanings in more depth. The advantage of making use of pre-existing images is that it may be possible to show historical changes, for example, to capture how the portrayal of bullying and harassment has changed over time and to assess how this relates to changes in social or economic concerns of the time. However, if you are making use of pre-existing images, you will not necessarily know the intentions and purpose of the person who created or generated the image and it is difficult to know what has been excluded. For example, the context surrounding a photograph may be difficult to understand, and it is possible that the image may have been 'photoshopped' or cropped in a way that distorts the original picture (Ray and Smith 2012).

An important first step in analysis of an image is a cataloguing of 'seen' elements (Banks 2007), something that requires you to look for details in the image and to take the context of its production into account. When assessing the images you have selected, for example, you will need to make detailed notes about the layout of the image, the activities depicted, facial expressions and so on. Items in an image or set of images can then be counted and compared in a similar way as word frequencies may be counted in an analysis of the text of policies and procedures. Alternatively, it is possible to identify and compare key issues, patterns and themes that are evident in images. The examination of images from corporate websites, for example, as well as 'messages' from company newspapers or copies of written communications relating to a particular topic might be qualitatively analysed, establishing and examining themes and categories in chronological order or some other sequence.

INDUCTION AND DEDUCTION

The analysis of organisational evidence can be undertaken in one of two different ways, which are illustrated in Figure 6.1 and which link to the different approaches of relating theories and evidence that are discussed in Chapter 5.

Figure 6.1 Categorising and analysing organisational evidence

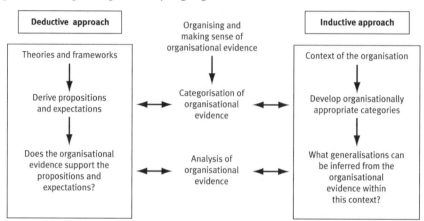

A deductive approach towards the analysis of documents would make use of a theory or framework of practice that has already been established and consider the extent to which the organisational evidence indicates that this theory is occurring in practice. Thus the basis on which the evidence is analysed (the analytical framework) is derived from the literature.

Alternatively, it is possible to analyse the information from the context of the organisation from which it has been generated. In this way data from the evidence are organised using contextually appropriate categories and further detailed interpretation – on the basis of which conclusions are drawn – takes place from this more inductive approach to analysis. Yin (2009) argues that researchers should choose one or the other of these analytical strategies. However, as different types of organisational evidence may lend themselves to different analytical approaches, and the boundaries between the inductive and deductive approaches may not be as clear as Yin's approach would suggest, the use of both could be appropriate (Gill et al 2010, Saunders et al 2012, Bryman and Bell 2007).

QUALITATIVE AND QUANTITATIVE ANALYSIS

A key theme of this chapter has been the diversity of organisational evidence and the potential of these forms of information to add value to research projects provided that there is a clear rationale underpinning the data-gathering and evaluation process. In addition, it is necessary to ensure that data are analysed in a systematic and rigorous way and treated with as much care as would be accorded to other forms of data. Given that organisational evidence is characterised by diversity, there are also a range of different approaches to analysis. Qualitative analysis may be appropriate for some of the organisational data and quantitative analysis may be required for other forms of information. Some of the evidence you have obtained may be suitable for both qualitative and quantitative analysis processes.

Activity 6.7 demonstrates how both qualitative and quantitative analysis may be used. It also provides an illustration of a situation where an HR issue can be researched without access to any one organisation and through making use of organisationally generated documents (job advertisements).

ACTIVITY 6.7

CATEGORIES FOR ANALYSIS

Visit an online HR jobs site and go to the section which advertises training and development posts (for example, http://hr-jobs.peoplemanagement.co.uk/jobs/training-learning-and-development/).
Imagine that you are undertaking research into the effect of contemporary economic conditions on learning and development job roles. The site will provide you with information about a range of posts.

DISCUSSION QUESTIONS

1   Decide how you would go about analysing the information about role expectations for training and development professionals.

2   What opinions might you have about the sampling strategy for this approach to research?

FEEDBACK NOTES

To begin the analysis you will need to generate some categories. Possible categories that you might try to use when undertaking your analysis of the role expectations of training and development professionals might include:

- responsibilities of the job
- range (and types) of work
- levels of qualification expected
- job title.

In addition, it is likely that when you start to compare the texts of the different advertisements you notice particular words that seem to be significant (such as 'strategic', 'results orientated', 'complex problems', and so on). However, you might also wonder whether choosing a 'random' week in which to assess the advertisements would be representative (suppose you undertook your search on a different week or month?). Equally you might ask whether the choice of one source of job advertisements is representative; why not use other online sites or paper-based journals more specifically directed to training and development specialists rather than to broadly defined HR roles?

This activity highlights a range of key issues for the use and analysis of documentary forms of data (Bryman and Bell 2007):

- **Sample selection:** if you propose to find documents from the public domain, which media will be chosen and why? If you propose to find documents from within the organisation, what selection criteria will you use? In both cases, what time period will you select from?

- **Subjects and themes:** having identified the documents you will select, what subjects or themes do you wish to focus on? How will you go about this (qualitative or quantitative approach or both)?
- **Evaluating the sources:** none of the information referred to in this chapter is likely to have been generated with your research project in mind. Key questions to ask will be: what kind of person produced the item (for example, HR director, news reporter, online blogger)? Who or what is the main focus of the item you are considering? What is the context in which the document was generated (annual report, redundancy announcement)?
- **Coding and categorising:** having identified the key issues or themes you wish to investigate using organisational or secondary sources, it is important to assess how you will make sense of your data. You are likely to need to simplify and summarise what you have found (which may well amount to many pages of written words and/or numbers). Some thought needs to go into establishing a set of categories and a method of cataloguing and recording the data you have gathered so that you can get a sense of (and communicate about) the 'intensity' or prevalence of your themes within the selection of data that you have gathered.

SUMMARY

- The range of sources of information about any organisation or HR issue includes materials produced within organisations for internal or external use, materials produced externally about organisations, and administrative records and data.
- The term 'organisational evidence' refers to artefacts, films, images and websites as well as those things more usually referred to as documents.
- These sources of information can add value to any organisational research project. These can help you to establish the context of the organisational situation that you are investigating, provide specific details about relevant events and corroborate and augment evidence from other sources.
- Most, but not all, organisational evidence is inadvertent – it will not have been generated for the purposes of your research. It will contain 'witting' and 'unwitting' evidence that may be useful to you.
- Key issues when evaluating organisational sources are: access and confidentiality; data quality and reliability; and relevance of the data to the research questions.
- Effective use of organisational sources requires identification and location of evidence that is relevant to the research questions and effective sample selection.
- Key issues when evaluating organisational evidence are: the authenticity and credibility of the sources, how representative the sources are and the meaning and significance of what they contain.
- Organisational evidence and secondary sources can underpin an inductive and/or a deductive approach to analysis.
- Documentary evidence is diverse in its form and nature. To make sense of the information may require qualitative and/or quantitative analysis.

Self-test questions

1   Which of the following are documentary forms of evidence about any organisation?

    a)   minutes of executive committee meetings

    b)   email exchanges between an employee and their manager

    c)   newspaper articles about the organisation

    d)   all of the above

2   What is the disadvantage of using organisational sources within your research project?

    a)   provides contextual information about the situation or issue that is being researched

    b)   difficult to achieve access within data protection regulations

    c)   provides specific details about relevant events

    d)   can be used to supplement evidence from other sources

3   What issues need to be considered when evaluating sources of evidence about an organisation?

    a)   the hand-in date of your research report

    b)   whether the organisation is well known or not

    c)   whether you are an employee of the organisation

    d)   access and confidentiality; data quality; relevance to the research questions

4   What criteria are helpful for assessing the quality of organisational sources of evidence?

    a)   objectivity, subjectivity, accuracy, significance

    b)   authenticity, credibility, representativeness, significance

    c)   credibility, reliability, pictorial clarity, ease of access

    d)   meaning, subjectivity, volume, validity

5   What issues should you take into account if you decide to make use of evidence from published diaries, memoirs or autobiographies?

    a)   they were produced for commercial intent

    b)   it is likely that they will describe, flatter and justify rather than evaluate

    c)   they may have been 'ghost-written' by an author who was not present at the time of the events being described

    d)   all of the above

6   What problems are presented by analysing photographs as a form of visual data?

    a)   they capture different features of what you are researching into

    b)   they can supplement other evidence that is available to you

    c)   they can show historical changes in work organisations

    d)   the context of the photograph's production may be difficult to understand

7   What challenges are presented by making use of evidence about organisations taken from website sources?

    a)   they are difficult to reference in a research report

b)   website data is always less
     reliable than proper data

c)   the visual images are
     distracting

d)   the motivation of the author
     and the context of their
     contribution may be unclear

8   Qualitative analysis of
     organisational sources of evidence
     involves:

a)   counting the number of times
     a word or feature appears in
     artefacts

b)   more creativity and
     imagination than other forms
     of analysis

c)   engaging in an interpretive
     understanding of the source
     in the context of its
     production

d)   deciding in advance what to
     look for and making sure you
     find it

Review questions

REVIEW AND REFLECT

1   What sources of organisational
    evidence (primary and secondary
    data) may help you to answer your
    research questions?

2   What are the views of your
    supervisor about the use of
    organisational sources of
    evidence?

3   Who might be helpful in arranging
    access to organisational forms of
    evidence?

4   What are the implications for
    confidentiality and ethics if you
    make use of internal information
    sources?

Questions for reflection

REVIEW AND REFLECT

This final part of the chapter enables
you to reflect about your professional
development and develop your skills
and knowledge. This will enable you to
build your confidence and credibility,
track your learning, see your progress
and demonstrate your achievements.

Taking stock

1   To what extent are you so familiar
    with the organisation that your
    knowledge of many of its features
    is 'tacit'? What sources of evidence
    would justify your understanding

through making your knowledge
explicit?

2   To what extent might images and
    photographic evidence help you to
    answer your research questions or
    provide a useful context for your
    analysis?

3   In what ways may data from any
    HR information system be useful
    to achieving your research
    objectives? What would be the
    most helpful format for the data?

Strengths and weaknesses

4   What level of skills would you need to generate specific queries and reports from information management systems? How might you develop the skills you need? Who would be the best person to help with this?

5   What information search skills do you need to identify and select appropriate documentary sources? How might you develop these?

6   To what extent are you interested in, and able to contribute to, Web 2.0 applications (such as blogs, social networking sites, wikis, podcasts and so on) that can provide information and ideas for your research project?

Being a practitioner-researcher

7   What level of permission will you require to use data from an HR information system (whether paper-based or electronic)?

8   How can you check on the meaning and significance of some of the terms and expressions used within any organisational sources that you study?

9   How might you ensure that you take into account any biases (such as a management perspective) in the documents that you analyse?

EXPLORE FURTHER

Reading

Banks, M. (2007) *Using visual data in qualitative research*. Thousand Oaks, CA: Sage.

Bauer, M.W. and Gaskell, G. (eds) (2000) *Qualitative research with text, image and sound*. London: Sage.

Bryman, A. and Bell, E. (2007) *Business research methods*. Oxford: Oxford University Press.

Gill, J., Johnson, P. and Clark, M. (2010) *Research methods for managers*. London: Sage.

Robson, C. (2011) *Real world research: a resource for social scientists and practitioner-researchers*. Oxford: Wiley.

Saunders, M., Lewis, P. and Thornhill, A. (2012) *Research methods for business students*. Harlow: Pearson Education.

Yin, R.K. (2009) *Case study research: design and methods*. Thousand Oaks, CA: Sage Publications.

CHAPTER 7

Collecting and Recording Qualitative Data

CHAPTER OUTLINE

- How to use this chapter
- The value of qualitative data in HR research
- Observation and participation
- Data from individuals
- Focus groups
- Sample selection for qualitative research
- Making sense of the data
- Summary
- Review and reflect
- Explore further

LEARNING OUTCOMES

This chapter should help you to:

- consider how qualitative data can add value to your research
- assess how participation or observation might provide some data for your project
- highlight how to collect and record interview- and diary-based data
- discuss the use of focus group and other group interview techniques in HR research
- consider the use of electronically obtained qualitative data
- determine an appropriate sample of respondents to provide trustworthy data.

HOW TO USE THIS CHAPTER

Nearly all HR research projects undertaken in work organisations make use of qualitative data of some sort and this chapter sets out some of the options. Many HR practitioners find they need to ask questions in depth of one or more 'key individuals' when they are conducting research, so this chapter is likely to be relevant whether you are undertaking a CIPD 'investigation of a business issue' for an advanced or postgraduate course or whether your research project is at intermediate level. You may be tempted to go straight to the material about interviews or focus groups, but if your project is likely to be influenced by your own observations of the work environment, you should make sure to consider the issues involving participation and observation.

The process of gathering qualitative data is far more effective if you give some thought to how you will analyse your information before you 'launch into action' with organising interviews or collecting data of other types, and so it is worth reading Chapter 8 before you make final decisions about your data-gathering process. When you come to write the methodology section of your report, you will need to reflect on your data-gathering process as well as your sampling decisions and analysis process. These are covered in this chapter.

CASE ILLUSTRATION 7.1

 TQM and training in a multinational enterprise

Talel was a distance learning student who was undertaking his research project into his own work organisation. The company was a large multinational enterprise with a strong manufacturing base which had invested heavily in total quality management (TQM), an approach to improving the quality of products and processes through continuous improvement. The TQM approach promotes the view that quality improvement is the responsibility of everyone in the organisation and cross-functional training and employee involvement are important features. Talel was asked by the HR director in his organisation to investigate and evaluate the relationship between training and development and TQM processes. Talel's immediate focus was on the relationship between training and development and TQM in parts of the organisation based in the Middle East and Asia, although his director

indicated that he may, at some stage, be asked to expand his focus to include parts of the company situated in Europe. Talel agreed with his director that, as TQM involved a 'hearts and minds' approach, the first stage in his research should involve finding out the perceptions and expectations about learning and training by those responsible for quality in sites throughout his region, and comparing this with the perceptions about the contribution of learning of those in each site with responsibility for training and development. On the basis of this qualitative data, there was a possibility that Talel might then be asked to develop a more quantitative approach to complete his investigation.

Discussion Questions

1   What sort of information would Talel need to gather to find out about the different perceptions of managers from the various

sites about the main issues connected with quality and training in different parts of the organisation?

2　How might he gain access to the information he needed?

3　What issues might impact on the reliability of the qualitative data that Talel would gather?

FEEDBACK NOTES

To find out about perceptions of the impact of TQM on learning and training, Talel needed to explore different factors that influenced the views of managers in different sites and variations in perception of those responsible for quality as well as those responsible for training and development. He wanted to know about how different people understood learning and career development issues in each country, the extent to which the focus on TQM had encouraged greater engagement by managers with learning and training issues and the extent to which some features of learning and career development might be overlooked. He needed to find out what the issues were from the perspective of quality managers in different parts of the organisation in the Middle East and Europe. In addition, he wanted to hear the views of the training and development managers.

At this stage of his project Talel felt that it was important to gather information in the form of words and language which reflected the context and situations of those involved. He decided to interview the managers responsible for TQM and to interview one training manager from each site. In addition, he requested permission to attend and observe meetings of the training and development teams and some of the team meetings of manufacturing staff to learn more about the issues from different perspectives.

Accessing such information was not easy. 'Watching' people in meetings is not a popular thing to do and can lead people to behave in a more self-conscious way or to 'tweak' agendas and discussions to present issues in a particular way. Talel was also concerned that interviewees might tell him what they thought their own site director wanted them to say rather than giving their 'honest' opinion. In addition, Talel was fairly fluent in both English and Arabic, but he became conscious that these were not the first or second languages of some of the managers (particularly in Asia and Europe) and he became concerned that they may be less able to express their thoughts and experiences because of this.

THE VALUE OF QUALITATIVE DATA IN HR RESEARCH

The issues highlighted in this case are common for many HR research projects, particularly those that are organisationally based. While quantitative data can identify the extent to which things are, or are not, occurring in organisations, it is less helpful in answering the question 'why' things are the way they are. Most organisationally focused HR projects, therefore, will include the use of some qualitative data. This chapter considers the key issues with gathering and recording qualitative data. Chapter 8 considers the data analysis process.

Qualitative data can be broadly categorised as encompassing **information in the form of words and language** from:

- observation and participation
- one-to-one interviews or conversations
- individual accounts or diaries (digital, 'virtual' and paper-based) of events and/or activities
- focus groups (or other group interviews).

As the data generated by such activities take the form of words, it is not readily quantifiable. Qualitative data are often generated through a process that is less structured and where questions posed are not standardised. As such the preconceptions and categories of the researcher are suspended, as far as is possible, and the language and expressions of the 'informants' is valued and used.

In-depth, unstructured and semi-structured interviews, where the language, expressions and meanings of the informants are recorded and used for analysis 'in their own terms', generate qualitative data, whereas structured interviews do not. Structured observations of work activity, where a very systematic approach to recording and counting the number of incidences of particular behaviours, contributions or interactions is used, also generate quantitative, rather than qualitative data. Such data can be useful, but they are considered in Chapter 9, whereas this chapter focuses on gathering and recording qualitative data.

Figure 7.1 Types of qualitative data

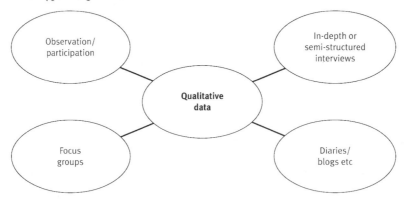

Working with qualitative data as part of your project is not an easy undertaking. Although proficiency in maths and statistics is not required, there are a lot of other skills that have to be developed if you are to take seriously and to faithfully reflect the information gathered from your sources. Qualitative data analysis involves working with small sample sizes but, to obtain information of good quality, you often need to establish a closer level of contact. As a result, the information you can gather is quite detailed, rich and extensive, and it is necessary to undertake an in-depth and 'open' analysis of your information to interpret it and 're-present' it in an appropriate way.

Qualitative data can add value to your research in different ways and can support both inductive and research approaches (O'Reilly et al 2012). You may choose to keep a direct (empirical) record of your observations or the experiences of those included within your research sample and then make sense of the evidence to answer clearly defined questions. Alternatively, you may work within an interpretivist 'world-view' (see Chapter 5). Seeking to make sense of complex situations and contexts, you may want to 'get beneath' the 'situation' through developing an informed awareness of research participants' (and your own) 'pre-understandings' of what is going on and to make sense of what you see, hear and read through a reflective process of familiarisation with the data, seeing issues as part of a 'whole' rather than breaking it down and 'making sense' of events through conceptualising what may be occurring.

Qualitative data helps you to explain or understand issues in their organisational context and can enable you to develop a 'rich picture' of processes that are taking place. If you are undertaking an action-orientated approach, where your project forms part of a wider change initiative, you can use a qualitative approach to help you interact with different stakeholders as part of your data collection strategy and so explore some of the issues as they emerge over time. Alternatively, you may choose a qualitative approach to develop a case-study-based understanding of an HR issue from the (perhaps multiple) perspectives of those who have to participate in it.

One thing is clear: qualitative research is unlikely to add value if the only reason you choose to undertake it is because it seemed like an 'easier' process.

OBSERVATION AND PARTICIPATION

An obvious way of finding out information about people's behaviours and actions at work is to watch and listen to them. If you are undertaking a project in an organisation in which you already operate – either as an employee, as an intern or as part of a paid work placement – there are likely to be plenty of opportunities for participation in, or observation of, organisational processes. However, if these practices are to be used as part of a systematically undertaken research project, it is important to distinguish between different types of observation and participation and the uses to which data gathered in this way may be put.

Ethics awareness training for managers

As a result of her studies at university, Gina had become very interested in issues associated with business ethics. She was particularly concerned with what she considered to be 'ethical tokenism' in many different business organisations. Gina was a self-employed training consultant and had developed a short two-day course on ethical management, which she delivered 'in-company' for organisations wishing to enhance their corporate social responsibility processes. For her master's-level programme, Gina decided to investigate the extent to which her training programme made a lasting impact on the behaviours and attitudes of the participants on her courses. Her idea was to gather data about participants' attitudes towards ethical issues before they attended her course, observe a group of course participants throughout the two-day programme and then undertake 'follow-up' research, by interview, a few weeks after the programme had been completed.

Discussion Questions

1   In addition to interviews, Gina wanted to make use of observation of people participating in her training courses. In what way might this 'add value' to the findings of the research? List what you think are the advantages and the disadvantages of using observation as part of a research project in HR.

2   What problems might emerge for the researcher, the situation being observed and the organisation in which observation is being undertaken? What issues need to be taken into account in such situations?

FEEDBACK NOTES

A major advantage of gathering data by watching people's behaviour is its directness; rather than asking people about their feelings, you can watch (and later make notes about) what they do and say and also reflect on your own experience as part of the analysis of the situation. What people say about their experience at work is valuable, but new insights can be achieved through direct observation of (and reflection about) the experiences of those that are being researched. Gina also found that, as she reflected on observations she made, she found herself thinking differently about some of the issues and so an additional 'loop' of (self-reflective) data was generated by this method.

However, and this was particularly pertinent given the subject of Gina's research (ethical behaviours), there are important ethical and legal issues that must be taken into account if observation is used, particularly if it may be interpreted as covert surveillance (see Chapter 4). There are also practical disadvantages. One such difficulty is the time commitment. Although Gina was already involved in delivering the training programmes, other researchers find the time commitment involved in working 'alongside' people in their work roles to achieve observational data is difficult to fulfil. In addition, it is possible that your presence as a researcher might influence behaviour one way or another, and so it is still difficult to know what would have happened if you had not been part of the situation.

Other issues that are important to take into account are (Iacono et al 2009):

- **Bias:** being a participant watching and listening is easy but, as you have been part of the situation, how can you be sure that the data you record is not biased in some way? This leads to further questions:

  1 **What to record:** when you are observing a situation, how will you know what to look out for?
  2 **How to record:** another question is the format you will use to record your data. Many HR students claim to have undertaken some observation but are less clear about how they recorded and then analysed their data. Relying on your memory and on anecdotes is not a good strategy and so effective methods of recording data are essential. Robson (2011) recommends noting down 'memory sparkers' within a few hours of the event that will help you recall and record more details of what happened. Other researchers keep some form of diary that they update on a daily basis. Records not made within 24 hours of any observation will be particularly unreliable.

- **Ethics:** as already discussed in Chapter 4, there are a number of ethical concerns relating to observation. Being explicit about the purpose of your observation and obtaining informed consent overcomes many of the difficulties, but may also influence the nature of your findings. For these reasons it is important that you discuss any plans to use some form of observation with your supervisor or tutor.

Although there are difficulties, observation and/or participation, in the context of your research project, can provide opportunities to record, describe and interpret people's behaviour. It is important, however, to be clear about the purpose of any observation and the way in which it will be carried out. Robson (2011) describes a range of different approaches to participation and observation (see Figure 7.2) and these are briefly described now:

Figure 7.2 Participation and observation

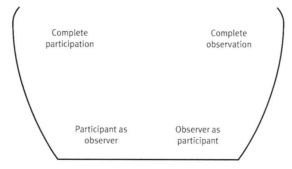

- **Complete participation:** the observer becomes as full a member as possible of the group or organisation being studied. Employment within an organisation provides many opportunities to undertake this (Easterby-Smith et al 2003), although the ethical implications of concealing the purpose of your participation need to be clearly thought through and discussed with your supervisor.
- **The participant as observer:** the observer makes clear to those involved that research is their explicit role, although they may also participate in the activity in one way or another. This is not an easy option and it is important to gain the trust of those involved. It does, however, provide opportunities for you to ask people to explain what is going on and why. Some students use an approach of 'interrupted involvement' (Easterby-Smith et al 2003) and complement it with in-depth interviews of key participants after the activities that have been observed.
- **The observer as participant:** this approach (referred to in Robson 2011 as the 'marginal participant') occurs when your main role is 'merely' to observe but, to some degree, you unavoidably become a participant in the situation as a result of your very presence. A researcher who wishes to find out the extent to which new corporate values really have become 'embedded', for example, may 'loiter' or spend time near a coffee machine or a photocopier to observe what issues people really do discuss when not at their desks. The very fact of their presence, however, may mean that the researcher becomes drawn into conversation or may influence in some way the conversations of those around them.
- **The complete observer:** this is someone who takes no part in the activity but the research purpose and the role as an observer is known to the participants. In many ways there is little distinction between this end of the spectrum and being an observer/participant because it is hard to see how the presence of someone to 'observe' would not affect the behaviour of those being observed.

If you are considering some form of participation or observation, it is important to adopt a systematic and justifiable approach to what you plan to do. Recording data appropriately is one of the key challenges of this approach. DeWalt and DeWalt (2002) indicate three broad types of data that may be generated:

- **Primary observations:** those 'field notes' made at the time, or very near to the time, usually in some form of jot-notes, diary or journal.
- **Secondary observations:** how other people that were there 'saw it' – generated through asking participants as closely to the time of the events as possible.
- **Experiential data:** how you 'felt' about what you were observing and experiencing as time passed. Here a diary format is usually used, and it is helpful in enabling you to record how your feelings or values have developed or changed as a result of the research process.

Observation and participation are valuable ways of obtaining qualitative data, but it is important to think ahead to ensure that time invested in this approach is productive.

Key issues that underpin the planning process are summarised in Table 7.1.

Table 7.1 Preparing for observation

Clarify what you need to know	What are your research questions? What information do you require to answer them?
Is observation the most appropriate way of obtaining the information you need?	Consider alternative ways of data-gathering.
What aspects of the situation(s) do you need to find out about?	Are you interested in process or content? Are all subjects equally interesting?
What times are most appropriate to carry out your observations?	Will the timing of your observations affect what you find out?
Access and permission	What permission do you need to undertake this observation? What level of authority is required? With whom should you discuss any plans for observation?
'Blending in'	How 'visible' will you be? Will what you wear, your gender, your age, and so on, affect how people behave when you are observing them?
Recording data	How will you record what you observe? Will the data be sufficient to enable you to form conclusions?
Roles and responsibilities	If you are going to participate as well as observe, how will you balance the demands of both activities?
Pilot your methods	Observation is an 'unrepeatable method' so mistakes cannot be rectified. Pilot your approach first before committing yourself fully to it.

(Robson 2011, Bryman and Bell 2007, Iacono et al 2009)

DATA FROM INDIVIDUALS

INTERVIEWS

Interview data are probably the most frequently used information in HR practitioner research. Qualitative data are obtained by in-depth, unstructured interviews and can also be generated from semi-structured interviews. Structured interviews generate quantitative data and are considered in Chapter 9.

Figure 7.3 Types of research interview

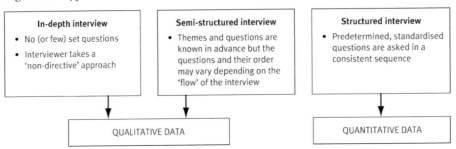

A key issue with interviewing, often overlooked by HR students, is to determine the type of interview that is most suitable to answer your research questions. Each different type of interview has implications for the approach you will take to questioning, recording and analysing data. There are also choices to make about the 'media' and 'method' of the interview. Most interviews are undertaken on a face-to-face basis. Increasingly, however, telephone interviews or electronic conversations/chat are used in HR research, and some researchers also choose to follow up their data-gathering with some form of electronic 'conversation' using email with some or all of their respondents.

 Researching the experience of 'interns'

CASE ILLUSTRATION 7.3

Chris was a full-time student who was struggling to find employment and was increasingly encouraged by careers advisers, course tutors, family and friends to get more relevant work experience to complement his (excellent) academic qualifications. However, he was also aware of controversy about the extent to which employers offered unpaid 'internships' rather than offering paid employment. Chris decided to make internships the focus of his research project. Two years prior to his current course he had undertaken a well-organised but unpaid work experience project with a prominent employer and he had maintained his contacts with the placement organisation. Mindful of the poor publicity that was being generated about internships in general and hopeful that Chris's research would show the positive features of the process for their interns, the organisation agreed to participate in

Chris's study and to give permission for him to undertake semi-structured interviews with placement managers and with interns on three occasions: before the commencement of their placement; at the mid-point of their placement; and at the end of their placement. The aim was to explore the motivations and intentions of placement managers and interns throughout the internship process. Chris wanted to examine how different parties in the internship process made sense of their contextualised experiences and to incorporate the perspective of both the employer and the interns.

Discussion Questions

1   In what ways might data generated by semi-structured interviews enable Chris to answer his research questions?

2   What problems might he encounter in collecting data in this way?

FEEDBACK NOTES

Chris envisaged that interviews would help him to explore and investigate underlying themes or issues related to the individual internship experience of managers and interns. Semi-structured interviews offer the possibility of modifying 'lines of enquiry' in a way that a questionnaire or structured interview would not. Answers can be probed, enabling interviewees to explain or build on what they have said. In this way data of a 'rich' quality can be gathered that allows for people to provide information about their experiences, feelings and motives. Indeed, the responses of one interviewee might alert you to a line of enquiry that you had not previously thought of and so allow for some form of incremental development of thinking to enhance the quality of your research outcomes. In addition, Chris hoped that the interns would find the interview opportunity helpful as a way of reflecting on their own career development.

However, Chris encountered a number of problems. Semi-structured interviews are time-consuming. His tutor told him that any interview of less than half an hour would be unlikely to generate qualitative data of much value, but pressures and deadlines at work made it unlikely that interviewees (particularly the managers) would be available for more than an hour. The time-intensive nature of interviewing meant that the number of participants had to be quite low, and Chris also started to worry about the extent to which he could generalise his conclusions given the highly contextualised nature of his interview data.

Another problem Chris experienced was the issue of recording data. He was very aware that the interns needed a positive 'end of placement' report and would be hoping to ask their placement manager as a reference for any future employment applications that they might make. Therefore, he anticipated that they would be reluctant for their interviews to be audio-recorded. In addition, transcribing a long conversation into (what would be) about 20 pages of closely typed text was a daunting prospect. However, Chris was conscious that note-taking during the interview might distract both him and his interviewees and provide only a partial record of what was said.

Although Chris was given access to people for face-to-face interviews, there were one or two participants whose internship involved travel to different locations and it proved impossible for Chris to undertake all his interviews on a face-to-face basis. One option he considered was for telephone interviews and the other was the use of Skype. This raised some interesting issues. Conducting interviews in this way was easier to arrange across a wide geographical area. However, he was worried that it would constrain the interpersonal relationship between him and his interviewees, which might detract from the quality of the data. Chris was concerned that Skype might limit the extent to which probing questions would be possible as non-verbal 'cues' are somewhat distorted in Skype-type conversations.

Once his project was under way, and with the consent of the organisation and all the participants, Chris also decided to expand his range of qualitative data-gathering by organising a web-hosted discussion group for this sample of interns. As he was not much older than his participants, he was familiar with the social networking opportunities and protocols of 'Web 2.0' and this enabled him to add to the range of his qualitative data.

PREPARING FOR THE INTERVIEW

Key issues to take account of to maximise the usefulness of data gathered in unstructured or semi-structured forms of interviewing are:

Interview design

Allocate time for preparation for all the interviews you intend to carry out. Clarify what research objectives or questions your interview data will contribute towards answering and identify the key themes that you need to explore. Your initial themes may arise as a result of your literature review; from discussions with your tutor or from other activities such as reviewing organisational documents. A process for designing interview themes or topics is shown in Figure 7.4. For each of the themes that you identify, write down a number of questions that you could ask. Be prepared to be flexible in the way you ask your questions. It is also important to be open to the possibility of new aspects or issues that may arise from the interviews. At this stage, therefore, you are clarifying what ground you need to cover and ensuring you have some way of checking, as the interview progresses, the extent to which you are achieving this. At the planning stage it is important to make sure that you are not being overambitious with your range of questions. Your interview will be time-limited (although you may find that some people will be happy to talk for much more than the initial time they promise to give to you). A common mistake is to try to gather data on too many issues and then find that there is no time to explore the themes in a deeper way. Another error, frequently made, is a tendency to ask ambiguous or leading questions. Before you start your interviews you would be wise to ask your tutor or supervisor to 'approve' any questions that you plan to ask in advance (this is a requirement in many universities). This checking process is important because mistakes in the interview will impact on the data you gather and may limit the value of your findings.

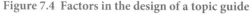

Figure 7.4 Factors in the design of a topic guide

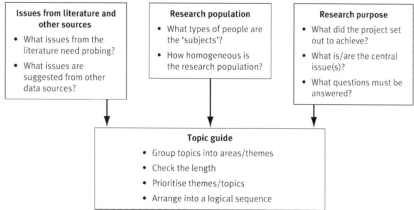

Preparation of the interviewee(s)

You are likely to get more co-operation from your interviewee(s) if they feel fully briefed and confident of your competence as an interviewer and as a researcher. It may be appropriate, for example, to provide your interviewees with a list of your question areas in advance of the meeting. Many people, once briefed, may also be prepared to give you documents that are relevant to your research, and this provides a useful basis for 'triangulation' (see Chapter 5). If you think you would like to ask more sensitive questions, however, it may be better to establish a rapport with your interviewee before you start asking about these issues.

Preparation of the interviewer

As with all forms of interviewing, first impressions are important. In recruitment processes the candidate wants to make a favourable impression on the interviewer. In a research interview the situation is somewhat reversed. You need to make an appropriate impression if a rapport is to be developed to allow for a productive interview. This means thinking carefully about what you will wear and the language that you will use. Clothes that are too smart or imposing may inhibit responses from employees who dress differently and student-quality jeans may be less than appropriate when interviewing the HR director of a work placement organisation. Undertaking some prior research into the key issues for the organisation (key challenges or successes for example) can be advantageous in two ways. First, by drawing on relevant examples during the interview your credibility may be enhanced. Second, your prior research may also allow you to assess the accuracy of some of the information generated by the interview.

      ACTIVITY 7.1

RESEARCH INTERVIEW SKILLS

Think back to any interview skills training that you have participated in – either as a trainee or

as the trainer. If you have never attended an interviewing skills course, think back to recruitment interviews that you have been involved in, either as the candidate or the interviewer.

1   Make a list of all the key skills necessary for effective interviewing.

2   To what extent are the skills needed for recruitment interviewing the same as those needed for undertaking effective qualitative interviews for research purposes?

FEEDBACK NOTES

An activity such as this, once it gets going, can fill pages of A4 or flipchart paper. The main points that tend to be made (and which all have relevance to conducting in-depth or semi-structured interviews) are:

- the interview environment
- structuring the interview
- opening the interview
- using appropriate questions
- listening actively
- using silence
- using appropriate language
- observing body language
- probing answers
- moving from one question to the next
- using summaries
- closing the interview
- keeping accurate records.

Key issues for effective research interviews are very similar to the skills developed for other interviews. However, there are some differences. Most HR practitioners use a structured approach to interviewing to allow comparisons to be more easily made between different candidates. With in-depth or semi-structured interviews, however, the aim is to gather data that reflects the experience of unique individuals. As such a less structured approach is used and this can be a challenge for a practitioner-researcher who is used to a more controlled form of interview with behaviourally structured questions that have been more or less predetermined.

The key skills and issues that underpin successful research interviewing are summarised below:

- **The interview environment:** the environment in which the interview takes place will be very important for the extent to which the interviewee feels 'safe' in articulating their thoughts and experiences. An unfamiliar or noisy environment is likely to inhibit a nervous interviewee. 'Phones off' must be a rule for the interviewer. In preparing for the interview it is also important to get across to the interviewee how helpful it will be if they can give you an agreed spell of time for the interview with no disturbances.

- **Structuring the interview:** although the questions and format of responses may be unstructured, it is still necessary to ensure some framework within which the interview can take place. This will normally involve:

  1 opening/introduction
  2 'warm-up' questions
  3 main body – exploring the main themes in a logical way
  4 'cool-off' questions
  5 conclusion/ending – thanking the interviewee, explaining the next steps in the research process and so on.

- **Questioning and listening:** your job is to get interviewees to speak freely and openly. To achieve this it is important that you listen more than you speak and that you express your questions in a clear, understandable and open way. People will only 'open up' if they feel you are interested in what they are saying, and it is also important to ensure that your behaviour and body language do not influence the opinions they offer. Active listening, involving verbal and non-verbal signs of your continued interest in the conversation, is necessary. Although some research interviews will explore general issues about the experience and perspective of the interviewee, it is also possible to focus more on 'critical incidents' or situations that may lead to the identification of behaviours or attitudes that are relevant to the research questions. This may involve identifying the important aspects of a situation or incident, as perceived by the interviewee, before going on to consider the effect of the situation as experienced by the respondent and others. Whatever the nature and purpose of the research interview, the most productive types of questions to ask are:

  1 open questions where the interviewee is encouraged to describe or explain an experience
  2 probing questions such as 'tell me more about…' or 'what factors contributed to …?' 'how did you feel when…?' which enable interviewees to reflect on issues in more depth or for responses to be further explored.

  Within an in-depth or a semi-structured interview it is unlikely that specific or closed questions will be appropriate. Multiple questions, long questions, leading questions and also those involving jargon should be avoided.

- **Probes:** in addition to the use of specifically probing questions, successful research interviewers will also use other non-verbal methods of encouraging interviewees to talk more about a topic. Robson (2011) indicates four useful techniques of probing in unstructured interviews:

  1 allowing a period of silence
  2 offering an 'enquiring glance'
  3 using verbal signals such as: 'mmhmm'
  4 repeating back all or part of what the interviewee has just said.

- **Summaries:** as with other forms of interviewing, the use of summaries at appropriate times can fulfil a very useful function. Sometimes, once started, an interviewee just cannot stop talking or repeating themselves. The use of a summary to check understanding and then 'build' on the contribution by asking a different, but related, question can allow some 'steering' of the interview. Where complex issues are being discussed, it may also be appropriate to offer a summary to check understanding or to allow the interviewee to clarify where there may be some misunderstanding.

- **Keeping accurate records:** a key issue with unstructured interviews is the approach that is taken to recording the data. This is something that you must explain about in the methodology section of your report. The two most commonly adopted options are to audio-record the interview or to make notes during it.

    1 **Audio-recording your information:** the advantages of audio-recording are that you can concentrate on the process of questioning and listening rather than being distracted by the need to take notes. You can also be confident of the accuracy of the record and you can listen more than once to the recording. However, the interviewee may feel inhibited by the recorder and your relationship with the interviewee may be affected. You cannot rule out the possibility of a technical 'hitch' and you must also ensure that the recording device has sufficient capacity and battery life so that it will not stop part way through the interview. In addition, the time necessary to transcribe the entire conversation is extensive. Secure audio transcription services are available on a commercial basis but these can be expensive if you have a lot of 'audio minutes'.
    If you do decide to use an audio-recorder you should explain why you are doing so and seek the respondent's permission, allowing them, if necessary, to turn off the device part way through the interview if they feel uncomfortable with it (see Chapter 4 for the ethical issues of audio-recording and data storage).

    2 **Taking notes:** there are many different approaches to taking notes. Some people have a sheet with spaces between headings as well as a spare space for unforeseen ideas and responses to be recorded. Others generate something more like a mind map or a concept map as a basis for noting down key pieces of information that are generated during the interview. One advantage of making some notes, even if you are recording the conversation, is that it encourages you to remain focused on what is being said and not to 'drift'. Whatever approach is taken it is important to make more detailed notes of the meeting shortly after it has been concluded. Your record of the interview will be based on the short notes that are already made but you should also note down your reflections about the environment, the body language of the interviewee and the main information that was provided in as much detail as possible. Notes taken in this way (extended summaries) will form the basis for the initial analysis of your qualitative data (see Chapter 8). These notes also provide you with the opportunity to reflect on what you have learned and to incorporate any unexpected directions, indicated by the interview data, into subsequent data-gathering activities.

Table 7.2 provides a summary of what to do and what not to do in research interviews.

Table 7.2 Qualitative interviews: what to do and what to avoid doing

Do	Avoid
Be gently assertive – you want to hear what the interviewee has to say in a sympathetic way but you also need to guide the discussion through your research topics/themes.	**Do not ask more than one question at a time** – take great care to avoid multiple questions.
Ask both sides of a question – for example, if you ask what someone likes about something, also ask them what they dislike.	**Avoid being led too far from the point** – keep the objectives of the interview clearly in your mind. Some diversions lead to areas of interest, but these are very rare.
Tackle difficult or sensitive areas with discretion – when sensitive issues are discussed, make sure you reassure the interviewee of the confidential nature of the process and of the maintenance of their anonymity.	**Avoid giving your own opinion** – if you do this it is likely that you will influence many answers that the interviewee gives.

Where face-to-face interviews are not possible, it may be feasible to undertake a telephone interview or Internet-based interview. These are particularly useful when it is impossible to travel in order to achieve a personal meeting. The options for data-recording are the same as with face-to-face interviews but, unless the interviewer is very skilled, interviews undertaken in these ways tend to be shorter and the information may be less 'deep' as a result of the lack of visual cues that can occur.

ELECTRONIC COMMUNICATION

The use of electronic communication (Twitter, Facebook, LinkedIn, chat rooms, discussion boards, contributions to blogs, email exchanges and so on) have also increased in popularity as potential ways for data to be gathered, particularly where 'physical' access to a sample of respondents is very difficult. One advantage is that time-zone constraints can be minimised and a 'conversation' between people in different regions of the world is more possible. Internet technology (for example, Skype) also makes it possible to undertake 'interviews' on a synchronous basis.

 ACTIVITY 7.2

RESEARCH USING DISCUSSION THREAD DATA

Imagine you are undertaking research in a small-sized organisation into pay and reward. You have interviewed the sales director, and she feels strongly that bonuses should be introduced as a way to motivate people to achieve discretionary effort. Because the organisation is very small, you want to access data from a wider range of sources, and your

friend suggested you might find some discussion about these issues online. Visit http://www.cipd.co.uk/community/subjects/subject?ForumID=39

On this site there are many discussions relating to pay and reward and you can scroll down or search for discussion threads that may be particularly relevant. Take a few minutes to scan their contents.

DISCUSSION QUESTIONS

1   What do you see as the advantages and disadvantages of obtaining qualitative data from one or more of these discussion threads?

FEEDBACK NOTES

A number of issues are raised by the use of electronic communications as part of a qualitative data-gathering strategy. With Internet-based research the issues of sample size become more problematic: to what extent can you estimate the extent to which the views of contributors may represent the wider population? Quite often you will find that discussion threads receive a high number of 'hits' but fewer contributions are made. On the other hand, you might argue that the people who contribute are most interested in the topic and may represent thoughtful and informed opinions. As discussed in Chapter 4, anonymity is not possible because the identity (although it may be an 'assumed identity') of contributors is shown within the discussion thread. However, as a supplement to other forms of data, perhaps as a way of informing the development of other data-gathering instruments, these forms of data can be very useful.

DIARIES AND BLOGS

Another way of exploring aspects of people's experience in a particular context is through the use of narratives and stories (Elliott 2005). Some form of diary, journal or blog, written by different participants in events, may well be worthwhile as part of a data-gathering strategy. These form something of a reflective record of an individual's or a group's actions over a defined period of time. A detailed record might be kept for just a few days (or even hours) or it might be undertaken less intensively over a period of weeks or months. 'Entries' can be written electronically, using pen and paper or spoken into an audio or video recorder.

ACTIVITY 7.3

DATA FROM BLOGS

Visit http://www.cipd.co.uk/blogs/ cipdbloggers/b/john_mcgurk/archive/ 2012/05/02/roy-hodgson-character-trumps-charisma.aspx and skim through the blog contribution and the comments associated with it. This is a blog posting about leadership and leadership styles. Imagine that your research is focused on examining 'authentic leadership' (Avolio and Gardner 2005) and you hope to identify different understandings of qualities that may affect leadership effectiveness.

DISCUSSION QUESTIONS

1   What advantages might the analysis of the content of one or more blogs focusing on leadership qualities offer as a source of data for your research? What other benefits might the use of data from some form of diary provide within a research project?

2   What problems might be experienced with the use of diaries or blogs as a method of data-gathering?

FEEDBACK NOTES

The use of blogs and other forms of journal can provide a different, and often useful, 'reflective' perspective on a situation or on issues relevant to your research and can be a helpful complement to other forms of data. This allows for some degree of 'triangulation' (see Chapter 5). In addition, the use of diaries, blogs or other forms of journal might provide information about events that it is not possible to observe, but which can provide for more 'immediacy' than would be possible through an interview.

Like all other methods of data-gathering, of course, there are a number of issues that must be taken into account, particularly if you are asking people in leadership positions to keep a diary or blog specifically for your project. Not all potential bloggers are able to communicate systematically in a written or an oral form and many people are not natural diarists; it is likely that they may 'give up' along the way or only turn to the blog in (untypical) moments of exasperation or exuberance. Therefore, it is important to keep in touch and to encourage them – to reinforce how important it is to understand their perceptions of the particular situation or context. Linked with this is the issue that blogging is time-consuming and people should not be pressured into maintaining the process. Second, where the journal process is 'intentional', it is important that those completing one are clear about what to record. It may be that you want them to note down any reflections, feelings and motivations in response to what is happening in their lives. However, it is more likely that it is appropriate to provide guidance about what should be recorded, stemming from the research questions that are being answered.

A third area of difficulty is the inhibition people may feel about recording what they 'really' think about things or how they 'really' spend their time at work. Data confidentiality is not possible on the Internet. The final issue to bear in mind is that of representativeness. How can you be sure that the weeks or months during which your blogger was writing was a 'typical' period? Choice of timeframes for the period you choose to draw down data for analysis is important.

FOCUS GROUPS

An enduringly popular way of gathering qualitative data in HR projects is through focus groups. Focus groups are a form of group interview where a process of dialogue and discussion between participants about a particular topic provides the data to help you answer your research questions.

ACTIVITY 7.4

OBTAINING DATA ABOUT FLEXIBLE WORKING

Imagine that a large organisation has asked you to research into the awareness of employees to its existing Internet Use and Misuse Policy and to explore views and opinions about the possibility of 'outlawing' social media activities during working hours. The organisation has agreed that focus groups would be an appropriate way of gathering these data.

DISCUSSION QUESTIONS

1   How many focus groups would you plan to hold and who should participate in them?

2   How would you decide what questions/issues to ask about?

3   What key skills would be required to facilitate the group(s) in an effective way?

4   How would you record the data from the focus groups?

FEEDBACK NOTES

Focus groups provide an opportunity to find out about a range of attitudes and values to different topics (Krueger and Casey 2000). You might feel that, if your aim is to familiarise yourself with a range of attitudes towards the use and abuse of Internet and social networking sites in relation to work, two focus groups would be sufficient. However, it is possible that people's opinions may depend, in part, on their age, the level of their familiarisation with 'Web 2.0' applications and their role or position within the organisation. Therefore it might be necessary to organise a larger number of groups, each with between 6 and 12 participants. One focus group will provide interesting data but would be insufficient as a 'sole method' to ensure data validity and reliability.

It will also be necessary to make sure that each group consists of similar kinds of people, with enough in common that they will not feel inhibited about contributing their views but with enough differences that a range of perspectives may be represented. In this case it would be important to ensure that people with different roles and contexts are included. The inclusion of men and women from different age ranges would also ensure an inclusive approach to data collection.

To find out people's views it would be necessary to pose a sequence of questions that stimulate and encourage a flow of discussion. The questions would need to be fairly broad ranging, but also relevant to the particular research purpose. Although you are seeking to explore opinions and feelings, it is also important to remember that participants may have personal sensitivities and these must be handled carefully. You will also be seeking to obtain data that are specific and detailed, so it is important to encourage people to avoid talking only in generalisations and to explore why they may hold the opinions that they do.

To achieve this you are likely to want to pose about six–seven questions, which move from the more general to the more specific. In a semi-structured interview the flow of conversation may be quite flexible, but the group nature of a focus group suggests that the order of your questions is maintained each time. As facilitator you would also be able to probe, steer and legitimise seemingly 'unpopular' viewpoints. The prevention of some individuals over-dominating the opinions of the group is another key issue.

Recording data from focus groups also needs careful thought and preparation. The energy and concentration you will require for facilitating the group is likely to mean that you will be unable to take many notes. Some people ask a colleague to join the group in the role of note-taker. Others obtain permission to audio-record the discussion, although, if only one person does not consent, you have a problem and transcribing focus group recordings is a difficult process. Another way to ensure some initial record of the data is to use flipcharts, white boards and so on. The data contained on these can then act as a trigger for you to produce a fuller account of the discussion as soon as possible after the end of the group meeting, and certainly within 24 hours of it.

In addition to face-to-face focus groups, it is also possible to organise 'virtual' focus groups, making use of Internet or video-conferencing facilities (Stewart et al 2007). As a method of research within HR these have the advantage of being quite 'acceptable' for many organisational stakeholders. There are, however, disadvantages as well as advantages of the method and these are summarised in Table 7.3.

Table 7.3 Advantages and disadvantages of focus groups

Advantages	Disadvantages
They are cheaper than individual interviews (in terms of the time-cost) and can generate large quantities of data.	The large quantity of data may be difficult to summarise and to analyse.
Interaction between researcher and participant allows for clarification, probing and follow-up questions.	The facilitator may influence the participants too much and so affect the opinions they express.
Data can be collected in the participants' own words and take account of deeper meanings and interpretations.	There may be undue influence of some participants over others, affecting the quality of the data.
In some circumstances, more than one topic can be explored in each session.	The small number of participants (relative to the size of the research population) leads to concerns about generalisability of the data.
'Snowballing' of ideas can occur as participants respond to the contributions of others in the group.	The 'group dynamics' of the session may lead the researcher to attribute more significance to the data than is actually warranted.
Participants can feel empowered, especially in action-orientated organisational research.	A 'polarisation effect' may occur where people's attitudes become more extreme as a result of group discussion.

(Neuman 2011, Saunders et al 2012)

To maximise the effectiveness of the focus group approach to data-gathering, it is important to take some process issues into account (Stewart et al 2007). These include:

- Carefully work out the boundaries of the topic you wish to be discussed. This must link closely with your research questions/objectives.
- Think carefully about who should be included (sample selection). Ensure that the sample will be appropriate to provide insights to a range of perspectives.
- Facilitating focus groups requires a high level of interpersonal skills. If you doubt your abilities here, you could ask someone else to facilitate and you could be the note-taker.
- Think ahead to how you will ultimately analyse the data. Allow decisions about analysis to influence how you record the data from the focus groups.
- Generate and pre-test/pilot the questions you propose to ask. As part of this process you can plan how to keep the discussion focused without leading it in an obvious way.
- Introduce the purpose of the focus group. This should be clear at the beginning, which is also an opportunity to communicate appropriate 'ground rules' and process issues.
- Build a good rapport with the group. It is important that people think that they can speak freely to each other as well as in front of you.
- Ensure that everyone has an equal opportunity to contribute to the discussion. It is important to make clear that all contributions are valued.

- Clarify feedback arrangements. Be clear about whether you propose to feed back the results of the focus groups to the participants and communicate this at the time.

SAMPLE SELECTION FOR QUALITATIVE RESEARCH

A key issue that has been raised many times already in this and previous chapters is that of data quality – validity and reliability. This is a particular issue with qualitative data, which is why the choice of participants (the sample selection process) must be clearly thought through and justified within your research report.

Sampling is the deliberate choice of a number of people to represent a greater population. In a very small organisation it may be possible to gather data from everyone, but in most cases it is necessary to choose a sample of people from whom information will be obtained.

There are two main ways of determining an appropriate sample. Probability sampling involves determining a sample that is statistically representative of the research population as a whole and so should reflect the characteristics of the population. This means that, provided you ask exactly the same questions to everyone in the sample, you should be confident that you can generalise the conclusions that you derive from the data to the wider population. Research enquiries that use a quantitative approach are likely to adopt probability sampling – more information about this is contained in Chapter 9.

Most qualitative data-gathering, however, operates from a basis of non-probability sampling, which is considered now.

 Determining an appropriate sample

CASE ILLUSTRATION 7.4

Researching into perceptions of professionalism

Amir was an HR student who wished to investigate the different understandings of 'professionalism' among HR practitioners in different roles within different types of organisation. He wanted to find out about the perspectives of those within HR functions working in different areas such as 'service centres', business partner roles and HR executive-level positions. Amir's reading around the subject of professionalism in general and the HR function in particular highlighted a range of ambiguities. He

decided to undertake semi-structured interviews with people who worked in HR.

Discussion Questions

1   How might you go about accessing interviewees if you were undertaking this project? In your answer, decide who you would include in your sample.

2   How many interviews might constitute a 'sufficient' sample size to explore the different perceptions of HR practitioners about HR as a profession?

FEEDBACK NOTES

Amir chose two different approaches to gathering his data. He first determined the criteria of those that he wished to interview: namely those who had been employed in an HR role for at least two years. He had to use his network of contacts and organisations to identify people who met this criterion and then he set about making contact with them. Amir had a target of ten interviews and, through his network, managed to make contact with individuals from two different organisations (one from the public sector and one from the private sector) who met the criteria. However, a number of those that he contacted were not able to agree to an interview, often as a result of pressure of work. Therefore, Amir revised his sampling approach and used snowball sampling, whereby people he approached were willing to refer him to other possible interviewees they knew from their local CIPD network who they knew also met his criteria.

There are different ways of tackling non-probability sampling, and Amir's approach involved purposive sampling (associated with criteria for selection in the sample), whose perspectives may typify important viewpoints pertinent to the research questions. These are described more fully below (Swanson et al 2005)

NON-PROBABILITY SAMPLING

- **Accidental sampling:** this is where the sample is chosen for reasons of convenience or practicability. Many students implicitly operate an accidental sampling approach to any observation that they undertake as part of their data-gathering process. The advantages are that it is convenient and that time and expense trying to undertake a more representative sample selection process are avoided. However, it is possible that the data may not be representative of the 'wider picture'.
- **Purposive sampling:** this involves choosing people whose experience and perspectives are deemed to be important to the investigation. There are different ways of choosing a purposive sample. First, you may identify key informants, people who have specialised and unique knowledge and experience of the issue you are trying to find out about. Many HR projects involve a key informant interview with the HR director, for example, or someone with particular knowledge and expertise in the area of the investigation.
  Second, it is possible to undertake a sliced sample whereby respondents are chosen because they occupy positions at different parts of the organisation. 'Slicing' is possible horizontally (a selection of middle managers from a range of different functions) and/or vertically (respondents from the top, middle and bottom of the hierarchy). Third, snowball sampling involves finding new people from which to gather data on the recommendation of those already included within the sample.

Each of these approaches has the advantage that you feel confident that the data gathered will reflect perspectives that are pertinent to the research being undertaken. However, the people and situations from which you gather data may not be 'typical', something which is worth exploring during the data-gathering process (by asking people how typical they feel they are) and when formulating your conclusions.

- **Quota sampling:** this involves choosing a sample that reflects as far as possible the diversity of the wider research population in the same proportions. Thus, if you know that the organisation you are researching has a proportion of 40:60 men to women, your sample would seek to ensure that you included 4 women for every 6 men. Similarly, if you know that the age distribution of 'under 30s', '30–45s' and '46–60s' is 40:40:20, you would try to choose a sample that reflected this proportionately.

  The advantage of this approach is that you can indicate it is broadly representative. However, it still does not mean that every employee had an equal chance of being included. Quota sampling can also be applied to observations (Neuman 2011). For example, if you are observing interactions or other management processes, it may be important to be sure to include all the different times of the day. Where different locations are involved (for example, in production, administration, reception areas, and so on), it may also be important to observe in a proportionately representative way, at different locations.

There are, therefore, a range of processes that can be used to select a sample within a qualitative approach to data-gathering. It is also important to determine how big the sample size should be. With probability sampling there are statistical 'rules' about sample size, but with qualitative enquiries things are less clear and informal considerations will often be quite important. The ideal sample size occurs when new 'cases' (either respondents or observations) cease to add new information or insights. This is sometimes referred to as data saturation and this is a matter of judgement. It is also important to be able to justify the lower limit to the size of a sample. If the characteristics of the sample are fairly consistent, and the research question is rather a limited one, a smaller-sized sample may be adequate. Where the research questions are broader and the sample is characterised by greater levels of variety, the sample would have to be larger.

Non-probability approaches to sample selection as a whole have the advantage of flexibility and are often more organisationally acceptable. They also provide opportunities for collaboration within a problem-solving and action-orientated project. The data that they generate provide scope for interpretation and judgement during the process of analysis. However, the disadvantages of them must be taken into account when you explain and justify your approach to data collection.

MAKING SENSE OF THE DATA

Unlike quantitative data-gathering, with qualitative data there is a close link between the processes of data-gathering and initial analysis (Burnard et al 2008). This is because the process of 'writing up' notes following from qualitative data-gathering processes provides an opportunity to reflect on and develop the research enquiry. Jankowicz (2005) suggests a series of questions to help with initial evaluation and analysis of qualitative data that can also 'feed in' to further data-gathering on an incremental basis:

- How do the data compare with the other data already obtained? Are there any apparent trends? What picture seems to be emerging?
- What concepts and research from the literature seem relevant to the data?
- What feelings were engendered by the data-gathering process just undertaken – does the information 'ring true'?
- In what ways might initial impressions formed by this information be 'checked out'?
- How much did you as researcher influence what was said? How significant was this influence? Should anything be discounted as a result?
- What unexpected information was gathered? How can its relevance be checked within the ongoing data-gathering process?

SUMMARY

- Qualitative data-gathering forms a part of many organisationally focused HR research enquiries. It may involve activities such as observation and participation, one-to-one interviews or conversations, electronically posted information, individual accounts, blogs, diaries of activities and focus groups.
- With qualitative data, the organisational context can be taken into account and data focused on particular themes and issues can be generated. Data relevant to 'real time' activity as well as past events can be obtained.
- Qualitative data-gathering processes must endeavour to limit bias on the part of the 'subjects' as well as the researcher by clarifying what information is to be obtained and how it will be recorded.
- Observation and/or participation in organisational processes provide an opportunity to obtain 'direct' data about organisational features and perspectives. A range of options for observation and participation of behaviours and processes in the workplace is possible, ranging from complete participation to complete observation.
- Particular care must be taken to ensure data confidentiality The ethical implications of observation or the use of data communicated through electronic media must be taken into account.
- Semi-structured interviews are a common way of gathering qualitative data. These require careful preparation and execution. Key skills for research interviews include: asking open questions, active listening, using silence, using appropriate language, using non-verbal communication and steering the interview.
- There are advantages and disadvantages to gathering qualitative data through audio-recording or through some form of note-taking. Permission to record activities and conversations must always be obtained.
- Where face-to-face interviews are not possible, data may also be obtained through email conversations, Web 2.0 applications and diary entries. These types of data allow people to reflect on their feelings and experiences but lack the face-to-face interaction that is possible in interviews, focus groups and forms of participant observation.
- Focus groups are a form of group interview where data are gathered through a facilitated process of dialogue and discussion about a particular topic. One focus group on its own is never sufficient to generate reliable data.

- Focus groups are often organisationally acceptable ways of gathering data as they are more time-effective than individual interviews and can involve and empower participants within a problem-solving or action-orientated process. However, they can also lead to a polarisation of opinions among participants and the data generated may be hard to analyse.
- Most sample selection processes, for qualitative research, involve non-probability sampling. Approaches to non-probability sampling include: accidental sampling, quota sampling and purposive sampling. Purposive sampling can include the selection of key informants, 'sliced' samples and 'snowball' sampling techniques.
- The nature of the research questions and the homogeneity of the research population will influence decisions about minimum sample size. The upper limit of sample size is a matter of judgement and is reached when it appears new 'cases' are not generating any 'new' or unexpected insights.
- The process of initial data recording and analysis can lead to an incremental development of the research project.

 Self-test questions

REVIEW AND REFLECT

1 What is purposive sampling?

a) deciding about the people you want to include before you have worked out your research questions

b) ensuring that your research sample provides an equal chance for all members of the research population to be selected

c) choosing a sample of respondents who are most likely to provide relevant information

d) asking your friends to recommend others to form part of your sample

2 Which of the following best describes a qualitative interview?

a) the researcher seeks rich, detailed answers

b) 'wandering' away from the topic is expected

c) the questions are standardised

d) the interview can be undertaken in ten minutes

3 Why is it important to prepare an interview guide or schedule before you undertake a semi-structured interview?

a) so that you can work out the statistical inferences from the answers

b) to make it easy to analyse the data using a computer software program

c) to increase the reliability of your research

d) so that data from different interviewees will be relevant to your research questions

4 What is a 'probing question'?

a) a question that asks indirectly about people's opinions or feelings

b) a question that encourages the interviewee to say more in response to your original question

c)   a way of finding out sensitive or highly personal information

d)   a way of summarising what someone has said before moving on to the next topic

5   Which of the following is a characteristic of a focus group?

a)   it has two or three participants

b)   it enables you to study decision-making processes in a group situation

c)   it is a way of get people to clarify your research methodology for you

d)   it is a form of group interview involving a facilitated process of dialogue and discussion about a particular topic

6   What is the role of the facilitator in a focus group?

a)   to evaluate the performance of the group relative to the questions being answered

b)   to encourage discussion and keep the conversation 'on track'

c)   to sit apart from the group to observe the behaviour of different members

d)   to ask leading questions

7   Which of the following is an advantage of focus groups?

a)   the facilitator cannot control how the discussion proceeds

b)   they can produce a large volume of data that represents a range of different experiences and opinions

c)   they show how reality is socially constructed

d)   they can lead to a polarisation of opinions among participants

Review questions

1   How likely is it that some form of semi-structured or in-depth interviews would be an acceptable form of data-gathering within the organisation?

2   What opportunities may exist within the organisation(s) in which your research is to be based for the use of some form of participant observation? To what extent would such approaches to data-gathering help to answer your research questions?

3   Who might be 'key informants' for your research project? What

access arrangements would be necessary to incorporate them into your sample?

4   To what extent might qualitative data from some Web 2.0 applications contribute to the achievement of your research objectives or questions?

5   What sample selection process is most appropriate for your project? How confident are you (and your tutor or supervisor) that your sample will be sufficient to provide data of good quality?

Questions for reflection

REVIEW AND REFLECT

This final part of the chapter enables you to reflect about your professional development and develop your skills and knowledge. This will enable you to build your confidence and credibility, track your learning, see your progress and demonstrate your achievements.

Strengths and weaknesses

1   How confident are you of your skills as an in-depth research interviewer, or facilitator of focus groups? How might you further develop your skills in these areas?

2   How clear are you about the purpose of the different types of data-gathering you plan to undertake? How clearly developed are the themes to be explored? How clearly are these themes derived from your literature review, other data-gathering activities, your research questions, and so on?

3   How well developed are your skills as a note-taker? What system can you develop to ensure that any notes you take while engaged in

qualitative data-gathering are formulated accurately and in detail?

4   If you plan to audio-record some of your data, how equipped are you to subsequently transcribe the dialogue into a written form? What arrangements might you make for this?

Being a practitioner-researcher

5   What organisational and ethical issues need to be considered if you decide to undertake some form of participant observation? What might be the best way to take this forward?

6   How aware are you of your own personal 'bias' in what information you expect to gather? What steps can you take to limit the influence of your personal perspective on the data that is generated?

7   What steps will you take to maximise the confidentiality of the data you gather and the anonymity of your 'subjects'?

EXPLORE FURTHER

Web links

There are some excellent web-based resources relating to qualitative data-gathering and analysis. These include:

http://onlineqda.hud.ac.uk/

http://hsc.uwe.ac.uk/dataanalysis/qualIssues.asp

http://www.learnhigher.ac.uk/analysethis/main/qualitative.html

Reading

Other excellent books that focus on some of the issues explored in this chapter include:

Bryman, A. and Bell, E. (2007) *Business research methods*. Oxford: Oxford University Press.

Elliott, J. (2005) *Using narrative in social research: qualitative and quantitative approaches*. London: Sage.

Krueger, R.A. and Casey, M.A. (2000) *Focus groups: a practical guide for applied research*. Thousand Oaks, CA: Sage.

Robson, C. (2011) *Real world research: a resource for social scientists and practitioner-researchers*. Oxford: Wiley.

Saunders, M., Lewis, P. and Thornhill, A. (2012) *Research methods for business students*. Harlow: Pearson Education.

Swanson, R.A., Holton, E.F. and Holton, E. (2005) *Research in organizations: foundations and methods of inquiry*. San Francisco, CA: Berrett-Koehler.

CHAPTER 8

Analysing Qualitative Data

CHAPTER OUTLINE

- How to use this chapter
- The process of qualitative analysis
- Categorising and coding data
- Different approaches to analysis
- Data display processes
- Evaluating explanations and formulating conclusions
- Use of software for qualitative data analysis
- Writing up your analysis
- Summary
- Review and reflect
- Explore further

LEARNING OUTCOMES

This chapter should help you to:

- work out an appropriate way to analyse your qualitative data

- identify themes and categories emerging from the data

- group different items or units of data and examine potential relationships between them

- evaluate the trustworthiness of your data-gathering and analysis process

- explore alternative explanations and formulate credible conclusions

- find out more about computer-assisted qualitative data analysis software in relation to your project objectives.

HOW TO USE THIS CHAPTER

This chapter aims to help you find ways of **analysing**, rather than merely describing, qualitative data. Because the processes of data-gathering, data description and data analysis are so integrated, it is best to read this chapter before you start your data-gathering process. However, if you have already gathered a huge volume of data and are now wondering what to do to make sense of the information, this chapter is also for you. Many practitioner-researchers, especially those involved with investigating a business issue and producing a business research report, find that they do not need to make use of any specialised software. Therefore the section concerned with software is placed towards the end of the chapter. However, if you think you will make use of some qualitative data analysis software, it would be worth reading this section first, before you get started on the data-gathering process.

ACTIVITY 8.1

IMPLEMENTING CHANGES TO PENSION PLANNING

In 2012 the Government introduced a range of pension reforms which became known as 'auto-enrolment'. Automatic enrolment into pensions was phased in from October 2012, starting with larger employers. It applies to UK workers aged between 22 and state pension age who have earnings of at least £8,105 (value in 2012/13). Employers can auto-enrol employees into their own 'qualifying' scheme or the Government's National Employment Savings Trust (NEST) and minimum contribution levels apply.

This process changes the responsibilities of those with responsibility for pay and rewards in organisations as it introduces a regulatory requirement to automatically enrol 'eligible jobholders' and to communicate their right to 'opt out' and respond to opt-out and opt-in requests, process contributions and maintain records, and so on. This leads to a number of practical issues around payroll and HR technology:

- HR and payroll systems, employee data and supporting processes have to distinguish between the different categories of employees (eligible jobholders, non-eligible jobholders, entitled workers, and so on) to ensure employers satisfy their duties for each category.
- Pension enrolment, opt-out and contribution refund processes have to be put in place to process information to pension provider systems.

- HR and payroll systems need to cope with the pensions implications of flexible benefits or salary sacrifice schemes and so on.

Imagine that you work in a large organisation that wishes to get prepared for the auto-enrolment process. Your organisation recognises that the HR department will need to establish a range of new systems to ensure that employees and managers understand what must be done to minimise confusion and maximise the benefits of the process. Work processes will have to be reorganised and this will present a range of challenges. Your manager has suggested that this will be a great topic for your research report. She wants you to explore the issues from the perspective of employees (how much do they know and understand about auto-enrolment?) and the HR function and to identify equipment, systems and communication issues that will need to be addressed.

To gauge the issues that are likely to arise, you have interviewed a selection of employees, from different operational areas of the organisation as well as those responsible for pensions and the HR systems experts in your HR function. You are taking a qualitative approach and you have undertaken semi-structured audio-recorded interviews, each lasting for about an hour. You have also spent time with the pensions staff to observe and record how they currently go about their tasks. As a result of this you have amassed a huge volume of data, stored on memory sticks, audio-recording devices and in notes that you made for yourself at the time as well as notes you have made about what you saw and heard when you were working with the pensions specialists.

DISCUSSION QUESTIONS

1   What steps might you take to make sense of this data to achieve your research objectives? Identify what you will 'do' with the audio recordings, notes, screen shots, and so on.

2   List four or five problems you might encounter when formulating 'objective' conclusions on the basis of the data that you have.

FEEDBACK NOTES

There are many activities that you might undertake to 'make sense' of the data you have collected. The main challenge, at the start, is its sheer volume. The first challenge of qualitative data analysis is one of information management. Some way or another must be found to establish a sense of control and identification of what is 'in there'. Once that has been achieved, it is possible to identify and explore key themes or patterns that the data may suggest. Only then will it be possible to draw conclusions.

You may have identified a number of other problems with analysis of qualitative data. Data overload is a common challenge. Another anxiety is that data that are analysed 'early on', when the researcher is relatively 'fresh', receives more careful attention than information that is considered later in the process. In addition, you might worry that you never know when you have 'enough' material. Perhaps some of your interviewees are too embarrassed about what they feel is their 'ignorance' of pensions issues and so have not really provided honest information about important gaps in their knowledge (or their existing pensions arrangements). If you have heard a range of different experiences and opinions expressed by interviewees, can you be sure that all of their accounts are equally 'reliable'?

A further challenge, although it can also be seen as an opportunity, is that there is no 'one right way' of going about the analysis of qualitative data. Whereas with quantitative data analysis (see Chapter 10) there are procedures and processes that provide some degree of confidence in the conclusions, there is no such consensus with the analysis of qualitative data. There are, however, different approaches that are more or less appropriate for research projects with different objectives, and the purpose of this chapter is to outline some of them.

THE PROCESS OF QUALITATIVE ANALYSIS

FROM DATA-GATHERING TO DATA ANALYSIS

The idea of data analysis can be a difficult one for first-time practitioner-researchers. Gathering data often takes longer than expected and so the time available for analysis, particularly with a submission date looming, may be very limited. However, analysis of data is fundamental to the quality of the outcomes of your research project. **Data analysis involves more than describing what people said or what you saw.** Indeed, raw data, on its own, has only limited value.

Analysis is a **process of thought**. Analysis enables you to understand the nature of what you are investigating, the relationships between different variables in the situation and the likely outcomes of particular actions or interventions. Analysis, therefore, involves using data to find answers to your research questions by considering issues such as what? why? and how? If the answers to your research questions are to be trustworthy, it is important that you treat the evidence fairly and you are careful to include all possible interpretations, rather than the one you (or your project sponsor) would prefer.

To achieve this you need to: understand and assess the information that you have; reduce it to manageable proportions; abstract information from the different sources of data that you have acquired; explore key themes and patterns; and then develop and evaluate a range of alternative explanations from which you can formulate conclusions. This process is illustrated in Figure 8.1.

Figure 8.1 Doing qualitative data analysis

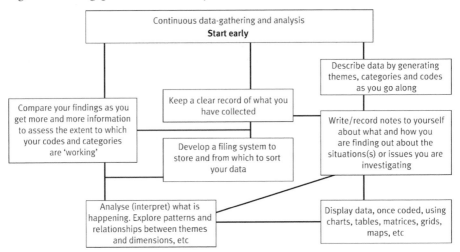

Trust issues in different organisations

CASE ILLUSTRATION 8.1

Jeanna was a full-time student undertaking a master's-level project. She had become intrigued by newspaper stories suggesting a 'crisis of trust' in many large organisations. She decided to investigate the extent to which people had lost trust in the leaders of their work organisations. Jeanna had undertaken a work placement in a large private sector 'blue chip' company, and the HR manager was keen to support any data-gathering process that Jeanna wanted to undertake for her master's dissertation. In addition, she was working part-time for a 'fast food' organisation, and the area manager also indicated her support for Jeanna to gather data. Jeanna decided that she would interview people at different levels of these organisations and, in addition, she wanted to find out if the age, gender or 'functional area' in which people worked might influence their sense of trust. Specifically, she decided to undertake semi-structured interviews with senior managers and staff at different levels to allow for the emergence of key factors and interrelationships that impact on people's trust in their leaders. She wanted to achieve a cross-section of interviewees to provide insights from different organisational 'positions' and contexts.

One challenge that Jeanna faced was to decide what questions to ask her interviewees. As a result of her literature search she identified some possible survey questions, but these were rather restricted and not suitable for her qualitative data intentions. However, after some diligent searching on Internet search engines she found two dissertations undertaken by other research students in the USA and was able to get some ideas for questions from here. She also felt that this would enable her to compare her findings with those of others who had undertaken research in a similar area. However, she was not sure how 'productive' these questions would be and wanted to 'try them out' with people other than her intended interviewees.

Discussion Questions

1   To achieve her research objectives, what sampling strategy should Jeanna adopt?

2   What are the strengths and weaknesses of Jeanna's approach to formulating interview questions?

3   How might Jeanna go about making sure her interview questions would be 'productive'?

FEEDBACK NOTES

Jeanna proposed to undertake her interviews in two different organisations, something that would enable her to compare responses 'across cases' as well as within each organisation. Because she also wanted to assess the influence of other factors such as age, gender and area of work on matters of trust, she needed to undertake a 'purposive' approach to sample selection whereby she would make sure that she had at least one person from each organisation in each of her 'categories'. In this way the purposive choice of individuals to participate in the research would affect the analysis process and her likely analysis process affected the sample selection process.

As indicated in Chapter 7, two broadly different approaches are possible when establishing the questions to be asked in any semi-structured interview situation. One approach is to start with a wide basis of general questions, often generated from the literature, for the first few interviews and then to build up subsequent questions in an incremental way, taking into account information from the first few interviews. The advantage of this is that it can more adequately reflect the reality of what is being investigated as it 'takes seriously' the meanings and interpretations articulated by respondents. An alternative approach, which Jeanna found herself drawn to, was to make use of questions that had already been used in other research. In this way the researcher might feel confident that the data-gathering and analysis process would build on and add to the knowledge already available from the work of other researchers. The choice of approach will be influenced, at least in part, by the purpose of the research. Exploratory research is likely to use an incremental approach 'from scratch'. Research that sets out to probe more deeply into an issue about which there is already some general knowledge might make more use of existing categories and variables in making sense of data. These different approaches are referred to as 'grounded theory' and 'analytic induction' (Bryman and Bell 2007).

An additional thing for Jeanna to undertake was a piloting process of her interview questions. Here you might suggest that she 'try out' her questions on people who are similar to those in her intended sample group. As far as possible she needed to ensure that her questions were as meaningful to older and younger people, those who occupy senior positions and those who fulfil other occupations. In this case Jeanna got two of her course colleagues to agree to participate in a piloting process and also made contact with associates from her part-time employment that she knew well (and had decided to eliminate from her actual research sample). The piloting process led to a reconsideration of the wording of one or two of her questions, and it also enabled her to 'polish' her own research interviewing and note-taking skills.

THE ROLE OF DATA ANALYSIS IN QUALITATIVE RESEARCH

Qualitative data analysis is different in many ways from the analysis of quantitative data. Most people who undertake quantitative data analysis are engaged in a process intended to present their findings as **facts**. However, a key assumption of the interpretevist 'world-view', within which most qualitative research is undertaken, is the intention to present research findings as **interpretations** of what is happening in different contexts or from different 'positions'. In addition, whereas quantitative data analysis is often a linear, standardised, staged set of procedures, qualitative data analysis is a continuous process, closely linked with ongoing data-gathering. The methods used in qualitative data analysis are less standardised. Since analysis is the search for explanation and understanding, it is reasonable to begin the analysis process early on while data are still being collected. Therefore, evidence and concepts are 'blended' and assessed for plausibility on an ongoing basis and the analysis process is iterative rather than being a fully distinct 'last stage' of a project. There are no unambiguous procedures about 'how to' undertake an initial analysis of qualitative data but three key steps are required, which are:

- to understand and assess the information you have collected
- to reduce the information to manageable proportions
- to explore key themes and patterns.

Different people tackle the initial process of understanding and assessing the information in different ways. One person might produce a summary of the information that has been gathered in note form. Another might prefer a 'spider diagram' or some other form of chart or table. However it is undertaken, the process of initial analysis involves asking 'what is the essence of what this data is communicating?' and 'what seem to be the dimensions of the issues?'

This process of questioning the data leads to the next stage: that of reducing the data to manageable proportions and making judgements about what is there.

This can be a daunting process because volumes of data that are generated by qualitative research are always large. As part of the data reduction process it is a good idea to undertake a 'write-up' of your notes in summary form. Such a summary forms part of the analytical process. It should occur close to the time that the data-gathering event occurred and is, in many ways, a 'memo to self' about what the data contains and your thoughts and ideas about it. In this way it is important to summarise 'what was said' but also to include your own reflections and thoughts, remembering to make a clear distinction in the notes between 'your thoughts' and what was actually said. A template for the production of a summary/memo is included as Table 8.1.

Table 8.1 Template for qualitative data summary/memo

Data for summary	My reflections
Who/what was involved? Names/events Date Time Location	Who else might be a useful source of similar data? How might the date, time and location have influenced the data-gathering process and the information obtained?
What issues were covered?	What issues were omitted and why? Were any 'unplanned' issues included? What prompted this?
What data of relevance to the research questions were obtained?	What was surprising about the information?
Were new concepts or issues suggested?	What are the implications for subsequent data collection?

Having summarised the data and reflected on it, you can then read through your notes carefully with a view to devising categories for the data, and then it is possible to assign a code to each category, in the form of abbreviations or short words or phrases that you will recognise and remember. Having coded chunks of your data, you are able to look for possible relationships and patterns within and between different categories. This process, which is cyclical and iterative, allows the 'testing' of alternative explanations about what it going on. Figure 8.2 provides an indicative overview of the steps in the process of qualitative data analysis.

Figure 8.2 The qualitative data analysis process

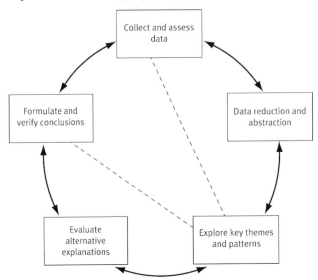

Although there are no standardised 'rules' for qualitative data analysis, Silverman (2011) provides five 'tips' for an effective process:

1   Start early – don't wait until all your interviews or observations have been completed.

2   Try out different approaches to analysing the data – find what 'works for you'.

3   Avoid thinking you have 'the answer' or 'a hypothesis' too soon – keep exploring and keep an open mind for as long as possible.

4   Don't get 'obsessed' with one or two productive (or 'telling') interviews or cases so that you neglect what other information you have. It is important to analyse **all** your data in a fair and thorough way.

5   Focus your early attention intensively on a small (and appropriate) part of your overall data set. Allow yourself to look for sequences and 'nuances' within the data and then expand your focus onto the data set as a whole.

CATEGORISING AND CODING DATA

Coding is at the very core of qualitative data analysis. A code is a label designed to 'catch the meaning' of part of your data. Coding is the process of identifying themes, ideas and categories from within your data set so that you can make comparisons and looking for regularities and different characteristics of the situation you are investigating. A category is a grouping of behaviours, descriptions or particular events that have shared characteristics. Remember that coding is an iterative process. The initial codes that you devise are likely to result from a range of different features of your project. Some may represent categories that are derived from your research aims and objectives; others may be issues you have decided to look out for as a result of a review of the literature and will be reflected in the question structure that you may have used. However, as your research proceeds you might include new codes that result from your reflections about what you have heard or seen when you produced initial notes following (say) an interview.

Once you have established some codes you can 'mark up' and code your data so that you can easily locate material relating to the same issue when you need to. Codes are nothing more than labels that you attach to chunks of text that represent a 'unit of meaning'. The size of 'chunks' of data that you associate with codes may vary considerably. It might be specific words that are coded, it might be a phrase or it may be a paragraph of your notes. Often it is a combination of the three. It is also possible (and often highly desirable) that one 'chunk' of data may be categorised in more than one way and therefore assigned more than one code. There are four levels or types of code:

- **Descriptive codes:** these tend to be the first (and almost obvious) codes that you assign. In many ways they are your route to summarising what is in the text. Neuman (2011) refers to them as 'manifest' or 'obvious' codes. They reflect what is going on 'on the surface'. These codes describe features and may be useful to you later as you undertake some comparisons within the data. In addition you may notice that specific terms, keywords or phrases seem to recur within all or part of the data and you may choose to code these for further analysis.
- **Organisational (demographic) codes or attributes:** these are very similar to descriptive codes: they are your way of grouping together data/respondents depending on (say) their age grouping, the type of organisation they work for, their occupation, and so on. These are very obvious but also very useful as they provide a basis for you to compare the extent to which these 'variables' seem to influence different experiences and interpretations within the people or organisations that comprise your sample.
- **Analytical codes:** these are generated as you go beyond an initial categorisation. They relate to what may be happening 'beneath the surface'. Such codes may be based on themes, topics, concepts or ideas that you identify within the data. Neuman (2011) refers to these as latent codes and Silverman (2011) refers to them as interpretive codes. These 'second level' codes require judgement and interpretation as you set about assessing the data for meaning as well as for description.

Descriptive and analytical codes are very important and, having identified them, it is important to assess whether some of them can be grouped together and whether some of them are also part of a 'hierarchy' where you can identify one main code and then a series of 'sub-codes' in what might look like a 'family tree'. Indeed, some qualitative researchers sometimes refer to 'parent' and 'child' codes and others refer to 'tree codes':

- **Axial codes:** sometimes called **relationship codes** or **pattern codes**, are a further useful level of analysis. Here you are looking for potential connections or relationships between or within categories and sub-categories. You would not usually assign these codes until you have identified some descriptive and analytical codes and really started to make sense of the data. When assigning relationship codes you would read your data set to find all the examples of the relationship you think might exist. Each time you find it you allocate it your chosen relationship code.

Shaping the future

CASE ILLUSTRATION 8.2

Extracts from CIPD. (2011) *Shaping the Future: Final Report*. With the permission of the publisher, the Chartered Institute of Personnel and Development, London (www.cipd.co.uk).

Shaping the Future research programme

The importance of sustaining organisation's people, financial, environmental and societal contribution over time needs to be a top priority for HR and business leaders. We designed a longitudinal, action research programme, using 'deep-dive' case study methods, semi-structured interviews and focus groups to examine the drivers of performance for the long term. We examine the case studies as complex, adaptive systems (Ford 2008), learning from experience, improvising and responding innovatively to both internal and external pressures. It is important to take both the internal and external context into account to appreciate the real business environment (Damanpour and Gopalakrishnan 1998). Dopson et al (2008) say that many studies acknowledge the role of context in change but for this research it is a particularly important variable of study.

An extensive literature review indicated that the drivers of sustainable organisation performance can be categorised within three main themes: leadership, engagement and organisational development, and these therefore initially guided phase 1 of our research. In the intervening period between phases 1 and 2, we maintained contact with our case study

organisations to follow them on their journeys. In both phases we conducted semi-structured interviews and focus groups in each organisation, taking a 'deep slice' by talking to people at different levels and across functions.

Analysing the data

The extensive data we collected across the six case studies through 47 interviews and 15 focus groups was analysed systematically. We developed a coding process linked to the existing six themes from phase 1 and expanded the coding system when we saw evidence of further, emergent themes. We remained open to data that both supported and contradicted the importance of the themes. Having coded the data, we then examined it through a process of discussion facilitated by an external partner to the research team, who challenged and probed our themes. Within the broad areas of engagement, organisational development and leadership, our analysis confirmed the importance of the six themes from phase 1 of the research and helped us further develop them. Two further themes also emerged: agility and capability-building. We spent time within each case study organisation and kept a journal to note our thoughts and observations, especially during the action phase, to deepen our understanding of context and themes. Simultaneously collecting and analysing data enabled us to 'take advantage of emergent themes and unique case features' (Eisenhardt 1989) and allowed consideration of alternative explanations of our findings. Having a team of four researchers, we took steps to maximise inter-interviewer reliability by ensuring a standard list of questions was used in the semi-structured interviews, ensuring that two researchers were present at interviews and that all interviews were recorded and transcribed. In addition, researchers outside of the team acted as challenging 'devil's advocates', probing key assumptions, insights and findings (Eisenhardt 1989).

Discussion Questions

1   How did the analysis process take place in this case?

2   What are the advantages and disadvantages of having more than one person involved in the data analysis process?

FEEDBACK NOTES

This case illustration provides an example of researchers devising initial categories from the basis of a literature review. The analysis process then enabled them to 'populate' their categories to learn more about what was going on 'beneath' the surface and to identify new codes and categories that emerged from the data. This process was undertaken by a group of researchers to enable a comparison of outputs and provide some reassurance that the possibility of subjective bias that might have arisen from one researcher acting alone was minimised. This case illustration gives a clear sense that an orderly and systematic process was undertaken, an important feature of any qualitative analysis if the conclusions that are drawn are to be persuasive.

Moving forward with the analysis process, key questions for any qualitative researcher, once the data have been coded, are:

- Are there any themes, trends or patterns from groups of people or organisations?
- Are there similarities and differences between the different data groups?
- Are there interrelationships between different parts of the data?
- What interesting issues emerge from the data?
- Do the findings suggest that additional data might usefully be collected?
- Are there deviations from the main patterns or trends that might be identified?

Although there are a range of different types of qualitative data and a range of different approaches to qualitative analysis, there are also some general principles for the process that have been identified by researchers who have engaged in case study research and in areas of social sciences research, such as in education, health and social policy (see, for example, Robson 2011, Neuman 2011, Silverman 2011, Yin 2009):

Clarify the research questions and the data sources that are required to answer them

Starting with organisational documents or pages of interview notes, diary entries or focus group discussions and wondering what they may be able to tell you can be a recipe for time-wasting. You will achieve a more effective analysis if you are clear about what questions you need to answer and the data that will be relevant.

Make use of an appropriate sampling strategy

Sample selection for qualitative data was considered in Chapter 7. Analysis of qualitative data is always time-consuming. It is detailed work that is difficult to hurry. A justifiable sampling strategy will be necessary. You may, for example, decide to study half of the 'company email bulletins' of the organisation, or 20% of the available appraisal forms. In selecting focus groups or interview respondents, it is important to be able to justify the criteria and methods of selection that you adopt.

Decide on the categories for your analysis

It is important to work out how you will deal with and make sense of the information you propose to analyse. This will very much depend on the research questions you are trying to answer. You may establish categories in terms of the **subject matter** (in response to different interview topics). You may be investigating aspects of an organisation's culture and values, so categories that allow you to record and analyse **attitudes** may be appropriate. Alternatively, you might want to analyse different **methods** of work or activity (for example, electronic, paper-based, one-to-one meetings) or different **characteristics** of people (as, for example, depicted by respondents in focus groups).

Piloting

Before investing too much time in a full-scale analysis of a large volume of data, try out your categories on a small selection of your data. Is your approach to categorisation clear and fairly unambiguous? Are there some things for which there do not seem to be any appropriate categories? At this stage it is worth getting someone else to help you with the pilot process. You might both look at the same data so that you can assess the extent to which you have both coded in a similar way. This provides you with a measure of the reliability of the process (see Chapter 5) and will help you to make revisions to enhance the trustworthiness of your process before going forward with the main analysis.

Proceed with the analysis

Once the preparation is complete you can carry out your analysis. This will mean using the categories you have devised to make sense of the data. As noted already, this process itself may lead to the identification of further codes which can be incorporated in the analysis of the data that is subsequently gathered. Activity 8.2 demonstrates how a coding procedure may be undertaken.

 ACTIVITY 8.2

CODING QUALITATIVE DATA

Imagine that you are undertaking a research project into the contribution of HR to innovation. Visit the podcasts page of the CIPD website (www.cipd.co.uk) and search for relevant podcasts. In particular, you may find it worth visiting Episode 67: *Innovation and HR* and Episode 30: *Building Sustainable High Performance*. You can download these podcasts in an audio format or read the transcript. For this exercise it is preferable to read the transcripts.

Read the transcript summaries and identify possible:

- descriptive categories
- organisational (demographic) categories
- analytical categories.

FEEDBACK NOTES

One of the interesting things about qualitative data analysis is that two analysts may categorise data in different ways. This is because data analysis is affected by the personal assumptions and interests of the analyst – something that must be reduced as far as possible. Your assumptions will be influenced by your interests – if you 'want' a particular outcome you may also, unconsciously, 'see' things in a way that you feel is expected in a given context. It is important, therefore, to be aware of the difference between 'is' and 'ought' and to undertake the categorisation with as open a mind as possible. It is also very important to value (and code) data that does not 'fit' with what you expect.

Some of the demographic categories that you may have come up with might reflect the contextual questions about the individual organisation that each of the participants in the different podcasts come from, such as:

- organisation size
- business sector
- interviewee background.

Descriptive categories might include:

- definitions of innovation
- collaboration/participation
- rewards
- entrepreneurship/capability
- culture.

Analytic categories that you may have identified might include:

- leadership
- risk
- vision.

Having established your categories, you are in a position to develop a list of codes. The next step is to go back through all your data and 'mark up' the text where each code is evident. As you do this you may find that you identify new items that you missed the first time, so your list of codes is likely to grow in a cumulative way and there will come a time when you may need to reorganise it, sort it, combine categories where appropriate and discard or extend categories for further analysis.

A possible coding list from this activity is shown in Table 8.2.

Table 8.2 Illustrative coding list

Organisation size	**Size**	
Business sector	**Sector**	
Interviewee background	**Background**	
Definitions of innovation	**Defs**	
Collaboration/participation	**Collab**	Internal
		External
Rewards	**Rewards**	Intrinsic
		Extrinsic
Entrepreneurship/capability	**Capability**	Management
		Entrepreneurial
Culture	**Culture**	
Leadership	**Leadership**	Participative
		Directive
		Paternalistic
Risk	**Risk**	Attitudes to risk
		Risk management
Vision	**Vision**	Alignment
		Communication

Data coding forms the first part of your qualitative data analysis process. It enables you to 'make sense' of and reduce the information you have and to compare the evidence from a number of different sources, identifying similarities, patterns and themes. The process also means that you can generate ideas to help you work out what features of your data may be particularly important. The quality of your coding activity is very important for the quality of your analysis. Sloppy coding will lead to a poor analysis. It may look sophisticated but it will actually have very little value. For this reason, particularly if you have had to code for long periods of time to meet a deadline, you should review the codes you have applied to the text on a subsequent occasion to make sure that you are allocating text to codes in a meaningful way.

Maintaining a researcher's diary, in which you can reflect about events and record thoughts and ideas that occur to you as you are working with data, is also a key part of the qualitative data analysis process. Indeed, the most successful students all invest time in keeping a provisional running record of their analysis and interpretation processes, and this gives them a basis to follow up on ideas and evaluate alternative explanations. Although the process of data analysis means that you will become very close with the data (something to be encouraged), it is also important to take care to limit the influence of your prior assumptions on the interpretation you generate. Therefore, as you think about your data, try to 'distance yourself' and to consider it from more than one perspective. It is especially important that you value (rather than ignore) data that do not fit with what you expect to find. Once you have undertaken some initial coding, therefore, it is highly advisable to meet with your tutor and ask them to act as a 'devil's advocate' – looking for interpretations or features of the data that you may have overlooked or overemphasised.

DIFFERENT APPROACHES TO ANALYSIS

Having reduced your data, there are many different ways to carry out the analysis. The options that you choose will depend on the purpose and objectives of your research and the types of data you have gathered.

CONTENT ANALYSIS

Those researchers who, in spite of setting out to gather and analyse qualitative data, find themselves more comfortable working with proportions and 'numerical' reasoning processes are often drawn to content analysis. This works best with textual data (so you need transcripts) and visual images. The principles behind content analysis are to:

- determine the categories you wish to analyse (from the literature AND from the data themselves)
- establish some coding 'rules' (what 'counts' as being in this category and what would be 'out of bounds')
- carefully scrutinising your data to apply the codes (this works in a similar way to the process explained in the previous section)
- establishing a data file where you gather together all the instances of each of your categories and then assess their 'frequency' (how many of your sample group exhibit evidence of these codes?) and 'intensity' (how many times do these codes recur within the data set: do people keep on about some things or just make only one passing references to others?).

Content analysis undertaken in this way allows you to understand how the data 'breaks down' and to formulate your interpretation. However, if you engage in this form of data analysis, it is important that you do not get drawn back into a wholly quantitative assessment. Most qualitative researchers would argue that these 'numbers' are just to give you an overall idea about what is there in the data. The really interesting analysis occurs when you get to a 'deeper' and 'richer' level of analysis through analysing the underlying 'narrative' of what is going on.

NARRATIVE ANALYSIS

It is perfectly possible to undertake narrative analysis without first undertaking content analysis, although it is also possible to move from one to another. Important questions to ask yourself when you are looking for the underlying narrative of your data are:

- What kind of 'story' are your respondents expressing to you?
- What is their 'position' and context in relation to what they have told you?

- If they are referring to other people, organisations, departments, and so on, how are these 'characters' positioned in relation to one another and in relation to your research participants?
- How do your respondents describe their 'identity'? What claims are they making about who they are and where they 'fit' in your research area?

The actual responses (the words) are very important to understanding what may be going on but, in addition, you may need to look beneath 'just' the words that are spoken. It may be interesting, for example, to wonder why your participants focused on one aspect of the issues you were discussing before getting to others. This is what some qualitative researchers refer to as trying to analyse both the 'form' and the 'function' (the structure and the purpose) of the story the respondent is narrating in response to your prompting.

DATA DISPLAY PROCESSES

Data display is another pillar of qualitative data analysis (Lee and Lings 2008). Data display illuminates the data – it helps you to explore possible relationships within categories and between categories. Having undertaken an initial analysis of your data, figurative depiction can be used to **describe** how things link together and can also be used to **explain** what seems to be happening. You may choose to undertake 'within case' data display (this is most common for practitioner-researchers), but if your research spans more than one 'case' (and remember that a 'case' may be a department, an individual or an organisation) you can undertake cross-case data display. The objective is to find a way that can bring different categories of relevant data together. Experimentation with different forms of data display is a productive way forward.

DEDUCTION OR INDUCTION?

Data display can form the basis of both inductive and deductive approaches to analysis. The differences between inductive and deductive approaches to research are highlighted throughout this book (see Chapter 5 in particular). Many practitioners who are new to academic research assume that induction requires a qualitative approach and deduction requires a quantitative approach. However, a deductive approach to research is frequently plausible with qualitative data. Concepts from the literature review can guide the initial coding process and data display enables you to undertake a comparison of the evidence with propositions that relevant theories lead you to expect. Robson (2011) and Bryman and Bell (2007) indicate that the use of a tentative hypothesis, even in qualitative research, can be useful in assessing the extent to which the data compares with what might be expected. Indeed, it would be possible for the analysis of qualitative data to be as useful in a theory modification process as might be expected with a deductive approach to research.

A 'pure' inductive approach to research is associated with 'grounded theory' (see Charmaz 2006, Silverman 2011). This is where you undertake data coding in an emergent way through careful and close reading of your 'texts' and a process of 'memo-writing' (notes to self) about what categories are evident in the data. Once you have started this process you then keep gathering new data to add detail and depth to the properties of your emergent categories and to widen out the contexts/situations from which the data are drawn to examine whether the emergent concepts still seem to 'work'. The process of continuous and purposive data-gathering, which incrementally increases your sample size, is known as 'theoretical sampling'. You keep going until you find that new cases are not adding new conceptual insights – something referred to as 'theoretical saturation'. As you are undertaking this process it is important to engage with and continuously revise your data display as you undertake constant comparisons to modify or broaden your initial categories. Therefore, you will find yourself moving constantly between your data, the memos you are writing for yourself and the concepts/categories that you are developing.

In some instances it may also be that your project involves both deduction and induction. You might start with concepts from the literature and then, as a result of the process of analysis, examine new areas and insights that are evident in the data.

METHODS OF DATA DISPLAY

There are no hard and fast 'rules' about how data must be grouped or assessed, but the following sections briefly describe some alternative ways of displaying your data. Most people find that, through a process of trial and error, they can find the most appropriate ways to display their data to assist them with taking forward their interpretive work (Miles and Huberman 1994).

Lists, typologies, grids and matrices

One way of making sense of data, particularly in the early stages of analysis, is to use a grid where one dimension (for example, the rows) represent one set of categories and the other dimension (for example, the columns) represent the evidence from different sources. An example of the use of a grid is shown in Table 8.3. In this fictional example the grid is used to describe the outcomes where people from each different function have been asked similar questions but, following a coding process, it becomes apparent that there are the similarities and differences of response.

Table 8.3 Fictional example of a data grid: why bother with corporate responsibility? – responses from different functional areas

Department	Behavioural focus	Attitude	Why
HR	Compliance Focus on employee engagement	Functional leadership Importance of societal expectations	Corporate reputation Corporate values

Department	Behavioural focus	Attitude	Why
Sales	Business as usual Short-term decisions dominate	Denial	Concern for revenue targets Short-term sales model
Finance	Compliance Focus on investors	Importance of cost–benefit analysis	Investor confidence Short-term financial model

Another use of the grid is to generate a matrix to examine, explore and display possible patterns that you find in your data. Table 8.4 shows an example of a matrix which provides a typology of the relationship between different management beliefs about workplace bullying and behaviour towards allegations of bullying.

Table 8.4 Fictional data matrix: managers' beliefs about bullying

		Taking responsibility	Shifting responsibility to others
Management beliefs about how to deal with bullying	Relationship resolution	Get involved personally with the aim of finding a mutually acceptable and feasible 'resolution'	Refer the person who has reported bullying to HR or counselling
	Business as usual	Expect ongoing, if fluctuating, levels of interpersonal conflict and try to 'keep a lid on things'	Ignore problems like this and hope they will go away
	Punishment	Investigate promptly and take strong disciplinary action quickly	Expect HR to know about the situation and to solve it

The important thing with any data display is that you must be confident that the data you have gathered really provide evidence for the cells you have identified, and you will need to demonstrate this by the use of illustrative examples from your data. This requires a fair amount of 'data management' and there are different ways of doing this. For small projects it is possible to undertake it with pen and paper. A large surface, such as a whiteboard, or a generous covering of the floor with coded extracts from the original data are quite common. Even for larger projects it is possible to compile matrices making use of database functions for common computer software packages (Hahn 2008). Specialised qualitative data analysis software (see below) will also enable the production of any number of matrices to help you assess the extent to which there may be patterns or trends in your data.

Another popular way to represent data is to present issues in a hierarchy format. Figure 8.3 provides an example of data displayed as a hierarchy relating to factors affecting decisions and implementation of a new HR information system.

Figure 8.3 Data display using a hierarchy

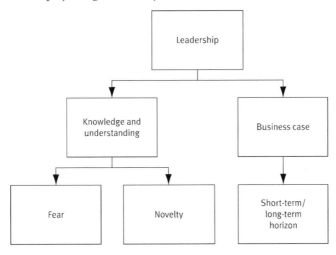

Yet another way of displaying your data is to organise it in some form of order, for example, by timeframes, length of service, size of location, and so on. An example of such a display is shown in Figure 8.4.

Figure 8.4 Fictional example of a time-ordered display: experiences of participants in a fast-track talent management programme

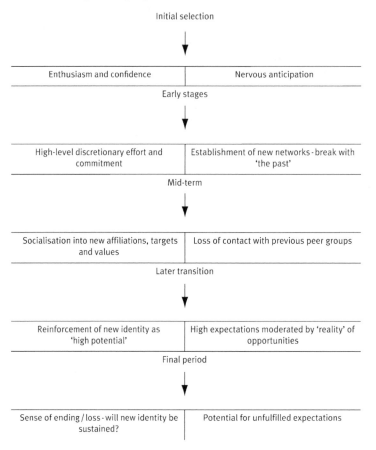

Initial selection

Enthusiasm and confidence	Nervous anticipation

Early stages

High-level discretionary effort and commitment	Establishment of new networks - break with 'the past'

Mid-term

Socialisation into new affiliations, targets and values	Loss of contact with previous peer groups

Later transition

Reinforcement of new identity as 'high potential'	High expectations moderated by 'reality' of opportunities

Final period

Sense of ending / loss - will new identity be sustained?	Potential for unfulfilled expectations

Display by modelling

Modelling provides another useful approach to considering the relationship between different categories of data. There are a number of different ways that data can be 'modelled'. A popular and fairly straightforward way is to 'draw' the layout of a work situation or a 'flowchart' of a number of processes, perhaps to extract and describe the different actions that led to particular outcomes that you have been investigating. While this can be a useful way of proceeding in an inductive way, it is also possible to use this approach in a more deductive way by devising an overall flowchart of what you expect a process to involve and then to compare reality, as suggested by your data, with it. This approach also enables you to map out any critical paths, decision points and supporting evidence that emerge from the data. Once you have an initial flowchart, perhaps generated from data from a few of your sources, you can assess the extent to which it also represents what you learn from other sources within your sample.

Figures 8.5 and 8.6 show two slightly different models, both of which relate to different research areas: Figure 8.5 displays concepts emerging from research into the career influences of executive-level HR professionals and Figure 8.6 is an example of a network diagram suggesting causal influences on the success of apprenticeship schemes.

Figure 8.5 Influences on the career experiences of executive HR professionals

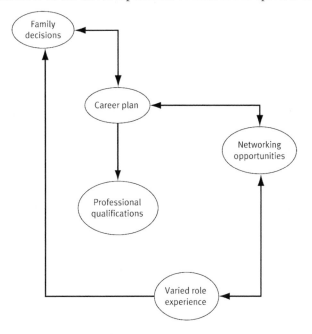

Figure 8.6 Network diagram for apprenticeship success

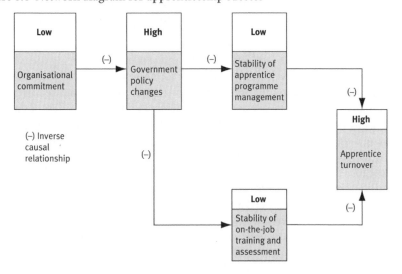

ACTIVITY 8.3

Discussion Questions

1   What are the advantages of the data display and modelling processes?

2   What challenges do they present?

FEEDBACK NOTES

The process of generating a model is a useful way of examining interrelated features of the phenomena or situation that you have examined in a qualitative way because it helps to represent patterns of experience and the relationships between them. Often it is helpful to try out different forms of data display before arriving at a model that best 'suits' your findings. One of the challenges of qualitative data analysis is determining how to start and where to stop. A further concern is the issue of the extent to which, as you get engrossed in making sense of your data, there is a tendency to produce a lovely diagram or figure and then wonder (or your assessor may wonder) to what extent the data really do support your interpretation. Effective qualitative research requires you to include the evidence to support the model and also evaluate the weaknesses of your model as a vehicle for explaining what is going on, as well as its strengths. In many cases an iterative process is required of: data display; model formulation; re-examination of the data; revision of the model; and so on. A good tip is to keep a note of your different drafts of data display and models as they evolve. Then, when you write up your analysis you will be able to explain how the model was amended and improved to take better account of all of your data. This will greatly enhance the credibility of your conclusions as well as the mark you get for your dissertation or research report.

Taken as a whole, therefore, qualitative data analysis involves testing ideas and hunches that you may develop as you think about and try to make sense of your data. It is important to look for emerging themes that may be scattered over different places in your data set or which occur from data from different data-gathering episodes. There is a strong likelihood that the process of analysing your data, using data display and modelling will involve you in subdividing and recoding some of your original categories and you may end up integrating one or more categories. This is time-consuming and, if you have left the analysis to the last minute, you will find it very frustrating. However, the quality of your final outcome will be much enhanced and, if you keep a clear record of what each of your categories mean (their definitions), you should be able to build in an incremental way as you continue with your data-gathering and analysis processes.

EVALUATING EXPLANATIONS AND FORMULATING CONCLUSIONS

The iterative nature of qualitative data analysis also applies to the process of formulating plausible conclusions on the basis of the evidence that has been gathered. With quantitative forms of data-gathering and analysis there are a number of fairly delineated 'stages'; drawing conclusions follows neatly at the end of a process where you first gather all your data and then undertake statistical analysis (see Chapter 10). The process is less 'clear cut' with qualitative data. The process of moving from data-gathering to data reduction and then to analysis and the evaluation of explanations to formulate conclusions is an iterative one without a clearly defined 'end point'. At some point, however, ideally when new 'cases' shed no new light on the topic of investigation (data saturation), you should reach a point where alternative explanations have been evaluated and one or two interpretations seem fairly plausible and others are quite unlikely.

The data analysis process, therefore, as illustrated in Figure 8.2 towards the beginning of this chapter, involves the generation of a range of possible explanations and/or propositions and the evaluation of these in the light of the evidence that has been gathered. The criteria by which alternatives might be evaluated (see Collis and Hussey 2009, Neuman 2011, Silverman 2011) can include asking questions about:

- **Credibility:** to what extent are the different explanations supported by evidence from different sources (triangulation)? How explicit have you been about the theoretical stance of your interpretation? Has this 'promoted' some explanations and excluded others?
- **Transferability:** to what extent are the explanations context-specific? Could they be applied to another situation? How clear are you about the limits of transferability?
- **Dependability:** how well documented is the research process? Are there things that the people or organisations in the research may have 'hidden', either purposely or inadvertently? To what extent might there have been unconscious non-reporting (on the part of the practitioner-researcher) or have commonplace events been overlooked? Has coding/categorisation been undertaken in a consistent way?
- **Meaning in context:** to what extent are the interpretations understandable within their holistic context? Has the process of analysis fragmented the evidence such that its analysis is out of context? This is something to think about if you undertake content analysis.
- **Recurrent patterning:** to what extent can the explanations be seen to relate to more than one particular timeframe? Is the sequencing within the explanations plausible?

Having evaluated the alternatives, conclusions about what is highly unlikely and what explanations are plausible can be drawn. The content and format of conclusions drawn from qualitative data are also characterised by diversity (Robson 2011). Different factors that can help with the formulation of conclusions based on the analysis of qualitative data are shown in Table 8.5.

Table 8.5 Factors in drawing conclusions from qualitative data

Factor	Example
counting	less than half of the interviewees perceived…
patterning	recurrent patterns in the analysis of the organisational documents were…
clustering	responses from focus groups in location B reported particular difficulties with … whereas those closer to … suggested…
factoring	key factors underpinning the perceived effectiveness of the appraisal scheme were…
variables	the analysis suggests that the practice of … occurs when … but it is unlikely to take place when…
causal networks	the following model indicates the relationships between the six different factors…
relationship to theory	the incidences of … that the analysis has identified may best be understood within the … theory relating to…

(Robson 2011, Neuman 2011, Yin 2009)

The nature of the conclusions that you draw will depend on the nature of your research questions as well as the broad (deductive or inductive) approach that you have adopted. The way that conclusions are drawn, however, is something of a point of convergence between these two different approaches.

Figure 8.7 Evaluating explanations and formulating conclusions

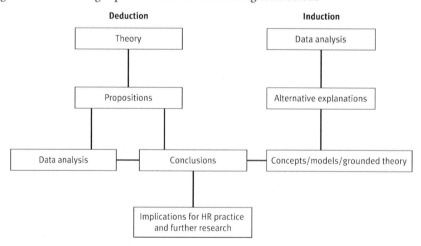

If you have used a deductive approach and have compared your data with theory, you will need to consider the evidence and the extent to which it supports propositions or explanations from relevant theories. The conclusions of the analysis will then be able to indicate areas where the propositions are plausible (note – not 'confirmed') and areas where the explanations stemming from the propositions are unlikely. The implications of the analysis for further research as well as for HR practice can be considered as a result of this.

If you are adopting a more inductive approach, you will also be able to draw conclusions and reflect on the implications of your analysis for further research and practice. The 'path' to this point, however, will involve gathering and analysing data without using prior theories or frameworks to explore 'what is going on'. The output of this iterative process (the conclusions) may be a model or an explanatory framework. Reflections about the implications for HR practice and further research to explore the conclusions will also be appropriate.

USE OF SOFTWARE FOR QUALITATIVE DATA ANALYSIS

Qualitative data analysis involves dealing with high volumes of data, expressed as words and/or pictures and possibly audio and video files. This is time-consuming and it is difficult to keep track of different items of data. Some form of database management system is likely to be required; merely storing printed text in a box file will not suffice. To operate without any computer software you need to make multiple copies of the texts and images that form the data and, as you undertake your coding, different chunks of data can be copied, cut, marked with appropriate codes, referenced to the original source document and then pasted into some form of filing system.

Initial stages of patterning or grouping, therefore, often involve 'laying out' the various relevant items. The main difficulty with this manual approach is the difficulty of 'keeping track' of all the different data. The transcript of a one-hour interview is likely to take up 20 pages of close-typed text and the volume of the data can lead to errors in the manipulation process, thus affecting the validity and reliability of the conclusions. However, if the quantity of qualitative data for your project is fairly limited, this approach may work well for you. Hahn (2008) provides some useful advice about using proprietary software, such as Access and Excel, to help with the data management and coding process.

Opinions vary about the usefulness of more specialised computer-aided qualitative data analysis (CAQDAS) software packages (see, for example, Atherton and Elsmore 2007), although the users of software packages are beginning to outnumber those who prefer not to use them. Most software tools include: functions to assist with coding, searching, reporting, retrieving, images and modelling. A useful comparison of the different packages available is provided by the online qualitative data analysis learning resources site funded by the UK Economic and Social Research Council (ESRC), which can be found at http://onlineqda.hud.ac.uk/Which_software/ which_package_comparison_table.php

If you are considering using some form of qualitative data analysis software, it is important to be clear about what the program can offer before you get too far into the collection of your data. This means that you can make use of the software throughout the duration of your project. The first step, therefore, is to find out if any qualitative data analysis software is available to you from your university or college and then find out how you can access training to use it. You may have to purchase the software yourself, in which case find out the cheapest way to get a personal licence for limited time duration at an 'education rate'. Demonstration and trial copies are also available for all the different products, but sometimes the trial period (say 30 days) is far too short to be of any value for your project. It is very important that you are 'at ease' with the software before you begin the data analysis process because you don't want to lose too much time finding out how to work it when your deadline is looming.

Remember also that qualitative data software does not code or do the analysis for you – your judgement and intellect are still required. If you code things in a sloppy way, you will get a sloppy analysis – however sophisticated the software makes it look.

The main functions of one commonly used CAQDAS software package (NVivo) are provided here, and it is possible to find out more about the functions of all of the software packages through websites from the software houses.

DATA MANAGEMENT FEATURES

- **Data storage:** NVivo, like other CAQDAS software packages, enables you to store all the source materials relating to your research. This will include all your 'raw data' (in the form of text, audio files, visual images and so on). In addition it provides you with the opportunity to maintain a reflective journal and write notes to yourself about your ideas and the progress you are making, making it possible to keep a record of the incremental process of data-gathering and interpretation. As it has significant storage capacity it is also possible to store other documents associated with your research (perhaps your research proposal, ethical approval form, and even some of the key literature sources that may be important as the analysis proceeds).
- **Coding facility:** within NVivo codes are referred to as 'nodes' and the software enables you to code (and then retrieve as appropriate) descriptive codes, analytical codes and relationship codes. NVivo provides the opportunity for you to work with emergent codes (called 'free nodes') as well as with a more structured or hierarchical system of codes (called 'tree nodes'). You can also assign attribute values to your participants' 'case nodes' (for example, age; gender; organisational size) in the form of numbers, dates or words. Once you have assigned these attributes you are able to view the data according to the attributes that you have chosen and so make comparisons between the codes and issues that emerge for the different groupings.
- **Data grouping functions:** most qualitative data analysis software enables you to group together data in different ways according to different characteristics. In NVivo such groupings are referred to as 'sets' and, once you have established these, you can carry out a specific analysis within particular groups or compare issues across the groupings.

ANALYSIS FEATURES

As indicated earlier in this chapter, there are many different approaches to qualitative data analysis but, at some stage or another, you will find yourself needing to identify and explore possible relationships both within your categories and between different categories. To help with this most software has a number of different 'query' functions:

- **Search and query functions:** the NVivo software works like a web-based search engine which creates an index to all the words in all your sources. Therefore, it is easy to carry out a range of different text searches to find data that meet your search criteria. As qualitative data analysis is an iterative and incremental process, it also allows you to save your queries for future use so that you can re-run them when your data set has changed and you can also edit them to make a similar but different search. It is also possible to view the results as a preview or to save the results in the form of a new code (node) or group (set). Four types of query are available using NVivo: text search (words; phrases; combinations of words or phrases); coding search (retrieve one code restricted in a particular way or retrieve a combination of codes); matrix coding (to gather responses with particular attributes); or a compound search where a text and coding combination is interrogated. If you are searching over a combination of codes, you can use the 'boolean' operators (and, or, not) and also give proximity operators (near content; preceding content; surrounding content) to examine data that may be relevant.
- **Modelling function:** almost all CAQDAS packages have a modelling function through which you can generate 'live' models so you can undertake initial model design, then carry out more analysis, then redesign your model on an ongoing basis. It is also possible to save each tentative model as you proceed and so have a record of your developing ideas.

Access to specialised software can be problematic for practitioner-researchers. Although many universities have site licences for SPSS to enable quantitative data-gathering, provision for qualitative data analysis is less widespread. Most software providers offer an 'educational' list price for a single user licence, usually for a defined one-year period, that may be more convenient and appropriate. Qualitative data analysis software takes time to learn to use. For projects where a limited amount of qualitative data has been gathered, the required investment in both money and time may not be sufficient to justify specialised software. Where large quantities of data have been gathered, however, it is likely that a more thorough analysis will be possible.

The use of software programs for qualitative data analysis, while making it possible to manage greater volumes of data, does not take away the requirement to think in a logical, evaluative and systematic way as part of the analysis process. Software packages organise data but the initial conceptualisation and the interpretation process still remain the province of the person undertaking the research.

WRITING UP YOUR ANALYSIS

The analysis processes outlined in this chapter should enable you to identify relationships between different aspects or features of the situation that you are investigating and to evaluate different explanations in the process of formulating a trustworthy conclusion. As you immerse yourself in the data you will become very familiar with all its features, but other people who read your work will not have this level of knowledge. Therefore, when the project report is 'written up', it is important that readers can know and understand three things:

1   How you went about reducing the data and the subsequent grouping and analysis processes – this is usually included within the methodology section.

2   The themes and categories that you identified from the data – this probably 'stood out' to you because you worked your way carefully through the minutiae of the evidence, but it needs to be explained to your readers. The most common way to do this is to offer an overall summary of the main features of the themes and then to illustrate them with a quotation or some other form of example. There are two main implications of this for your practice as a researcher. First, the quotations must be representative (don't squeeze the evidence to fit your preferred explanation). Second, it is important to have a strategy for recording and referencing quotations accurately so that you are able to access them when you need to provide an illustration.

3   The justification for the conclusions that you reached – you will demonstrate this in the analysis section by indicating the different explanations that you have evaluated on the basis of the data and the reasoning behind your conclusion as being the most plausible.

SUMMARY

- Qualitative data are concerned with language and meaning attached to different phenomena. Qualitative data are not 'standardised' and are characterised by 'volume' and 'messiness'.

- Analysis is the thought process that underpins understanding of the relationships between different elements in situations and the likely outcomes of particular actions or interventions. It involves finding answers to your research questions using the data that you have gathered by exploring the relationships between different categories and themes.

- Qualitative data analysis is an integrated and iterative process. It informs data-gathering and the formulation of conclusions. Data analysis involves data reduction and categorisation, grouping and display, and the evaluation of alternative explanations before conclusions are reached.

- Data coding is at the heart of qualitative data analysis. Coding involves labelling 'chunks' of data in relation to their meaning. Chunks of data may vary considerably in size, from individual words to a phrase or paragraph. One unit of data may be categorised in more than one way and therefore be assigned more than one code.

- Codes can relate to contextual information or they may be thematic. Categories and codes can emerge from the data, be developed from the aims, objectives and research questions of a study, be derived from concepts in the literature, or follow from the analysis of other sources of data.

- It is important to analyse the data from a range of perspectives and value data that does not 'fit' with what is expected.

- Qualitative data analysis may include some element of counting or quantification as well as the identification of patterns, clusters, factors, variables, causal relationships and the development of a theory, model or framework.

- Maintaining a diary in which notes, ideas, reflections and procedures are recorded assists with the ongoing analysis process and can provide a basis for evaluating the degree of 'detachment' that you have achieved.
- Qualitative data analysis can be undertaken using an inductive, deductive or 'mixed' approach.
- Content and narrative analyses are two common ways that people use as part of their analytical approach.
- Data display processes that can underpin analysis include: lists, grids, typologies, matrices, charts and figures.
- The evaluation of alternative explanations is an important part of qualitative data analysis and leads to the formulation of conclusions on a basis of likelihood and plausibility.
- A range of qualitative data analysis software products such as ATLAS/ti and NVivo are available which can enhance data manipulation processes for text-based, visual and audio forms of data. It is important to evaluate available software at an early stage in your research so that the software functions can be used throughout the research process.
- It is important to clarify and justify the analysis process that has been undertaken. Information about the data recording, reduction and coding processes and the overall analytical approach should be included within the methodology section. A description of the main themes that have been identified – illustrated from the data – and an indication of the way the evidence has been used to evaluate alternative explanations should be included in the section(s) devoted to data presentation and analysis.

 Self-test questions

REVIEW AND REFLECT

1 When undertaking qualitative data analysis why should you start coding your data as soon as possible?

   a) because you will get short of time when the deadline approaches

   b) because it is a fun thing to do

   c) to ensure that you find the interpretation that you manager is hoping for

   d) to sharpen your focus and identify areas to look out for in future data-gathering processes

2 The generation of charts, grids, hierarchies, matrices, and so on, are all forms of:

   a) template analysis

   b) data display

   c) grounded theory

   d) analytical induction

3 Keeping a chronological record of your ideas and reflections as your research project goes along, to help you develop your analysis, is known as:

   a) research summaries

   b) data transcripts

   c) research diary

   d) self-memos

4 Which of the following would be suitable for content analysis?

   a) interview transcripts

b)   newspaper articles

c)   website content

d)   all of the above

5   The purpose of keeping a record of your codes in some form of 'coding manual' is to:

a)   test your knowledge of statistics

b)   provide you with a reminder about what each of your codes represent

c)   formalise instructions about how to code the data

d)   list everything that you have decided to omit from your research

6   What does the acronym 'CAQDAS' stand for?

a)   complicated analysis of qualitative data and statistics

b)   constant analysis, qualitative data and simplicity

c)   computer-assisted qualitative data analysis software

d)   content analysis, qualitative data software

7   Which of these could be considered to be advantages of CAQDAS packages?

a)   you can find concealed data

b)   report-writing is straightforward

c)   you can re-analyse data easily

d)   no training is necessary

8   Which of the following is not a type of node used in NVivo?

a)   tree node

b)   case node

c)   free node

d)   shrub node

 ## Review questions

1   How organised are the data that you have collected so far? What sort of filing process might be applicable?

2   In what format are your data at present? Do they require transcription or summarising?

3   What software options may be available to you through your study centre for the analysis of your qualitative data?

4   What is your tutor's opinion about the quantity and quality of the data you have collected?

5   Does your supervisor have specific expertise in data analysis that would be helpful for you?

6   How clear are you about your research questions? What are the main themes that you are likely to explore when you analyse your data? What initial categories will you use for the analysis?

Questions for reflection

REVIEW AND REFLECT

This final part of the chapter enables you to reflect about your professional development and develop your skills and knowledge. This will enable you to build your confidence and credibility, track your learning, see your progress and demonstrate your achievements.

Strengths and weaknesses

1   How skilled are you at producing useable summaries of data-gathering 'events' that will remain meaningful in a number of weeks? Is there some way you could practise in advance?

2   How successful have your early attempts at coding data been? What have you learned from these early attempts and how might you apply what you have learned to subsequent coding activity?

3   To what extent will you need to use individual quotations as examples of the categories you identify? How will you ensure you can identify, store and retrieve them?

Being a practitioner-researcher

4   How might you use a 'research diary' throughout the duration of your project to inform your thinking?

5   What organisational factors might influence the way that you interpret your data? What strategies can you use to maintain a detachment from the data?

6   What explanations of the data might be 'organisationally preferred'? What alternative explanations might there be? What might enhance your ability to develop and evaluate a range of explanations as part of the analysis process?

7   What actions can you take to maximise the credibility and dependability of the data that you analyse? How can you ensure that the organisational and personal context in which the data has been generated is not lost as a result of the fragmentation involved in the data analysis process?

Web links

There are some excellent resources focused on issues associated with qualitative data analysis, which can be found at:

http://onlineqda.hud.ac.uk/

http://hsc.uwe.ac.uk/dataanalysis/qualIssues.asp

http://www.learnhigher.ac.uk/analysethis

Other useful webre sources are:

http://www.researchsupport.com.au/QDA_with_NVivo.htm

http://www.sagepub.co.uk/richards/

http://blogs.warwick.ac.uk/ahariri/entry/nvivo_9_tutorials

http://www.dur.ac.uk/resources/its/info/guides/52NVivo9.pdf

Internet addresses for software houses where further information about CAQDAS packages is available are:

http://www.qsrinternational.com

http://www.atlasti.com

http://www.qualisresearch.com

Useful Reading

Other useful sources of reading about analysing qualitative data include:

Atherton, A. and Elsmore, P. (2007) A dialogue on the merits of using software for qualitative data analysis, *Qualitative Research in Organizations and Management: An International Journal*, 2(1): 62–77.

Bazely, P. (2007) *Qualitative data analysis with NVivo*. London: Sage.

Bryman, A. and Bell, E. (2007) *Business research methods*. Oxford: Oxford University Press.

Charmaz, K. (2006) *Constructing grounded theory: a practical guide through qualitative data analysis.* London: Sage.

Collis, J. and Hussey, R. (2009) *Business research: a practical guide for undergraduate and postgraduate students*. Basingstoke: Palgrave.

Echlin, B. (2011) *NVivo 9 essentials*. Lulu.com.

Eisenhardt, K.M. (1989) Building theories from case study research, *The Academy of Management Review*, 14(4): 532–50.

Elo, S. and Kyngas, H. (2008) The qualitative content analysis process, *Journal of Advanced Nursing*, 62(1): 107–15.

Hahn, C. (2008) *Doing qualitative research using your computer*. London: Sage.

Lee, N. and Lings, I. (2008) *Doing business research: a guide to theory and practice*. London: Sage.

Miles, M.B. and Huberman, A.M. (1994) *Qualitative data analysis: an expanded source book*. London: Sage.

Neuman, W. (2011) *Basics of social research: qualitative and quantitative approaches.* International edition. Harlow: Pearson Education.

Richards, L. (2009) *Handling qualitative data: a practical guide*. London: Sage.

Robson, C. (2011) *Real world research: a resource for social scientists and practitioner-*

researchers. Oxford: Blackwell.

Silverman, D. (2011) *Interpreting qualitative data*. London: Sage.

Yin, R.K. (2009) *Case study research design and methods*. Thousand Oaks, CA: Sage Publications.

CHAPTER 9

Collecting and Recording Quantitative Data

CHAPTER OUTLINE

- How to use this chapter
- The uses of quantitative data in HR research
- Sources of quantitative data
- Undertaking your own survey
- Collecting, organising and presenting quantitative data
- First-level data analysis
- Summary
- Review and reflect
- Explore further

LEARNING OUTCOMES

This chapter should help you to:

- consider how quantitative data can contribute to your research
- discuss different sources of numerical data
- design and evaluate an effective survey instrument
- administer a survey to an appropriate sample of respondents
- collect, organise and store quantitative data in an effective way
- describe and present a summary of data you have collected.

HOW TO USE THIS CHAPTER

It would be almost impossible to investigate an HR problem or issue without the use of some numerical data. This chapter aims to give you some ideas about where to look for quantitative data, how to evaluate the extent to which numerical information will help you to address your research questions and how to collect quantitative data. The focus of the chapter is on gathering, presenting and describing data; Chapter 10 will help you to analyse and interpret your data in order to formulate meaningful conclusions. This chapter does not require you to become an expert in statistical techniques or specialised software programs.

ACTIVITY 9.1

MAKING SENSE OF THE NUMBERS

Visit the survey reports page of the CIPD website (http://www.cipd.co.uk/hr-resources/survey-reports) and examine either: a *Labour Market Outlook*, an *Employee Outlook* or an *HR Outlook* report, which you will find there. For this activity you do not need to read the findings carefully – skim-read the report and answer the following questions:

DISCUSSION QUESTIONS

1   What information does the report provide? What does it **not** tell you?

2   How is the information presented in this report? In what ways is the presentation helpful (or not)?

3   What information would you need to evaluate the trustworthiness of the data on which the report is based?

FEEDBACK NOTES

Depending on the report you have chosen you may feel either very interested by the information it contains or you may feel that it is not immediately relevant to your concerns in relation to your work and/or your research. These reports contain a lot of charts in various formats. Depending on your background and learning style, you may find these helpful or you may find numerical and statistical data of this sort to be boring or somewhat alienating. Nonetheless, these reports contain useful information about general trends in employment, labour markets and the development of HR. The figures and charts that are provided offer a useful **description** of some trends relating to employment and HR. Survey information itself cannot **explain** the reasons for the trends, although the context at the time the data were gathered is always discussed as part of the report. You may think that further information would help you to make more sense of the data. It would, for example, be interesting to know if the trends discussed varied in line with the size of organisations or whether they differed in relation to regions of the UK or for different types of work.

To evaluate the trustworthiness of the report you have chosen, it is also necessary to know more about it. The CIPD 'outlook reports' are usually published fairly close to the data collection on which they are based, so you might comment that one of the good features of the report is its 'up-to-date' quality. Questions that might also occur to you include: how were the questions put together? To what extent are the roles fulfilled by the survey respondents (all of whom were CIPD members) representative of all the employers in the UK? How confident can you be that the response rate to the survey (often around 15% of CIPD members) reliably represents the views of all those involved in employing people in the UK?

These issues and others underpin this chapter. Quantitative data is likely to form part of any assessment of an HR issue or problem, and it is important to be clear about its purpose and to use the data in an appropriate way. This chapter provides a framework through which to consider how best to use quantitative data in HR studies.

THE USES OF QUANTITATIVE DATA IN HR RESEARCH

All research needs data. Quantitative data is the term given to data that can be counted and quantified to shed light on features of organisational and employment situations. Such data deal in **variables** that can be counted, measured, described and compared. Quantitative data have an important part to play in answering research questions. Using quantitative data, you can describe a current situation in terms of:

- **Frequency:** how many people over the age of 50? How many times were certain behaviours manifested?
- **Central tendency:** what is the average salary of employees?
- **Dispersion:** how wide is the difference between the lowest and highest rates of absence between different departments?

You can compare this information with data from other sources (maybe from other parts of the organisation) and you can describe trends (spend on training over a four-year period, and so on). These procedures are common in most organisations and underpin decision-making and the evaluation of achievements. However, quantitative data can also be more fully analysed to explore potential relationships between different variables and to assess their significance. Therefore, although much quantitative data in HR is used **descriptively**, it is also possible to use it to help to **explain** different phenomena.

 Sources of quantitative data

CASE ILLUSTRATION 9.1

Yammeh was a part-time student who was a trade union member and had recently become a safety representative in his organisation, a large provider of transport services. For his dissertation he decided to research into the concerns of trade union safety representatives. However, Yammeh discovered that the Trades Union Congress (TUC) itself commissions a survey of safety representatives every two years. In the most recently published survey report, the TUC indicated that stress, bullying and harassment, back strains, trips and falls, and overwork were the most commonly cited issues of concern, although there were regional variations in the data (http://www.tuc.org.uk/

extras/safetyrepssurvey2010.pdf). To take his research forward, Yammeh decided to find out about the health and safety concerns of employees in different parts of his own organisation across the country and then to compare the findings with the TUC's national survey.

Discussion Questions

1   What information would Yammeh need to undertake the comparative research he wished to pursue?

2   What variables or issues might he want to identify and analyse?

FEEDBACK NOTES

You have probably commented that, if Yammeh wanted to undertake his comparison, he would be wise to find out what survey questions were asked in the TUC survey and then to try to replicate these in his own research. As this survey is undertaken every two years, it is reasonable to assume that the questionnaire itself asked the same questions as in previous years, and it may be interesting to examine trends over time and also to assess relationships between variables.

Variables that you may have identified that Yammeh might be interested in include: hazards in the workplace; stress at work; occupational health provision; safety audits; counselling services. In addition other variables that Yammeh might be interested in for his research might include demographic features such as: the age of his respondents; the nature of their work; their length of service as a safety rep; and their geographical location. Having obtained this sort of data it is then possible to 'interrogate it' in order to try and draw conclusions about health and safety issues and compare the transport sector with the overall picture presented by the TUC survey.

SOURCES OF QUANTITATIVE DATA

Much of the quantitative data used in HR research comes from surveys of one sort of another. However, useful information can also be generated from structured observations, from content analysis of texts and from other artefacts. HR information systems are another rich source of quantitative information.

There are three main sources of survey data:

- **Published surveys:** these are undertaken for purposes other than your research. WERS 2012 is an example of such a survey (see http://www.bis.gov.uk/policies/employment-matters/research/wers). Surveys such as these are useful sources of secondary data.
- **Unpublished surveys:** undertaken for purposes other than your research (regular employee engagement survey data, for example). These are further examples of secondary data.
- **Surveys undertaken as a part of your specific research:** including postal or online surveys, telephone interviews and structured face-to-face interviews.

Most of this chapter considers issues relevant to undertaking a survey of your own, but some information about published surveys is provided first.

DATA FROM PUBLISHED SURVEYS

Practitioners undertaking HR research projects, particularly those that are organisationally based, often make little or no use of published surveys although the data might offer a useful point of context or comparison. The data from most surveys, in tabulated form, are available electronically, mostly through an Internet link. Registration is often required but does not usually involve a cost. Useful data might include:

- **Census data:** many countries collect data from nearly all of their population from time to time. In most countries completion is required and there is a wide range of questions.
- **Regular surveys:** many regular surveys are likely to be of interest to those working in HR. These include surveys undertaken on behalf of the Government, research organisations or professional institutes (such as the CIPD). Some examples are shown in Table 9.1.
- **Ad hoc surveys:** these are often undertaken for particular purposes and are sponsored by those with a particular interest in the issues being examined. The CIPD website has links to a range of survey reports, which can be found at http://www.cipd.co.uk/onlineinfodocuments/surveys.htm

Table 9.1 Examples of regular surveys

Name	Sample / frequency	Sponsor	Description
Labour Force Survey	60,000 households / quarterly	UK Office for National Statistics http:// www.ons.gov.uk/ons/ guide-method/surveys/ list-of-surveys/ survey.html? survey=Labour+Force +Survey	A quarterly sample survey of 60,000 households to provide information on the employment circumstances of the UK population. It is the largest household survey in the UK and provides the official measures of employment and unemployment. The LFS is carried out under a European Union Directive and uses internationally agreed concepts and definitions. It is the source of the internationally comparable (International Labour Organization) measure known as 'ILO unemployment'.
National Employer Skills Survey	175,000 employers	UK Learning and Skills Council http:// nessdata.ukces.org.uk/ ness/KMS/News.aspx	Data relating to employment from the perspective of employers about issues such as recruitment and retention, skills gaps, training and workforce development activity. Responsibility for this survey changes quite often as changes in local employment support arrangements have been made. Currently it is managed by the UK Commission for Employment and Skills.

Name	Sample / frequency	Sponsor	Description
Workplace Employee Relations Survey	3,000+ managers, 1,000+ employee reps., 20,000 employees. Undertaken initially as WIRS and later as WERS in 1980, 1984, 1990, 1998, 2004 and 2012.	Acas, DTI, ESRC, PSI, NIAS http://www.bis.gov.uk/policies/employment-matters/research/wers	Survey collects information relating to employment relations in workplaces in the UK. Data on issues such as union recognition, negotiating structures, collective bargaining, procedures and agreements, pay systems, consultation and communication, workforce composition, performance measures, and so on.
Reward Management Survey	Reward specialists and people managers in about 500 organisations / annual	CIPD http://www.cipd.co.uk/hr-resources/survey-reports/reward-management-2011.aspx	An annual survey of UK reward management is based on responses received from organisations, across all industrial sectors. The main aim of the research is to provide readers with a benchmarking and information resource in respect of current and emerging practice in UK reward management.

Table 9.2 Examples of cross-national surveys

Name	Sample / frequency	Sponsor	Description
European Commission Public Opinion Analysis	Ad hoc + weekly 200 telephone interviews in each member state 44 weeks of each year	European Commission http://ec.europa.eu/ public_opinion/ archives_en.htm	Data from both quantitative and qualitative surveys undertaken on behalf of the European Commission.
European Social Survey	Biennial survey monitoring attitude change in over 30 European countries	Economic and Social Research Council (UK) + other country funding bodies http:// www.europeansocia lsurvey.org	Data from quantitative surveys from over 30 countries. Data available to registered users (free to register).
GLOBE (Global Leadership and Organisational Behaviour Effectiveness) Research Project	A multi-phase and multi-method project. Data from 50+ countries / cultures	Collaborative project involving a network of 200 social scientists from different parts of the world. http:// www.thunderbird.e du/wwwfiles/ms/ globe/pdf/ GLOBE_Phase_2_A lpha_Questionnaire .pdf	Quantitative and qualitative data from over 60 countries. Data-gathering instruments available with permission.
GEM (Global Entrepreneurship Monitor)	Annual national surveys of 2,000+ in each participating country about attitudes towards entrepreneurship + an annual 'expert' survey	Collaborative project led by Global Entrepreneurship Research Association http:// www.gemconsortiu m.org/What-is-GEM	Quantitative data from over 40 countries. Data sets available to registered users (free to register).

UNDERTAKING YOUR OWN SURVEY

Surveys are perhaps the most widely used method of gathering data in business and management and HR projects are no exception. As with any form of data-gathering, surveys can contribute to the achievement of a range of different research objectives. A key issue, if you plan to use a survey, is to be clear about its purpose. Some surveys operate from within a **deductive** approach where the researcher aims to test the relationships between variables. A hypothesis is formulated and then the data are analysed to test the propositions derived from the hypothesis. (See Chapter 5 for a fuller discussion of the deductive and inductive approaches to research.) Gill et al (2010), however, point out that some surveys fulfil a more exploratory and **inductive** purpose, by indicating patterns and frequencies that can contribute to theory-building. Other surveys have a comparative purpose, seeking to describe data and consider similarities with data from other research populations. The surveys undertaken in many HR projects, particularly for the purposes of CIPD management research reports, tend to fulfil a descriptive purpose, although those at master's level should go further than data description.

DETERMINING A SAMPLE

The issue of sample size and selection is crucial to the usefulness of any survey and the trustworthiness of the findings. As noted already in previous chapters, sampling is the deliberate choice of a number of units of analysis to represent a greater population. There are two main approaches to sampling. Non-probability sampling (discussed in Chapter 7) is most often used for qualitative data-gathering. For quantitative data, probability sampling is more appropriate. This involves determining a sample that is statistically representative of the population as a whole and so should reflect its characteristics such that you could be confident that your conclusions can be generalised to the wider population.

There are two key decisions with any survey. First, you must determine the size of the sample that you will select. Second, you will need to work out how you will select the respondents for your survey.

Sample size

A common question asked by student researchers is: 'how large must my sample be?' and there are no simple answers. Some books (see, for example, Saunders et al 2012) give calculations for desired sample size for cross-sectional research which follow from a decision about how closely you want your sample to resemble the research population. However, these calculations are often not feasible if you are including quite a few variables in your study (see, for example, Lee and Lings 2008). This means that you may be influenced as much by practicalities as by calculations. One practical issue to think about is the likely rate of return of your survey questionnaires. Another issue to take account of is your plans for data analysis because some statistical tests require larger samples. A further practicality to consider is the nature of your research question. If you are undertaking some form of longitudinal study (admittedly quite rare for many HR student projects), you may need to develop and justify your sampling strategy and ratio in a different way from the approach you might use for cross-sectional research. For example, it is likely that, as time passes, some of your original sample group may withdraw from your project and so you will need to build this risk into your initial sample selection process.

The following general principles (Neuman 2011) are helpful:

- The smaller the population, the bigger the ratio of sample size to population size (sampling ratio) should be. Thus:
    1. For very small populations (fewer than 500) a ratio of at least 50:100 (50%) is advisable.
    2. For small populations (500–1,000) a ratio of about 30:100 (30%) is advisable.
    3. For populations of between 1,000 and 10,000, a ratio of about 10% may be acceptable.
    4. For populations of over 15,000 a ratio of 1% may suffice.
- The higher your requirement for accuracy (and generalisability), the greater your sampling ratio should be.
- The higher the degree of diversity in the population, the higher the sampling ratio should be.
- The higher the number of different variables to be examined in the analysis of the data, the higher the sampling ratio should be.

Some of these factors are illustrated in Figure 9.1. Table 9.3 indicates the recommended sample sizes for different populations (associated with a reasonable degree of statistical accuracy) that Hart (2010) recommends.

Table 9.3 Indicative sample size

Population size	Sample size	Population size	Sample size
10	10	175	122
20	19	200	134
30	28	250	153
50	44	300	172
60	52	350	187
80	66	400	201
100	81	500	222
125	96	750	258
150	110	1000	286

Figure 9.1 Influences on sample size

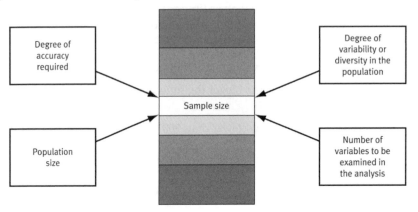

Degree of accuracy required

Degree of variability or diversity in the population

Sample size

Population size

Number of variables to be examined in the analysis

 Determining a sample size and method of sampling

Sarah was an operations director for a medium-sized charity employing 350 people operating a large number of food banks to provide emergency help and support for people in the UK experiencing a crisis. The charity operated through local partners (for example, religious groups or community organisations) and the strategic objective of the charity was to increase its number of food banks to provide support to every town in the UK.

As part of its social responsibility strategy, the charity employed a large number of disadvantaged people in its warehouses and distribution centres, and there were particular challenges with their training and development. In addition to responsibility for operations, Sarah also had responsibility for training and development throughout the warehouse and distribution functions of the charity. For her research project she wanted to focus on achieving greater consistency and effectiveness of training in different warehouse locations. Like Sarah, all of the 'trainers' in the organisation had been given their training responsibilities

without any prior background or training in HRM or HRD and, for her project, Sarah decided to evaluate the benefits that might be achieved if trainers in the organisation were encouraged (and sponsored) to study for some form of training qualification.

She decided to issue two questionnaires: one questionnaire would investigate the trainers' perspective on this issue, and another questionnaire was to be completed by a sample of warehouse and distribution centre managers to assess the extent to which they would feel it would be beneficial and whether the cost (in both time and money) could be justified. She also decided to investigate the ways that other similar charities tackled this problem. Before she set about devising the questionnaires, however, she had to decide who to select to complete them and how many responses would constitute a representative sample.

Discussion Questions

1   How might Sarah select potential survey respondents to ensure that her sample(s) would be representative?

2 What sampling ratio would you recommend for a) the survey to trainers and b) the survey to managers?

approach to sampling would she need to think about?

3 How might she get information from other charities and what

FEEDBACK NOTES

Decisions about the sampling ratio must take a number of factors into account. Although the organisation was quite small, Sarah needed to know how many managers and how many trainers were employed because it is these groups that would form her 'survey populations'. She knew that there were 50 people involved in different training roles across the organisation and Sarah decided to sample all of them (a 100% sample). There were just over 100 managers and she thought about approaching a 70% sample. However, Sarah's supervisor discussed with her the likelihood that very few of these managers would bother to respond and Sarah anticipated that it might be hard to get a good response rate. Therefore, she decided to sample them all in the hope that she would get sufficient responses overall. This also meant that managers from smaller warehouses would have an equivalent chance of being invited to complete the survey. Having decided on the sample, Sarah needed an accurate listing of all those whose role involved training and all those who were line managers; she obtained this information from the payroll listing. This list formed the 'sampling frame'. When she glanced through the list she realised that she would need to do some more work because she noticed the names of people that she knew to be on long-term sick leave. Sarah then had to decide whether these people should remain within the sampling frame.

Sarah faced a different set of sampling issues when considering getting data from other charities. Here there was very little chance that she could undertake a randomised probability sample; she would need to make a deliberate choice of which organisations to approach. This is known as a non-probability sample (which was discussed in Chapter 7). As this case illustration demonstrates, even the most simple situation involves decisions: there are no hard and fast 'rules' about sample size and selection; your judgement will be needed and you will need to justify your decisions in the methods chapter or section of your report. The process of sample selection is illustrated in Figure 9.2. When reading the research of others, it is worth critically evaluating their approach to sample selection and sample size, as well as being prepared to discuss the benefits but also the limitations of the approach that you have taken for any sample you select as part of your project.

Figure 9.2 The sample selection process

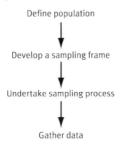

Define population

↓

Develop a sampling frame

↓

Undertake sampling process

↓

Gather data

Sample selection methods

- **Simple random sampling:** this is the most basic type of probability sample which should eliminate the possibility of undue bias within your group of respondents in terms of their general characteristics. This approach requires the development of an accurate sampling frame and then the use of a mathematically random procedure (usually the use of published random number tables) to select the elements (the respondents) from the sampling frame. Random number tables are published in many statistical textbooks and are also readily available on the Internet (see, for example, http://www.randomnumbergenerator.com; http://www.graphpad.com/quickcalcs/randomN1.cfm; http://stattrek.com/Tables/Random.aspx). Begin the sampling process by giving each potential respondent (all the cases in the sampling frame) a number – the first is 0, the next is 1 and so on. It is important to have as many random numbers as there are cases (elements) in your frame. Go to the random number tables and choose a number at random. This is the first selection for your sample and you can read off more random numbers in a systematic and regular way (this can be along the rows of the sheet of numbers, every fifth number, and so on) until you have chosen the number of respondents you require. This approach does not guarantee a perfect representation of the population, but it does mean that you will be close to it. In addition, it is possible (see Chapter 10) to calculate the level of confidence, or probability, of the sample being inaccurate. However, having used a random approach it is very important that you actually deliver your survey to every respondent represented by the random numbers – hence the importance of an accurate sampling frame. Also remember that every non-respondent diminishes how representative your sample can be considered to be.
- **Systematic sampling:** this approach also requires numbering of all the elements or cases in your sampling frame. However, instead of using a randomised approach you determine a set sampling interval or ratio. So, for a 10% sampling ratio, you would choose one respondent randomly and then 'count down' one in every ten cases. While this might seem easier than the random number approach, it is important to remember that you may not achieve a random sample if the sampling frame (for example, the listing from an HR information system) is itself organised in some form of pattern or cycle, perhaps by grade or by department or even alphabetically.

- **Stratified sampling:** with this approach the sampling frame itself is divided into sub-populations (perhaps by department, by grade or by age group) and you then draw a random sample from each one. This approach may be particularly useful when one of the sub-populations is quite small and so could be missed by a simple random or stratified approach.
- **Cluster sampling:** here you identify sample clusters (units) from the overall population and then you draw a random or a systematic sample from within each of your clusters. This multi-stage approach is often cheaper and easier than a simple random approach when the population is very dispersed and difficult to access. However, each stage in the clustering and selection process introduces sampling errors and so limits the reliability of the data.

SURVEY CHOICE OR DESIGN

Surveys are a very popular method within HR research. Sometimes they are adopted because it is felt it will be easier and quicker than undertaking interviews. In reality, however, surveys are equally challenging. Survey instruments that are valid and reliable are difficult to construct. Poorly designed surveys, which have limited validity and reliability, mean that your data will be very difficult to analyse and the quality of your findings will be diminished. If you decide to pursue a cross-sectional survey within your research design, you might be well advised to find out what instruments have been used by other researchers in your area and to consider using a pre-validated survey. However, if like many students, you and/or your organisation have decided that you should design your own survey instrument, it is important to keep in mind some important features of effective questionnaire design. There are two main 'golden rules' for survey design: the first is to **maintain clarity** and the second is to **keep the respondent's perspective in mind** (Neuman 2011).

SURVEY STRATEGY

Before launching into the design of the survey it is important to clarify key issues. First, what is the purpose of your survey? What are your research objectives or questions and what important variables do you need to examine? Do you intend to compare data you gather with data from other surveys? If so, you must carefully identify the basis on which the data in the other survey(s) was gathered. What form of analysis will you hope to achieve? If you want to test the relationships between different variables, you must ensure that your questions allow you to do this. To what extent are open as well as closed questions appropriate, given the purpose of your survey? How will non-responses to some of your questions impact on the subsequent analysis?

Question structure

This part of the thinking and decision process involves considering a range of issues such as the question format and the method of response. Although paper-based surveys are used in HR projects, they are increasingly being replaced by surveys distributed by email or hosted on a webpage. Do you want respondents to 'click' boxes, circle numbers or make some other form of response? Will respondents be asked to make one choice from a range of options? Will they make a choice somewhere between two dichotomous ends of a 'scale'? Is some form of ranking of alternatives going to be appropriate? These are crucial decisions which will influence the success of your analysis process. The implications of these are outlined next (Robson 2011, Collis and Hussey 2009, Gill et al 2010, Zikmund 2009).

- **Open vs closed questions?** The issues around the use of open questions have been considered in Chapters 7 and 8. Although quantitative surveys will mainly use different forms of closed questions, a few open questions are sometimes included. This enables people to clarify their answers, provide additional detail and show the logic, or thinking process, underpinning different choices. Subsequent analysis requires thought, however, and 'statistics' will not be possible. Closed questions, by contrast, offer a range of advantages. They are easier and quicker for a respondent to 'tackle'; answers will be unambiguous and can be more easily compared. It is also possible to repeat the survey at another time or with another research population. However, there are also disadvantages with closed questions. It is possible that by providing a 'menu' of answers in your survey instrument you are suggesting things to people that they would not otherwise think of (but may now choose). Also, respondents with no knowledge or opinion may still opt to 'choose an answer' or become frustrated that the answer they would like to give is not provided as one of the choices. A further difficulty is that there is no check as to the level of understanding of the question by the respondent and simplistic choices may be 'forced'. Whether you decide to use open or closed questions, don't forget the golden rule of survey questions: leading questions are never effective!

Decisions about the form of questions in a survey are crucial as they impact on what you can do with the data once the surveys have been returned. The material that follows describes the main options. To illustrate the different approaches to formulating questions, I have used the scenario of trying to find out about management training and development.

Nominal scale data

Sometimes called category scales, these relate to data that describe things and allow you to classify responses into different groupings. Questions that ask respondents whether they are male or female, or which department they work in, allow you to count 'how many' there are. Data in categories such as these have no 'arithmetic value' (you cannot calculate the average gender, for example) but they are very useful. If you were researching into management training and development, you could compare the proportion of women who have attended a management training course in the last 12 months with the proportion of men, or you could compare the proportion of people from different ethnic groups who have attended a management training course. The inclusion of these 'biographical' or 'situational' variables within a survey, therefore, allows for a range of comparisons to be made. As you start devising your questionnaire think about the nominal categories you will need to include.

Ordinal scale data

This is an approach that involves inviting responses to reflect a degree of **ordering**. Different points on the 'scale' show greater or lesser amounts of the phenomena, relative to other points on it. A question in a survey asking about the level of satisfaction with the training someone had received might range from 1 = low level of satisfaction; 2 = fairly satisfied; 3 = satisfied; 4 = very satisfied. Another approach to ordinal scale data is to ask respondents to 'rank' a set of attributes from the most preferred to their least preferred. For example, ordering the importance of attributes (for example, participative activities; clarity of communication by the trainer; learning environment; quality of handouts) that respondents feel contribute to their satisfaction with management training programmes. Again, however, other than counting the numbers of responses, and establishing the 'order', such responses will not enable you to undertake many calculations or perform statistical tests because there is no clear distance between the points on the scale. What **is** the distance between 'fairly satisfied' and 'satisfied', for example, and would every respondent understand the distance in the same way?

Interval scale data

Questions using interval scales are similar to ordinal scales, but the distance between the points **is** known **and** the intervals represent equal quantities. Measures of IQ that are calculated from most intelligence tests, for example, work on the basis of '100' as the norm and other points indicating the distance of the score from the average. As such you cannot achieve an IQ of zero, but the distance between two people with an IQ of 85 and 100 is known to be the same as the distance between two people with an IQ of 100 and 115. The **Likert scale** is a well-known example of an ordinal scale:

I felt more confident in my management ability after the training.

This example shows that an interval scale does not have a 'zero'; you cannot go lower than '1'. For this reason statisticians are uncomfortable with calculations (such as averaging) being performed, although you are likely to find research that does use mathematical processes on interval scale data.

Ratio scale data

These data represent the highest level of precision. A ratio scale does have a zero (for example, height, weight, time) and so it is possible to say that something lasts for twice as long or costs three times as much. However, the nature of research questions underpinning many HR surveys, particularly in organisational enquiries, tends to mean that ratio scale questions are quite rare.

ACTIVITY 9.2

QUESTIONNAIRE DESIGN

Extracts from: CIPD. (2009) *Coaching at the sharp end: developing and supporting the line manager as coach* [online] http://www.cipd.co.uk/hr-resources/practical-tools/developing-line-manager-coaching.aspx With the permission of the publisher, the Chartered Institute of Personnel and Development, London (www.cipd.co.uk).

Questions about you

1   **Are you:**

Male	☐
Female	☐

2   **Your age range:**

Under 25	☐
25–34	☐
35–44	☐
45–54	☐
55–64	☐
over 34	☐

3   **How many people directly report to you?**

—

4   **Which best reflects your level in the organisation hierarchy?**

First-line manager	☐
Middle manager	☐
Top-level/board manager	☐

Questions about training and support

In an ideal world what would help you improve the way you manage your people?

Please choose the appropriate response for each item:

5   **In-house training course**

Very helpful	4	☐
Helpful	3	☐
Not very helpful	2	☐
Not helpful	1	☐

6   **External training course**

Very helpful	4	☐
Helpful	3	☐
Not very helpful	2	☐
Not helpful	1	☐

7   **Being given space to learn by trial and error**

Very helpful	4	☐
Helpful	3	☐
Not very helpful	2	☐
Not helpful	1	☐

8   **Advice and guidance from a senior manager/mentor**

Very helpful	4	☐
Helpful	3	☐
Not very helpful	2	☐
Not helpful	1	☐

9   **One-to-one coaching from my manager**

Very helpful	4	☐
Helpful	3	☐
Not very helpful	2	☐
Not helpful	1	☐

Questions about the people you manage

Please select the number which best describes your level of agreement regarding the people you manage:

Please choose the appropriate response for each item

10   **I admire their professional skills**

Strongly agree						Strongly disagree
1	2	3	4	5	6	7
☐	☐	☐	☐	☐	☐	☐

11 I respect their knowledge and competence on the job

Strongly agree						Strongly disagree
1	2	3	4	5	6	7
☐	☐	☐	☐	☐	☐	☐

12 I work for them beyond what is specified in my job description

Strongly agree						Strongly disagree
1	2	3	4	5	6	7
☐	☐	☐	☐	☐	☐	☐

13 I am willing to apply extra effort to further their interests

Strongly agree						Strongly disagree
1	2	3	4	5	6	7
☐	☐	☐	☐	☐	☐	☐

14 I do not mind working hard for them

Strongly agree						Strongly disagree
1	2	3	4	5	6	7
☐	☐	☐	☐	☐	☐	☐

15 I am impressed with their knowledge of the job

Strongly agree						Strongly disagree
1	2	3	4	5	6	7
☐	☐	☐	☐	☐	☐	☐

Questions about you

Please choose the number which best describes your level of agreement with each statement.

Please choose the appropriate response for each item

16 I can remain calm when facing difficulties in my job because I can rely on my abilities

Completely true					Not at all true
1	2	3	4	5	6
☐	☐	☐	☐	☐	☐

17 When I am confronted with a problem in my job I can usually find several solutions

Completely true					Not at all true
1	2	3	4	5	6
☐	☐	☐	☐	☐	☐

18 Whatever comes my way in my job I can usually handle it

Completely true					Not at all true
1	2	3	4	5	6
☐	☐	☐	☐	☐	☐

19 My past experiences in my job have prepared me well for my occupational future

Completely true					Not at all true
1	2	3	4	5	6
☐	☐	☐	☐	☐	☐

20 I meet the goals that I set for myself in my job

Completely true					Not at all true
1	2	3	4	5	6
☐	☐	☐	☐	☐	☐

21 I feel prepared for most of the demands in my job

Completely true					Not at all true
1	2	3	4	5	6
☐	☐	☐	☐	☐	☐

DISCUSSION QUESTIONS

1 Study the extracts from this questionnaire and identify which questions use nominal, ordinal, interval or ratio scale.

2 Critically evaluate the usefulness of the data that would be gathered from the questions shown in this extract from the survey.

FEEDBACK NOTES

You should have identified that most of the early questions in this survey use a nominal scale which records characteristics of different respondents. Although it is not possible to perform 'statistics' on these types of question, they can be useful in assessing whether respondents in one category have responded in a greater or lesser way to subsequent questions. As such the variables in these categories are 'independent', and it may be possible to see if there is some form of relationship with other 'dependent' variables (such as remaining calm in my job). Question 3 provides for ratio data where people can put the exact number of people in their team. Questions 5–9 use an ordinal scale. There is some degree of ordering but the 'distance' between each of the points within the order is not quantified and is not necessarily regular. Although these questions have the potential to yield interesting information, the extent to which data from this survey can be analysed, beyond descriptions of the frequency with which different categories were chosen, is somewhat limited. To establish interval scales would require a more obvious numbering scale visually representing equivalent distances between each point, something which occurs from question 10 onwards.

You may also have noticed that on some occasions a four-point scale is used, on other occasions a six-point scale appears and then sometimes a seven-point scale has been included. Different questions are also associated with scales of different length and so direct comparisons between the responses to these different items will not be meaningful.

This extract demonstrates, therefore, how the question design process impacts upon the subsequent opportunities for analysis of the data. Careful planning is necessary with survey design. This involves clarifying what analysis will be required to answer the research questions or achieving the research objectives to ensure that the questions, and their scales, are appropriate and effective.

SURVEY DESIGN

The next stage in the survey process involves the design of the questionnaire itself. It is important to consider its length, structure, the order of the questions, the layout and the method of administration (telephone, post, email, online and so on). A summary of the main features of appropriate survey design is shown as Table 9.4.

Table 9.4 Effective survey design

Initial request/ instructions	• Explain the purpose to all participants (a covering letter or email is often used). Ensure that all requirements for informed consent are met. • Establish the timescale, processes for return and confidentiality/anonymity arrangements.
Layout	• Ensure the questionnaire looks neat and attractive and is a reasonable page length. • It must be easy to read with clear instructions. • Provide enough space and clear instructions for respondents to mark their answer. • Establish a logical order for the questions. • Use a numbering or sub-lettering system to show groupings of questions.
Questions	• Begin with 'warm-up' questions. • Keep the questions as simple as possible. • Check that all questions are relevant – ask 'need to know' rather than 'nice to know' questions. Be clear about what the objective of each question is in relation to your research questions. • Avoid jargon, specialist language, slang or abbreviations. • Phrase each question so that only one meaning is possible. • Ensure the language of your questions is not 'emotionally loaded'. • Check that there are no multiple or leading questions. • Edit out any 'double negatives' from the questions. • Use 'filter' questions where some questions may not be relevant for all respondents.
Final thanks / return arrangements	• Thank respondents for taking the time to complete your survey. • Establish the return arrangements clearly. • Do not commit to more feedback after the research than you are sure you can provide.

(Collis and Hussey 2009, Neuman 2011, Robson 2011, Lee and Lings 2008)

WEB-BASED SURVEYS

Although many survey instruments are distributed and completed using a paper-based format, you may prefer to use some form of electronic method of distributing your survey. You could attach your survey to an email that is sent to potential respondents. The idea here is that the respondent opens the attachment and completes the survey before sending it back, often using the 'reply' command, to its originator. Here it is vital that those receiving the email know what is expected and know how to send the completed survey (rather than the blank original attachment) back to the researcher. In addition there are implications for anonymity as the email carrying the completed questionnaire as an attachment can be traced to a named individual. Therefore you must be very clear about the arrangement you will make to save completed questionnaires separately and delete evidence of the name of the sender.

An increasingly popular approach, which overcomes many of these disadvantages, is to design and use a web-based questionnaire. Here the survey is hosted on a webpage that respondents access through a hyperlink. Anonymity is easier to manage and the survey software will also gather together the data from all the responses into some form of spreadsheet. The software underpinning web-based questionnaires is not difficult to use and a number of commercial organisations can provide it at a charge which varies with the number of questions to be asked, the time that the survey is to be 'live' and the number of respondents that are anticipated (see, for example, http://www.surveymonkey.com and http://www.zoomerang.com).

The survey design principles outlined in Table 9.4 are equally applicable to surveys distributed electronically, but Table 9.5 highlights some additional issues that should be considered if using a web-based survey design.

Table 9.5 Web-based survey design

General layout and features	• Begin the survey with a welcome screen that will motivate the respondent to proceed to the first page. • Only use colour as a visual cue to simplify the survey instrument – don't get too 'carried away'. • Provide clear instructions and consider a 'help button' for clarifications. • Avoid pop-ups – these distract and annoy respondents.
Page / screen features	• Use hyperlinks if necessary to add help or additional information without adding to the apparent length of the survey. • Pre-programme the survey to check for errors / validate responses (for example, if input items do not add up to the required 100%). • Pre-programme a 'skip pattern', for example, if a response of 'no' means to go to a later question. • Only have a few questions on each screen – too much scrolling can be a burden to the respondent and they may quit your survey without completing it.
Buttons / check boxes	• Remember that the 'radio button' size does not change even when the font size of the question changes. • Radio buttons are best used for 'select only one' options for mutually exclusive items. • Avoid 'default-filled' radio buttons because respondents may not answer the question but a response would automatically be recorded. • Too many 'check box' options for each question can be confusing. Consider using a simple matrix question instead (see Table 9.6 for an example). • Use 'check all that apply' as an instruction sparingly as respondents may get 'carried away'.
Drop-down boxes	• Drop-down boxes require three clicks whereas other responses require only one – this means three times the opportunity for error! • Avoid the use of drop-down boxes where multiple selections are permitted.
Text input options	• Make sure that the size of the box is appropriate for the information you require.
Confidentiality / anonymity	• Consider a PIN to limit access to authorised users and inhibit anyone from completing the survey more than once. • Use password-protected web survey software to ensure data security and avoid unlimited access.

(Cobanoglu et al 2001, Couper et al 2001, Dillman 1999)

Table 9.6 Example of a simple matrix structure for web-based survey questions

Please select the number which best describes your level of agreement to these statements: Please choose the appropriate response for each item.	1 Strongly agree	2	3	4	5	6	7 Strongly disagree
I feel a sense of loyalty to my organisation.	O	O	O	O	O	O	O
I respect my manager.	O	O	O	O	O	O	O
I am willing to work beyond what is specified in my job description.	O	O	O	O	O	O	O
I am committed to my own personal development.	O	O	O	O	O	O	O
I make suggestions for improvements in the way work is carried out in my department.	O	O	O	O	O	O	O

SURVEY PILOTING

Survey design is a complex process and it is easy to become so absorbed in it that potential errors are not picked up. However, if your survey has inappropriate features or questions, the data that it generates will be of limited value. For all research projects it is strongly advisable to pilot any survey, prior to its distribution, to answer the following questions (Robson 2011, Saunders et al 2012):

- Is the content of the questions appropriate for the research objectives/ questions? Have any important variables been omitted? Will the questions that have been asked provide the information that is sought (validity)?
- How long does it take to complete the survey? How acceptable would the length of the survey be to the respondents? Are the instructions clear?
- Are all the questions clear and unambiguous?
- Are any questions likely to be too sensitive for the respondent group?
- How appropriate is the layout of the questionnaire?
- How easy was it for respondents to follow the instructions and submit their answers?

It will only be possible to answer all these questions if your pilot process incorporates a range of different people. It is a good idea to ask a 'subject expert' for their opinion of the strengths and weaknesses of your draft survey instrument. Your project tutor, as a minimum, should have the opportunity to offer feedback. It is a requirement of many study centres that a tutor approve any data-gathering instrument, and this can form a useful stage in the survey design and piloting process. In addition, comments about the survey can be obtained from people who are similar to those in the respondent group. If your survey is web-enabled, you will also need to check that you know how to transfer the data to the software package you are going to use to analyse the data; the piloting process is a useful way of checking this.

 Make or borrow?

CASE ILLUSTRATION 9.3

Afrah was a student who was undertaking a course in the UK but wished to conduct comparative research for her dissertation involving some people working in a UK organisation and other people working in an organisation in her country of Kuwait. While undertaking a coursework assignment on knowledge management, Afrah became intrigued by the concept of social capital: the extent to which relationships in an organisation underpin effective performance. The essence of social capital theory is that relationships are the key to success, and Afrah was aware that work relationships in her country were more 'collectivist' than in the UK, so she was keen to find out the extent to which differences in social capital would be found in the UK and Kuwait.

Afrah decided that a questionnaire approach would be most appropriate to examine social capital issues and she had to design a survey instrument to investigate the extent to which social capital in organisations is related to enhanced work performance by employees. The first challenge she faced was that there seemed to be very little consensus in the literature about the concept of social capital, although there was general agreement that it involves networks and social relations between individuals and organisations which promote trust, rapport and goodwill.

In the process of undertaking her literature review Afrah found that a set of questionnaire items relating to social capital in organisations had been developed and published (Ellinger et al 2011) which measured individuals' perceptions of managerial behaviours that might represent 'organisational investments in social capital' and also came across some questionnaire items related with work-related performance (Babin and Boles 1996).

Discussion Questions

1   What advantages and disadvantages might there be for a research project that 'borrows' survey questions from another source?

2   What difficulties might you encounter in trying to obtain and use survey questions designed by another researcher or research institution?

3   What challenges would Afrah face when collecting questionnaire responses from two very different countries?

FEEDBACK NOTES

Making use of survey questions that have already been developed and piloted by other researchers has many advantages, but also some disadvantages. You may have identified the attraction of using 'proven' questions as a way of enhancing the level of reliability and validity of the survey instrument (assuming that your evaluation of the information about the survey instrument suggests that it does have a good level of validity). On the other hand, you might think that pre-existing questions might not be fully appropriate to the purposes of your research. In such situations you might choose to amend them, although this would mean that you could not be as sure of the 'statistical quality' of the amended items. You might also worry about issues of copyright permission and cost. All published questionnaire instruments are subject to copyright restrictions and it is necessary to obtain the permission of the publishers (for which there may be a cost or other conditions to be met). Research published in academic articles may well not carry the actual questionnaire, so it would be necessary to follow up on the contact details provided with the article and ask the author if you might have a copy and consider using some or all of their questions.

The third question raised here relates with the extent to which survey questions 'travel'. Cross-national research is becoming increasingly popular among HR students as interesting discussions occur about the extent to which traditional US or Western assumptions about people management issues apply in a straightforward way in other societies. The first issue to be faced is the need to translate questions from one language to another, and many students have learned that translation is not as easy as it sounds; equivalent words may not be available in the 'second' language or they may be differently understood (this issue is known as the problem of 'conceptual equivalence'). Therefore a basic check of translation involves 'back translation'; you translate your questionnaire and then get an independent native speaker in the second language to translate it back into English and examine the similarity between the original and the back-translated version.

ADMINISTERING SURVEYS

The final set of decisions regarding the survey will relate to its distribution. Your objective is to ensure that the survey reaches all those in your sample in a timely way to maximise the chance that they will answer your questions and return the completed survey to you. The higher the level of non-response rate, the less reliable will be your findings. The main options for survey distribution are:

- postal, self-administered questionnaire
- delivered and collected, self-administered questionnaire
- structured telephone interview
- structured face-to-face interview
- email questionnaire
- web-based survey.

Table 9.7 indicates the key issues to be taken into account with each of these, as well as the advantages and disadvantages of each of them.

Table 9.7 Administering and delivering surveys

Method of distribution	Key issues	Advantages	Disadvantages
Postal, self-administered	<ul><li>pre-survey contact will enhance response rate</li><li>covering letter</li><li>reply-paid envelope</li><li>follow-up after one or two weeks to enhance response rate</li></ul>	<ul><li>cheap</li><li>respondents possible across a wide geographical area within one country</li><li>respondents can complete when convenient to them</li><li>anonymity is possible</li><li>no interviewer bias</li></ul>	<ul><li>low response rate</li><li>late returns</li><li>conditions for completion are not controlled</li><li>clarification of questions is not possible</li><li>incomplete responses are more likely</li></ul>
Delivery and collection questionnaire	<ul><li>pre-survey contact and permissions on the basis of informed consent are necessary</li><li>personal explanation of purpose of survey</li><li>respondents can seal their completed survey and place it themselves in a collection box</li></ul>	<ul><li>good response rate is possible</li><li>respondents slightly more involved</li><li>anonymity is 'visible'</li><li>clarification of a question is possible</li><li>controlled conditions for survey completion</li></ul>	<ul><li>sample restricted to those that can attend at the given time and place</li><li>'reluctant' respondents may make more extreme responses</li><li>organisational authorisation may be difficult to achieve</li></ul>

Method of distribution	Key issues	Advantages	Disadvantages
Telephone interview	• initial contact with respondent may mean calling back at a more convenient time • clear explanation of the purpose of the study is required • decisions about how many calls to each respondent required	• survey can be completed in a shorter timeframe • geographical limitations can be overcome but time zone issues must be taken into account • clarification of questions is possible	• low response rate • some interviewer bias may occur • no scope for recording non-verbal information
Face-to-face interviews	• competence of interviewer is important • pre-survey contact necessary • possible areas for probes must be clearly specified	• good response rates • more probing of issues is possible	• possibility of interviewer bias • expense (time-intensive) • geographical constraints of reaching respondents
Email survey	• email addresses of sample are required • pre-survey contact enhances response rate • covering message required • attachments may not work if in a different software version • arrangements for anonymity required • follow-up message to enhance response rate	• speed of transmission • no geographical or time zone limits • no interviewer bias • respondents can complete at a time suitable for them	• respondent concerns about anonymity • different software can affect display of images and the format of questionnaire • poor response rate • lost data (particularly attachments) • potential for respondents to edit the questionnaire

Method of distribution	Key issues	Advantages	Disadvantages
Web-based surveys	• establish a website with online questionnaire • explain purpose and provide instructions for completion (replaces covering letter) • hyperlinks need to be operational	• questionnaire cannot be altered • possible to monitor 'hit rate' on the site over the period in which the survey is 'live' • no interviewer bias • more (but not full) control over image and format of questionnaire	• unclear sample unless respondents are emailed the link to the website • those without access to the technology cannot be included • security needs to be built into the web system to stop one person making multiple responses

(Neuman 2011, Saunders et al 2012)

Figure 9.3 Stages in survey design and distribution

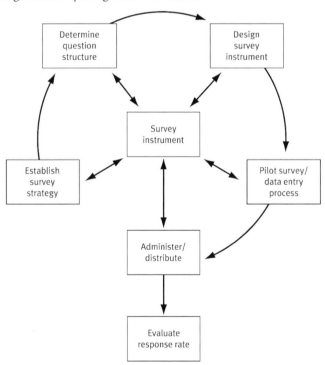

COLLECTING, ORGANISING AND PRESENTING QUANTITATIVE DATA

Quantitative data have no value in their raw state; data need to be organised and presented. Data collection can be an anxious time. After expending effort to devise and pilot the best-quality survey instrument that you are able to, once you send it to your planned respondents you lose control of the process; once it leaves you it is impossible to know whether and how people will respond to your questions. However, once the data begin to arrive back with you it is an exciting time – at last you can start to make sense of the information to answer your research questions.

As with all stages of any research project, a systematic approach is necessary. The first challenge that you may face is one of volume. A first-time researcher, faced with 100 returned questionnaires and an impending deadline, can feel very daunted about the prospect of manipulating the data to answer their research questions. You will need to describe the frequency of responses for different variables within your survey, and for this a spreadsheet package (most HR students use Excel) may be sufficient. Most students undertaking a CIPD business investigation or report (but not those working at master's level) will find that this will suffice. However, if you wish to analyse the data at a deeper level (see Chapter 10), the use of the SPSS (Statistical Package for Social Sciences) will be preferable. Such statistical software is not difficult to use for the questions you are likely to be addressing and the software should be available for student access at your study centre. Your project tutor or supervisor will be able to clarify this for you.

RECORD-KEEPING

To evaluate the information provided from your survey, it is important that you keep a record of non-responses. This should include:

- **number of non-located responses:** the number of respondents in your sampling frame who could not be found (for example, a postal questionnaire which was 'returned to sender' or an email survey that 'bounced back')
- **number of non-contact responses:** the number of respondents who were perpetually out (in a telephone survey) or were away during the time of the survey (postal, email or interview)
- **number of ineligible responses:** those respondents who, as a result of any errors in your sampling frame, fall outside your sampling criteria (joined the organisation too recently, work in a non-sampled department, and so on)
- **number of 'refusals':** those who were reached but would not participate in the survey
- **number of incomplete responses:** those who got part way through your survey but did not complete it fully.

For small-scale surveys (a sample size of fewer than 200), a simple 'tally sheet' will probably be sufficient.

ESTABLISHING A CODING STRUCTURE

This stage is where you work out how you will organise the software to record the different responses. Most software packages are organised in the same initial format as a simple spreadsheet, whereby the variables within your questionnaire are recorded in columns and each respondent's responses are contained within a row. For each reply option on your survey instrument there must be a discrete code. This will take a numerical form. The first item to code is the identity of the questionnaire response (not the individual). This is your 'audit trail' and ensures that you can identify each questionnaire in the future and, if necessary, return to check the data it contains. This is illustrated in Tables 9.8 and 9.9.

Table 9.8 Illustrative survey questions

				Tick box
Are you male or female?			Male	
			Female	
What is your age?			Under 25 years	
			25–35 years	
			36–45 years	
			46–55 years	
			56 or more years	
How long have you worked for your current organisation?			Less than 1 year	
			1–5 years	
			6–10 years	
			More than 10 years	
Please tick the most appropriate box for the following questions				
	A lot	Somewhat	Only a little	Not at all
To what extent do you trust your immediate line manager to look after your best interests?				
To what extent do you trust senior management to look after your best interests?				
In general, would you say you trust your company or organisation?				
	Yes – definitely	Yes – probably	No – probably not	Not at all
Do you feel you are fairly paid for the work you do?				
Overall, do you feel you are rewarded fairly compared with other people doing similar jobs to you?				

Table 9.9 Illustrative coding structure

Column	Variable name	Codes
A	Questionnaire ID	Questionnaire ID (start at 001)

Column	Variable name	Codes
B	Q1 – Gender	1 = Male 2 = Female 9 = non-response
C	Q2 – Age	1 = under 25 years 2 = 25–35 years 3 = 36–45 years 4 = 46–55 years 5 = 56 or more years 9 = non-response
D	Q3 – Length of service	1 = less than 1 year 2 = 1–5 years 3 = 6–10 years 4 = more than 10 years 9 = non-response
E	Q4 – Immediate manager trust	3 = a lot 2 = somewhat 1 = only a little 0 = not at all 9 = non-response
F	Q5 – Senior management trust	3 = a lot 2 = somewhat 1 = only a little 0 = not at all 9 = non-response
G	Q6 – Organisational trust	3 = a lot 2 = somewhat 1 = only a little 0 = not at all 9 = non-response

Column	Variable name	Codes
H	Q7 – Job pay fairness	3 = yes – definitely 2 = yes – probably 1 = no – probably not 0 = not at all 9 = non-response
I	Q8 – Comparative pay fairness	3 = yes – definitely 2 = yes – probably 1 = no – probably not 0 = not at all 9 = non-response

DATA ENTRY

Although rather laborious, once the coding structure is established the process of data entry is relatively quick. With web-based surveys the software will automatically provide the responses in a spreadsheet form, although you may find that you need to re-label the columns and cells. Manual data entry is also not difficult, although it can be boring and it is important to stay alert to ensure an accurate process.

It is a good idea to establish the coding structure for your questionnaire before you pilot it because the very activity of coding can highlight potential problems. You can also pilot the data entry process with the responses from your pilot study to establish any potential problems. There are a variety of methods of data entry. The most common for many student projects is for a manual process, but software packages will allow for structured interview data to be entered on a direct basis from a personal computer and some organisations have facilities for optical mark reading of questionnaire responses.

CLEAN THE DATA SET

When your data have been entered it is important to evaluate the accuracy of the process. It is extremely rare that no errors will have occurred, and it is important to identify them and correct them at the start of the data presentation and analysis process. First, you should carry out a visual check of the data can be made to look for 'impossible' codes. A coding of '6' when there are only four attributes, for example, is an indicator that the responses for that questionnaire need to be checked again. Second, it is worthwhile choosing a random sample of questionnaires and checking the entries for them. If there are too many errors in your sample, the whole data set should be checked again. Figure 9.4 provides an example of common data entry errors.

Figure 9.4 Illustrative data entry errors

ID	Q1	Q2	Q3	Q4	Q5	Q6	Q7	Q8
1	1	2	4	2	3	3	2	2
2	1	3	3	2	3	2	2	1
3	2	5	3	2	3	3	2	2
4	2	4	3	0	1	2	1	1
5	1	4	2	3	2	1	2	2
6	9	4	1	0	1	0	1	2
7	1	3	2	2	3	2	2	3
8	1	2	2	2	3	2	2	3
9	2	1	(11)	2	2	1	1	2
10	2	9	4	1	1	2	1	2
11	1	2	3	1	2	3	2	1
12	2	2	3	1	2	2	2	1
13	1	2	2	1	2	3	2	1
14	2	2	2	1	3	2	3	(11)
15	(22)	5	2	1	1	2	2	2
16	1	4	2	0	0	0	(11)	1
(178)	1	4	1	9	9	0	2	2
18	1	1	9	1	2	1	2	2
19	1	(33)	2	2	3	3	2	2
20	1	1	3	2	3	2	2	3
21	2	1	3	2	2	3	2	1
22	2	2	2	2	1	2	2	2
23	(21)	5	2	3	2	1	1	2
24	2	3	2	3	2	2	2	2
25	1	4	1	3	2	3	2	2
26	1	2	2	2	3	2	3	2
27	1	9	2	2	2	2	2	1
28	9	1	2	2	1	2	2	2
29	2	2	2	9	2	1	1	2
30	1	1	3	2	1	2	2	2

PRESENT THE DATA

Having entered and cleaned the data, the final stage in this part of the process is to describe and summarise the information using tables and/or charts. Both tables and charts (most often a judicious combination of the two) will provide you with some insight about possible associations between different variables.

This process of **descriptive analysis**, therefore, transforms raw data into a form that makes it possible to understand and interpret it. Although charts look attractive, it is important not to 'overdo it' with charts and diagrams. Use them sparingly to add value to the analysis and understanding process. The first stage of this is to describe the frequency of all the different attributes within the survey. If you plan to use SPSS for your data analysis, you will find the data presentation tools are easy and effective to use. To help those who decide to stick with Excel, the examples given below describe some of the actions you can take. These are written with the needs of absolute novices in mind: if you are nervous about numbers and nervous about Excel, read on. If you are confident and competent in this area, jump ahead to the next section of the chapter.

DATA PRESENTATION USING EXCEL

1. Organise your worksheet

Once you have 'cleaned your data set', you will want to make it easier to use.

1   Label the columns by positioning the cursor in the column heading you wish to label. What you type in will be shown in the ribbon above the worksheet.

2   Select the column you wish to work with and use the find and replace tool at the top right of the screen to re-label variables expressed as numbers with an appropriate label.

Figure 9.5 Labelling columns

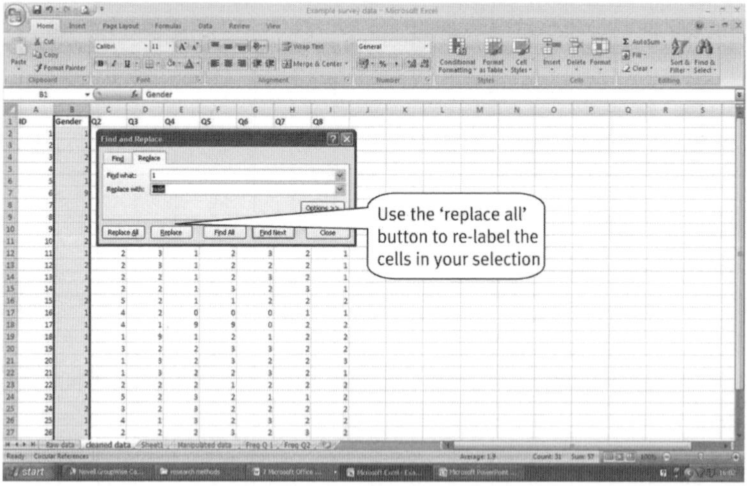

3   Label your worksheet by positioning the cursor over the tab at the bottom of the sheet and 'right-clicking'. Then choose 'rename' and type in the label you would like to use.

4   Excel can seem frustrating if you have a lot of data or a lot of variables because you can lose sight of the labels for your columns and rows. To overcome this use the 'freeze panes' command to make the column and row headings stay in view when you are scrolling down and across your data set.

You will find this on the 'view' tab on the menu options at the top of your screen. Before you use the command make sure you position your cursor underneath the top row and next to the first column of your data.

Figure 9.6 Freeze panes

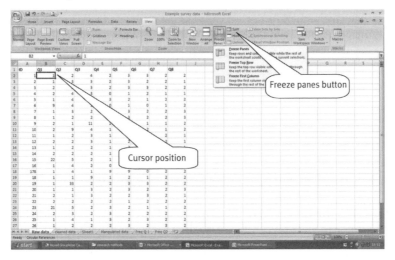

5   You can amend the row height (your data will seem less squashed!) by highlighting the data and then using the format button (part of 'cells' on the 'home' tab).

6   A quick and easy way to adjust the column width for your columns is to position your cursor at the top of the column you wish to alter (at its right-hand limit) and double-click. This will bring the column to fit the widest entry in that column (so don't bother with this until you have finished all your other labelling!).

2. Present your data using tables and charts

To undertake this process you need to 'flip' and summarise your data. For this you need to use the 'pivot table' command. To generate a pivot table, highlight the data range you wish to include and use the 'insert' tab to find 'pivot table'.

Figure 9.7 Pivot table command in Excel

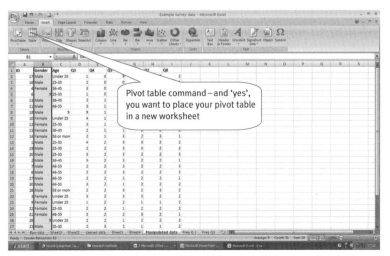

A dialogue box then appears. In the pivot table field list, tick the boxes that you want to include in your pivot table. Also drag the items into the 'values box'. As long as your data is formed of text labels, it will count the items for you.

Figure 9.8 Selecting fields for your pivot table

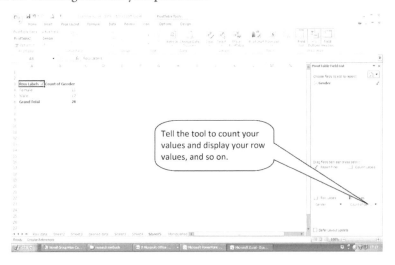

You can now tell Excel to calculate the percentages for you in the next column if you wish. Do this by using the '=' command in the cell to indicate a calculation and then highlight the first cell value you wish to include (b3 in this example) and then use the '/' symbol (divide by) and highlight the cell with the total count (b6 in this example). If you press return you will probably get a long decimal number, so tell Excel you want this as a percentage by using the 'number box' on the top ribbon.

Excel is quite good at charts too, once your data are nicely tabulated. To create a chart you highlight the row labels and the associated columns you wish to include and then go to the insert tab and choose from the range of charts available.

Figure 9.9 The chart options in Excel

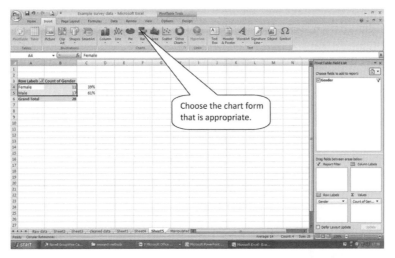

There is also a very useful tool on the 'chart layout tab' that will allow you to ask Excel to add the percentages to your chart. Once you have created your tables and charts, it is easy to copy them and paste them into a Word file.

Figure 9.10 Making use of the chart layout tab

The most common forms of chart that may be useful to present a summary of your data include:

- **pie charts**, where percentage data is represented as a series of categories that are compared within a circle, which represents 100% of all cases (see Figure 9.11)
- **bar charts**, where the length or height of the bars (depending on whether they are presented on the horizontal or vertical axis) represents an appropriate number or percentage (see Figure 9.12).

Figure 9.11 Example pie chart

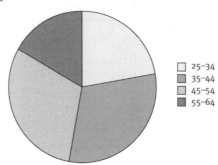

- [ ] 25–34
- [■] 35–44
- [ ] 45–54
- [■] 55–64

Figure 9.12 Example bar chart

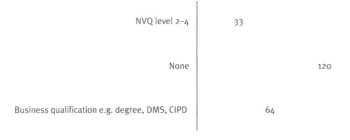

NVQ level 2–4	33
None	120
Business qualification e.g. degree, DMS, CIPD	64

These methods of presentation are particularly appropriate for presenting nominal scale (category) data. Other forms of graph can demonstrate the relationship between two variables. A **line graph** can represent the relationship of one variable with time (the trend in pay rates for different types of staff is often represented in this way, for example). For interval scale data, a **histogram** is also an appropriate way of representing the data you have collected.

Figure 9.13 Example of a histogram

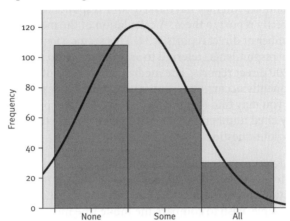

While a histogram looks similar to a bar chart, the regularity of the intervals means that the distribution of cases within the organisation can also be evaluated graphically and, where the intervals are the same, can be compared with the distribution in another sample group.

For most HR management research reports, the use of summary tables and charts, rather than histograms, is likely to form the main approach to presenting data. It is important not to get too 'carried away' with the charting potential of software packages. For students undertaking a master's qualification, a fuller consideration of the data is likely to be required. There are occasions where charts can advance understanding and comparison, but used too frequently, with little more than a decorative purpose, they diminish rather than advance the persuasiveness of your research report.

FIRST-LEVEL DATA ANALYSIS

Describing the frequencies of different questionnaire responses is helpful in enabling you (and those who will assess your project) to make sense of the data. In addition it is helpful to establish some measures by which you can compare the responses with different variables in a more concise way. The way that you approach this will depend on the type of data you have gathered. As noted already, with **nominal or ordinal data**, there is no defined 'distance' between the attributes of the variable. Therefore mathematical operations are not viable, although 'counting' the frequencies and describing these as **proportions, percentages or ratios** are possible and provide a means for comparison.

For **ratio and interval scale data** it is possible to calculate **measures of central tendency** (mean, mode and median) to assist comparisons between different variables. There are three forms of these:

- The **mode** is the most frequently occurring value.
- The **median** is the middle point of the range.
- The **mean** is the average value (calculated by adding all the values together and then dividing by the number of cases).

These can all be useful measures to help you make sense of the data that you have gathered. For example, you may have asked your respondents to indicate how many people directly report to them. A calculation of the mean may indicate that the 'average' number of direct reports is 38. This seems a very high figure, and it may reflect a few respondents (referred to as 'outliers') who have indicated that they have over 200 direct reports. The median (middle point of the range) and mode (most frequently occurring response) are more likely to be helpful here. In such a situation you may find that the median is 8 direct reports and the mode (most frequently cited number) is 6, and this gives you a better 'overall picture' of the responses to your question.

If you are using Excel to store your data, you may be pleased to read that you do not have to create pivot tables to work out measures of central tendency – you can use the function command for this. You can find this just above your data set. You may, for example, wish to compare the mode (the most frequently occurring variable) for responses to questions with a number of response options. To do this you take one question at a time: position the cursor at a suitable place (below the relevant column?), choose the function command and then choose 'mode' from the menu you are offered. Then highlight the range of values you wish to be included before pressing the OK or return button to see the value displayed where you left your cursor.

Figure 9.14 Using the function command in Excel for simple procedures

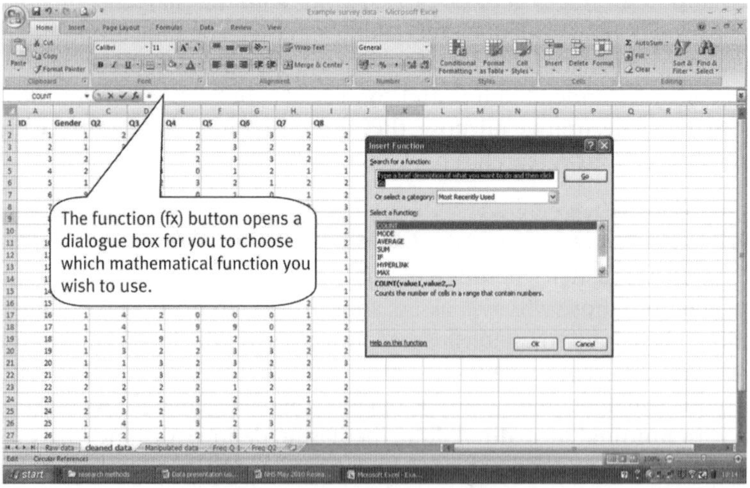

Another worthwhile characteristic to explore for single variables may be the spread or dispersion of the variables. This is interesting in its own right but also crucial to know about if you propose to do any data analysis along the lines outlined in Chapter 10. The calculation of an average length of service of 5.3 years for those who left an organisation during 2012 may mask the fact that one or two leavers had very long lengths of service and many others left with only a few months of employment with the organisation.

There are two main measures of dispersion. The **range** is the distance between the lowest value and the highest. This is the simplest measure of 'spread' but it can be misleading (if only one person had 38 years of service and the rest had less than one year). A more informative way of assessing dispersion is to identify the point at which 25% of the respondents (the distribution) have that 'score' or less and the point at which 75% of the sample have that score or less. These are referred to as the 25th and 75th **percentiles**. The 50th percentile is the median (the middle point of the range). It would also be possible to divide your sample up into ten percentile 'chunks'. A calculation of the 25th and 75th percentile, therefore (or the 10th and 90th), may be more informative about the dispersion of the values than a simple calculation of the range.

The most popular measure of dispersion that is derived from a calculation of percentiles within any sample is **standard deviation**. This is a measure of the average distance between all the values and the mean. The smaller the standard deviation, the more similar are the values within the distribution. Standard deviation is complex to calculate manually (and not covered here), but is a common function of software and calculator programs and so can be undertaken easily enough. It is, however, not an appropriate function when applied to nominal scale data and should not really be used (although you may well see it used) with ordinal scale data. Figure 9.15 provides an example of a line graph that represents the distribution of responses to the question. The highest point of the graph represents the mean value, and then the area underneath the line corresponds to the proportion of responses with a standard deviation more than (and less than) the central point. If your data approximate to an even 'bell curve', it is likely that your responses fall within what is termed a 'normal distribution' (see Figure 9.15). This is worth knowing about if you plan to undertake any of the analysis processes outlined in Chapter 10.

Figure 9.15 Example of a normal curve of distribution

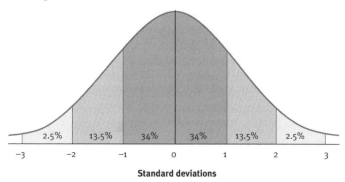

Assuming that you have some interval or ratio scale data, therefore, it is possible to calculate measures of central tendency and measures of dispersion as part of the analysis of your data, and these calculations provide a useful start with making sense of your data. However, it is much more interesting to assess the relationship between different variables. This and other statistical tools that can be used are outlined in the next chapter.

SUMMARY

- Quantitative data involves the measurement of variables that can be counted, described and compared.
- Quantitative data can be used as part of an inductive or deductive approach to research.
- In addition to surveys undertaken for a particular research purpose, quantitative data can be obtained from secondary sources, such as published surveys, that may be undertaken on a regular or an ad hoc basis.
- Effective sampling techniques are important if the data that are obtained are to be representative of the population being studied.
- The planning process for any survey must take into account the purpose of the research, the research questions, the advantages and disadvantages of different types of question and the format in which responses are sought. Response scales and structure will affect the forms of analysis that will be possible.
- A range of issues are relevant to the questionnaire design process. These include: the initial contact/request/instructions to respondents, the layout of the survey, the language of the questions and the arrangements for return.
- Piloting the survey and the process of recording and organising the data (data entry) will enhance the quality of the questionnaire and the usefulness of the data it generates.
- Surveys can be undertaken in a range of ways. The main options are: postal, self-administered; delivered and collected; structured telephone interviews; structured face-to-face interviews; email questionnaires; and web-based surveys.
- A coding structure, established in advance, enables data to be electronically organised and summarised.
- Following the initial data entry process, it is important to 'clean' the data of any data-inputting errors.
- Data can be presented in the form of summary tables and charts. These include pie charts, bar charts, line graphs and histograms. Use charts sparingly to add value to the analysis and understanding process.
- Analytical processes for single variables include the consideration of frequencies, proportions, percentages and ratios. For some types of data it is also possible to calculate measures of central tendency, such as the mean, median and mode, as well as the dispersion (range or standard deviation).

Self-test questions

1 Quantitative data is the term used to describe:

a) all the data you include in your research report

b) charts and tables

c) statistical tests

d) data in the form of numbers and measures

2 Which one of the following is the principal quantitative method of data capture in HR?

a) focus groups

b) surveys

c) participant observation

d) discourse analysis

3 Which one of the following scales is commonly used to measure opinions in a questionnaire?

a) ranking scale

b) nominal questions

c) Likert rating scale

d) open question

4 Which of the following is NOT part of the sampling process?

a) determining the sample frame

b) defining the research population

c) clarifying the research question

d) selecting an appropriate sampling technique

5 A sampling frame is:

a) the different stages involved in survey design

b) a list of all the people in the research population from whom the sample will be drawn

c) a set of random numbers

d) the structure of the questionnaire

6 Which of the following is a type of probability sample?

a) systematic random sample

b) snowball sample

c) convenience sample

d) purposive sample

7 Which of the following is NOT a measure of central tendency?

a) mode

b) middle

c) mean

d) median

8 Which of the following is not a type of graph?

a) box

b) pie

c) bar

d) scatter

9 Name a software package for analysing quantitative data:

a) Atlas TI

b) Microsoft Word

c) SPSS

d) Microsoft Access

Review questions

1   How clear are you about your research questions? How important will quantitative data be in answering them? Will this involve describing frequencies or undertaking a deeper level of analysis?

2   What depth of data analysis is required within the assessment criteria of your study centre for the qualification you are working towards?

Questions for reflection

This final part of the chapter enables you to reflect about your professional development and develop your skills and knowledge. This will enable you to build your confidence and credibility, track your learning, see your progress and demonstrate your achievements.

Taking stock

1   What sources of quantitative data may already be available that might be relevant to your research questions? How can you go about accessing and evaluating them?

2   Who might you approach for help with the piloting of your questionnaire and how might you make use of their feedback?

3   What software for data entry and analysis is available to you? What might you do to enhance your competence and confidence with using it?

Strengths and weaknesses

4   What experience do you have of survey design? What personal development areas are you aware of and how might you meet them?

5   How well do you understand the advantages and limitations of different sampling techniques in

relation to your project? What information or support might help you to develop your understanding and apply an appropriate sampling process for your enquiry?

6   How well do you understand the implications of different question structures for subsequent analysis of the data? Who can help you with this decision-making process?

7   How confident are you about the level of your numerical/statistical competence? What development activities would help enhance this?

Being a practitioner-researcher

8   Is there anyone in the organisation (often there is someone in marketing or planning) who would be able to offer advice and guidance on the survey design, administration and analysis processes? How might you find out about them?

9   How might you go about developing a sampling frame of good quality from which to select a sample? Who may be able to offer support with this process?

10 What organisational factors may influence decisions about sample size and selection? In what way

might that affect the quality of the data that you obtain?

11 What 'permissions' do you need to undertake a survey within the organisation? Who might be able to influence these decisions? What actions can you take to influence the response rate for your survey?

12 What level of feedback from the data is required by the organisation? How will this impact the way you collect, organise and present the data?

EXPLORE FURTHER

Web Links

http://lap.umd.edu/survey_design/questionnaires.html – focuses on questionnaire design for web-based surveys.

http://www.surveymonkey.com/ – online survey provider – prices vary depending on the number of questions and the time the survey will be 'live'. There is also a charge to retrieve your data.

http://zoomerang.com/online-surveys/ – online survey provider – prices vary depending on usage.

http://www.statistics.gov.uk/ – data sets and information on data sources from the UK Statistics Authority.

http://www.bis.gov.uk/policies/employment-matters/research/wers – information about the WERS 2012 data collection process.

http://www.cipd.co.uk/onlineinfodocuments/surveys.htm – surveys published by the CIPD.

http://gsociology.icaap.org/methods/surveys.htm

http://www.reading.ac.uk/ssc/n/resources/PlanningDataCollection.htm

Reading

Bourque, L.B. and Fieldler, E.P. (1995) *How to conduct self-administered and mail surveys*. London: Sage.

Bryman, A. and Bell, E. (2007) *Business research methods*. Oxford: Oxford University Press.

Bryman, A. and Cramer, D. (1997) *Quantitative data analysis for social scientists*. London: Routledge.

Cobanoglu, C., Warde, B. and Moreo, P. (2001) A comparison of mail, fax, and webbased survey methods, *International Journal of Market Research*, 43(4): 441–52.

Collis, J. and Hussey, R. (2009) *Business research: a practical guide for undergraduate and postgraduate students*. Basingstoke: Palgrave.

Couper, M.P., Traugott, M. and Lamias, M. (2001) Web survey design and administration, *Public Opinion Quarterly*, 65(1): 230–53.

deVaus, D.A. (2002) *Surveys in social research*. London: Routledge.

Dillman, D.A. (1999) *Mail and internet surveys: the tailored design method*. New York: John Wiley and Sons.

Fowler, E.J. (2009) *Survey research methods*. Newbury Park, CA: Sage.

Gill, J., Johnson, P. and Clark, M. (2010) *Research methods for managers*. London: Sage.

Hart, C. (2010) *Doing your master's dissertation*. London: Sage.

Lee, N. and Lings, L. (2008) *Doing business research: a guide to theory and practice*. London: Sage.

Neuman, W. (2011) *Basics of social research: qualitative and quantitative approaches*. International edition. Harlow: Pearson Education.

Oppenheim, A.N. (2001) *Questionnaire design, interviewing and attitude measurement*. London: Continuum International.

Peterson, R. (2000) *Constructing effective questionnaires*. Thousand Oaks, CA: Sage.

Robson, C. (2011) *Real world research: a resource for social scientists and practitioner-*

researchers. Oxford: Wiley.

Saunders, M., Lewis, P. and Thornhill, A. (2012) *Research methods for business students*. Harlow: Pearson Education.

Zikmund, W.G. (2009) *Business research methods*. London: Cengage Learning.

CHAPTER 10

Analysing Quantitative Data

CHAPTER OUTLINE

- How to use this chapter
- Quantitative data analysis in plain English
- An 'analysis routemap'
- Assessing the relationship between two variables
- Analysing data to answer research questions
- Summary
- Review and reflect
- Explore further

LEARNING OUTCOMES

This chapter should help you to:

- make sense of basic terminology used in quantitative data analysis
- undertake an initial analysis of your data
- discuss the reliability of the data you have gathered
- identify appropriate tools to interpret your data to answer your research questions
- draw appropriate conclusions based on your data.

HOW TO USE THIS CHAPTER

This chapter has been written to help those whose need to analyse rather than 'just' describe numerical data. Brett-Davies (2007) notes that the world is divided into two kinds of people: the first (quite small) group of people are those who are statisticians. The second group are the rest of us. If you are a statistician, you can work through this chapter very quickly and progress to more specialised statistical texts and discussions. If you are one of 'the rest of us' and you occasionally come close to a panic attack when statistical terms are used and multiple regression analyses or reliability coefficients are presented, this chapter is for you. It sets out to explain in 'plain English' the main issues to consider if you wish to interpret data and formulate meaningful conclusions on the basis of your analysis.

What you will not find in this chapter is a step-by-step guide to using statistical analysis packages. Textbooks about quantitative data analysis increasingly include some step-by-step instructions about the use of one or another of the available packages, particularly IBM SPSS (Statistical Package for Social Sciences). I have not done this here for two reasons. First, some students, particularly CIPD students who are researching into a business issue, may not wish to or be able to access the software and may have a preference to use a more generic database or spreadsheet package (such as Excel). Second, new versions of statistics software are frequently developed and the step-by-step instructions become out of date very quickly.

However, if you intend to undertake statistical analysis you will need to develop some familiarity with appropriate software. Excel will be required as a minimum and you will be able to get further faster with SPSS. Most study centre libraries have copies of SPSS that can be loaned and installed for discrete periods of time onto your own computer and there will be networked versions within the university or college itself. If you are a part-time student, it is worth asking if your employer already has a licence. If you are undertaking a master's level dissertation (or aiming higher), you should certainly arrange access to a copy.

 Help – I have collected data – what should I do next?

CASE ILLUSTRATION 10.1

Afrah was a student who was undertaking comparative research for her dissertation involving some people working in a UK organisation and other people working in an organisation in her country of Kuwait. Afrah was undertaking comparative research to investigate the extent to which social capital in organisations is related to enhanced work performance by employees (see Case Illustration 9.3). She spent some time devising a good-quality survey instrument to explore people's experience of social capital and work performance. In particular, Afrah was interested to examine the extent to which social capital and performance was differently experienced in Kuwait and the UK.

Afrah overcame a number of setbacks with collecting her data and was left with very little time to undertake the data analysis. Afrah had decided to use

SPSS for her data analysis and set about entering her data onto the software. However, once she had completed the data entry, Afrah realised that she did not know where to start with presenting and analysing her data. She found the way to generate some attractive-looking frequency tables to provide an overall description of her data along the lines explained in Chapter 9. After that, however, the software offered numerous statistical tools, none of which she understood, and she realised that she needed help fast if she was to interpret the data at a deeper level.

Discussion Questions

1   Why was it necessary for Afrah to explore the data more fully?

2   What questions did Afrah need to address to decide how to

move forward with her data analysis?	3	Where might Afrah go for help?

FEEDBACK NOTES

As noted in Chapter 9, descriptive statistics are very useful and they provided Afrah with a helpful summary of the main features of the data she had collected. It was possible to see 'at a glance' the frequency with which different variables were reported by those who responded to her survey. This enabled Afrah to get a sense of the trends involved. However, although the descriptive summary 'painted a picture' in numerical terms, it was not possible for her to assess the extent to which her results were purely due to coincidence or chance. Neither did the descriptive approach enable her to explore potential relationships between different variables, particularly the extent to which different groups (people in Kuwait and in the UK) responded to her survey questions.

To move forward with her data analysis, Afrah needed to remind herself of her specific research questions. With this in mind she could then begin to identify which statistical tools would be relevant to interpret her data and answer her research questions. Afrah consulted one or two 'how-to' books on statistical analysis using SPSS to take her project forward. For many students (and other researchers) these form an invaluable basis for survival during the data analysis process. It is also a good idea to consult any friends, colleagues or tutors who have an interest and expertise in quantitative data analysis because they can help you to work out the best way to interpret your results.

 ## ACTIVITY 10.1

FEAR OF HEIGHTS, SPIDERS OR STATS?

Think back to times when you have had to undertake a numerical analysis (maybe as part of your course or possibly when you were at school).

- Identify what worries you had when you started out.
- What helped you to 'get by'?
- What positive experiences did you associate with completing the numerical tasks?

FEEDBACK NOTES

In response to these questions, many people might confess to having 'bad memories' of maths from school. Maths, and other numerically based subjects, are often remembered as times where people recall frequently getting answers 'wrong' in classroom or homework situations. This can lead to a long-term 'aversion' to numerical work so that it is avoided rather than practised. In addition, students often say that it is easy to forget the numerical 'terms' and/or 'formulae', and the process of revising these again to undertake some form of analysis is time-consuming and often does not seem to be worth the effort. As a result many researchers, particularly those who either work in HR or who aspire to work in HR, lack confidence in their numerical abilities. However, solving a numerical 'puzzle' or using numerical data to shed new light on a problem or issue can be very satisfying (in the same sense that completing a Sudoku puzzle might be) and most people have a greater numerical aptitude than they think. Numerical reasoning is very similar in structure to musical reasoning – it is not something that is only for 'clever types'. Most people have little to fear from the sort of analysis that underpins a quantitative research project once a few basic issues have been clarified.

QUANTITATIVE DATA ANALYSIS IN PLAIN ENGLISH

One of the problems that can beset HR researchers who try to 'read up' about statistics is the specialised language that is often used. However, don't be put off by the technical terminology. As Rugg and Petre (2007, p168) point out, **statistics** are really nothing more complicated than 'describing things with numbers and assessing the odds'. Indeed, the meanings behind many statistical terms are quite straightforward. Also, you do not have to be an expert 'across the board' of statistics. Some features may not be relevant to your work and you should not feel forced to use them. Before a consideration of which statistical tests are most likely to be appropriate to your research project, therefore, some 'plain English' definitions and observations about some of these terms are offered here (Rugg and Petre 2007, Rugg 2007, Brett-Davies 2007, Bryman and Bell 2007):

- **Variable:** this is an important term and you will find yourself using it. It refers, simply, to something that is likely to vary. In HR research, for example, this may be an attribute of a person or an organisation (for example, size, age, level of commitment, and so on).
- **Independent variable:** this is the **cause** of something or some things that vary. For example, 'high levels of absence from work' (the independent variable) may **cause** or **lead to** 'low productivity levels'.
- **Dependent variable:** this is the thing that varies because it is **affected** by the cause. For example, 'low productivity levels' (the dependent variable) may be affected by 'high levels of absence from work'.
- **Probability:** this is pretty important to quantitative data analysis. Probability refers to the extent to which your findings can be explained (or not) as the result of random chance. Probability is important: if you can show, for example, that there is only a 1 in 1,000 chance of your findings being the result of coincidence, you can feel pretty confident in them. Probability is often referred to as 'p' (pronounced pee) and the values are usually stated as decimal figures. The main figures to take notice of are:

  1    $p = 0.05$ means 1 chance in 20 of a result occurring through coincidence
  2    $p = 0.01$ means 1 chance in 100 of a result occurring through coincidence
  3    $p = 0.001$ means 1 chance in 1,000 of a result occurring through coincidence.

- **Significance:** this is a nice term to use when you discuss your findings. Significance is no more than a verbal signpost about how confident you can be that your results (generated by a randomly selected sample) are generalisable to the wider research population. Expressions of significance stem from measures of probability (see above). When evaluating your findings you may want to use the following accepted expressions:

1 **'significant'** means 1 chance in 20 or beyond that this happened by coincidence (where p = 0.05 or less)
2 **'highly significant'** means 1 chance in 100 or beyond that this happened by coincidence (where p = 0.01 or less)
3 **'very highly significant'** means 1 chance in 1,000 or beyond that this happened by coincidence (where p = 0.001 or less).

- **Hypothesis:** this is an 'informed guess' that there may be a relationship between two or more variables. Once you have a hypothesis you can then analyse your data to test out whether they suggest that there is (or is not) a relationship and you can assess the significance (see above) of the association between the variables. If you do not feel confident about the whole 'hypothesis approach', you should not try to force yourself to produce one. You can still undertake very good research provided that you formulate good-quality research questions or objectives.

- **Null hypothesis:** this expression is the source of endless confusion and frustration to many non-statistical people. It is confusing because it works on a 'double negative' basis. Statisticians are good at double negatives; the rest of us find them bemusing. The null hypothesis actually means that when you test out the likelihood that your results occurred by chance (which is certainly worth doing), you make an assumption that there is NO relationship between the variables (that is the null hypothesis). Then you run an appropriate significance test (using software) to see whether you can disprove your null hypothesis (and therefore show that there IS a significant relationship).

- **One-tailed hypothesis and two-tailed hypothesis:** these are also confusing and frustrating terms if you are not a 'hypothesis type'. However, you will come across them in research that you read and also in the statistical tools that you use. A 'one-tailed hypothesis' is where you think (hypothesise) that there is an association between two variables **in a specific direction**. In HR research, for example, you may want to test whether stress levels lead to absence from work. Therefore you might write your hypothesis in note form as:

stress → absence from work

You have one 'point' on your arrow and so this represents a 'one-tailed hypothesis'.

For other relationships it may be unrealistic to assess the direction of the association. For example, you may want to test the association between 'manager self-confidence' and 'manager training undertaken'. Here it may be possible that training for managers improves their levels of self-confidence, but it is equally possible that those managers who are already self-confident may seek out more training and development opportunities. Therefore this hypothesis is expressed in note form as:

manager self-confidence ↔ manager training

Because the direction of the association could be either way, there are two points to the arrow and so you have a 'two-tailed hypothesis'. This may seem trivial but it affects the assessment you can make about significance, which is why the statistics software always refers to it. Usually probability values are calculated by the software for a two-tailed hypothesis. If you have a one-tailed hypothesis, you would need to divide the probability value by two. If you get very advanced with your statistics, there are also further tests that you can run for one-tailed and two-tailed hypotheses.

- **Parametric data:** this is another term that is a source of irritation for non-statisticians. However, it is no more than a way of categorising different kinds of data. Parametric is the term used to describe data that meets certain criteria. If your data are parametric, there are specific statistical tests that are appropriate to use. If your data are 'non-parametric', you simply use different statistical tools. To decide if your data are 'parametric', you must answer the following questions:

1 Is your data normally distributed or not? (See Chapter 9 for normal distribution.)

2 If you have gathered data from separate groupings and you wish to assess the differences between the groups (for example, in different companies, in different parts of the organisation or in different countries), are the sample sizes similar?

3 Have you asked all of the participants in your research the same questions? If you have asked different questions to different groups, you are unlikely to meet the criteria for parametric data.

4 Are your data generated from ratio scale or interval scale measures? (See Chapter 9 to revise what these measures look like.)

If (hand on heart) you can answer 'yes' to all of these questions, your data are suitable for statistical tests designed for parametric data. If (and this is more likely) you answered 'no' to one or more of these questions, you should use statistical tools designed for non-parametric data. This is not something that should unduly worry you. Non-parametric tests work differently but they still work. The different tests for parametric and non-parametric tests are shown in Table 10.11.

AN 'ANALYSIS ROUTEMAP'

The question of where and how to start with data analysis is a real worry to HR students who are unfamiliar with the quantitative data analysis language and 'world-view'. Figure 10.1 indicates the main steps you can take and the issues you should address as you set out on your 'journey' through the quantitative analysis process. The tests that are referred to in Figure 10.1 are explained later in this chapter.

Figure 10.1 Steps and options for quantitative data analysis

Step 1: Review your research questions

What questions do you need to answer by interpreting the data?

Step 2: Review your data

- Look through your data frequencies and description.
- Can you spot possible associations between variables?
- What seems to be there that you might expect?
- What surprises are there?
- What do you need to check?

Step 3: Choose your test(s)

Do you wish to test the effect of some category-based variables? For example: age; gender; ethnicity; grade; organisation type (public; private; non-profit); organisation size (large; small; medium)	Do you wish to test the association between variables measured on a scale and see whether they vary in a consistent way or whether one variable can predict the outcome of another? For example: the association between manager training; management style; manager self-confidence; length of management experience	Do you wish to examine whether a number of variables cluster together to represent something (that you might then treat as a new variable)? For example: what are the principal components of employee engagement in your organisation?
Tests of association and tests of difference	Tests of correlation and regression	Principal component analysis or factor analysis

ACTIVITY 10.2

PLANNING THE ANALYSIS

Visit http://www.partnersforlearning.com/instructions.html, where you should find information about the 'dimensions of the learning organisation' questionnaire. Use the link provided on this site to view the survey instrument itself. You do not have to complete the survey; merely review its structure and the questions that it asks. As you review it you will notice that the language is orientated towards respondents and organisations in the USA, but do not let this stop you from undertaking this activity. Imagine that you are researching into the learning organisation and have decided (with the permission of the authors) to use this survey as the basis for your data collection. You may imagine you plan to get a sample of people from within your organisation to complete the survey or you may imagine that you will get a sample of people from 'the general working population' to reflect on their experience in their own organisations.

FEEDBACK NOTES

There are a range of research questions that you might formulate. You might wish to examine whether those who are more highly paid or more highly educated respond differently to questions about the learning organisation. You may wish to investigate whether organisational factors (such as the sector, the employee numbers or the financial turnover) are important variables affecting the development of a learning organisation approach. To answer these questions you would look to cross-tabulations (sometimes referred to as contingency tables), where you generate a table in a matrix format to display the frequency distribution of the variables.

You might also find it interesting to see if individual, team or organisational factors are more significant for measures of organisational performance or whether there are particular variables within the groups of questions that are particularly significant in the effect they have on a learning organisation approach. To answer these questions you would need to use principal component or factor analysis, which help to indicate whether there are 'clusters' of responses or can suggest the presence of 'key variables'.

Alternatively, you might ask whether there is any association between the different variables within (say) the team and group level section of the survey and the performance measurement questions from the survey. To assess this you would use tests of correlation.

The important part about quantitative analysis, like other forms of analysis, is generating appropriate questions. To undertake a robust HR project it is important to clearly articulate the questions your research will address. Once this is achieved, it is not too difficult to select the most appropriate statistical tools to enable you to interpret the data to answer your questions.

ASSESSING THE RELATIONSHIP BETWEEN TWO VARIABLES

Bivariate analysis is the term used to refer to an examination of the extent of any relationship between two or more variables. Where there is **no association or relationship** between the variables, they are referred to as being **independent**.

If you are nervous of statistics, bivariate analysis is a good place to start. It is not difficult to undertake, although it takes patience if you decide to include a number of different variables in the process. You can move forward in a number of ways depending on the type of data you have collected.

CROSS-TABULATION (SOMETIMES CALLED CONTINGENCY TABLES)

You can construct these tables for any type of data and they are particularly useful for analysing nominal (category) data. Cross-tabulation involves assessing how the cases in each category of one variable are distributed into each category of a second variable. These require patience to construct manually but are easily produced using statistical packages. An example is shown as Table 10.1.

Table 10.1 Example of cross-tabulation: age and highest qualification

Highest qualification			Age					Total
			Less than 25	25–34	35–44	45–54	Older than 54	
O-level/GCSE	Count		1	20	48	24	9	102
	% within age		1.2%	2.7%	8.2%	10.3%	13.2%	6.0%
A-level	Count		4	49	53	44	12	162
	% within age		4.7%	6.6%	9.1%	18.8%	17.6%	9.5%
HNC	Count		0	7	16	19	4	46
	% within age		0.0%	0.9%	2.7%	8.1%	5.9%	2.7%
HND	Count		1	25	34	14	5	79
	% within age		1.2%	3.4%	5.8%	6.0%	7.4%	4.6%
Degree	Count		76	478	262	71	26	913
	% within age		89.4%	64.9%	44.8%	30.3%	38.2%	53.4%
Postgraduate degree	Count		1	117	63	15	3	199
	% within age		1.2%	15.9%	10.8%	6.4%	4.4%	11.6%
Professional qualification	Count		0	29	87	39	7	162
	% within age		0.0%	3.9%	14.9%	16.7%	10.3%	9.5%
Other	Count		2	12	22	8	2	46
	% within age		2.4%	1.6%	3.8%	3.4%	2.9%	2.7%
Total	Count		85	737	585	234	68	1709
	% within age		100.0%	100.0%	100.0%	100.0%	100.0%	100.0%

(n = 1,709)

Table 10.1 shows an example of a cross-tabulation where raw data have been turned into percentages to reflect the proportion of each subgroup that are represented in each of the cells of the cross-tabulation table. (If you are using SPSS you have to tell it to do this – if you don't it will present the 'raw data' only.) In this example there were over 1,500 respondents to a large-scale questionnaire. The proportions represented by the percentage figures, therefore, make it possible to consider the relationships between the variables (in this case the distribution of educational qualifications across the different age groups). To 'read' the table you look for the direction (if there is one) that the percentages indicate. Where there is no relationship in a table, the percentages will look roughly equal. Although percentages provide a useful mechanism for comparison, remember that where the numbers in the overall group are small (fewer than 50), it is probably more realistic to use numbers rather than percentages.

SCATTERGRAM

This approach is the most visually accessible form of analysis. It is appropriate if you have gathered interval or ratio scale data (see Chapter 9) but **never appropriate** if either variable is a nominal (or category-based) measure. It involves plotting a graph (using software or manually) where each axis represents the value of one variable. If the scatter pattern that emerges looks random, the relationship is one of independence. Where a tendency to a straight line is discernible, this suggests a linear relationship and a 'U' curve represents what is called a 'curvilinear' or non-linear relationship.

 ACTIVITY 10.3

PLOTTING A SCATTERGRAM

1 Use the data given below and plot a scattergram on the empty chart.

2 What does the scattergram suggest about the relationship between length of service and the number of days of sickness absence?

Employee ref. number	Days sick	Length of service (years)
01	6	1
02	4	1
03	5	2
04	6	2.5
05	2	2.5
06	5	3
07	4	3
08	4	3
09	3	3

Employee ref. number	Days sick	Length of service (years)
10	4	3.5
11	3	3.5
12	3	4
13	3	4
14	2	4
15	3	4.5
16	2	4.5
17	3	5
18	2	5
19	2	5
20	1	5
21	2	5.5
22	1	5.5
23	2	6
24	1	6
25	1	6
26	2	6.5
27	1	6.5
28	2	7
29	1	7
30	0	7
31	1	7.5
32	0	7.5
33	0	8
34	6	7
35	1	2

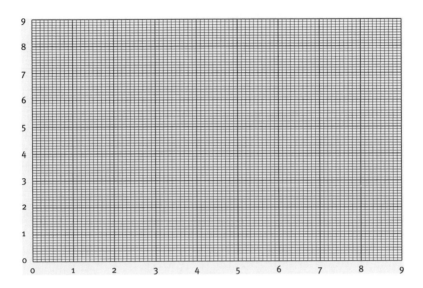

FEEDBACK NOTES

Before plotting this fictional data you have to decide and clearly label which 'axis' represents the 'days' sickness' and which represents 'length of service'. If you have plotted the 'co-ordinates' effectively, you should be able to see an overall declining trend (you could almost draw a straight(ish) line through the general direction of most of the points on the chart). This suggests a negative relationship between length of service and days of sickness absence. However, the presence of data that do not conform to this general trend also indicates that this is not a 'precise' relationship and that there are exceptions. A relationship with a high level of precision, therefore, would be characterised by the points 'hugging' the line.

Figure 10.2 shows a scattergram produced using Excel from the data given in this activity.

Figure 10.2 Scattergram produced using Excel

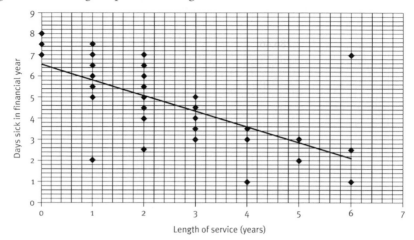

PROBABILITY AND SIGNIFICANCE

Scattergrams and cross-tabulations are visually accessible ways of interpreting data. The drawback is that they do not tell you about the likelihood that these results might have arisen through chance or coincidence, and this is an important feature of any discussion about the importance of your findings. Therefore, it is necessary to test the significance of the association between the variables. The most usual test to run is known as the 'chi-square test' ('chi' is pronounced kuy – rhymes with sky). You may see the chi-squared test represented as χ^2 in some articles. Karl Pearson proposed the chi-square test early in the last century and so (in SPSS at least) it still bears his name. It is widely used in research projects in the field of business and management generally because it can be used to evaluate whether there is an association between the rows and columns in a cross-tabulation (contingency) table.

The chi-square test works by calculating what you might **expect** the counts for each of the cells in your table to be if there was no association between the variables and what the **actual** count is. It then compares 'expected' with 'actual' (rather like a budgeting process) and from this comparison it calculates the extent of any deviation from the 'null hypothesis' (the assumption that there is no relationship whatsoever). The test is only reliable where there is an expected count of at least five in each cell. If your initial tests of association indicate that there might be a relationship between two or more variables, you may also wish to establish the strength of any 'co-variation' and you can examine this further using a test of correlation.

If you are using the SPSS software, you can ask for the chi-squared value to be calculated at the same time as the cross-tabulation is produced (look for the statistics tab at the right-hand corner of the dialogue box and find it in there). The chi-square calculation for the example cross-tabulation (Table 10.1) is shown below as Table 10.2.

Table 10.2 Chi-square example (chi-square tests from Table 10.1)

	Value	df	Asymp. sig. (2-sided)
Pearson's chi-square	286.468[a]	28	.000
Likelihood ratio	296.271	28	.000
Linear-by-linear association	30.706	1	.000
N of valid cases	1709		

a. 7 cells (17.5%) have expected count less than 5. The minimum expected count is 1.83.

On the face of it the results of the chi-square test relating to the association between 'age' and educational qualifications taken from Table 10.2 indicates that there is a non-coincidental relationship between these two variables. The larger the chi-square value, the stronger the likelihood of an association between the variables. However, it is also important to look at the column headed 'Asymp. sig (2-sided)' as this indicates the probability that these results might have occurred as a result of chance or coincidence. Table 10.2 shows that the probability figure is very low (in statistics the use of '0.000' connotes a value of less than 1 in 1,000), so the chance that this relationship occurred as a result of chance is coincidental; you can trust that the results would be replicable on other similar occasions.

TESTS OF CORRELATION

Tests of correlation are useful tools to measure the strength and the direction of association between different variables. They enable you to see whether two or more of them vary in a systematic way. For example, you might want to see whether the extent to which an organisation makes use of classroom training is related to the extent to which they also invest in e-learning, coaching and in the professional development of their employees. You can draw one of three alternative conclusions from tests of correlation. A **positive correlation** occurs when the variables (for example, spend on training courses and spend on coaching) both increase together or decrease together. A **negative correlation** occurs when one variable gets bigger as the other gets smaller. A non-existent correlation occurs when the size of one variable is unrelated to the size of the other.

The two most frequently used tests of correlation are the Spearman's correlation test (used for non-parametric data) and the Pearson's correlation test (used for parametric data). You may see the Spearman's test referred to as Spearman's rho (or r_s) and the Pearson's test uses the symbol 'r'. Both tests calculate a 'correlation co-efficient' ranging between -1 (perfect negative correlation) to **0** (no association) to +**1** (perfect positive correlation).

Where there is a probability that there is a less than 1 in 1,000 chance that the results were due to coincidence (p = 0.000), a correlation of 0.2 to 0.4 can be described as a good level of association; correlations of 0.4 to 0.6 can be described as strong and 'ratings' of 0.6 and above can be described as very strong in a business and management context (Collis and Hussey 2009).

Remember that a correlation test tells you whether variables are associated – it does not mean that one variable causes the other. To access both the Spearman's and Pearson's tests using SPSS, you follow the menu options for 'analyze', 'correlate' and 'bivariate'. You then choose the test you require. For most projects you will want to accept the 'two-tailed test of significance' and you will also want to ensure that the 'flag significant correlations' box is ticked.

ACTIVITY 10.4

Take a look at Table 10.3, which provides a copy of the Pearson's correlation test to assess the association (or lack of it) between different items contained in a survey.

1   How easy is it to make sense of these findings?

2   Which items seem to be most frequently correlated with other items?

3   What do the 'sig. (2-tailed)' figures represent?

Table 10.3 An example of a correlation table

		Gender	Age	Direct reports	Level	Quals	Tenure	Coaching	Relns	Confidence
Gender	Correlation coefficient	1.000	-.179**	-.194**	-.048	-.070	-.080	.124**	.047	.045
	Sig. (2-tailed)	.	.000	.000	.274	.110	.068	.005	.283	.300
	N	521	521	521	521	521	521	521	521	521
Age	Correlation coefficient	.179**	1.000	.050	.146**	.056	.298**	-.026	.028	.007
	Sig. (2-tailed)	.000	.	.257	.001	.204	.000	.550	.522	.866
	N	521	521	521	521	521	521	521	521	521
Direct reports	Correlation coefficient	.194**	.050	1.000	.147**	.063	.152**	.139**	.050	.073
	Sig. (2-tailed)	.000	.257	.	.001	.153	.001	.001	.259	.094
	N	521	521	521	521	521	521	521	521	521
Seniority	Correlation coefficient	-.048	.146**	.147**	1.000	.290**	.114**	.044	.018	.021
	Sig. (2-tailed)	.274	.001	.001	.	.000	.009	.322	.676	.625
	N	521	521	521	521	521	521	521	521	521
Qualifications	Correlation coefficient	-.070	.056	-.063	.290**	1.000	.029	.056	.029	.080
	Sig. (2-tailed)	.110	.204	.153	.000	.	.515	.202	.506	.067
	N	521	521	521	521	521	521	521	521	521
Tenure in this position	Correlation coefficient	.080	.298**	.152**	.114**	.029	1.000	.086	.024	.106*
	Sig. (2-tailed)	.068	.000	.001	.009	.515	.	.051	.586	.015
	N	521	521	521	521	521	521	521	521	521

		Gender	Age	Direct reports	Level	Quals	Tenure	Coaching	Relns	Confidence
Coaching	Correlation coefficient	.124**	.026	.139**	.044	.056	.086	1.000	.373**	.412**
	Sig. (2-tailed)	.005	.550	.001	.322	.202	.051	.	.000	.000
	N	521	521	521	521	521	521	521	521	521
Relationships	Correlation coefficient	.047	.028	.050	.018	.029	.024	.373**	1.000	.354**
	Sig. (2-tailed)	.283	.522	.259	.676	.506	.586	.000	.	.000
	N	521	521	521	521	521	521	521	521	521
Self-confidence	Correlation coefficient	.045	.007	.073	.021	.080	.106*	.412**	.354**	1.000
	Sig. (2-tailed)	.300	.866	.094	.625	.067	.015	.000	.000	.
	N	521	521	521	521	521	521	521	521	521

FEEDBACK NOTES

The first reaction of many of us to a correlation table like this is of confusion and panic. There seems to be no limit to the volume of numbers before our eyes and also the various 'stars' attached to some of the cells and not to others seem baffling. However, once you have got over the initial shock of the volume of data, correlation tables are relatively easy to interpret. The first thing to note is that all the data are provided 'in duplicate'. If you look along the labels for the rows you will see the variables listed and these also form the headings for the columns. This means that you only need to look at half of the data; the other half are repeat values. Which half you choose to look at is up to you. In Table 10.3 the 'line' dividing the duplicate sets of data is shaded grey and it covers the cells in the table where each question is (perfectly) correlated with itself. When looking at these tables, therefore, you may find it helpful to draw a line through the bottom or the top 'triangle' so that you only focus your effort on one set of figures.

The next step with interpreting the correlation table is to scan across the cells either above or below the 'diagonal middle line' (shaded grey in Table 10.3). You will see that some cells have (**) next to them, some have (*) next to them and some have no symbols whatsoever. The star symbols are based on the ever-favourite 'null hypothesis', which makes the assumption that there is NO association between any of the variables. The correlation test then examines the data to see where there is a deviation from the null hypothesis. In this table the items flagged by the software as (*) have a 1 chance in 20 (or 5 in 100) that the association that is recorded has occurred through coincidence. Where the item is flagged with (**), there is a 1 in 100 (or beyond) chance that the association results from coincidence and so these correlations may be more significant. Data analysis is about choices and judgement, so you next must decide if you wish to treat the cells with (*) as worthy of your attention. To provide a 'clearer view', some people will choose to highlight only the cells they wish to continue viewing on this basis and/or delete the cells on a copy of the table where there is no significant correlation.

As you assess the data you might be interested to see where the highest correlations occur and also the direction of the correlations. The negative correlations have a minus sign in front of the correlation co-efficient value. You might mark the 'positives' in one colour and the 'negatives' in another. This should make it easier to make sense of the correlation test results.

Another feature of the correlation table is that the 'sig. 2-tailed' figure is also shown. The significance figures might suggest different levels of probability of the result occurring through chance for different correlations and you should reflect on this in your interpretation. If the correlation test indicates only correlations where the 'best' results were flagged (*), you should reflect on the significance shown in the cells of the table to ensure you take account of the different levels of probability that they indicate.

Tests of correlation are not as scary as they may first seem and they can provide a very useful interpretation of the data that you have collected. The example provided here is fairly complex and contains a large number of variables. It may be that your research will require assessments of correlations that involve fewer variables and so will generate simpler-looking tables.

A consistent theme of this chapter has been that quantitative data analysis is a process of asking questions about the data and then choosing appropriate tests to use to answer those questions. Often, answering one question may lead you to 'wondering' about the answer to another question. In some cases this may lead to another statistical test. In Table 10.3, for example, it seems that 'coaching' is positively associated with 'relationships' and 'self-confidence', although smaller positive correlations are also evident relating to 'gender' and 'direct reports'. Having noticed this you may begin to wonder which out of 'gender', 'direct reports', 'relationships' and 'self-confidence' are stronger predictors of managerial coaching. To answer this question you would need a regression analysis.

REGRESSION

To undertake a regression analysis your data must be generated through ratio, ordinal or interval scales. Nominal data can be used but only where the item is 'dichotomous' – that is, there are only two possible responses (for example, gender). In addition, multiple regression analysis requires a large sample. The number of cases in your sample of participants must substantially exceed the number of predictor variables you intend to include in your analysis. The minimum is that you have five times as many participants as predictor variables. A more acceptable ratio is 10:1, but some people argue that the ratio should be as high as 40:1. If you have a small sample, therefore, it is not appropriate to undertake a regression analysis. In SPSS the commands to use are

With a regression analysis you will find that when you ask for a test you get lots of information. If you undertake a regression analysis on SPSS, you will find that the output file it generates provides you with six tables. Don't be put off – you will soon learn what to look out for. The first table describes the data in general terms. The second table (there is an example shown as Table 10.4) shows the correlations between different pairs of variables within the analysis using an example of an assessment of whether gross salary is predicted by employee gender, length of service in current job and/or length of time in employment. Here it is important to reassure yourself that there are not strong correlations between the predictor variables and the dependent variable. Notice here how the significance (p) values are for a one-tailed hypothesis because your hunch is that there is a one-way relationship between gross salary (the dependent or 'outcome' variable) and the independent (predictor) variables: gender, length of time in current job and length of time in employment.

Table 10.4 Example of correlations table within a regression analysis output

		Gross salary (£)	Gender	How long in current job	How long in employment
Pearson's correlation	Gross salary (£)	1.000	.225	.156	.596
	Gender	.225	1.000	.080	.140
	How long in current job	.156	.080	1.000	.418
	How long in medical sales industry	.596	.140	.418	1.000
Sig. (1-tailed)	Gross salary (£)	.	.000	.000	.000
	Gender	.000	.	.001	.000
	How long in current job	.000	.001	.	.000
	How long in medical sales industry	.000	.000	.000	.
N	Gross salary (£)	1534	1534	1534	1534
	Gender	1534	1534	1534	1534
	How long in current job	1534	1534	1534	1534
	How long in medical sales industry	1534	1534	1534	1534

Table 10.4 is important because the **Adjusted R Square** value tells you the extent to which the model of prediction you are using accounts for variance in the outcome variable. In Table 10.5 you will see that 38.5% of variance is accounted for by these variables. Therefore, it is likely that other factors are also important in determining gross salary. Nonetheless, the 'model' used here represents almost 40% of what is going on.

Table 10.5 Example of model summary table

Model	R	R square	Adjusted R square	Std. error of the estimate
1	.622[a]	.387	.385	7186.686

a. Predictors: (Constant), How long in medical sales industry, Gender, How long in current job

The important part of Table 10.6 (ANOVA) is the significance column because it indicates the probability that any regression relationship occurred through coincidence. The **'Sig'** figure in Table 10.6 indicates there is a less than 1 in 1,000 chance that the results of this regression occurred through coincidence; this is good news!

Table 10.6 Example ANOVA table

ANOVA[a]						
Model		**Sum of squares**	**df**	**Mean square**	**F**	**Sig.**
1	Regression	49814950757.485	3	16604983585.828	321.500	.000[b]
	Residual	79022137184.887	1530	51648455.676		
	Total	128837087942.371	1533			

a. Dependent variable: Gross salary (£)

b. Predictors: (Constant), How long in medical sales industry, Gender, How long in current job

Finally, you arrive at a table reproduced here as Table 10.7, which has the regression data. Here it is important to look at the **standardised coefficients (beta)** numbers, which give a measure of the contribution of each variable to the regression model you are testing. A large value indicates that a unit change in this predictor variable has a large effect on the outcome variable. In Table 10.7 you will see that length of time in employment has a much higher value than the others. In addition, the 't' and 'Sig (p)' values give an indication of the impact of each predictor variable – a big absolute t value and small p value suggests that a predictor variable is having a large impact on the outcome variable. Here again we see from Table 10.7 that length of time in employment has the largest predictive value, although smaller contributions are also made by the other two variables.

Table 10.7 Example of coefficients table from a regression analysis

Coefficients[a]						
Model		Unstandardised coefficients		Standardised coefficients	t	Sig.
		B	Std. error	Beta		
1	(Constant)	8158.784	930.050		8.772	.000
	Gender	2706.586	371.111	.148	7.293	.000
	How long in current job	−752.446	142.263	−.117	−5.289	.000
	How long in employment	4945.609	175.939	.624	28.110	.000

a. Dependent variable: Gross salary (£)

TESTS OF DIFFERENCE

Tests of association are very useful approaches to use to interpret your data to answer your research questions. However, they are a clumsy way of assessing whether there are differences in responses to some of your questions made by members of different groups within the sample. Afrah, from Case Illustration 10.1, for example, wanted to know whether people from two different countries responded differently to questions about social capital. There are two main tests that will enable you to form a judgement about differences between groups. If your data are parametric, the most appropriate tool is the t-test. If your data are non-parametric (which is often the case in HR master's level projects), the Mann-Whitney test is appropriate.

The t-test can be found on SPSS easily enough using the 'analyze' and 'compare means' menu options. The Mann-Whitney test can also be easily undertaken from SPSS, but you will find it via the 'analyze' and 'non-parametric' tests and then choose '2' (or '3' if appropriate) independent samples from the drop-down list. Table 10.8 provides an example of the results from the Mann-Whitney test.

The Mann-Whitney test outcome shown here enables an interpretation of the extent to which there was a difference between the responses of two groups of managers from different countries to questions associated with management behaviours included in a survey used in some comparative research.

Table 10.8 Example of Mann-Whitney U output

	Choice	N	Mean rank	Sum of ranks
Developing people	UK	222	278.85	61904.00
	Kuwait	284	233.69	66367.00
	Total	506		
Giving feedback	UK	222	285.91	63471.50
	Kuwait	284	228.17	64799.50
	Total	506		
Goal-setting	UK	222	276.58	61400.00
	Kuwait	284	235.46	66871.00
	Total	506		
Asking for opinions	UK	222	254.12	56415.00
	Kuwait	284	253.01	71856.00
	Total	506		
Communicating plans	UK	222	264.69	58762.00
	Kuwait	284	244.75	69509.00
	Total	506		

Test statistics[a]

	Developing people	Giving feedback	Goal-setting	Asking for opinions	Communicating plans
Mann-Whitney U	25897.000	24329.500	26401.000	31386.000	29039.000
Wilcoxon W	66367.000	64799.500	66871.000	71856.000	69509.000
Z	−3.741	−4.894	−3.455	−.093	−1.679
Asymp. sig. (2-tailed)	.000	.000	.001	.926	.093

[a] Grouping variable: Country.

Yet again, if you use SPSS you will find that when you ask for a test you get lots of information and need to work out what to look out for. The first table produced in Table 10.8, for example, shows 'the workings' and the second table gives the outcome. Here it is possible to see the Mann-Whitney U test statistic and the ever-important 'Asymp. sig. (2-tailed)'. As with all other tests there is a 'null hypothesis' that there is no difference between the groups. The significance measure indicates whether the test result can be seen as reliable. Here you may notice that the test suggests that there is a highly significant difference between the groups for three of the questionnaire items (goal-setting, giving feedback and developing people), which have high Mann-Whitney scores (look at the 'Z') and a probability of only 1 in 1,000 or beyond that these results occurred through chance. However, the test also enables us to see that responses to the questions relating to communicating plans and asking for opinions show a probability figure that suggests that the results may have occurred by coincidence.

EXAMINING FEATURES REQUIRING 'MULTIPLE INDICATORS'

A key challenge for researchers in HR is that most of the interesting things that we want to examine cannot be directly observed and measured. For example, although variables such as people's age, length of service, gross pay, and so on, are interesting, you may feel far more curious about less directly measurable issues such as: organisational culture, engagement, leadership style, and so on. These latter variables are referred to as 'latent constructs'. If you want to measure them, you are unlikely to get a very reliable or valid result if you ask one question (for example: do you have an empowering management style?). If you ask very 'obvious' questions, it is highly likely that people will tell you what they think you want to hear or their responses may be 'skewed' by what they believe to be the 'right answer'. In such cases you will need to make use of multiple indicators that, taken in combination, will help you to measure what you are interested in. However, deciding which indicators within a 'batch' of questions really are indicative of the variable you are interested in and which are less effective as indicators takes some working out, and for this a technique called factor analysis can be very useful.

FACTOR ANALYSIS

Factor analysis is useful in two main ways. First, it can assess whether responses to some of your questions indicate that there are patterns or 'clusters' of responses that might indicate a coherent construct (such as 'empowerment' or 'assertiveness'). Second, it can assess whether the responses to the questions you have asked suggest the presence of 'key variables'. Factor analysis and principal component analysis tests form part of two related 'families' of statistical procedures. The underlying maths is quite complicated (and I am not going near to touching on it here) and the principles underpinning them are different in places, but the reasoning behind factor analysis and principal component analysis is fairly simple. They involve assessing how strongly each of your variables is correlated with each of the other variables and so identifying:

- 'clusters' of variables that all correlate fairly strongly with each other
- the extent to which one or more variables account for all of the variation in the data set.

Therefore, factor analysis is useful as a way of assessing the validity of questionnaire items (taken together) because it provides a mechanism to determine whether the questions in your survey actually do relate in a coherent way to the concept that you are trying to measure.

ACTIVITY 10.5

SURVEY DESIGN AND FACTOR ANALYSIS

Imagine that you have decided to conduct research into 'levels of anxiety in HR students about statistics'. You have to devise a

questionnaire that will try to capture the different features of this (possibly common) occurrence. You organise your questionnaire with the 'biographical' questions first and then a series of ten statements against which survey respondents can give their measure of 'agreement/disagreement' on a scale of 1–5. Try to generate ten questionnaire statements that you might include in your survey to examine 'anxiety about statistics'.

FEEDBACK NOTES

Writing survey questions 'out of the blue' is a difficult task. If you were doing this 'for real' you might decide to interview some people first to get an idea of the things that might comprise overall 'anxiety about statistics' and then use your interview data as a basis for designing your survey questions. Having done this, it would be a good idea to try your ideas out on your supervisor or some other experts and get them to tell you which of your questions they think 'make sense' and which should be changed or eliminated. Some of the items that you may have come up with might be along the lines of:

	Strongly disagree 1	2	3	4	Strongly agree 5
I cannot understand the basis of calculations in statistics.					
I do not feel confident in using software such as 'Excel'.					
Words mean more to me than numbers.					
I would rather read quotations than look at tables of figures.					
I am afraid that I will make miscalculations.					
Statistical packages such as SPSS are a worry to me and I do not wish to use them.					

Once you have got a set of items you think might represent 'anxiety about statistics', you will need to try them out 'for real' by devising a survey and collecting responses. You could send out your survey to as many HR students as possible (let's be optimistic and pretend you have got 300 responses). Factor analysis can then indicate for you whether all of your questions cluster in a coherent way and also whether there might be sub-categories (for example: anxiety about computers; preference for words over numbers) in the data you have collected. Using SPSS and other statistical software packages, it is possible to identify clusters and their effect on the variance within the overall responses.

To undertake a factor analysis using SPSS, start with the 'analyze' menu and choose 'data reduction' and then 'factor'. At this point you select the variables that you wish to include and then turn to the many optional screens accessed by the buttons in the dialogue box. In the 'extraction' dialogue box make sure that you tick the 'scree plot' option. In the 'rotation' dialogue box ask for the 'varimax' method. The output from this process is quite extensive and if you can find a friendly statistics adviser (your tutor or someone recommended by them?), they will be able to help you to use and interpret the outputs appropriately.

Tables 10.9 and 10.10 provide an example of some of the outputs from a principal component analysis. After outputs with 'the workings', the output contains a table that indicates the proportion of **variance** that is accounted for by the 'factors' or groups of items that the software has identified. Opinions vary between disciplines (such as engineering, medicine, business and management) about what proportion of variance is significant and worth 'taking note of'. For HRM projects a contribution to variance of over 40% can be seen as interesting given the complexity of the phenomena that are being researched. Table 10.9, which reproduces a factor analysis output, indicates that two 'components' (clusters) accounted for just over 49% of the variance within the responses. You will see the term 'eigenvalue' used in this chart. This should not worry you; it refers to the total test variance that is accounted for by a particular factor (where the eigenvalue is less than 1, there is no contribution to variance).

Table 10.9 Example of principal component analysis output Total variance explained

Component	Initial eigen values			Rotation sums of squared loadings		
	Total	% of variance	Cumulative %	Total	% of variance	Cumulative %
1	3.136	34.842	34.842	2.721	30.231	30.231
2	1.228	13.642	48.484	1.643	18.254	48.484
3	.929	10.325	58.810			
4	.781	8.678	67.488			
5	.707	7.854	75.342			
6	.669	7.433	82.774			
7	.581	6.452	89.227			
8	.497	5.523	94.750			
9	.473	5.250	100.000			

Extraction method: principal component analysis.

The effect of the clustering can be visually displayed by SPSS in the form of a 'scree plot', reproduced here as Figure 10.3. Making sense of scree plots can be rather baffling for 'non-scree plotters', but the trick is to look at the gradients between the points. The plot provides a graphic representation of the eigenvalue for each of the factors. Where there is almost no gradient and the curve is 'flat', this indicates that there are no 'worthwhile' clusters. The scree plot shown for these items, for example, indicates one quite powerful cluster (where there is a sharp 'fall' between co-ordinates on the graph). This reflects the 'descent' from a quite high eigenvalue for factor one and then a further (but much smaller) difference between the second and third eigenvalues shown in the table. This is a visual suggestion that there are two clusters, one being much more significant than the other in explaining variance within the responses as a whole.

Figure 10.3 Example of a scree plot

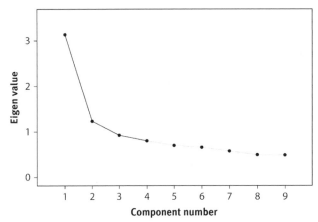

The 'rotated component matrix' for the data is shown next as Table 10.10. This is much easier to read than an additional output (not reproduced here) of an 'unrotated component matrix'. The column headings for the rotated component matrix indicate again that two clusters have been identified and the contents of the columns represent the 'factor loadings' of the questionnaire items within the two 'components' (or clusters). Most researchers would not take much account of anything with a factor loading below 0.6, and using this criterion you can identify which questionnaire items are associated with each cluster. The data in Table 10.10, for example, indicate a cluster of responses within component one, all of which have factor loadings above 0.6 as follows:

Cluster one: 'observing'; 'action plans'; 'developing individuals'; 'feedback'; 'training'. A second cluster (**cluster two**) comprises only two variables with factor loadings of more than 0.6: 'problem-solving' and 'use ideas'. The other two items – 'questioning' and 'share decisions' – have a much lower factor loading, indicating that there is less probability that they make a significant 'contribution' to the variance accounted for by this cluster.

Table 10.10 Example of a component matrix: Rotated component matrix[a]

	Component:	
	1	2
Observing	**.772**	−.002
Action plans	**.768**	.089
Developing individuals	**.694**	.086
Feedback	**.654**	.247
Training	**.634**	.338
Problem-solving	−.077	**.803**
Use ideas	.093	**.628**
Share decisions	.389	.470
Questioning	.239	.437

Extraction method: principal component analysis.

Rotation method: Varimax with Kaiser normalisation.

aRotation converged in 3 iterations.

If you have followed this explanation so far you may be wondering whether all the effort is worth it. However, factor analysis 'opens the door' for further useful analysis. Case Illustration 10.2 provides an example of the use of factor analysis as a basis for constructing new 'composite' scales. The relationship between these new scales and other variables within the data can then be explored. In addition, if you have devised a questionnaire with a number of items which, collectively, you intend to measure a more general (latent) variable and one or two of the items do not cluster effectively, this provides a useful basis to consider removing these items from your analysis because the test suggests that they may not be 'fit for purpose'. With this in mind, if you have decided to devise your own survey instrument you may decide to include factor analysis as a useful part of any piloting process to help you assess the validity of your questionnaire items.

Factor analysis as a basis for further analysis

CASE ILLUSTRATION 10.2

Extracts from Hashim, J. (2010) Human resource management practices on organisational commitment: the Islamic perspective, *Personnel Review*, 39(6), 785–99. © Emerald Group Publishing Limited all rights reserved.

... Religious influences on human resource practices are important but are rarely highlighted in literature. The specifications of right and wrong, reward and punishment, work and spirituality, as well as relation to others and God address human resource issues directly and indirectly (Ali **et al** 2000). In most countries, the influence of religion on human resource management (HRM) is formally incorporated in the rules and regulations governing employee–management relations, some more explicitly than others. These rules and regulations can be related to the employees' individual rights, such as equal employment opportunities, job security, and wage levels. They can also be related to the employees' collective rights, such as unionisation and participative decision-making.

... This paper aims to examine the management of human resources from the Islamic perspective and its effects on organisational commitment among selected employees in Islamic organisations in Malaysia. ... The influence of Islam and its teachings on HRM, which are prevalent in certain countries, could be of interest to people and organisations that wish to do business with them, such as multinational organisations...

The study employed a self-developed questionnaire. ... Data were collected from eight Islamic organisations in Malaysia ... well known as Islamic organisations among the Malaysians. Six of the organisations are in the Islamic banking and financial business, and the other two are in Islamic services business.

The total respondents were 121 Muslim employees, who vary in positions and were purposively selected to represent each of the eight organisations. To ensure the respondents understand and are familiar with their organisations' HRM practices, the respondents selected were required to have worked for the organisation for at least three years and they must have performed some of the HRM functions (selection, performance appraisal or training) themselves, i.e. they are supervisors.

Based on the interpretation of ... related verses mentioned in *Al-Qur'an* and *Hadith*, a specially constructed questionnaire was developed in order to gather the data. The instrument consisted of 54 items seeking information about the organisations' background and HRM practices among these selected organisations. Specifically, there were four questions enquiring of the organisation background, the name of the organisation, the number of employees

employed, and the type of organisation's ownership. There were ten items each enquiring about the recruitment, selection, performance appraisal, training and development, and compensation practices. For each of these functions, the respondents were asked to indicate the extent to which each of the activities in the questionnaire are being practised in their organisations by using the seven-point Likert scales (1=never, 2=very rarely, 3=rarely, 4=occasionally, 5=frequently, 6=very frequently, 7=all the time).

Organisational commitment was measured by a 12-item short version of the Organisational Commitment questionnaire developed by Mowday **et al** (1979). Before the actual data collection was conducted, a pilot test was conducted for the instrument.

... Reliability test was conducted for 50 items for internal consistency purposes. The reliability coefficient for all 50 items was 0.951. Next, another reliability test was conducted for the ten items in each of the five HRM functions [recruitment, selection, performance appraisal, training and development, and compensation]. If they are reliable, then factor analysis would be conducted for each of these five functions. If the factor analysis produced more than two factors, then the most reliable factor between them will be selected for subsequent analysis in measuring the HRM practices.

For recruitment there were ten items asking how the organisations recruit new employees. The reliability coefficient for recruitment was 0.787. Factor analysis was then performed for all these ten items. The analysis produced one factor and it was reliable thus the factor was selected. Next, the same process was repeated for selection practices. The reliability coefficient for ten items in selection practices was 0.919. The factor analysis produced one factor and since it was reliable, all the ten items were used for the next analysis. For performance appraisal, the factor analysis produced three factors, and Factor 1 was chosen because it has the most loaded items and it was most reliable compared to Factor 2 and Factor 3. Factor 1 consisted of seven items. A reliability analysis was done on these seven items and it shows reliability coefficient value of 0.890. Meanwhile, factor analysis conducted for training and development function produced two factors, and Factor 1 was selected because it was more reliable than Factor 2. Its reliability coefficient was 0.891. For compensation function, the factor analysis produced three factors. Factor 2, which comprised four items, was selected because it was the most reliable factor among the three factors with coefficient value of 0.855. For the organisational commitment variable, a confirmatory factor analysis was done and it produced one factor.

Discussion Questions

1   In what ways has factor analysis been used in this extract?

2   What are the strengths and weaknesses of the approach described in this extract?

FEEDBACK NOTES

Factor analysis has been used here to identify coherent clusters of questionnaire items that can be said to comprise different features of Islamic HRM. As a result of this analysis the researchers are able to 'discard' questionnaire items that do not coherently correlate together. This means that new scales, derived from the original responses, can be created for: recruitment, selection, performance appraisal, training and development, compensation and organisational commitment.

Instead of trying to deal with 66 different individual variables, therefore, it is possible to create 6 composite variables to represent these multidimensional constructs. This then allows for a test of association between the new variables and, in this case, a composite measure of organisational commitment.

In evaluating the strengths and weaknesses of the research described in this extract you might have observed that the sample size was small. In addition, while developing a measure of Islamic HRM using data from Islamic organisations is an interesting exercise, it would be very interesting to now examine whether respondents from non-Islamic organisations would respond in similar or different ways to the questions. You may have noticed the frequent reference in this extract to 'reliability coefficients'. These refer to the Cronbach alpha (symbolised as 'α') test. You will find that this is frequently used in the analysis of quantitative data. It has been used as a measure of internal consistency (and hence reliability) of questionnaire responses since the 1950s. The calculation on which it is based will result in an output which varies from zero to 1, and higher values of alpha (values of 0.7 or higher) give greater confidence in the quality of a questionnaire and the extent to which a set of items measure a single construct. The reliability coefficients shown in this paper, therefore, give some confidence (although the sample size is still a concern) of the reliability of the instrument as a whole and the six scales that were created following the factor analysis.

ANALYSING DATA TO ANSWER RESEARCH QUESTIONS

If you have persevered this far with the chapter, you may now be feeling that the possibilities for analysis are endless and that you may never be in a position to formulate any conclusions as you will be spending all your hours on generating tests and trying to 'read' the results. Indeed, it is very easy to get fixated by all the tests that the statistical analysis packages can undertake and to feel the need to 'try them all'. This would be a mistake. Statistical packages are a **tool** and it is important to use your own judgement about the most appropriate way to use the tool. Analysis is fundamentally a thinking process and even the most expensive and up-to-date packages will not do the thinking for you.

The starting point for your analysis must be your research questions or objectives. They form the basis for your interpretation of the data and they are also what those who mark your project will expect to be the focus of your conclusions. Having reviewed your research questions, it is also important to then look over the type of data that you have collected. There are two important issues here. First, what measurement scales did you use? Did your questionnaire instrument generate:

- nominal or category data
- ordinal data
- interval scales
- ratio scales?

If you are planning to analyse nominal or ordinal data, you will need to make use of non-parametric tests. Second, is your data normally distributed? If the spread of the data across the extremes does not reflect a normal curve of distribution (with a 'hump' in the middle), again, you should use non-parametric tests.

If you are clear about your research questions and you are clear about the types of data you have collected, you are well placed to identify the most appropriate analysis tools to use. Table 10.11 provides an indication of the main options for parametric and non-parametric data (Collis and Hussey 2009, Brett-Davies 2007).

Table 10.11 Analysis options and choices

Test purpose	Non-parametric data option	Parametric data option	Types of data	Notes
Test of association	Cross-tabulation (see page 323)	Cross-tabulation (see page 323)	All types. Especially useful with nominal (category) data	Need to report the significance of the association
Test of association	Scattergram (see page 325)	Scattergram (see page 325)	Interval or ratio scale data only	Need to report the strength of the association as well as the significance
Assessment of significance of association	Chi-square (χ^2)	n/a	All types	
Test of difference	t-test (t)	Mann-Whitney test (U)	Never for nominal data	Report probability of chance (p) result as well as the test 'result'
Test of correlation	Spearman's rho (r_s) (see page 329)	Pearson's correlation (r) (see page 329)	Never for nominal data	Report probability of chance (p) result as well as the test 'result'
Principal component / factor analysis	Factor / principal component analysis	Factor / principal component analysis	Never for nominal data	Report Chronbach's alpha (α) correlation coefficient as well as the test result

Another useful depiction of analysis options and choices, provided by Cavana et al (2001) and recommended by one of the reviewers of this book, is shown as Table 10.12.

Table 10.12 Analysis options and types of variable

Dependent variable				
		Nominal / category scale	**Ordinal scale**	**Interval or ratio scale**
Independent variable	**Nominal / category scale**	Chi-square test for independence	Mann-Whitney U test	Analysis of variance (ANOVA) t-test
	Ordinal scale		Spearman's correlation	
	Interval or ratio scale	Analysis of variance (ANOVA)		Regression analysis Pearson's correlation

(adapted from Cavana et al 2001)

As you proceed with the analysis process it is likely that you will want to explore the relationships between different variables using different tests (as appropriate and depending on your research questions). It is also likely that you will need to 'pick up' and 'put down' the analysis process over a number of different occasions. Therefore the following tips are offered to ensure that your time, on each occasion, is used to best effect and that you are able to formulate credible conclusions:

- Back up your work frequently (every 20 minutes is not excessive with data analysis).
- Work as neatly as you can. Keep a record of what tests you have done and what still needs to be done. Label all your outputs in a logical way so that you can find them again later. Repeating tests because you have 'lost' the output is a luxury that a student with a deadline cannot afford.
- Double-check your numbers and outputs. Results that look too good to be true usually are too good to be true.
- Check that the scoring you used on your scales all works in the 'same direction'. You might see what you think is a negative correlation but this may turn out to be a scale which went 'against the flow' for some reason.
- Double-check that you are using appropriate tests for appropriate types of data.
- If you are using SPSS, remember that you can copy your outputs into a Word file. This is important because it means that there is no danger that you will make a mistake in typing data into your report document. Also, you can edit the headings and tidy up the data for presentation within the research report or dissertation itself.
- Remember that the larger the sample, the more likely it is that a relationship will appear to be significant. With a smaller sample you might assert a reasonable level of significance of $p = 0.01$ or even $p = 0.05$, but with a larger sample you would need to look for significance of $p = 0.001$.
- Don't be tempted to overdo it with charts and diagrams. Use these sparingly where they add value to the analysis and understanding process. Remember

that your tutor will not award marks for attractive charts – your tutor will reward meaningful charts. Quality will outweigh quantity.

SUMMARY

- Statistics can be defined as: 'describing things with numbers and assessing the odds' (Rugg and Petre 2007, p168).
- IBM SPSS is the most commonly used software package to help with quantitative data analysis in HRM and most other business and management disciplines.
- It is important to use your own judgement about the most appropriate way to use statistical packages and which tests to undertake. Analysis is fundamentally a thinking process and even the most expensive and up-to-date packages will not do the thinking for you.
- Before you choose your statistical tests, you should review your research questions or objectives and review the types of data that you have gathered and the extent to which they are normally distributed.
- Cross-tabulation allows for an assessment of the relationship between any two variables. It is particularly useful for nominal (category) data.
- A scattergram involves plotting a graph where each axis represents the value of one variable. This method of data analysis is never appropriate for nominal (category) data and is most appropriate for interval or ratio scale data.
- The chi-square test (χ^2) is a useful way of evaluating the probability that results in tests of association occurred through chance.
- The Mann-Whitney U test and the t-test are useful tools with which to assess different patterns of responses across different sample groups.
- Tests of correlation measure the strength and direction of association between different variables. The two most frequently used tests are the Spearman's correlation test (for non-parametric data) and the Pearson's correlation test (for parametric data). Both tests calculate a correlation co-efficient that ranges between –1 (a perfect negative correlation) and +1 (a perfect positive correlation).
- Regression analysis enables you to examine the extent to which different variables may 'predict' the strength of a dependent variable, but this procedure requires a minimum sample size to be reliable.
- Factor analysis can assess whether there are 'key variables' in the data or whether some variables can be grouped or clustered together to form a coherent (multidimensional) composite variable.
- The Cronbach alpha ('α') test provides a measure of internal consistency (and hence reliability) of questionnaire responses. Higher values of alpha (values of 0.7 or higher) give greater confidence in the quality of a group of questionnaire items to measure a single one-dimensional latent construct.
- Charts and diagrams can be a powerful way of presenting parts of your analysis but use them sparingly, and only when they are directly relevant to your research objectives or questions.

Self-test questions

1   The terms 'parametric' and non-parametric' refer to:

   a)   two main groups of data types that are linked to different groups of statistical tests

   b)   measures of statistical significance

   c)   alternative forms of data display

   d)   forms of questionnaire response scale

2   Tests of probability that a test result occurred by chance is known as:

   a)   multiple regression analysis

   b)   chi-square test

   c)   significance testing

   d)   Cronbach alpha

3   A reliability coefficient is a measure of:

   a)   the difference between two variables

   b)   the strength of the relationship between two different variables

   c)   the extent to which the responses to a group of variables are internally consistent

   d)   whether the data are measuring what you think they are measuring

4   What information can a cross-tabulation provide?

   a)   It shows the results for all of your questionnaire items.

   b)   It lists different measures of significance.

   c)   It summarises the frequencies of different variables so that they can be compared.

   d)   It compares the different results from a regression analysis.

5   A perfect positive correlation between two variables in a test of correlation would give a result of:

   a)   −0.123

   b)   +1

   c)   0

   d)   −1

6   A commonly used 'test of difference' for parametric data is known as:

   a)   Mann-Whitney Test

   b)   Cronbach alpha

   c)   factor analysis

   d)   t-test

7   Factor analysis can be used to:

   a)   assess whether some variables can be grouped or clustered together to form a coherent composite variable

   b)   work out the extent to which two variables are co-related

   c)   identify the extent to which different variables can 'predict' the strength of an independent variable

   d)   divide results by a multiplier

Questions for reflection

This final part of the chapter enables you to reflect about your professional development and develop your skills and knowledge. This will enable you to build your confidence and credibility, track your learning, see your progress and demonstrate your achievements.

Taking stock

1   What quantitative data analysis software is available to you through work or your study centre? Do you have (or can you obtain) a personal copy?

2   What books or manuals might you obtain to help you through the data analysis process?

3   How clear are you about your research questions and the implications of them for choosing appropriate quantitative data analysis tests?

4   How realistic do your outputs look? Might some of them really be 'too good to be true', meaning that you need to carefully check the appropriateness of the test and the way it has been undertaken?

Strengths and weaknesses

5   What are your strengths and weaknesses with numerical reasoning? Where might you look for help with statistics (family member, work colleague, fellow student, colleague, tutor, friend)?

6   What are the strengths and limitations of the data you have collected? What are the implications of the sample size and response rate for your analysis? What seem to be the main features of the data you have collected?

7   What steps can you take to build your confidence on the statistics software you have decided to use?

Being a practitioner-researcher

8   What help is available at your place of work with running statistical tests and making sense of the findings?

9   What are the data security and ethical issues with storing your data in paper or electronic form? What password protection do you need to use to ensure that no unauthorised access occurs?

EXPLORE FURTHER

Reading

Brett-Davies, M. (2007) *Doing a successful research project: using qualitative or quantitative methods*. Basingstoke: Palgrave Macmillan.

Collis, J. and Hussey, R. (2009) *Business research: a practical guide for undergraduate and postgraduate students*. Basingstoke: Palgrave.

Diamantopoulos, A. and Schlegelmilch, B. (1997) *Taking the fear out of data analysis*. London: Dryden.

Rugg, G. (2007) *Using statistics: a gentle introduction*. Maidenhead: Open University Press.

Rugg, G. and Petre, M. (2007) *A gentle guide to research methods*. Maidenhead: Open University Press.

Walker, J. and Almond, P. (2010) *Interpreting statistical findings: a guide for health professionals and students*. Maidenhead: Open University Press.

My favourite books related to SPSS are:

Field, A. (2009) *Discovering statistics using SPSS for Windows*. London: Sage.

Pallant, J. (2010) *SPSS survival manual*. Maidenhead: Open University Press.

EVALUATE AND REVIEW

CHAPTER 11

Writing up Your Project and Making Recommendations

CHAPTER OUTLINE

- How to use this chapter
- Why, what, when and for whom to write
- Structuring and organising your writing
- Writing your conclusions, recommendations, abstract and personal reflection
- Style and expression issues
- Reviewing, revising and submitting your work
- Summary
- Review and reflect
- Explore further

LEARNING OUTCOMES

This chapter should help you to:

- clarify what is required by different audiences with whom you will communicate about your research
- draft a research report or dissertation
- revise, redraft and proof-read your work to maximise its credibility and accuracy.

HOW TO USE THIS CHAPTER

When you reach this chapter you will rightly feel that you are on the 'home run'. Many of the previous chapters of the book contain suggestions about how to 'write up' specific sections of your final report. However, the conclusions, recommendations and personal reflections sections do not have their 'own' chapters. Therefore, an additional section has been added to this chapter to provide you with a starting framework for thinking about how to write these important chapters or sections in an effective way.

The focus of this chapter is on helping you to communicate the results of your research in a credible way. Academic 'audiences' for your work have different priorities from those in work organisations, and this chapter should help you to clarify the expectations of both sets of stakeholders. Although I would like to think that you will read this chapter before you start the writing process, I recognise that most of those who are now staring at this page will be acutely aware of the need to write fast to meet a rapidly approaching deadline. All the activities in this chapter, therefore, are focused on helping you to develop the skills you need to write effectively and submit on time.

 Finding the right style

CASE ILLUSTRATION 11.1

Lorenzo was a training director in a large, diversified, manufacturing and services organisation. He had transferred into his role after an initial career in operations management and had never previously undertaken any training or HR qualifications. His university days, when he had studied engineering, were in the distant past and had been undertaken in Italy. Having moved into the training area Lorenzo was keen to pursue some studies as he hoped to remain in his 'new' profession over at least the medium term. Lorenzo enjoyed his course and the opportunity to study a range of HR topics. He was confident in his use of English, particularly when speaking and listening, but he was much less confident when it came to written work and had mixed feelings about the dissertation process. Lorenzo's planned research topic was talent development and so his investigation was directly relevant to his role at work. However, tutor feedback on his assignments had stressed that his work was not characterised by sufficient 'depth'; that his reading was too 'operational' and that his style was 'prescriptive and descriptive'; he made too much use of bullet points and was not sufficiently evaluative and analytical. Lorenzo became increasingly anxious about the extent to which he would be able to deliver a much longer dissertation document to meet the 'academic' requirements of his tutors. He had always taken a very thorough approach to his studies but was baffled about the distinction between 'description', prescription, analysis and evaluation.

Discussion Questions

1   What advice would you give to Lorenzo to help him feel more confident of developing an appropriate writing and thinking style?

FEEDBACK NOTES

This case illustration highlights a number of challenges that many students, particularly those who are studying part-time or for whom English is not their first language, experience when faced with the requirement to 'write up' their research report or dissertation. Like Lorenzo, many people are baffled and confused by tutor comments (often not well explained) on the text of assignments saying things such as 'too descriptive' or 'lacks critical evaluation'. Perhaps the best advice you might offer Lorenzo is to try to 'stand back' from what he reads about his topics and make a 'rounded assessment' of strengths and weaknesses. Lorenzo might be well advised to think about the issues from more than one perspective. The perspective of a fairly senior manager came easily to him, but what about the perspective of those affected by the talent development processes he is reading about or developing in practice?

While bullet points may be useful to summarise key points and to show Lorenzo 'knows about' things, they are less helpful in convincing an academic reader that he understands the things he has listed. Lorenzo might also be well advised to try comparing different themes and issues that occur in the literature rather than listing them one at a time.

This chapter explores ways in which the writing process can be managed effectively and can become a rewarding part of the overall research process.

WHY, WHAT, WHEN AND FOR WHOM TO WRITE

WHY AND WHEN TO WRITE?

Like many HR practitioners you may feel that 'academic writing' seems dry and uninteresting and that the seemingly endless references that are cited within the text are distracting rather than helpful. Writing a lengthy project report or dissertation in an academic style can seem daunting. Some students find the writing process makes them feel clumsy and inarticulate. Some find they have plenty of ideas in their head but that translating these into words on paper (or a screen) is nearly impossible. However, for other people, the opportunity to create a piece of writing can be a rewarding opportunity for reflection and 'sense-making'.

Whether you hate or love writing, there are a number of very good reasons for doing it. First, once the writing process is finished you can submit your work and reclaim a significant part of your life: you can do some of the things you have been promising yourself you will do 'after the course'. Second, writing about your research helps you to reflect on and communicate what you have found out. Third, provided that you meet all the assessment criteria for your course, you can be awarded credit for your achievements: you can qualify!

These are powerful motivators, but writing is 'a good thing' for other reasons too. Saunders et al (2012) point out that by engaging in the writing process you are forced to clarify your thinking. It is difficult to commit ideas on to paper but the more times you try, the clearer your thinking becomes. Within this process some ideas will be discarded, others may be reformulated but, as time goes by, what you are trying to explain will become clearer to you and to those with whom you need to communicate.

Writing and reflection go hand in hand. Therefore, writing is a learning process and the way to learn to write is by writing (Neuman 2011). The more you write **at all stages of the project**, the more you will reflect on what you are doing and the more guidance you will be able to receive from your tutor or supervisor. The message, therefore, is write often and write throughout the project process. If you have not done this and now have to face up to writing 'from scratch', don't fret too much – many others have been in your position and they have survived.

WHO IS THE AUDIENCE FOR YOUR RESEARCH AND WHAT ARE THEY LOOKING FOR?

As you write your dissertation, the most important and urgent stakeholder to focus on is your university or study centre because they will assess your work and determine whether it meets the criteria for a pass.

ACTIVITY 11.1

KNOWING YOUR READERS

Draw up two short checklists. One list relates to your tutors; the other relates to any organisation sponsor(s) or client(s) who may want a report about your research. For each checklist identify:

- why the reader needs to read about your research

- their professional background and how this may influence what they expect to see in your report
- their attitude towards the research process
- what they really need to know about.

FEEDBACK NOTES

The two lists that you have compiled may well have some similarities, but it is likely that there will also be some differences. Your tutors will read your report because they have to mark it. Assessors are interested in your level of knowledge and understanding, as well as your ability to apply a consistent and appropriate research methodology to investigate a defined HR issue, problem or opportunity. They are looking for analysis, critical evaluation, different perspectives and synthesis of information from different sources. They will be particularly interested in the implications of what you have found for their understanding of HR more generally.

THE ACADEMIC REPORT – CLARIFYING INSTITUTIONAL REQUIREMENTS

It is very important to remind yourself about the details of what your particular study centre is expecting. In particular, find out about:

- **Length:** what is the minimum and maximum word count?
- **Structure:** what sections must be included?
- **Style:** what conventions are expected with regard to 'first or third person', what 'tense' to use (present or past) and so on?
- **Format:** what line spacing? What margins? How should the title page be laid out? What font size and typeface?

- **Assessment criteria:** you will have been given a copy of the criteria by which your work will be assessed. Find this again now – take a good look at the requirements and then refer to them frequently while you are writing up.

RESEARCH REPORT OR DISSERTATION?

At the end of the research project some courses require the submission of a **business or management research report** (this is the general requirement for a CIPD advanced-level qualification). Other courses (at undergraduate and leading to a master's-level qualification) require a dissertation. These different forms, and the different word lengths that you may be given, can generate anxiety, so here are some comparisons. First, the difference in expectations between **undergraduate- and postgraduate-level** work is expressed in Table 11.1. Here the difference is essentially one of 'depth'. Postgraduate-level researchers are expected to probe more deeply and work at a higher level of uncertainty, achieving outcomes at a more 'professional' level than are undergraduate students.

Table 11.1 Comparison of expectations for research reports at undergraduate and postgraduate levels

	Undergraduate-level expectations	Postgraduate-level expectations
Knowledge and understanding	Systematic understanding and coherent and detailed knowledge of the subject area	Systematic understanding and knowledge of the area, including theoretical and research-based knowledge at the forefront of the topic
Analysis	Use of established techniques of analysis in the subject area	Comprehensive understanding of the techniques of analysis in the subject area
Conceptual understanding	Ability to develop and sustain arguments and analysis relevant to the topic area; ability to describe research and scholarship in the field	Critical evaluation of advanced scholarship in the area; evaluation of methodologies of scholarship in the field
Thinking skills	Application of thinking skills and appreciation of levels of uncertainty with awareness of the provisional nature of knowledge	Ability to deal with complex issues and make sound judgements in the absence of complete data
Learning skills	Ability to manage own learning	Demonstration of self-direction, autonomy and originality to advance knowledge and understanding and develop new skill

(Adapted from QAA 2008)

If you are undertaking an advanced-level CIPD qualification, the general CIPD requirements for a management research report are that you:

1   Identify and justify a business issue that is of strategic relevance to the organisation.

2   Critically analyse and discuss existing literature, contemporary HR policy and practice relevant to the chosen issue.

3   Compare and contrast the relative merits of different research methods and their relevance to different situations.

4   Undertake a systematic analysis of quantitative and/or qualitative information and present the results in a clear and consistent format.

5   Draw realistic and appropriate conclusions and make recommendations based on costed options.

6   Develop and present a persuasive business report.

7   Write a reflective account of what has been learned during the project and how this can be applied in the future.

The difference between a business research report and a dissertation

Some general marking criteria of a dissertation (adapted from Fisher 2007, Brown 2006, Fox et al 2007) are shown here, and this is followed by CIPD guidance about the marking criteria for a business research report at advanced level.

General assessment criteria for a master's-level dissertation

- **Research objectives:** clear and relevant objectives, derived from an identification and definition of a valid and practicable project.
- **Research design:** the research design and methodological approach and issues of access and co-operation are appropriate and justified to generate sufficient quality and quantity of data. An evaluation of issues of research ethics and the reliability and validity of the data, taking the methodological approach into account, is undertaken.
- **Literature review:** relevant literature drawn from a range of appropriate sources is analysed and critically reviewed. The literature review provides a structure and focus for the dissertation. Concepts are defined and structured and an appropriate analytical framework is developed to give a theoretical grounding and focus in the dissertation.
- **Data collection and analysis:** primary and/or secondary data that are relevant to the research objectives are gathered and presented. Data are analysed in a thorough and critical way, using (where appropriate) the analytical or conceptual framework derived from the literature review.
- **Conclusions:** these are clearly expressed, supported by the evidence and derived logically from the analysis. Where recommendations are also appropriate they are practical, imaginative and relevant.
- **Presentation:** clear written expression using a style and use of language and referencing that is credible and appropriate for academic purposes.
- **Integration of academic knowledge:** the research process demonstrates originality or use of initiative, and there is evidence of a 'learning process' for the researcher.

If you compare the general assessment criteria for dissertations with the generic assessment criteria for CIPD research reports, which is shown in Table 11.2, you will see that there are more similarities than differences. **Both** sets of criteria emphasise the importance of clearly expressed and relevant research aims and objectives, a review of relevant literature, the use of appropriate methods to collect data and the analysis of that data in an integrated and appropriate way. Although individual study centres operate slightly different assessment criteria, these components would be expected in any postgraduate-level project report. A CIPD advanced-level **management research report** tends to be shorter (7,000 words is the norm) and there is greater emphasis on the use of the analysis of primary data to generate business-focused, practical, costed, timely and realistic recommendations.

Table 11.2 CIPD assessment criteria

CIPD general assessment criterion	Where found
Clarity and relevance of terms of reference/aims and objectives or research question	Introduction
Critical analysis of the most significant contribution to the literature, drawing on recent published research and practice	Literature review Findings, analysis and discussion
Justification and use of appropriate methods of data collection	Research methodology
Focused and relevant discussion of organisational context, evidence of systematic data collection and clear presentation of findings	Introduction, Findings, analysis and discussion
Comprehensive analysis and interpretation of findings in a holistic/integrated manner	Findings, analysis and discussion
Appropriateness of conclusions in the light of terms of reference and empirical work	Conclusions
Realistic, timely and cost-effective recommendations and action plan	Recommendations
Satisfactory presentation of material and argument, and clear and accurate referencing	Whole report
Evidence that personal learning has been reviewed, including comments from organisation if appropriate	Final section

If you are undertaking master's-level research, therefore, you will be expected to focus more on the:

- analytical focus, scope and contribution of the literature review
- evaluation of different research design and methodological issues and the skill with which methods of data collection are undertaken

- analysis of the data – particularly its thoroughness, the questioning nature of the approach you use and the analytical links with the literature review
- reasoning process behind the formulation of your conclusions and the links between the conclusions and your analysis of the literature and the primary data.

STRUCTURING AND ORGANISING YOUR WRITING

GETTING STARTED

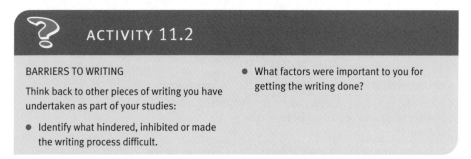

ACTIVITY 11.2

BARRIERS TO WRITING

Think back to other pieces of writing you have undertaken as part of your studies:

- Identify what hindered, inhibited or made the writing process difficult.

- What factors were important to you for getting the writing done?

FEEDBACK NOTES

Everyone (even your tutor) feels daunted when faced with writing a long document. The more anxious you become, the more you may be tempted to put off the moment of getting started. People often worry that they do not have enough information or they delay starting as they feel the word limit is too long (or too short). In addition, interruptions to writing, pressure of other work and an inability to concentrate are common concerns, all of which can contribute to 'writer's block'.

Other delaying factors, which may well have affected you at some stage in your studies, might include those expressed in Figure 11.1.

Figure 11.1 Factors that can delay progress with writing

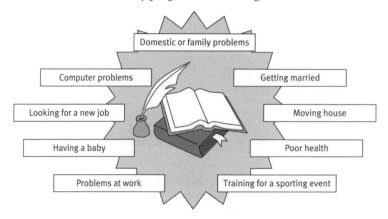

The factors illustrated in Figure 11.1 as well as the concerns you may have listed in response to Activity 11.2 can be difficult to cope with and, when it comes to the writing process, it is important to try to deal with the things that are partly within your control so that you are better able to manage in spite of those that are outside of your control.

A key issue for any writer is to overcome any tendency to procrastination and to work through writer's block. Some suggestions for this are provided in Table 11.3. No one will find all of these 'tips' appropriate, so it is important to take what works for you and use it in your own way.

Table 11.3 Making yourself write

Planning to write	• Divide up the word limit and set sub-limits for each of the chapters or sections.
	• Set yourself a writing timetable and deadlines.
	• Draft out the structure for the section or chapter you are about to write.
	• Break down main parts of the section or chapter into smaller parts – it is much less daunting to produce 200 words than 2,000.
	• Set up a word processing template for each chapter: set the correct font and point size; line spacing; margins; style for heading and sub-headings. This can save you about a week at the end of the writing process.
	• Use outlines, structures and plans to keep you focused.
When to write	• Begin early – the closer you get to the deadline, the more the pressure mounts up. If you write something now, there will be time to improve on it.
	• Create time ('prime time') for writing – put off other jobs so that you are not exhausted when you begin writing.
	• Write regularly and develop a pattern or rhythm of work on the report. Try to never to miss a writing session.
	• If the going is getting tough, try writing at a different time of the day or time of the week.
	• Write up a section as soon as possible.
	• Reward yourself for little achievements – try to look forward to what you are about to achieve.

Develop your own individual writing 'habits'	• Engage in your own personal writing rituals that might help you to get going (music in the background; sharpen your pencils; cup of tea).
	• Begin wherever it is easiest – start in the middle if that is what it takes!
	• Don't expect perfection – you are drafting something – you can improve on it later.
	• Reduce interruptions – do what it takes to work for a defined period without distractions. Turn off your mobile phone for defined writing periods. Do not check your emails until you reach a predetermined 'break time'.
	• Find a regular place for your writing (particularly if you are using a laptop). Familiarity with the surroundings means they won't distract you. Don't waste time getting everything out and putting it away again if you can avoid it.
	• If you need to, start by speaking your ideas aloud. You might also consider using voice recognition software if you find it easier to speak than to type or write.
	• Take a short break if you get 'stuck' and then come back to it after a walk/cup of tea, but don't leave it for too long. Try not to stop mid-way. If you can struggle through to the end of a 'troublesome section', you can revisit it another day when you are fresh and you will find that you can improve it then.
	• Where possible, stop writing at a point from which it is easy to resume work again the next time.
Monitoring your progress	• Set yourself a target for writing a given number of words each week or month.
	• Reward yourself when you achieve significant 'word targets'.
	• Allow someone else to oversee your writing progress (partner, child, colleague, fellow student?). Get someone else to read what you have written. This is hard but well worth it because they can comment on how understandable your material is and suggest some easy ways of making your work much better.
	• Ask your supervisor/tutor to read your drafts so that you can identify any writing 'issues' early on and deal with them.
	• Plan to finish – look forward to the day when you submit the project report or dissertation and can then forget about it if you want to.

(Blaxter et al 2006, Robson 2011, Neuman 2011, Jankowicz 2005, Hart 2010)

SAFETY FIRST

If you can develop an approach that enables you to plan each section within the overall report, and use personal strategies so that you maintain a habit of writing, you should be able to achieve your objective of finishing and submitting your report on time. However, there are other technical obstacles that may seem trivial but can afflict anyone at any time and cause misery. Most tutors have had occasion to commiserate with a student whose computer has crashed less than a week before the submission date and who have no back-up copy of their work, or whose printer has failed for no apparent reason. Writing is hard work and these technical problems are dispiriting and, in extreme cases, can cause total despair. The following suggestions (written from the heart) are, therefore, offered:

- Save your work every 1,000 words or every hour, whichever is the soonest.
- At the end of each session (or more frequently), back up your work to at least one other computer device.
- If you are working at home, think about saving your work to your PC and flash drive, but also email it to yourself.
- Never trust your writing to a networked system – always back it up so you can continue outside of the network.
- Once each section is drafted, save it with a version number (one is never enough!) and print off a hard copy as your ultimate back-up. This may be expensive, although print options to print two pages on one sheet and to print 'double-sided' will make some savings to your print bill. A hard copy is an insurance policy against more than one crisis occurring at the same time.
- Don't keep your back-up (for example, on a flash drive) in the same case as the laptop you are using. If one is stolen, the other will disappear too.
- Have in mind two alternative printers you can use when the time comes to print the final version. Ensure that you have a back-up copy of your work in a format that both printers can work from.

PLANNING YOUR WRITING

Students tend to adopt one of two approaches for their writing. Some plan the contents of each section to a greater or lesser extent and then work through their plan, amending it as necessary as they proceed. Although this is the approach recommended by almost every tutor, anecdotal evidence suggests that only a minority of students follow this advice. Many students, it appears, have a rough (often implicit) idea of where they will go in their writing and start writing just 'hoping for the best'.

The 'hoping for the best' approach is not for the faint-hearted. As noted in Table 11.3, breaking down what must be written into smaller parts makes writing less daunting. It also promotes structure and coherence. Writing that is undertaken without much of a plan usually has to be significantly revised and restructured two or three times until coherence gradually emerges. Work that has been planned is still likely to need revision, but the process is less extreme and quicker to achieve.

There are a number of ways to plan your writing, and it is likely you use them in other aspects of your work and life outside study. These techniques can be used in isolation or in different combinations to facilitate the planning process:

- **Brainstorming:** use this technique (you could work with a colleague) to generate a list of all the possible ideas or items you need to include in the section you are concerned with. Then set about taking out the ideas that are not relevant, editing out repetitions and putting the remaining ideas into a logical order.
- **Mind-mapping:** construct a mind map that represents different ideas or themes and how they branch out from one another. Use the 'shape' of the map to identify the main sections and the more detailed points to include within them.
- **Concept mapping:** this is a more structured form of 'mapping'. Start with your main topic at the top of a large piece of paper. Use 'post-it' notes to write down all the associated concepts and issues that are relevant and then arrange them on the paper. Draw lines (in pencil) to indicate the links between them AND the nature of the relationship between the concepts or issues (for example, 'stems from', 'leads to' or 'requires'). You will find you move your post-its around on the page and edit your lines quite a lot before you are 'happy'. However, the end result will be a hierarchically arranged, graphic representation of the relationships between concepts. This will provide you with the basis to structure what you write and you are more likely to achieve the analytical approach that your tutors are looking for.
- **Linear planning:** jot down the main themes you feel are relevant for the section you are planning. Under each one write down points that 'drop out' from it. Put the main themes into some kind of order (it might be chronological, by category or by significance to the issue being researched).
- **Post-its:** write headings for all the different points you need to make onto different post-it notes. Then, on the basis of each heading, break it down into sub-points (rather like task analysis if you are engaged in project planning). The sub-points also go onto post-it notes and you can organise and display your notes visually on the wall in front of your computer. This means that you can visually check your progress by removing post-its from the wall or flipchart as you have covered them in your writing.

STRUCTURING YOUR REPORT

Your study centre will have given you guidance about the structure of the report, although most will allow for some variation where it is appropriate to the nature of the topic and the research approach that has been used. In brief, your report or dissertation needs to tell the reader why, how and when you carried out your research; what you found; what it means; and how it compares with other research and practice in your field.

The main areas that will be incorporated within most project reports and dissertations are:

- **Title page:** title of the report; your name; date of submission; any other information required by your study centre.

- **Summary or abstract:** a very short overview that indicates the issue being researched, the research questions, the approach taken to the investigation, the main findings and the conclusions. The next section in this chapter provides some more thoughts about writing a good abstract or summary.
- **Contents page.**
- **Introduction:** an introduction to the topic and its significance for the organisation and/or HR practice more widely as well as an explanation of the research objectives, aims, terms of reference or the principal research question to be examined. If you are required to make organisational recommendations, make sure that you include the need to make recommendations as one of your report's objectives. There should also be a brief overview of the logic of the forthcoming sections or chapters.
- **Literature review:** this is where you set your research in its wider context and indicate how your research builds on what is already known. Make sure you show how the review of the literature has informed your research questions as well as the research approach you have adopted. By the time the reader has finished reading your literature review, they should be clear about: the way that your issue or topic is defined (by others as well as by you); the important concepts; the strengths and weaknesses of previous studies; and how your research can add to knowledge and/or practice in this area
- **Research methodology:** an explanation of how you investigated your topics as well as a description of procedures you carried out to gather, record and analyse data. In addition, discuss the ethical issues you took into account, any logistical problems that you encountered as well as an evaluation of the strengths and weaknesses of your approach. By the time the reader reaches the end of this chapter, they should be clear about: what data you collected and what data you did **not** collect (and why), what methods, tools and sampling procedures you used and what data analysis procedures you undertook. Chapter 5 provides more detail on how to write the methodology.
- **Findings/results:** this chapter sets out the results of your data-gathering activities. The way this is presented will depend on the research approach you adopted. This section is where you **describe** what you found (the facts) rather than your interpretation of your findings. Tables rather than graphs are more appropriate in this section. Save the graphs and figures for the analysis chapter. Remember, if you have a low number of respondents (fewer than 50 responses), use 'whole numbers' rather than percentages to describe the frequencies. Chapters 7 and 9 indicate different ways of presenting qualitative and quantitative data.
- **Analysis:** for some research approaches, the analysis of the data may be integrated within the findings chapter/section. For others, it is possible (and preferable) to differentiate between the presentation of data and the data analysis. Lee and Lings (2008) point out that in general terms your research will lead to one of three outcomes, illustrated in Figure 11.2.

Figure 11.2 Research outcomes spectrum

| You found what you expected to find. | Some of what you found was expected but there were also anomalies or fresh insights. | What you found was not what you expected to find. |

Each of these 'outcome positions' requires discussion and interpretation and, in addition, the analysis chapter provides you with the opportunity to answer the 'so what' questions by interpreting your data in the light of the research objectives and questions. Chapters 8 and 10 indicate different approaches to writing about your analysis of qualitative and quantitative data.

- **Conclusions:** this part of the report should provide a summary of the main features of your analysis and the implications for both the study of HR and for practice. Make sure your conclusions are clearly drawn from the **evidence** rather than from your opinions. Highlight any areas where further research would be beneficial. The next section in this chapter offers more suggestions about how to tackle the conclusions.
- **Recommendations** (where appropriate): where these are required (for example, for CIPD research reports) they should be action orientated, indicating costs, timescales, accountabilities and contingencies. Whereas your conclusions are orientated to the past (they relate to what you found out), the recommendations are future orientated and indicate your views about what should happen next. The next section in this chapter offers more suggestions about how to tackle the recommendations.
- **Personal reflection:** if you are undertaking a CIPD qualification, there is an expectation that you will write a reflective account of what you have learned during the project and how you can apply your learning in the future. The next section in this chapter offers more suggestions about how to tackle the personal reflection element of your report.
- **References:** if you do not reference your work appropriately you may be penalised for plagiarism, which is a serious form of cheating. It is wise to ask your tutor for feedback about your referencing technique and obtain any necessary guidance to ensure your work provides evidence of good academic practice.
- **Appendices:** these will include copies of your research instruments (questionnaires, interview schedules, and so on) and other material that is relevant to the understanding of the main report. Research reports should 'make sense' without having to refer to the appendices. Avoid using the appendices as a way around the word limit.

WRITING THE CONCLUSIONS, RECOMMENDATIONS, ABSTRACT AND PERSONAL REFLECTION

Most of the other sections of the report or dissertation have been given a chapter in their own right with information and ideas about what to include and how to structure each chapter. However, the abstract or summary, conclusions, recommendations and personal reflection have not had their 'own' chapters and so I have produced an additional section for this edition of the book which focuses on these important chapters or sections of your report.

The abstract (see below) is the first element of your report or dissertation that will be seen by any of your readers and it is important that this provides a 'solid start'. Although it is the first part of the report, most people find they have to wait until they have completed all the sections of their report (including their conclusions) before they are able to write the abstract. Following this logic, you will find some ideas about how to write the abstract after the material relating to formulating the conclusions and recommendations.

THE CONCLUSIONS SECTION

By the time you get to write your conclusions chapter or section, you are likely to be very close to the submission date and you will probably have been working long hours on your report for the previous few weeks. Like many others, you may be tired and feel fed up by the time you get to the conclusions chapter, wondering what else to write that would not be a repetition of what you have covered already. As a result, you may be tempted to 'write anything' to fill two or three pages so that you can finish the project and move on with your life.

This is a temptation to be resisted as, in many study centres, the conclusions carry a lot of marks; underperformance here can be costly in terms of your grade! However, do not despair. The conclusions chapter should not require more work or research, just one last effort of serious thinking. This is the point where things need to come together. In the conclusions chapter or section, you discuss your own findings in the light of the literature and the context of the wider frameworks of HR in which you are working. It is also the point where you need to reassure your reader that the research questions you set out to address really did 'drive' the research design and your interpretation of the data. If, on reflection, you find that your conclusions seem to be addressing rather different questions or issues, it might be worth redrafting some of the material in the introduction chapter.

To help you develop your conclusions in a meaningful way, try following this 'template' for the chapter structure:

1   **Introduction to the conclusions chapter**
    - Remind your readers about the aim and the research objectives or questions you have addressed in your research. This is one place where a copy and paste word for word of your research aim and objectives from the introduction would be acceptable.
    - Indicate that this chapter will discuss the significance of the research findings and evaluate the implications for both the study of HR and for practice.

2   **Research design**
    - Summarise the way you designed your research (and your reasoning) and provide a short reflection on the strengths and limitations of your research process.

- Indicate the extent to which your findings may be generalisable for HR practice generally and/or across different types of organisation and context.
- Highlight areas where your project findings indicate a need for further research. Remember that all knowledge is 'provisional'; you will get credit for identifying what your research has shown but also what needs further examination.

3   **Taking one objective/question at a time**

- What were your main findings and how do they relate with the literature/theories?
- What was surprising in what you found and how does the literature help you to understand what may be happening? What issues came up that the literature does not fully reflect?
- What are the implications of what you have found for the study of HR?
- What are the implications of what you have found for HR practice and practitioners?
- Taking your research as a whole, what is the 'big thing' that emerges from the project findings? Highlight the 'added value' of your project – end strongly and confidently!

THE RECOMMENDATIONS SECTION

The requirements for master's-level dissertations at your institution may or may not require you to formulate an implementation plan or some recommendations at the end of your report. However, a set of feasible and costed recommendations is expected in CIPD management research reports. Many students feel unsure about how to go forward with these, particularly in relation to the costings element. Again, provided that you are prepared to do some thinking, you should be able to achieve a good mark for this section. You will get more marks if you include an implementation plan showing timescales and accountabilities. A discussion about possible barriers/points of resistance and how these might be overcome will earn you even more marks.

A useful way to think about your recommendations is to set them out in a tabular form, rather like the template shown as Table 11.4.

Table 11.4 Template for recommendations

Action	Priority	Timescale	Accountability	Resource implications
Indicate in this column the actions you propose	High?	Immediate (within four weeks?)	Indicate clearly who should be responsible for making sure this is implemented	If you can estimate a direct cost, do so (work in round numbers)
Make sure they follow from your data / evidence rather than from your assumptions	Medium?	Short term (within three months?)	HR (who specifically?)	Your resource estimate may relate to time needed rather than to financial estimates
	Low?	Medium term (3–6 months?)	Line managers?	

Starting out with a table can provide a helpful basis for you to think through what actions you recommend that follow from the conclusions that you have drawn from your research. It is important to convince your readers that your recommendations are based on the data and the analysis. The value of the report will be extremely limited if people feel that you could have made your recommendations without undertaking the project in the first place. You may be tempted to 'make do' with just a table for this section of your report, but if you can supplement this table with some additional text setting out what alternative 'ways forward' you considered and why the ones you have put forward seem most appropriate, your recommendations will seem more persuasive. You can do even better with a brief discussion of the potential points of resistance to your recommendations and some ideas about how these might be overcome or what 'fall-back' plans are possible.

THE ABSTRACT OR SUMMARY

This part of the report may well not 'count' in the overall word count but its function is to be a 'taster' of what is contained in the full report and it is important to communicate the 'essence' of your report in an effective way. Check out how many words or pages you are 'allowed' for the abstract or summary by your study centre. Some indicate no more than one page, others 250 words, and so on. A common mistake in writing the abstract or summary is to reproduce a few parts of the introduction, but this part of the document should contain a more general overview of what you have researched, your research questions, your methods of inquiry and your main findings and conclusions. It is daunting to condense all this into one page. The template below (adapted from Biggam 2011) might help you to plan what to include:

- This research examines…
- The study is important because…
- Data for this study were gathered in the following ways(s)…

- The findings suggest that…
- The main conclusions from the study are…
- (If appropriate) the main recommendations arising from this report are…

THE PERSONAL REFLECTION SECTION

If you are undertaking a CIPD-accredited programme, this section is likely to be a requirement, but the ability to undertake reflective and reflexive thinking is an important characteristic of all HR professionals. Therefore, even if this section is not required for your dissertation, it would be useful for you to include some form of personal reflection in your continuing professional development processes. The personal reflection section is the place to write about what you, as a person, have learned: what challenges did you face and how did you overcome them? What would you do differently in the future as a result?

This is likely to be a short section within the overall word count of your report, but it will carry marks and it would be a shame if you missed out on them. Some suggested areas for you to reflect on and write about are:

- What was your level of skills, knowledge, attitudes, and so on, relating to research at the beginning of the project?
- What has changed?
- What problems did you encounter and how did you overcome them?
- What strengths have you been able to build on and what development areas have you become more aware of?
- How will you set out to apply the skills, knowledge and attitudes you have developed over the duration of the project in your work role or future career?
- What are your priorities for your further development?

STYLE AND EXPRESSION ISSUES

Working out a structure for your report will help you clarify **what** to write. It is also important to develop an appropriate style (**how** to write) to enable successful communication with your academic readers.

 ACTIVITY 11.3

WRITING FOR DIFFERENT PURPOSES

Think back to all the texts, tweets, Facebook postings, emails and (occasional) letters that you have received during the last week at home and at work. Try to classify them as to:

- their purpose (why they were sent to you)
- the different styles used by the authors to communicate with you and achieve their purpose.

FEEDBACK NOTES

Predicting the contents of someone's email in-box and social media alerts is impossible, but it is likely that your mail has included:

- **Junk:** these general communications (paper-based, texts, electronic mail, Internet 'pop-ups', unwanted postings) were not written for you personally but encourage a rapid response. They use a style that suggests you 'must' or 'should' respond in some way, or that you would be foolish (or churlish) not to respond. Although expressed in quite emotive terms, these are not memorable and you may have forgotten about them already.
- **Letters, cards, emails, postings from family and friends:** these may be to thank you for something, to wish you luck, to send birthday greetings, to send you news/updates, to suggest a social gathering, and so on. As well as giving some information, these usually express feelings and are often written in a semi-humorous or 'chatty' style.
- **Bank statements, insurance documents, payment reminders, pay-slips, and so on:** these are not at all 'chatty' and their purpose is to provide you with information on which you may want or need to take action. Their style is impersonal and official, and people rarely read all the information (the small print) that they provide.
- **Everyday communications:** these provide snippets of information or suggestions and questions. They are partial and often only understandable to the people involved in the communication. They rely on participants being able to 'read between the lines'.

Activity 11.3 indicates in a very simplistic way how the purpose of different forms of writing influence the style that is appropriate for it. The purpose of your research report is to provide a formal record of your research process as well as your findings. This enables others to evaluate what you have done and to learn from your research. Most often, the appropriate style to achieve this purpose will be succinct and will express some 'distance' from the subject matter. Research reports are not the place for language that moralises, is humorous or is 'chatty'. The purpose of the report is to inform rather than to entertain. Try to avoid the temptation to advance one position while ignoring other points of view. However, it is also important to produce a report that is more interesting than the small print on a broadband bill or direct debit statement. While adopting a formal style, therefore, it is also important to maintain the interest of the reader and to organise what you write to communicate the logic of the document.

The report as a whole will have a 'storyline', something like the one illustrated in Figure 11.3. Each of the main sections of the report will also require a framework through which the purpose of the section can be explained, fulfilled and the progression to the next section is indicated. A framework through which this might be achieved is shown as Figure 11.4.

Figure 11.3 Developing a project report 'storyline'

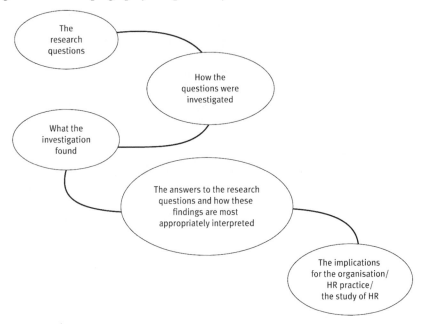

Figure 11.4 Outline framework for each section/chapter

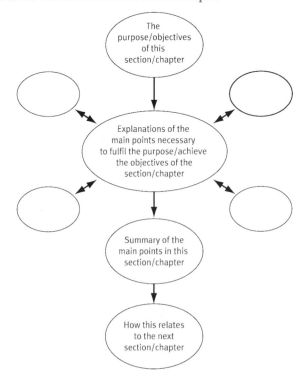

The framework indicated in Figure 11.4 shows that it is advisable to subdivide each of the main chapters or sections, using sub-headings, and to have an introduction and a conclusion to each of the sections. This provides some form of 'signposting' to enable your reader to follow the logic of your report. Other stylistic 'hints and tips' are included below (Robson 2011, Saunders et al 2012, Blaxter et al 2006, Collis and Hussey 2009, McMillan and Weyer 2008):

- **Write clearly and simply:** many students assume that academic language should be more complex and sophisticated than 'normal' writing. In fact, clear communication is enhanced by the use of simple sentences. Where you have drafted a long sentence, check tosee if you could rewrite it as two shorter ones.
- **Avoid using too many direct quotations:** you will get credit for your own thinking and your ability to express what is already known in your own words. Using other people's expressions too often makes the report look 'second hand'. Use quotations sparingly and to support a point rather than to 'prove' a point.
- **Avoid using jargon, slang and abbreviations:** written communication is different from the spoken form. Abbreviations such as 'don't' should be written as 'do not'. Avoid informal language such as 'the flip side of this is…'. Use words that are precise rather than over-generalised and objective rather than emotive. Where you have to use technical terms, include a glossary.
- **Use a new paragraph for each new idea:** ideas cannot normally be expressed in one sentence. If you find you are using a new paragraph every one or two sentences, check that you are explaining your ideas fully or see whether two paragraphs really relate to the same idea and could be combined.
- **Avoid repetition:** make sure that you have not repeated yourself in two different sections. Look particularly carefully at the introduction to see if some expressions occur again in the same form in the literature review or in the conclusions. Where this is the case, redraft one of the passages.
- **Be consistent (and appropriate) with the 'person' and tense:** different study centres have different expectations about the 'person' with which you write. Most formal academic communication is written from the 'third person', as in the example below:

> The process undertaken for the research was as follows. First, a literature review was undertaken and key themes were identified. A questionnaire was then devised to…

Some research projects, particularly those adopting a more action-orientated and qualitative approach, can be appropriately written in the first person, provided that this is acceptable at your study centre. An example of this is shown below:

> At the beginning of the research process I reviewed the literature about. … To explore the key issues about … I then organised a focus group consisting of…

Some study centres permit the use of the third person in some sections or chapters of the report and the first person in others. Having decided what 'person' to write from, however, it is important to maintain a consistent approach to it within each section or chapter. The same consistency is required with regard to the 'tense' with which you write. The normal convention is to use the present tense when you are referring to work that is published, as in the examples below:

> Jones (2003) highlights four key aspects of … and these are briefly described now…

> XYZ Ltd is a large employer situated in the north of England. The firm produces … for high street retail outlets.

Where you are referring to primary data that you gathered for your study and the process by which you gathered it, however, the past tense may be more appropriate:

> Questionnaires were issued to 78 people and 62 completed returns were received.

● **Avoid discriminatory language:** to maintain an objective stance within your writing it is necessary to avoid using language that can be interpreted as offensive or discriminatory. Check your writing and eliminate such expressions. Writing should be as 'gender neutral' as possible. Thus, 'her manager said that he…' can be more appropriately expressed as, 'the manager indicated that…'. Some other expressions that can occur within writing about HR, and which need to be appropriately expressed, are indicated in Table 11.5.

Table 11.5 HR language – avoiding discriminatory language

Try to avoid	Alternative expression
businessman	business manager
committee chairman	committee chair
manpower	staffing
manpower planning	HR planning
manning levels	staffing levels
spokesman	representative

REVIEWING, REVISING AND SUBMITTING YOUR WORK

EVALUATING WHAT YOU HAVE WRITTEN

Achieving perfection in one draft is not likely to occur. Once you have a draft report or dissertation, it will be necessary to revise and edit it. This will help you to clarify your thinking and communicate more effectively. You will need to 'clean up' or 'tighten up' your writing as well as undertake more significant revisions such as inserting some new sections, deleting some material and moving material around within the structure. Key questions to be addressed when evaluating your early drafts are (Saunders et al 2012, Brown 2006, McMillan and Weyer 2008):

● How clear and appropriate is the structure of the report as a whole and the structure of each section or chapter?

- Are the research objectives or questions expressed clearly and consistently throughout the report? Have you achieved them?
- Is the meaning clear? What passages seem obscure or 'clumsy'? Are all your terms clearly defined?
- Are there occasions where you have inadvertently used biased, emotional or imprecise language?
- To what extent does the literature review inform the methodology and the data analysis?
- To what extent does your literature review describe what others have written, analyse the issues **and** advance a line of argument?
- Where are the missing references?
- Have you presented **and** analysed your data in a way that readers can follow?
- How close to the word limit are you (too long or too short?)
- How **logical** and well explained are the points made in each chapter? Do they follow on in a sensible way from each other?
- How **trustworthy** or reliable is the evidence that you have presented in your chapters?

Honest answers to these questions should help you to prioritise your work as you set about revising what you have written. Your tutor may also be able to provide a useful evaluation (but not at the last minute). Family and friends, although not 'technically' knowledgeable, may also be able to spot the areas that need more careful explanation.

LOSING OR FINDING MORE WORDS

At the beginning of the project process you may have thought you would never have enough words to write to meet the required word length of your dissertation or research report. At this stage, however, you may be facing the opposite problem and experiencing difficulty staying within the word limit. The prospect of losing words can seem very painful, especially if you struggled to write some of them in the first place. For a minority of students, the problem is the reverse; you may discover that your report is 'thin' or that some sections of it are not as long as your tutor expects. Some ideas about how to tackle these opposite areas of difficulty are provided in Table 11.6.

Table 11.6 Losing or adding more words

Making more into less	Making less into more
Check each sub-section in each section. Which one(s) are not central to your argument and analysis? Lose the 'nice to have' but make sure you retain the 'need to have' sub-sections.	Add new sections. Identify which section(s) might benefit from a fuller explanation or discussion.
Shorten lengthy, descriptive passages by using tables, charts or diagrams.	Do you have a lot of appendices and not enough text? Consider working material from one or two of the appendices into the text (but don't engage in 'padding').
Take a good look at the quotations you have used. Do they repeat ideas you have already explained? Do you really need them? Could you express the ideas they articulate in a more concise way?	Look for more references or quotations on the subjects or issues you are writing about.
See if you can summarise the ideas in two or more sentences, or even in a whole paragraph, into one (shorter) sentence.	Are you making too many assumptions? Build up sentences into paragraphs by developing your argument or making your line of thinking more explicit.
Engage in 'word weeding' (a form of literary gardening). Remove unnecessary, qualifying or repetitive words from sentences.	Go further in your evaluation of different aspects of your methodology and how appropriate it was. (This section is often not discussed in enough length – particularly in management or business research reports.)

(Blaxter et al 2006)

DESCRIBING AND ANALYSING

In writing your report it is important to minimise description of the work of others and undertake more analysis. Description involves summarising what other people have written or said, more or less in the terms of the original author. **Analysis,** however, is a search for **explanation and understanding**. If you are concerned that some parts of your work are too descriptive (or your tutor has indicated this to you), try the following steps. Steps 1–3 should help you make your writing more critically evaluative. Steps 4–7 should help you make your writing more analytical.

Being critical

1   For each theory, framework, concept, research procedure or method that you describe, write beside it the words *'prove it'*.

2   On a post-it note try to note down possible objections to each 'prove it' point where the opposite or a different situation might apply.

3   Redraft your work into a more critical and evaluative style by using this thinking process to highlight the limitations as well as the strengths of the ideas you are describing.

Being analytical

4   Read through your work again and after each idea that you have evaluated, write the words '*so what*'.

5   Redraft your work again, attempting to answer the 'so what' questions in the light of your research objectives or questions.

6   Read your work again. You may find that some of the answers to some of the 'so what' questions are the same. If so, this means you are starting to identify some analytical themes. This is a very good sign.

7   Have a go at reorganising your work so that you tackle one theme at a time. This will involve considering more than one author's work at a time. There may also be implications for the order with which you consider the data in your findings section. If this is the case, give yourself a reward, as it means you have probably started to think and write in a more analytical way.

FINAL CHECKS

The process of drafting and revising your report can be both frustrating and rewarding. As the submission date approaches there are some important final checks to make prior to printing the final version. The aim at this stage is to arrive at a form of presentation that is as near to perfection as can be achieved. Look carefully at the text to ensure that spelling errors have been eradicated and that the punctuation and grammar are correct. This is something that cannot be hurried. It is also necessary to check the formatting. Have all the section numbers, table numbers and labels for the appendices been consistently applied? Are all the font sizes consistent? Are there any 'glitches' in the page layout? Are there still any missing references? Is the list of references at the back in the right order and formatted in a consistent manner?

The first few pages of the report are crucial. Check the title page – does it have all the necessary information? Are all the pages numbered and are the page numbers on the contents page still accurate? Have you listed the appendices on the contents page? Is the abstract or summary still appropriate or does it require revision in the light of redrafting you have recently undertaken? Are the research objectives and questions explained clearly in the introduction? Do you need to include a copy of a completed ethical review process?

Once you are satisfied, you can print your work. Before making any subsequent copies, make a final visual check to ensure that the printer has not inserted the odd blank page or the numbering system has not been disrupted by a section break. Then make sufficient copies and securely bind them ready for their journey to your study centre.

SUMMARY

- The process of writing about your research underpins the learning process. It enables you to reflect on what you have found, clarify your thinking and communicate more effectively about your research.
- Readers in different contexts have different expectations of what they read. **Academic readers** expect a formal and objective style of writing and a

demonstration of your knowledge and understanding of your subject area. They will want to assess how you have applied and evaluated an appropriate research methodology for your enquiry. **Managers and other organisational sponsors** expect a more persuasive and accessible written style and a report that focuses on recommendations and implementation that can contribute to the resolution of HR problems, issues or opportunities.

- All research reports or dissertations, whatever level or type of qualification they are associated with, should clearly express the research aims and objectives, review relevant literature, report the use of appropriate methods of data collection and analyse data in an integrated and objective way. Business research reports have more emphasis on the generation of practical, costed, timely and realistic recommendations. Master's-level dissertations have more emphasis on the analytical focus, scope and contribution of the literature review, the evaluation of different research design and methodological issues, the analysis of data and the reasoning process linking conclusions with analysis of the literature and other data.
- To overcome factors that inhibit the writing process, it is important to develop 'writing habits', to write regularly, to plan your writing, to reward yourself when you achieve your writing targets and to ensure that everything you write is regularly 'backed up'.
- Planning can reduce the stress of writing. Useful techniques that can enhance the planning process are: brainstorming, mind-mapping, concept mapping and linear planning.
- It is important that readers of any report can follow its 'logic' through the structure, style and expression. Effective writing is expressed clearly and simply with appropriate paragraphing and a consistent system of headings and sub-headings. Jargon, slang, abbreviations, informal, emotive and discriminatory language are not appropriate.
- Involving others in evaluating your draft report, or sections of it, will enable you to prioritise the revisions that are required to ensure that it meets the assessment criteria by which it will be judged.

 Self-test questions

REVIEW AND REFLECT

1 Which of the following are **not** normally found in a research report or dissertation?

   a) research objectives or research questions

   b) contact details about research participants

   c) methods or methodology

   d) critical review of the literature

2 The introduction chapter or section of a dissertation or research report should:

   a) set out the conclusions in advance

   b) establish the focus and research questions or objectives for the study

   c) include promotional material about the organisation in which the research was carried out

d) provide an acknowledgements section

3 What is the principal purpose of the conclusion in a research report or dissertation?

  a) to justify the methods and methodology

  b) to provide a detailed review of other research and practice developments in the area of the study

  c) to discuss the main findings in relation to the literature and the research questions or objectives

  d) to explain the processes of the design or choice of research instruments

4 A research report written from an interpretivist perspective is likely to include:

  a) a decision to accept or reject a hypothesis

  b) detailed summaries of statistical frequencies and correlations

  c) explanation of the ways in which variables have been operationalised

  d) a discussion of the 'position' of the researcher in the research process and the possible ways that the project affected research participants and the resulting interpretation of the data

5 Which section or chapter of the research report or dissertation is likely to describe the purpose of the research and the principal research question?

  a) introduction

  b) methodology

  c) results

  d) appendices

6 The methods chapter or section of a research report or dissertation would **not** normally include:

  a) sampling strategy

  b) response rates

  c) recommendations for future research

  d) details about research instrument design

7 The recommendations section of a research report should:

  a) provide costed suggestions for future action

  b) discuss implications for HR research

  c) highlight what the organisation is incapable of achieving

  d) be written in the past tense

8 When data are presented in the findings it is important to:

  a) include information about sample and response sizes

  b) conceal data that does not 'fit' what you hope to show

  c) leave out information about the response scales

  d) make use of quotations from only one or two responses to the 'open questions' you included

REVIEW AND REFLECT

 Questions for reflection

This final part of the chapter enables you to reflect about your professional development and develop your skills and knowledge. This will enable you to build your confidence and credibility, track your learning, see your progress and demonstrate your achievements.

Taking stock

1   What written reports about your research are required by your study centre, employer or other sponsor or client? How clear are you about the required length, format and content required by these different readers?

2   How much time do you have before the submission date for your research report? Who can help you to evaluate your draft sections? What lead time will they require to review your work and offer feedback?

3   Where will you undertake your writing? What steps do you need to take to have the 'space' to write without distractions?

4   What arrangements will be necessary to ensure your work can be printed, copied and bound when the time comes?

Strengths and weaknesses

5   Look back at previous written coursework assignments that you have submitted. What comments have your tutors made? What improvement areas have they highlighted with your writing and how might you develop the skills that you need?

6   Consider your strengths as a writer. What steps can you take to ensure that you tackle the 'difficult' sections in a timely and effective way?

Being a practitioner-researcher

7   What writing conventions or styles are you most comfortable with? How compatible are they with the expectations for academic writing?

EXPLORE FURTHER

It is very difficult to read about writing. The best way to learn to write is to critically evaluate the writing of others, get going with your own writing and then seek feedback about it. Therefore, the process of reviewing the literature will help you to learn to write. It is also worth reading projects submitted by past students at your study centre to identify the ways in which other students have communicated in an objective and reasonable way. To make sure that you are able to learn from the more effective writers, make sure you only review the work of those who achieve a mark equivalent to a 'merit' or higher.

Web Links

You can find information about voice recognition software from: http://www.bbc.co.uk/accessibility/guides/voice_recognition/

The market leader for 'paid for' software seems to be:

Dragon (Nuance)

http://shop.nuance.co.uk/store/nuanceeu/en_GB/Content/pbPage.PS_44_uk_D12_11BAS?resid=UEyrvgoHAtUAABQWMp4AAAAW&rests=1347201982596

Reading

Biggam, J. (2011) *Succeeding with your master's dissertation*. Maidenhead: Open University Press.

Blaxter, L., Hughes, C. and Tight, M. (2006) *How to research*. Buckingham: Open University Press.

Brown, R.B. (2006) *Doing your dissertation in business and management: the reality of researching and writing*. London: Sage.

Fisher, C. (2007) *Researching and writing a dissertation: a guidebook for business students*. Harlow: Pearson Education.

Hart, C. (2010) *Doing your master's dissertation*. London: Sage.

Marsen, S. (2007) *Professional writing*. Basingstoke: Palgrave Macmillan.

McMillan, K. and Weyer, J. (2008) *How to write dissertations and project reports*. Harlow: Pearson Education.

CHAPTER 12

Developing Effective Links Between Research and Practice

CHAPTER OUTLINE

- How to use this chapter
- Routes to knowledge about HRM
- Communicating what you have learned with non-academic audiences
- Bridging the gap between research and practice
- Developing effective practitioner-researchers
- Summary
- Final review and reflect
- Explore further

LEARNING OUTCOMES

This chapter should help you to:

- take courage and 'go public' with your work to share what you have learned
- communicate your findings to non-academic audiences in a credible way
- examine why HR researchers and practitioners seem to operate in different 'worlds'
- identify how researchers and practitioners might collaborate better to co-produce a richer knowledge and understanding of HR issues.

HOW TO USE THIS CHAPTER

All of the previous chapters of the book have focused on the achievement of an academic research report or dissertation. The focus of this chapter is on life after the dissertation. Once you have submitted your research report or dissertation, you may feel as though you never want to hear or write another word about your topic. However, it is likely that you will have to. Once you have had a break you may even feel that you want to disseminate what you have learned beyond your tutors. There are many people who will be interested in learning about what you have found as a result of your research. The organisation(s) that have been involved in your research process, clients or sponsors that have helped make your research possible may all expect to receive a project 'output'. Other (non-studying) practitioners and researchers might also be interested in learning more about your findings and their implications.

It takes a brave person to 'go public' with a piece of research, but this chapter provides some ideas about how you might communicate the results of your research in a credible way to non-academic 'audiences' once your research report has been completed. The early part of this chapter focuses on ways of communicating about your research. This is not too difficult. Once your 'long' research report is written, you will find that producing a 'punchier' and shorter summary for non-academic purposes is usually relatively straightforward.

In addition, this chapter identifies how you might build on the skills of systematic research you have developed through the research process to develop your role and contribution to organisational change and effectiveness. Hopefully you might be encouraged to reflect on ways in which you can make use of your research skills in new contexts and situations to the benefit of both organisational performance and developing wider knowledge and understanding of HRM.

ROUTES TO KNOWLEDGE ABOUT HRM

 ACTIVITY 12.1

HOW DO YOU AND YOUR COLLEAGUES LEARN ABOUT HRM?

This activity requires you to brainstorm the different ways you have come to learn about different elements of HR throughout your career. If you are a part-time student with some experience as an HR practitioner, reflect on both the practical and taught 'avenues' to knowledge. If you are a full-time student who is undertaking a course to develop a career in HR, reflect on what and how you learned in any work placement or internship as well as on your course. There may also have been important learning 'moments' in your life as a part-time or full-time worker at other times of your life or through experiences that your friends and family have also shared with you.

FEEDBACK NOTES

If this activity has stimulated you to think back to a time before you started your current course (which must seem a long time ago now), you may have reflected that, before you became a student, you learned very little about HRM from a scholarly book, lecture or journal article. Most practitioners (not just HR professionals) prefer websites, practitioner-focused books, reports from government or specialist organisations, or social and less formal forms of information-sharing through practitioner conferences, seminars or workshops. Indeed, you may have reflected that your own personal network of contacts has been your most important 'route to knowledge' about HRM.

This diversity of routes to knowledge is not surprising given the diversity of backgrounds of most HR practitioners and their different learning styles and preferences. This means that there are many different, overlapping 'ways of knowing' about HRM. This has implications for you if you wish to share the findings of your research, particularly within the practitioner community. Although 'non-academic' audiences may be very interested in what your research can do for the organisation and its performance, they will be less excited than your academic tutors about your extensive knowledge of the literature and they are possibly indifferent to the finer points of your methodological approach. For practitioner and management-level readers, the 'so what' points they are interested in are the recommendations for action. The next section of this chapter focuses on different options to communicate what you have learned with these important stakeholders.

ACTIVITY 12.2

STAYING UP TO DATE

This activity requires you to undertake a little bit of 'simple' research.

1 Compile a list of the ways you and your colleagues keep up to date with developments in HRM. Ask your boss, your colleagues, people who are younger and older than you.

2 Take a look at the list you have generated. What ideas does this give you for how to 'get the message out' about your research findings?

3 From your list choose **three** dissemination opportunities that you might engage with. What challenges would they present to you?

FEEDBACK NOTES

In response to this activity you may have identified a number of internal and external ways of keeping up to date. Within organisations there are a range of organised information dissemination processes, such as centralised email updates and alerts, 'brown bag' events, which include short presentations by people who need to share information with other interested people on more of a face-to-face basis, or knowledge-sharing events through team briefings or database facilities where your experiences can be recorded so that others can benefit from them.

In addition, you may have identified externally generated information updates that you or others find helpful. Social media sites have transformed the way that many practitioners communicate and these all provide a range of ways to help you stay up to date. Professional bodies such as the CIPD, for example, provide facilities for you to engage with them on many social networking sites and also maintain their own 'internal' members-only discussion boards. Many practitioners subscribe to regular news updates from the CIPD or from *People Management* and use social bookmarking to save, organise and share useful information links with others. It is possible that you follow the blog content or Twitter comments of influential people in HRM. Many people also stay up to date by joining groups on social networking sites such as LinkedIn and Facebook.

In addition, YouTube and Myspace are popular ways for many people to watch and review talks and training demonstrations. A more specialised HRM social and professional network is *HRM: The Journal* (http://hrmthejournal.ning.com/?xg_source=msg_mes_network), the aim of which is to bridge research and practice for HR leaders.

Remember that social networking is often an 'all or nothing' activity. Different people either engage fully with almost all forms of social networking or they hardly make any use of any of them. Therefore, you may also have included other more traditional ways of information-sharing in your list of ways to stay up to date, including attending specialist conferences or workshops, reading *People Management* and so on. You may make a point of going along to CIPD branch meetings to hear presentations about practice innovations as well as to chat with other practitioners about the work that they are engaged with. Having compiled an extensive list of potential ways to share what you have learned through your research project, you might now identify three to five ways that you feel would be appropriate for you to take forward and work out what challenges these would present and how you might plan to undertake them.

COMMUNICATING WHAT YOU HAVE LEARNED WITH NON-ACADEMIC AUDIENCES

Most practitioner-researchers' work remains a well-kept secret, known only to them and a few other close friends. Interestingly, in spite of the acknowledged benefits of knowledge management and knowledge exchange, many HR professionals are strangely modest when it comes to sharing their research findings. This is regrettable; a lot of work will have gone into your project and it is a shame not to share what you found with others who might be able to develop their own thinking and decision-making as a result.

There are other reasons that might make you reticent about sharing your research. Anxiety about people 'dismissing' your work may loom large in your mind. In addition, your existing work commitments are another problem. However, there are a number of benefits from engaging in some form of 'knowledge-sharing'. These include:

- **personal recognition**, both professionally and within your work organisation, to increase your profile and (possibly) your career prospects
- **recognition for your organisation** if you disseminate your research externally
- an opportunity for the **further clarification** of your thinking by revisiting ideas and reflecting on them.

Before you move on with these opportunities, however, you must ensure that you will not be contravening any ethical assurances you gave to your research participants (individuals and organisations). Organisational concerns about confidentiality and anonymity must be taken into account. If you indicated that information you gathered would only be used for your academic study purposes, you must seek the permission of your research participants for any further dissemination.

Assuming that ethical issues are not a problem, the main challenge with disseminating what you have learned from your research is the need to write (and speak) more succinctly. Having spent a number of months learning to communicate in what seemed like excessive detail, you now have to reverse the process. The following steps can help you with this (Day 2008).

CLARIFY THE PURPOSE, SCOPE AND VALUE OF WHAT YOU DID

It is important to be clear about your research problem and its context so that you can articulate it to those who will read your work or hear what you have to say. Useful questions to ask yourself include:

- What did I investigate and why?
- How far did I decide to look and why?
- What related issues did I not examine and why?
- What constraints impacted on my work and why?

In any dissemination that you undertake you should communicate what you have found out and what this means for your readers/audience. Day (2008) suggests that a good way of preparing to communicate about your research is to write down an answer for yourself, in no more than 20 words, to the question: 'what do I want to say and why should anyone care?' This is a challenging thing to do and will probably take at least five attempts (and even then you may still not achieve the 20-word target). Having done it, however, you will find you have a useful focus to the preparation process of any dissemination about your research.

SUMMARISING YOUR WORK

Once you have clarified the purpose, scope and value of your research, you can go on to express the following aspects of your work, in no more than one paragraph each:

- **Findings:** what did you find out? In what ways do your findings matter?
- **Literature:** what did it say and how did it affect your research?
- **Methodology:** what did you do and how did it affect the findings?
- **Analysis:** how did the techniques you used to analyse the data affect your findings?
- **Implications:** what are the implications of what you found for potential answers to your research problem? How far are you prepared to go and why?

Writing these paragraphs enables you to establish what you have to communicate and, from this point, you can develop presentations or write papers or articles to meet the expectations of the audience/readership. Some will be longer and fuller than others, but you have a basis on which to build.

DISSEMINATION OPPORTUNITIES

Organisational reports

If your HR project has been organisationally based, it is likely that you will have to submit some form of report to the manager that has sponsored your project. Most managers will not have the time to work their way through the detail of your full dissertation. Before you begin writing your organisational report, it is worth finding out what your organisational 'audience' expect from you in terms of document format and length. Although you will be able to draw extensively on the material you prepared for your dissertation or research report, there are likely to be a number of differences in what you produce:

- **Less detailed content suitable for a 'manager in a hurry':** you will need to write in a more accessible style, with less use of 'academic-speak'. Focus on the broad issues rather than the detail.
- **Well-thought-through recommendations:** this is likely to be a key issue for the organisational sponsors of your research. Make sure your recommendations are clearly derived from the data and expressed in direct and practical terms. Consider presenting recommendations as a set of options. Be clear about accountabilities, costs, timescales, priorities and contingencies.
- **Write persuasively:** indicate the benefits of implementing your recommendations.

Making presentations

You will find many opportunities to talk about your research on an informal basis, but the occasions where you will 'present' your research more formally are likely to be as presentations to different groups of staff within the organisation or through a presentation made at a conference, workshop or a local CIPD branch meeting (which you might also consider making more widely available through social media opportunities).

Commercial conferences

These are advertised quite widely, take place in comfortable venues and delegates pay to hear from experts about good practice and research relating to particular topics. The format tends to involve a range of expert speakers making a 40–50-minute presentation, with short question and answer sessions following each of them. The emphasis is on the practical implications of the topic being presented and delegates are interested in what it means for them and their organisations. Conference organisers usually 'source' their speakers through a fairly extensive system of networking and 'colleague referral'. If they approach you, they will be fairly explicit about what is expected in terms of the length of the presentation and any supporting material they require, as well as any fee they may be prepared to pay.

It is likely that your presentation will be supplemented with some additional information. Copies of the PowerPoint or Prezi slides you have prepared will be expected. While restricting your supplementary information to 'visuals' may suffice for internal presentations within your own organisation, for any other external presentation, this may be something of a lost opportunity. Provision of more detailed information, for which there will not be time during the presentation, will enable you to disseminate your work more fully. Robson (2011) suggests a 'pamphlet form' using an uncluttered layout and use of photographs, tables and diagrams.

Academic conferences

Other conferences are more **academic** in focus. These are usually less 'glossy' and delegates are likely to be academics undertaking research in similar areas. Here an organiser will make a 'call for papers' 9–12 months before the intended date of the conference. This 'call' may be published in relevant journal publications, through Internet databases and via university networks. Potential speakers submit a paper to the conference organisers, who will then decide whether to accept the contribution. If you are interested in this sort of opportunity, it would be a good idea to ask your dissertation supervisor to suggest appropriate conference opportunities. See, for example, conference information at: http://www.ufhrd.co.uk/wordpress/ and http://www.emccouncil.org/eu/public/annual_conferences/index.html

The audience at these conferences will be interested in the academic as well as practical context of the research, the methodology and the way in which data were analysed. If your paper is accepted, it is likely that the organisers will suggest you submit a fuller version to them, which they will copy for all the participants at the conference. You will also make a presentation about your paper (usually about 20 minutes in length). Often these presentations are to smaller numbers of people (up to 50). There will be scope for questions at the time of your presentation, and it is possible that those who were interested in what you have to say will contact you later (either in person or via email) for a further discussion of your work.

Although these presentations may be rather daunting, they are a useful way of clarifying your thinking and for making contact with people who are also interested in similar areas. The feedback that you receive as a result of the process is also very valuable if you are thinking about going further and publishing your findings in a written form.

The content of presentations for different types of conferences, therefore, varies considerably although the overall structure of the different presentations may be similar and is likely to involve:

1   Objectives of the presentation

2   Research purpose/problem/context

3   Methods of enquiry

4   Findings (what did you expect to find and what did you actually find?)

5   Implications – for practice and for further research

6   Final summary – main interest of the findings for you and for the HR profession more widely.

Aim for three 'summary sentences':

- Sentence 1 – the purpose
- Sentence 2 – the main points and methodology
- Sentence 3 – the main conclusions.

Poster presentations

A less stressful contribution to make at an academic conference is to present a poster about your research. This is where you design and print a large poster (usually A1 in size), which summarises what you have done and any plans for further research or implementation. You do not have to make a spoken presentation but you need to be present at the conference so that those who see your poster and have similar interests can make contact with you to offer suggestions and feedback and discuss ideas for the future. If you decide to produce a poster about your research, remember that posters are a visual presentation of information about your research – not a simple reproduction of your written work. This is your chance to be creative with design so that your poster is attention-catching and understandable to the 'reader' without the need for verbal comment.

Table 12.1 Hints and tips for poster preparation

Information	**Make sure your project title and your name are prominent and eye-catching. Make your poster title the 'punch line' so that it will be seen during the first 11 seconds of the time a person spends looking at your poster.**
Narrative	Tell a story. Provide a clear flow of information from the introduction to the conclusion.
Focus on your major points	A common fault is to try to cover too much – people are not likely to read everything on your poster, so get to the point. Keep the word count low.
Visuals	Use graphs, tables, diagrams and images where appropriate. Use boxes to isolate and emphasise specific points.
White space	Use all the space but do not cram – white space is important. Take out all unnecessary text or visual distractions, including borders between related data and text. This will help the 'reader' to assimilate your ideas easily.
Colour	Use colour sparingly for emphasis and differentiation. Have a white or muted colour background and avoid colour combinations that clash or cause problems for people with colour-blindness.
Layout	Use layout to make the flow of information clear; avoid using too many arrows. Communicate information in a **spatial sequence**. People (in the West) tend to look at things: vertically from centre (top to bottom) and horizontally from left to right. Put the most important message in the centre top position followed by the top left, top right, bottom left, and finish in the bottom right corner.
Labels	Label diagrams/drawings and provide references to them in the text where necessary.
Font	Choose a clear font: Arial, Verdana, Georgia, Calibri. Title text: at least 48-point text; body text: at least 24-point text. The use of multiple fonts in a poster can distract from the message.

You do not need specialised software to create a poster – you can use Microsoft Word or PowerPoint. In **PowerPoint**, create your poster as a single slide. **Set the page size when you start (Design > Page Setup)**. PowerPoint also allows you to add guidelines to help you line up the poster elements. Use View > 'Grid' and 'Ruler'. In **Word**, create your poster as a single side of A4 and scale it up when you come to print it. Word does not have guidelines as such, but you can get a grid by showing the Drawing toolbar (Insert > Shapes > New Drawing Canvas). For the ruler and gridlines go to View > Ruler and View > Gridlines. In both applications, use the Drawing toolbar to add text boxes to the screen. This allows you to control the way the text is positioned on the page. When the initial poster design is complete, convert it to a PDF file for printing. The conversion process is often problematic: edges of words and images may be cut off near to the margins, images may appear degraded or misshapen, poster elements may have shifted and become overlapping. However, by dealing with these problems at the conversion stage, you avoid nasty surprises later when you come to print your poster. When the PDF looks good, you can be pretty confident that the printed version will also work well.

Writing articles and papers

You might be tempted to share your findings through internal, local or professional publications or contributions to social media sites. Your organisational supervisor/mentor will be a good source of advice about potential avenues for dissemination. If you wish to pursue academic means of dissemination, you may aim to publish your work in an academic journal. Here your academic supervisor would be able to provide you with some guidance. Some ideas about how to go about these different forms of communication are given below.

News releases

These might be for a local intranet site or directed at the editors of local press and social media outlets. Editors are always in a hurry and need to find the easiest ways possible to present topical news stories. A news release should be shorter than one side of A4 (or its electronic equivalent) and written in a lively style with a 'catchy' heading. You should also provide a contact number for editorial enquiries. If your release is used it is likely that the journalist who authors the item will use some of your text on a word-for-word basis (hence the need to write in a topical and accessible way). However, you should be prepared to read something that is not wholly familiar to you as they may also add their own 'spin'. It is very important to check the PR policy of your organisation and gain any necessary 'permissions' before sending out any news releases. It is also important to render anonymous any organisations or participants in your research if there is even the slightest chance that they are not comfortable with media coverage. (See Chapter 3 on research and professional ethics.)

Professional journals

Most professional and industry sector associations produce a monthly (or more frequent) journal publication which might provide an opportunity for you to disseminate your research findings in print or on the Web. The word limit here, for a feature article, is likely to be 2,000 words at most and an accessible writing style is expected. If you are considering offering a contribution, it is worth contacting the editor with a short (500 words maximum) summary of your contribution, explaining how your paper would be of interest to readers. Useful headings for such a summary would be:

- target readership
- aims of the intended contribution
- implications of your findings
- treatment (style, etc)
- your contact details.

Use your covering email to make clear your name and the working title of your paper, providing a brief paragraph describing the contents and explaining why you chose this outlet.

Often an editor will not respond for many weeks or months, if at all. If the editor does wish to go ahead, the deadline is likely to be fairly prompt. However, once agreement in principle is achieved, the writing of the article can be achieved quite quickly and may be structured in a similar way to a presentation.

Peer-reviewed journals

These are the most demanding articles to write. If you think you would like to submit your work to a peer-reviewed journal (such as *Human Resource Management Journal, European Journal of Training and Development, Human Resource Development International, Journal of Management Development, Journal of Workplace Learning*, and so on), you should first find and read the guidance for authors that is provided in each copy of the journal and on the journal's website. This will indicate the sort of papers that are expected. If you wish to proceed, you would write your paper and submit an electronic copy to the editor. If the editor believes the paper may be acceptable, it will be sent, without the details of the author(s), to a number of 'reviewers' whose job is to critically evaluate the article and to indicate whether it might be appropriate for the journal as well as how or where it should be improved. This is a lengthy process, rarely taking less than three months. It is very rare for an article to be accepted without revisions, and the process of further enhancing the paper means that many articles are not accepted for publication for at least a year from the date of their original submission. There is also likely to be a further delay of 3–12 months before the paper appears in a volume of the journal.

This process is quite daunting but can be very rewarding when your paper finally appears. Some 'first-time' researchers choose to publish in a non-refereed section of an academic journal first. Others, who wish to achieve a peer-reviewed paper, find it helpful to 'team up' with a more experienced academic writer, often their supervisor or someone recommended by them.

ACTIVITY 12.3

THE DIFFERENT WORLDS OF RESEARCH AND PRACTICE

Human Resource Management Journal is a UK journal you should already have come across as part of your professional studies. It is a scholarly journal which claims to address HRM issues of interest to both academics and practising managers. It is the only HRM journal to be endorsed by the CIPD and it sets out to publish papers that have both academic and HR practitioner relevance. In 2011, to celebrate the twenty-first anniversary of the publication of the journal, a number of respected academic scholars were invited to produce 'provocation papers'. Make use of your electronic library access to find *Human Resource Management Journal* (2011) Volume 21, Issue 3, pp221–35. Read the first part of the introduction to this paper.

1 Identify what the authors believe to be the main problems with HR practice in contemporary organisations.

2 To what extent do you agree with their assertions about HR practitioners?

FEEDBACK NOTES

This paper makes a number of strong assertions about perceived 'failings' of HR practitioners. The authors accuse most HR practitioners of making 'knee-jerk' business decisions, uncritically embracing 'fads' and engaging in implicit guesswork about the effectiveness of different HR practices. They argue that these failings have unfortunate implications for organisational performance and sustainability. The authors allege that HR practice is characterised more by 'blind faith' than critical thinking.

In response to these strongly worded points, you might have reflected that many managers choose not to engage with academic 'theory' and 'research' as it seems to be remote from the 'real world' and irrelevant to the day-to-day, business-focused perspective that they need to underpin their decisions and actions. What the authors of this paper fail to acknowledge is that those involved with HRM in organisations have to undertake work that is inherently challenging and, at the same time, to cope with significant limits to their power and influence. However, there is a paradox. HRM academics invest time, energy and their careers in undertaking systematic research and engaging with theories relevant to people management and development, but many practitioners do not value their work, findings and insights. Practitioners are 'information-hungry', but they rarely look to academic research outputs to inform their practice.

Academics and business practitioners, it seems, 'walk on different sides of the street'. One side of the street focuses on generalised (and sometimes slow-moving) theories and concepts. The other focuses on business imperatives and is results-orientated.

However, the argument underpinning this book is that business-relevant and good-quality HR practitioner research provides an opportunity for a 'bridge' between robust research and excellence in HR practice. Indeed, such a bridge might overcome the dangers of exclusive reliance by practitioners on 'experience', which can lead to a situation of 'superstitious learning' where past experiences are replicated without any evaluation of issues such as 'cause', 'context' or 'important factors' and which can lead to operational inefficiencies and strategic failures. Your own experience or your reading of business pages in newspapers or news websites might provide you with examples where this has occurred; perhaps where a new chief executive or director has joined an organisation and tried to replicate the system that was successful in their last company only to find that the approach is not as transferable as was assumed and a crisis occurs. Such a scenario can also occur at a national level where national policy relating to HR or human capital is formulated in one country to 'copy' the HR practices that have been developed in other continents, only to find that there are unexpected (and often very significant) factors that make these approaches much less successful.

Accessible HR research can transform HR practice and excellent HR practice innovations have much to offer for 'theory development'. In an area such as HRM and HRD, a productive relationship between research, policy and practice is highly desirable but remains stubbornly problematic for three main reasons.

TIME PRESSURES, DEMANDS, REWARD SYSTEMS AND PRIORITIES

An important reason for the gap between academic and practice communities is the different time pressures, demands, reward systems and priorities of the two communities. This leads them to make different judgements about the 'value' of different types of HRM knowledge and to formulate different views about information quality and relevance. For academics, institutional and government cultures and policies mean that they have to prioritise conceptual work that has the potential to make a lasting 'contribution to knowledge'. As a result, research projects tend to go on for a long time and focus on 'depth' and analysis. In addition, there is a potential 'time-delay' of up to five years between an original research process and its publication in a scholarly journal. Research of this type is highly unlikely to be appealing to many HR practitioners.

Management initiatives rarely occur as an idealised process of logical planning, control, communication and co-ordination. In reality, managerial work, in HR as elsewhere in organisations, is fragmented and characterised by the need to deal with many different issues at the same time (Gifford 2007, Hutchinson and Purcell 2007). For HR practitioners the priority is to achieve multiple results in a short timeframe and to provide a rapid response to changing management priorities. As a result, practitioners find themselves launching new initiatives and organisational processes that require rapid evaluation and, in such circumstances, 'practice' runs ahead of 'theory'. Developments in managerial coaching, talent management and human capital management are all examples of where this has occurred in recent years.

Managers under pressure, therefore, are always likely to prefer accessible research that is 'strikingly packaged' and well publicised, although there is a danger here because this can lead to oversimplified and naive forms of knowledge which, over time, have limited value.

MYSTIFICATION OF RESEARCH

Second, a factor that inhibits the impact of HR research is the perceived 'mystery' and jargon of the research process itself. It is not just international students who may find the language of research methods and of academics to be inaccessible; this is a common complaint of time-starved HR practitioners in demanding organisational roles. Equally, the 'business-speak' language used in many organisations can also seem mystifying to those 'on the outside' who do not understand the 'jargon'. As you will have discovered as you undertook your course, members of the academic community are encouraged to spend most of their time publishing 'high-quality' research in a small number of academic journals that are expressed in difficult and conceptual ways. However, practitioners, particularly once they have completed their course, hardly ever access these journals and prefer other forms of accessible information. As indicated in Chapter 1, higher status is given by governments and research-orientated higher education institutions to research that is focused on describing, explaining and predicting phenomena (sometimes referred to as 'Mode 1' research). This tradition has, over time, become progressively embedded within the academic community as an indicator of 'worth' and 'quality' and so academics give less time to the complementary (Mode 2) form of research which focuses on designing solutions to 'applied' problems with more immediate practitioner relevance. The preference for 'pure' or mode 1 approaches to research means that, even when highly relevant HRM knowledge is generated by researchers, these findings are rarely if ever communicated in a way that busy managers can access.

Dissemination and communication of research findings and outcomes is a key issue for any 'bridging' between the research and practice communities. It is not just academics who do not share their work with practitioners. Most practice-orientated student research reports or dissertations, once completed, are put somewhere safe and never read or discussed again. If research outcomes are to be applied and developed in practice, therefore, it is important that HR practitioner-researchers are willing and able to articulate the development of their understanding and learning so that those not directly involved in an investigation or piece of research can take something from it.

SEPARATION OF HR RESEARCH FROM HR POLICY AND HR PRACTICE

A third factor that inhibits the impact of HR research in practice may be a 'separation of roles' within the HR community. Large-scale research, for example, tends to be undertaken by and in university departments by those who specialise in it. Policy decisions, which may or may not be informed by such large-scale research, are made by a different group of people, such as those working in government departments or those in strategic decision-making roles in large organisations. The communication and implementation of those policy decisions is the responsibility of yet another group of HR practitioners and managers. The effect of the lack of 'ownership' is to diminish the impact of HR research. This separation of roles stems from an assumption by policy-makers and many academics of an 'objectivist' and linear process involved in research. (Objectivist assumptions about research are discussed in Chapter 1.) This assumes that knowledge is generated by academics as 'research outcomes' that are then disseminated to be adopted, adapted or applied by practitioners (Nutley et al 2007). While this is a convenient 'common-sense' understanding of research (which underpins the argument for evidence-based HR featured in Activity 12.3), there is very little evidence that this actually occurs. Both research and practice occur in dynamic contexts involving multiple stakeholders and are characterised by messy and often fragmented processes (Upton and Egan 2010).

The argument of this book is that the relationship between research and practice is best understood as a constructivist process (also discussed in Chapter 1) which is complex and multifaceted. Both academics and practitioners 'frame' and understand knowledge of HR in the light of their tacit knowledge and pre-existing experience. Rather than bemoan the lack of 'evidence-based HR practitioners' (Rousseau and Barends 2011), I argue for a more productive and synergistic relationship between practice-aware academic researchers and research-aware HR practitioners. This is possible if both communities engage in a process of interaction which accepts that knowledge of HR is 'provisional' and likely to be developed through 'messy' and socially interactive processes. In such circumstances, both academic and organisational cultures could play a mediating role to narrow the 'cultural gap' between the two 'worlds' to promote greater collaboration and co-production of relevant and robust knowledge and understanding of the HR field. Good-quality HR research and excellence in HR practice both involve systematically investigating people management and development issues to increase knowledge and underpin effective action. Therefore, HR research should be inextricably involved with the 'real world', driven by the need of practitioners to solve problems, to evaluate innovative practices and to develop and implement new forms of HR intervention. HR research, therefore, has the potential to help organisations change and, at the same time, to generate knowledge (Coghlan and Brannick 2009). This approach to practitioner research and to researcher-practitioners accepts a relationship between the research topic and methods and between researchers and participants. Such action-orientated forms of research can be undertaken by organisations of all sizes and sectors. It requires a systematic and rigorous approach to defining a research issue, problem or opportunity and also to gather and analyse data of good quality. These forms of practitioner-researcher partnerships have been used in a range of management development, organisation development, HRM and HRD settings (see, for example, Burgoyne and James 2006, Conklin and Hart 2009). However, it is difficult for academic researchers to 'let go' of traditional research assumptions and so action-orientated practitioner-researcher projects are largely overlooked by 'mainstream' academic traditions and very few systematic evaluations of the approach have been published.

There are a number of benefits that could be achieved if a closer relationship between HR practice and research were achieved. From a practitioner perspective, research enables practitioners to:

- recognise tensions in good practice
- identify alternative options and courses of action
- understand the issues involved in different practices to improve them
- enable fast, reflective action.

Theory and research will not provide you or any other practitioner with one 'prescription' for success. However, engaging with research processes and findings can help you to build up a set of alternatives. These can form part of any practitioner's repertoire when strategic, policy-level or practical issues arise. However, it requires that HR practitioners keep up their set of alternatives through engaging in research projects themselves and staying up to date with both research innovations and practice developments. Aspirations of finding 'one right way' or one 'quick fix' are likely to lead to disappointment over the medium and long term. However, engaging with and participating in research can make you aware of important concepts and give you insight into knowledge and understanding about important issues. On occasions, learning about (or discovering for ourselves) new research insights might change our attitudes, or those of important colleagues, and so it might lead to much needed changes in practice or policy. Equally, a practice-led research agenda has a lot to offer for the academic community. 'Experimentation' through the implementation of new practices can stimulate new concepts and understanding; theory can be refined by practice and new and relevant areas for research can emerge.

Although 'building a bridge' (or 'walking in the middle of the street') to make the best of both theory and practice is not the easiest of options for HR practitioners, it provides a more robust basis that can cope in times of economic challenge as well as growth. Being an effective practitioner-researcher should not involve trying to fulfil two separate roles at the same time, nor should it involve 'waiting' for academic researchers to disseminate the outcomes of their extended studies. Instead, the aim is to develop an approach to work that is neither typical practitioner nor typical researcher. Instead of seeing practitioners (on one side of the street) as people who 'consume' relevant knowledge that has been generated elsewhere and researchers who 'generate' knowledge on their 'side of the street', the practitioner-research role means that HR professionals can become part of and add value to the process of generating knowledge as practical experiences and issues are included in the process. In this way research and practice together can provide a valuable 'ingredient' in HR decision-making processes in organisations.

DEVELOPING EFFECTIVE PRACTITIONER-RESEARCHERS

If research and practice are to become more closely linked, there are implications for both practitioners and researchers. First, it is important to value the activity of systematic research within the role of HR practitioners at all levels and within all types of employing organisation. 'Applied' research within organisations is a valuable activity and, when done well, the activity deserves affirmation by both practitioners and academics (Robson 2011).

Second, it is important to see the 'research' process as a part of the 'HR toolkit' of effective practitioners. Good-quality HR research and theory can be just as relevant to operational as to strategic issues. The distinction between a professional 'HR researcher' and a professional 'HR practitioner' is a false one. Some professionals may engage more with 'research', others may engage more with 'practice', but it is only when the role of 'practitioner-researcher' is accepted as valid that the research process itself will be demystified. Those whose role focuses more on research can assist the 'demystification' process by communicating the outcomes of their research in ways that suit the timescales and priorities of practitioners and by using language that is accessible. At the same time, those engaged in HR practice should 'make a nuisance' of themselves to influence the research agenda of universities and research institutes and ensure that a balance is achieved between the rigour of an excellent research process and the relevance of the issue or topic that is being researched.

This book celebrates and encourage the contribution of research undertaken by 'practitioner-researchers' where 'local theory' (Coghlan and Brannick 2009), which is relevant to particular organisations, can be developed, evaluated and revised as appropriate. These forms of research are as valuable as specialised and highly theoretical projects undertaken by groups of researchers in universities and research centres. Where practitioner-researchers, and those who work with them, have been involved in gathering and analysing data relevant to organisational problems or issues, there is more chance of effective implementation of the solutions that their work suggests. As practitioner-researchers reflect on and learn from the research processes they engage with, there is also more chance that the benefits will be realised to the benefit of the individuals involved and the organisation(s) in which the research took place.

If the premise of this book – that systematic research is a valuable process – is accepted, it is also worth considering how HR research may develop in the future. One of the major themes of this book has involved a discussion about the usefulness of both objectivist and constructivist 'world-views' about research in HR, in business and in the social sciences more widely. Will HR research continue to be dominated by the assumptions of an objectivist and deductive approach? Will HR research increasingly try to access and understand individuals' perceptions of the world of work from more of an interpretevist or social constructivist perspective? Is the 'mixed methods' approach likely to be seen as the most appropriate way forward?

This book does not seek to negate the positive benefits of systematically undertaken research processes that **describe** current practices, but it sets out to raise the profile of research that **explores** the dimensions of HR issues and problems from the perspective of both practitioners and researchers. If practitioner-researcher projects, which are advocated in this book, become more integrated within professional practice, it is likely that a mixed methods approach, involving a justified use of both quantitative and qualitative data, will become a feature of HR research (Gill et al 2010, Bryman and Bell 2007).

Finally, it is important to explore the characteristics, or competences, that might underpin an effective 'practitioner-researcher'. The advantages and disadvantages of this role are considered in Chapter 1. Having explored the different features of the research process in the main body of this book, it is worth a consideration of the qualities of an effective practitioner-researcher (Coghlan and Brannick 2009, Nutley et al 2007):

- **Being critical and committed:** implicit preconceptions about issues and situations are inevitable if you are part of or close to the organisation being researched. The effective practitioner-researcher will, therefore, be able to critically evaluate and question 'received wisdom' at the same time as maintaining and communicating a commitment to the development of the organisation. In this way they will challenge organisational assumptions and encourage 'paradigm shifts'.
- **Encourage research enthusiasts but be realistic about limits:** organisational realities may make it difficult for some research to be undertaken or taken seriously. It is important, therefore, to 'aim high' but, at the same time, to be prepared and able to work within the limits of organisational realities.
- **Be independent and work well with others:** as a part of the organisation, practitioner-researchers have access to a range of contacts and sources of information. At the same time it is important to retain independence as grounding for the research process.
- **Take ownership of research through being proactive and reflective:** as well as being action-orientated the effective practitioner-researcher must reflect on the wider context of the problem or issue that is being researched, both within the organisation and with regard to practice and developments outside of the organisation. It will also involve promoting the dissemination of the findings of studies so that they can inform the development of practice and understanding in other organisations and contexts.
- **See 'insights for learning' as equally important as metrics-based 'return on investment':** practitioners who are only focused on the next or last three months are unlikely to be able to engage with the more enduring benefits of a research–practice synergy. Academic research rarely provides 'quick fixes'; its value is in the way it can help practitioners and organisations develop and sustain effective practice over the long term in work situations that are often messy and ambiguous.

Achieving good-quality practitioner-relevant research also requires members of the academic community to reassess their assumptions. Practitioner involvement in research will not occur unless those responsible for research projects are prepared to integrate practitioner involvement into their systems and practices, acknowledge the value of instrumental as well as conceptual knowledge, 'translate' their research findings into practitioner-accessible language and encourage people who are able to make links between organisations or practitioners with particular HR knowledge needs or opportunities and researchers who would be able to work with them to examine the issues in a scholarly and systematic way.

Achieving a bridge between the worlds of academic HR research and HR practice also requires action from institutional leaders. Practitioners working alone will not achieve a closer integration between the 'established domains' of academic research organisations, employers, professional bodies or sector-wide institutions. What is needed is:

- **institutional interaction** to embed research through meaningful research–practice partnerships and two-way flows of information
- **influence channels** facilitated by professional bodies such as the CIPD to foster research champions who can gradually change the mindsets and actions of practitioners and researchers
- **alignment of research with 'organisational excellence'** to generate a 'user-pull' focus and encourage research use to be seen as part of the professional development of any practitioner and as part of the organisation development of employing organisations
- **incentives and reinforcement** where the use of current research is affirmed and recognised through both extrinsic and intrinsic reward processes.

SUMMARY

- The role of many HR practitioners is fragmented and characterised by the need to deal with many issues at the same time. As a result managers tend not to access and evaluate the findings of many HR research projects.
- Within the HR profession the processes of 'research', 'policy formulation' and 'action and implementation' are undertaken by different groups of professionals. The lack of involvement in the process as a whole can limit the impact of research findings in HR.
- Many HR practitioners are reluctant to engage in research because they believe it is complex, difficult and mysterious.
- As practitioner-researchers reflect on and disseminate the outcomes of their research more widely, their work can have more impact within the profession as a whole and contribute to the development of HR practice in an incremental and credible way.
- There are many ways in which you can communicate your research findings to others. These include: internal reports, presentations and updates undertaken within one or more organisations and more 'public' means of communication through social media opportunities or through face-to-face networks and professional publications.
- Communicating your research insights to non-academic audiences requires that you produce less detailed content, use accessible language and focus on broad issues rather than the detail. Non-academic audiences are interested in hearing your recommendations for action and expect you to write persuasively and indicate the benefits of your findings for organisational performance.
- Research should make a positive impact on the contribution of HR to work organisations. The practitioner-researcher can add value to organisational

decision-making processes by undertaking robust research that is grounded in practice and organisational contexts.

- A key skill for all HR practitioner-researchers is to question implicit understandings of HR issues within their organisations.
- As more HR professionals engage with the role of 'practitioner-researcher' in organisations so the research process itself can become demystified.
- Different approaches to research are valuable in systematically exploring and examining people management and development issues to increase knowledge and underpin effective action; no one approach should be 'privileged' over others.
- Effective practitioner-researchers have to be critical and committed, independent and collaborative, ambitious and realistic, and proactive and reflective.

FINAL REVIEW AND REFLECT

As indicated in Chapter 11, research reports that are part of a CIPD professionally accredited qualification route are expected to provide some reflection about how the research process has contributed to your personal and professional development. This chapter urges you to go further. Having reflected on what you have learned through this demanding process, it urges you to consider how – as a result of the capabilities of effective research and scholarship you have developed – it would be possible to bring together the often separate worlds of academic researchers and HR practitioners to ensure a greater synergy between the two fields.

Taking stock

1   What opportunities might there be to disseminate the findings from your project? What skills will you need to share what you have learned more widely?

2   What features of your research benefited from your involvement with the organisation(s) in which you carried out your project? What have you learned about the organisation that you might not otherwise have been able to learn?

3   What relationships with practitioners have you developed to achieve your project objectives? What factors have helped you to achieve this?

4   What relationships with academics have you developed to achieve your project objectives? How might you build on these relationships to enable you to continue the dialogue between practice and research?

Future options

5   What skills and qualities, relevant to being a practitioner-researcher, would you like to further develop in the future? How might you go about developing in these areas?

EXPLORE FURTHER

Web Links (Social Media Sites)

HRM: The Journal – http://hrmthejournal.ning.com/?xg_source=msg_mes_network

CIPD Professional Communities discussion boards – http://www.cipd.co.uk/community

CIPD blogs – http://www.cipd.co.uk/blogs/

Twitter – https://twitter.com/

Facebook – http://en-gb.facebook.com/

LinkedIn – http://uk.linkedin.com/

YouTube – http://www.youtube.com/

Myspace – http://uk.myspace.com/

Reading

Day, A. (2008) *How to get research published in journals*. Aldershot: Gower.

Hayes, J. (2007) *The theory and practice of change management*. Basingstoke: Palgrave Macmillan.

Nutley, S.M., Walter, I. and Davies, H.T.O. (2007) *Using evidence: how research can inform public services*. Bristol: Policy Press.

Robson, C. (2011) *Real world research: a resource for social scientists and practitioner-researchers*. Oxford: Wiley.

References

Abratt, R. and Penman, N. (2002) Understanding factors affecting salespeople's perceptions of ethical behavior in South Africa, *Journal of Business Ethics*, 35: 269–80.

Ali, A., Gibbs, M. and Camp, R. (2000) Human resources strategy: the Ten Commandments perspective, *International Journal of Sociology and Social Policy*, 20(5/6): 114–32.

Alias, M. and Suradi, Z. (2008) Concept mapping: a tool for creating a literature review, in A.J. Cañas, P. Reiska, M. Åhlberg and J.D. Novak (eds), *Third International Conference on Concept Mapping.* Tallinn, Estonia and Helsinki, Finland [online]. Available at: http://cmc.ihmc.us/cmc2008papers/cmc2008-p048.pdf

Applied Ethics Resources on WWW [online] http://www.ethicsweb.ca/resources/research/index.html

Association of Internet Researchers. (2002) *Ethical decision making and internet research*[online] http://aoir.org/reports/ethics.pdf

Atherton, A. and Elsmore, P. (2007) A dialogue on the merits of using software for qualitative data analysis, *Qualitative Research in Organizations and Management: An International Journal*, 2(1): 62–77.

Avolio, B.J. and Gardner, W.L. (2005) Authentic leadership development: getting to the root of positive forms of leadership, *The Leadership Quarterly*, 16(3): 315–38.

Babin, B.J. and Boles, J.S. (1996) The effects of perceived co-worker involvement and supervisor support on service provider role stress, performance and job satisfaction, *Journal of Retailing*, 72(1): 57–75.

Bamber, G., Lansbury, R.D. and Wailes, N. (2004) *International and comparative employment relations: globalisation and the developed market economies.* London, Sage.

Banks, M. (2007) *Using visual data in qualitative research.* Thousand Oaks, CA: Sage.

Bauer, M.W. and Gaskell, G. (eds) (2000) *Qualitative research with text, image and sound.* London: Sage.

Bazely, P. (2007) *Qualitative data analysis with NVivo.* London: Sage.

Bell, J. (2005) *Doing your research project.* Maidenhead: Open University Press.

Bellizzi, J.A. and Hite, R.E. (1989) Supervising unethical salesforce behavior, *Journal of Marketing*, 53: 36–47.

Bergman, M.M. (2011) The good, the bad, and the ugly in mixed methods research and design, *Journal of Mixed Methods Research*, 5(4): 271–5.

Biggam, J. (2011) *Succeeding with your master's dissertation.* Maidenhead: Open University Press.

Birkinshaw, P. (2010) *Freedom of information: the law, the practice and the ideal.* Cambridge: Cambridge University Press.

Blaxter, L., Hughes, C. and Tight, M. (2006) *How to research.* Buckingham: Open University Press.

Boedecker, K.A., Morgan, F.W. and Stoltman, J.J. (1991) Legal dimensions of salespersons' statements: a review and managerial suggestions, *Journal of Marketing*, 55: 70–80.

Bourque, L.B. and Fieldler, E.P. (1995) *How to conduct self-administered and mail surveys.* London: Sage.

Boxall, P. and Purcell, J. (2003) *Strategy and human resource management.* Basingstoke: Palgrave Macmillan.

Brett-Davies, M. (2007) *Doing a successful research project: using qualitative or quantitative methods.* Basingstoke: Palgrave Macmillan.

Brocket, J. (2011) Stress tops list of long-term absence causes, *PM Online*, 5 October [online] http://www.peoplemanagement.co.uk/pm/sections/misc/search/all-of-people-management.htm?q=Stress%20tops%20list%20of%20long-term%20absence%20causes

Brown, R.B. (2006) *Doing your dissertation in business and management: the reality of researching and writing.* London: Sage.

Bryman, A. (ed.) (1988) *Doing research in organisations.* London: Routledge.

Bryman, A. (1989) *Research methods and organisation studies.* London: Unwin Hyman.

Bryman, A. (2006) Integrating quantitative and qualitative research, *Qualitative Research*, 6(1): 97–103.

Bryman, A. and Bell, E. (2007) *Business research methods.* Oxford: Oxford University Press.

Bryman, A. and Cramer, D. (1997) *Quantitative data analysis for social scientists.* London: Routledge.

Burgoyne, J. and James, K.T. (2006) Towards best of better practice in corporate leadership development: operational issues in mode 2 and design science research, *British Journal of Management*, 17: 303–16.

Burnard, P., Gill, P., Stewart, K., Treasure, E. and Chadwick, B. (2008) Analysing and presenting qualitative data, *British Dental Journal*, 204(8): 429–32.

Bushe, G.R. (2007) Appreciative inquiry is not (just) about the positive, *OD Practitioner*, 39(4): 30–5.

Cavana R., Delahaye, B. and Sekaran, U. (2001) *Applied business research: qualitative and quantitative methods.* Queensland: John Wiley & Sons Australia Ltd.

Charmaz, K. (2006) *Constructing grounded theory: a practical guide through qualitative data analysis.* London: Sage.

Chartered Institute of Personnel and Development. (2006) *The changing role of the trainer – people development in transition.* London: CIPD.

Chartered Institute of Personnel and Development. (2009) *Coaching at the sharp end: developing and supporting the line manager as coach* [online] http://www.cipd.co.uk/hr-resources/practical-tools/developing-line-manager-coaching.aspx

Chartered Institute of Personnel and Development. (2011) *Sustainable organisational performance: what really makes a difference?* [online] http://www.cipd.co.uk/binaries/5287STFfinalreportWEB.pdf

Chartered Institute of Personnel and Development. (2012) *Code of Conduct* [online] http://www.cipd.co.uk/about/code-of-conduct-review/profco.htm

Clarke, G.M. and Cooke, D. (1998) *A basic course in statistics.* London: Arnold.

Clegg, F.G. (1983) *Simple statistics.* Cambridge: Cambridge University Press.

Clough, P. and Nutbrown, C. (2007) *A student's guide to methodology.* London: Sage.

Cobanoglu, C., Warde, B. and Moreo, P. (2001) A comparison of mail, fax, and webbased survey methods, *International Journal of Market Research*, 43(4): 441–52.

Coghlan, D. (2007) Insider action research doctorates: generating actionable knowledge, *Higher Education*, 54: 293–306.

Coghlan, D. and Brannick, T. (2009) *Doing action research in your own organisation.* London: Sage.

Cohen, L. and Holliday, M. (1996) *Practical statistics for students.* London: Paul Chapman.

Collis, J. and Hussey, R. (2009) *Business research: a practical guide for undergraduate and postgraduate students.* Basingstoke: Palgrave.

Conklin, T.A. and Hart, R.K. (2009) Appreciative inquiry in management education: measuring the success of co-created learning, *Organization Management Journal*, 6: 89–104.

Cooper, R.W. and Frank, G.L. (2002) Ethical challenges in the two main segments of the insurance industry: key considerations in the evolving financial services marketplace, *Journal of Business Ethics*, 36: 5–20.

Cooperrider, D. and Srivastva, S. (1987) Appreciative inquiry in organizational life, in R.W. Woodman and W.A. Passmore (eds), *Research in organizational change and development*, Vol. 1, pp129–69. Greenwich, CT: JAI.

Cooperrider, D.I., Whitney, D., Stavros, J. and Fry, R. (2008) *Appreciative inquiry handbook: for leaders of change.* Brunswick, OH: Crown Custom Publishing.

Cottrell, S. (2008) *The study skills handbook.* Basingstoke: Palgrave Macmillan.

Couper, M.P., Traugott, M. and Lamias, M. (2001) Web survey design and administration, *Public Opinion Quarterly*, 65(1): 230–53.

Cowton, C.J. (1998) The use of secondary data in business ethics research, *Journal of Business Ethics*, 17(4): 423–34.

Creswell, J. (2009) *Research design: qualitative, quantitative and mixed methods approaches.* London: Sage.

Damanpour, F. and Gopalakrishnan, S. (1998) Theories of organizational structure and innovation adoption, *Journal of Engineering and Technology Management*, 15(1): 1–24.

Day, A. (2008) *How to get research published in journals.* Aldershot: Gower.

Denscombe, M. (2010) *The good research guide.* Maidenhead: McGraw-Hill.

deVaus, D.A. (2002) *Surveys in social research.* London: Routledge.

DeWalt, K.M. and DeWalt, B.R. (2002) *Participant observation: a guide for field workers.* Oxford: Rowman Altamira.

Diamantopoulos, A. and Schlegelmilch, B. (1997) *Taking the fear out of data analysis.* London: Dryden.

Dillman, D.A. (1999) *Mail and internet surveys: the tailored design method.* New York: John Wiley and Sons.

Dochartaigh, N.O. (2007) *Internet research skills.* London: Sage.

Doherty, N., Dickman, M. and Mill, T. (2010) Mobility attitudes and behaviours among young Europeans, *Career Development International*, 15(4): 378–400.

Dopson, S., Fitzgerald, L. and Ferlie, E. (2008) Understanding change and innovation in healthcare settings: reconceptualising the active role of context, *Journal of Change Management*, 8(3–4): 213–31.

Dubinsky, A.J., Howell, R.D., Ingram, T.N. and Bellenger, D.N. (1986) Salesforce socialization, *Journal of Marketing*, 50(4): 192–207.

Dunfee, T.W. and Gunther, R. (1999) Ethical issues in financial services, *Business & Society Review*, 104: 5–10.

Easterby-Smith, M., Golden-Biddle, K. and Locke, K. (2008) Working with pluralism: determining quality in qualitative research, *Organisational Research Methods*, 11(3): 419–29.

Easterby-Smith, M., Thorpe, R. and Lowe, A. (2003) *Management research: an introduction.* London: Sage.

Echlin, B. (2011) *NVivo 9 essentials.* Lulu.com.

Eden, C. and Huxham, C. (1996) Action research for management research, *British Journal of Management*, 7(1): 75–86.

Eden, C. and Huxham, C. (2006) Researching organizations using action research, in S.R. Clegg, T.B. Lawrence and W.R. Nord (eds) *The Sage handbook of organization studies.* London: Sage.

Eisenhardt, K.M. (1989) Building theories from case study research, *The Academy of Management Review*, 14(4): 532–50.

Ellinger, A.D., Ellinger, A.E., Bachrach, D.G., Wang, Y-L. and Bas, A.B.E. (2011) Organizational investments in social capital, managerial coaching, and employee work-related performance, *Management Learning*, 42(1): 67–85.

Ellinger, A.E., Elmadağ, A.B. and Ellinger, A.D. (2007) An examination of organizations' frontline service employee development practices, *Human Resource Development Quarterly*, 18(3): 293–314.

Elliott, J. (2005) *Using narrative in social research: qualitative and quantitative approaches.* London: Sage.

Elo, S. and Kyngas, H. (2008) The qualitative content analysis process, *Journal of Advanced Nursing*, 62(1): 107–15.

Erickson, B.H. and Nosanchuck, T.A. (1992) *Understanding data.* Maidenhead: Open University Press.

Eurostat. (2002) *EU labour force survey.* Luxembourg: Eurostat.

Farquhar, J.D. (2012) *Case study research for business.* London: Sage.

Field, A. (2009) *Discovering statistics using SPSS for Windows.* London: Sage.

Fisher, C. (2007) *Researching and writing a dissertation: a guidebook for business students.* Harlow: Pearson Education.

Fitzgerald, S.P., Oliver, C. and Hoxsey, J.C. (2010) Appreciative inquiry as a shadow process, *Journal of Management Inquiry*, 19(3): 220–33.

Ford, R. (2008) Complex adaptive systems and improvisation theory: toward framing a model to enable continuous change, *Journal of Change Management*, 8(3–4): 173–98.

Fourage, D. and Ester, P. (2007) *Factors determining international and regional migration in Europe*. European Foundation for the Improvement of Living and Working Conditions, Report EF/07/09/EN [online]: www.eurofound.europa.eu/pubdocs/2007/09/en/1/ef0709en.pdf

Fowler, E.J. (2009) *Survey research methods*. Newbury Park, CA: Sage.

Fox, M., Martin, P. and Green, G. (2007) *Doing practitioner research*. London: Sage.

Fraser, D.M. (1977) Ethical dilemmas and practical problems for the practitioner-researcher, *Educational Action Research*, 5(1): 161–71.

Gerring, J. (2007) *Case study research: principles and practice*. Cambridge: Cambridge University Press.

Gifford, J. (2007) *The changing HR function*. CIPD survey report [online] Retrieved on 12 March 2009 from http://www.cipd.co.uk/NR/exeres/630F706F-573B-4B5C-BDEF-3705E71BF4E8.htm

Gill, J., Johnson, P. and Clark, M. (2010) *Research methods for managers*. London: Sage.

Grant, S. and Humphries, M. (2006) Critical evaluation of appreciative inquiry, *Action Research*, 4(4): 401–18.

Gundlach, G.T. and Murphy, P.E. (1993) Ethical and legal foundations of relational marketing exchanges, *Journal of Marketing*, 57: 35–46.

Hahn, C. (2008) *Doing qualitative research using your computer*. London: Sage.

Hammersley, M. (2005) *The politics of social research*. London: Sage.

Hantrais, L. (1996) Comparative research methods, *Social Research Update*, 13: 1–8.

Harris, L. (2007) The changing nature of the HR function in UK local government and its role as an 'employee champion', *Employee Relations*, (1): 34–47.

Hart, C. (2010) *Doing your master's dissertation*. London: Sage.

Hart, R.K., Conklin, T.A., and Allen, S.J. (2008) Individual leader development: an appreciative inquiry approach, *Advances in Developing Human Resources*, 10(15): 632–50.

Hashim, J. (2010) Human resource management practices on organisational commitment: the Islamic perspective, *Personnel Review*, 39(6): 785–99.

Hatch, M.J. (1997) *Organization theory: modern, symbolic and postmodern perspectives.* Oxford: Oxford University Press.

Hayes, J. (2007) *The theory and practice of change management.* Basingstoke: Palgrave Macmillan.

Hubeman, M. (1994) Research utilization: the state of the art, *Knowledge and Policy: The International Journal of Knowledge Transfer and Utilization,* 7(4): 13–33.

Hutchinson, S. and Purcell, J. (2007) *Line managers in reward, learning and development.* London: Chartered Institute of Personnel and Development.

Iacono, J., Brown, A. and Holtham, C. (2009) Research methods – a case example of participant observation, *The Electronic Journal of Business Research Methods,* 7(1): 39–46 [online] www.ejbrm.com

Institute of Business Ethics. *Codes of ethics: introduction to ethics policies, and programmes and codes* [online] http://www.ibe.org.uk/index.asp?upid=57&msid=11

Jankowicz, A.D. (2005) *Business research projects for students.* London: Thomson Learning.

Kane, E. (1995) *Doing your own research: basic descriptive research in the social sciences and humanities.* London: Marion Boyars.

Kirkpatrick, D. (1959) Techniques for evaluating training programs, *Journal of the American Society of Training and Development,* 13(11):3–9.

Knights, D. and Scarborough, H. (2010) In search of relevance: perspectives on the contribution of academic-practitioner networks, *Organization Studies,* 31: 1287–1309.

Kolb, D.A., Rubin, I.M. and McIntryre, J.M. (1979) *Organizational psychology: an experiential approach.* London: Prentice Hall.

Kristensen, S. (2004) *Learning by leaving: placements abroad as a didactic tool in the context of vocational education and training in Europe.* Luxembourg: CEDEFOP, Office for Official Publications of the European Communities.

Krueger, R.A. and Casey, M.A. (2000) *Focus groups: a practical guide for applied research.* Thousand Oaks, CA: Sage.

Lagace, R.R., Dahlstrom, R. and Gassenheimer, J.B. (1991) The relevance of ethical salesperson behavior on relationship quality: the pharmaceutical industry, *Journal of Personal Selling & Sales Management,* 11: 39–47.

Lee, N. and Lings, L. (2008) *Doing business research: a guide to theory and practice.* London: Sage.

Lewin, K. (1946) Action research and minority problems, *Journal of Social Issues,* 2: 34–6.

Lincoln, Y.S. and Guba, E. (1985) *Naturalistic enquiry*. Beverley Hills, CA: Sage.

Ludema, J.D. (2001) From deficit discourse to vocabularies of hope: the power of appreciation, in D.L. Cooperrider, P. Sorenson, D. Whitney and T. Yeager (eds), *Appreciative inquiry: an emerging direction for organization development*. Champaign, IL: Stipes.

Macfarlane, B. (2009) *Researching with integrity: the ethics of academic inquiry*. Abingdon: Routledge.

Marchington, M. and Wilkinson, A. (2008) *Human resource management at work: people management and development*. London: Chartered Institute of Personnel and Development.

Marsen, S. (2007) *Professional writing*. Basingstoke: Palgrave Macmillan.

Maslow, A.H. (1943) A theory of human motivation, *Psychological Review*, 50(4): 360–96.

Maylor, H. and Blackmon, K. (2005) *Researching business and management*. Basingstoke: Palgrave Macmillan.

McDonald, G. (2000) Cross-cultural methodological issues in ethical research, *Journal of Business Ethics*, 27: 89–104.

McLeod, D. and Clarke, N. (2009) *Engaging for success: enhancing performance through employee engagement* [online] http://webarchive.nationalarchives.gov.uk/+/http://www.bis.gov.uk/files/file52215.pdf

McMillan, K. and Weyer, J. (2008) *How to write dissertations and project reports*. Harlow: Pearson Education

McNiff, J. and Whitehead, J. (2011) *All you need to know about action research*. London: Sage.

Miles, M.B. and Huberman, A.M. (1994) *Qualitative data analysis: an expanded source book*. London: Sage.

Mitchell, W.J., Lewis, P.W. and Reinsch, N.L., Jr. (1992) Bank ethics: an exploratory study of ethical behaviors and perceptions in small, local banks, *Journal of Business Ethics*, 21: 197–205.

Mowday, R.T., Steers, R.M. and Porter, L.W. (1979) The measurement of organizational commitment, *Journal of Vocational Behavior*, 14(2): 224–47.

Neuman, W. (2011) *Basics of social research: qualitative and quantitative approaches*. International edition. Harlow: Pearson Education.

Nutley, S.M., Walter, I. and Davies, H.T.O. (2007) *Using evidence: how research can inform public services*. Bristol: Policy Press.

Oliver, P. (2010) *The student's guide to research ethics*. Maidenhead: McGraw-Hill.

Oliver, P. (2012) *Succeeding with your literature review: a handbook for students.* Maidenhead: Open University Press.

Oppenheim, A.N. (2001) *Questionnaire design, interviewing and attitude measurement.* London: Continuum International.

O'Reilly, K., Paper, D. and Marx, S. (2012) Demystifying grounded theory for business research, *Organizational Research Methods*, 15: 247–62.

Pallant, J. (2010) *SPSS survival manual.* Maidenhead: Open University Press.

People Management Online. (2012) *CIPD launches apprenticeship guidance: guide aims to ensure employers 'get full benefits' from schemes*, 3 February [online] http://www.peoplemanagement.co.uk/pm/articles/2012/02/cipd-launches-apprenticeship-guidance.htm

Peterson, R. (2000) *Constructing effective questionnaires.* Thousand Oaks, CA: Sage.

Quality Assurance Agency (QAA). (2008) *The framework for higher education qualifications in England, Wales and Northern Ireland* [online] http://www.qaa.ac.uk/Publications/InformationAndGuidance/Documents/FHEQ08.pdf

Quinton, S. and Smallbone, T. (2006) *Postgraduate research in business: a critical guide.* London: Sage.

Ray, J.L. and Smith, A.D. (2012) Using photographs to research organizations: evidence, considerations, and application in a field study, *Organizational Research Methods*, 15(2): 288–315.

Reason, P. and Bradbury, H. (2006) *Handbook of action research.* London: Sage.

Remenyi, D., Swan, N. and Van Den Assem, B. (2011) *Ethics protocols and research ethics committees.* Reading: Academic Publishing International Ltd.

Remenyi, D., Williams, B., Money, A. and Schwartz, E. (1998) *Doing research in business and management: an introduction to process and method.* London: Sage.

Richards, L. (2009) *Handling qualitative data: a practical guide.* London: Sage.

Roberts, B. (2007) *Getting the most out of the research experience.* London: Sage.

Robinson, S.A. and Dowson, P. (2012) *Business ethics in practice.* London: Chartered Institute of Personnel and Development.

Robson, C. (2011) *Real world research: a resource for social scientists and practitioner-researchers.* Oxford: Wiley.

Rogers, P.J. and Fraser, D. (2003) Appreciating appreciative inquiry, in H. Preskill and A.T. Coghlan (eds), *Using appreciative inquiry in evaluation*, pp75–83. San Francisco, CA: Jossey Bass.

Roma'n, S. (2003) The impact of ethical sales behaviour on customer satisfaction trust and loyalty to the company: an empirical study in the financial services industry, *Journal of Marketing Management*, 19(9/10): 915–49.

Roma'n, S. and Munuera, L. (2005) Determinants and consequences of ethical behaviour: an empirical study of salespeople, *European Journal of Marketing*, 39(5/6): 473–95.

Rose, D. and Sullivan, O. (1996) *Introducing data analysis for social scientists*. Maidenhead: Open University Press.

Rousseau, D.M. and Barends, E.G.R. (2011) Becoming an evidence-based HR practitioner, *Human Resource Management Journal*, 21(3): 221–35

Rugg, G. (2007) *Using statistics: a gentle introduction*. Maidenhead: Open University Press.

Rugg, G. and Petre, M. (2007) *A gentle guide to research methods*. Maidenhead: Open University Press.

Saunders, M., Lewis, P. and Thornhill, A. (2012) *Research methods for business students*. Harlow: Pearson Education.

Scott, J. (1990) *A matter of record*. Cambridge: Polity Press.

Scullion, H. and Collings, D. (eds) (2011) *Global talent management*. London: Routledge.

Selmer, J. and Lam, H. (2003) 'Third-culture kids': future business expatriates?, *Personnel Review*, 33(4): 430–45.

Sheldon, T. (2005) Making evidence synthesis more useful for management and policy-making, *Journal of Health Services Research and Policy*, 10(supp 1): 1–5.

Silverman, D. (2009) *Doing qualitative research: a practical handbook*. London: Sage.

Silverman, D. (2011) *Interpreting qualitative data*. London: Sage.

Smallbone, T. and Quinton, S. (2011) A three-stage framework for teaching literature reviews: a new approach, *International Journal of Management Education*, 9(4): 1–13.

Starkey, K. and Madan, P. (2001) Bridging the relevance gap: aligning stakeholders in the future of management research, *British Journal of Management*, Special issue 1: 3–26.

Steers, R.M. (1977) Antecedents and outcomes of organizational commitment, *Administrative Science Quarterly*, 22: 46–56.

Stephens, D. (2009) *Qualitative research in international setting: a practical guide*. Abingdon: Routledge.

Stevens, M. (2011) News review 2011: Phone hacking, *People Management Online*, 22 December [online]: http://www.peoplemanagement.co.uk/pm/articles/2011/12/news-review-2011-phone-hacking.htm

Stewart, D.W., Shamdasani, P.N. and Rook, D.W. (2007) *Focus groups*. London: Sage.

Swanson, R.A., Holton, E.F. and Holton, E. (2005) *Research in organizations: foundations and methods of inquiry*. San Francisco, CA: Berrett-Koehler.

Tashakkori, A. and Teddlie, C. (2010) Putting the human back in 'human research methodology': the researcher in mixed methods research, *Journal of Mixed Methods Research*, 4(4): 271–7.

Therborn, G. (2006) *Inequalities of the world: new theoretical frameworks, multiple empirical approaches*. London: Verso.

Trades Union Congress. (2010) *Focus on health and safety: trade union trends survey – TUC biennial survey of safety reps 2010* [online] http://www.tuc.org.uk/extras/safetyrepssurvey2010.pdf

Ulrich, D. (1997) *Human resource champions*. Boston, MA: Harvard University Press.

Upton, M.G. and Egan, T.M. (2010) Three approaches to multilevel theory building, *Human Resource Development Review*, 9(4): 333–56.

Van Aken, J.E. (2005) Management research as a design science: articulating the research products of mode 2 knowledge production in management, *British Journal of Management*, 16: 19–36.

Van de Ven, A. (2007) *Engaged scholarship: a guide for organizational and social research*. Oxford: Oxford University Press.

Walby, K. and Larsen, M. (2011) Access to information and freedom of information requests: neglected means of data production in the social sciences, *Qualitative Inquiry*, 18(1): 31–42.

Walker, J. and Almond, P. (2010) *Interpreting statistical findings: a guide for health professionals and students*. Maidenhead: Open University Press.

Watkins, S. and Mhor, B. (2001) *Appreciative inquiry: change at the speed of the imagination*. San Francisco, CA: Jossey-Bass Pfeiffer.

Watson, T.J. (2000) Management and interactive social science: critical participative research, *Science and Public Policy*, 27(3): 203–10.

Wells, P. (1994) Ethics in business and management research, in V.J. Wass and P.E. Wells (eds), *Principles and practice in business and management research*. Aldershot: Dartmouth.

West, M.A., Guthrie, J.P., Dawson, J.F., Borrill, C.S. and Carter, M. (2006) Reducing patient mortality in hospitals: the role of human resource management, *Journal of Organizational Behavior*, 27: 983–1002.

White, L. (2000) Changing the whole system in the public sector, *Journal of Organisational Change*, 13(2): 162–77.

Wotruba, T. (1990) A comprehensive framework for the analysis of ethical behavior, with a focus on sales organisations, *Journal of Personal Selling & Sales Management*, 10: 29–42.

Yin, R.K. (2009) *Case study research: design and methods.* Thousand Oaks, CA: Sage Publications.

Zikmund, W. (2009) *Business research methods.* London: Cengage Learning.

Glossary

Terms that may be useful in your research report or dissertation

Action research strategy	Research strategy concerned with changing activities or processes, which involves close collaboration between practitioners and researchers.
Analysis	The ability to break down data and clarify the nature of the component parts and the relationship between them.
Anonymity	The process of concealing the identity of participants in all documents resulting from the research.
CAQDAS	Computer-aided qualitative data analysis software.
Case study research strategy	An approach to research that uses a group of research methods to investigate a complex phenomenon where the boundaries between the situation and its context are not clear.
Categorising	The process of developing categories and subsequently attaching these categories to meaningful chunks or units of data.
Census	The collection and analysis of data from every possible case or group members in a population.
Central tendency measure	The generic term for statistics that provide an impression of those values that are common, middling or average. These are expressed as: the mean, the median or the mode.
Cluster sampling	Probability sampling procedure in which the population is divided into discrete groups prior to sampling. A random sample of these clusters is then drawn.
Comparative research strategy	The comparison of two or more cases to illuminate existing theory or generate theoretical insights as a result of contrasting findings uncovered through the comparison.
Concept	An abstract idea.
Confidentiality	Concern relating to the right of access to data provided by participants and in particular the need to keep these data secret or private.
Consent form	Written agreement of the participant to take part in the research and give their permission for data to be used in specified ways.
Contextual data	Additional data recorded when collecting primary or secondary data that reveals background information about the setting and the data collection.
Convenience sampling	Non-probability sampling procedure in which cases are selected opportunistically.
Correlation	The extent to which two variables are related to each other.

Correlation co-efficient	Number between –1 and +1 representing the strength and direction of two ranked or numerical variables. A value of 0 means the variables are perfectly independent.
Cross-sectional research	The study of a particular phenomenon across a range of cases at a particular time (a 'snapshot').
Data	Facts, opinions and statistics that have been collected together and recorded for reference or for analysis.
Descriptive statistics	Generic term for statistics that can be used to describe variables.
Dispersion measures	The spread of data within a data set. Two principal measures (the range and the standard deviation) express how the values for a variable are dispersed around the central tendency.
Empirical	Something which is observable by the senses.
Ethics (research ethics)	The application of fundamental moral ethical principles underpinning what are accepted as appropriate behaviours applied to research.
Experiential data	Data about the researcher's perceptions and feelings as the research develops.
Exploratory data analysis	The use of relatively simple techniques to understand the data.
Focus group	A facilitated group interview, composed of a small number of participants, in which the topic is clearly defined and interactive discussion between the participants is recorded.
Frequency distribution	Table for summarising data from one variable so that specific values can be read.
Grey literature	Sources such as government white papers and planning documents that are available in the public domain but are not the output of not a specific publishing house.
Hermeneutics	The study of the theory and practice of interpretation.
Histogram	Diagram for showing frequency distributions for a continuous data variable in which the area of each bar represents the frequency of occurrence.
Independent groups t-test	Statistical test to determine the likelihood that the values of a numerical data variable for two independent samples or groups are different. The test assesses the likelihood that any difference between these two groups occurred by chance alone.
Independent variable	Variable that causes changes to a dependent variable or variables.
Inductive approach	Research approach involving the development of theory or generalisations as a result of the observation of empirical data.
Informed consent	Position achieved when intended participants are fully informed about the use of research to be undertaken and their role in it, and where their consent to participate is freely given.

Interpretivist	A research approach that is concerned to understand how we as humans make sense of the world around us.
Interval data	Numerical data for which the interval between any two data variables can be stated but the relative difference between them is not meaningful.
Interviewee bias	An attempt by an interviewee to construct an account that hides some data or when they present themselves in a socially desirable role or situation.
Interviewer bias	Implicit or explicit attempt by an interviewer to introduce bias during an interview or where the appearance of behaviour of an interviewer has the effect of introducing bias in the interviewee's responses.
Line graph	Diagram for showing trends in data for a variable.
Literature review	Detailed and justified analysis and commentary of the merits and limitations of the literature in a chosen area, which demonstrates familiarity with what is already known about the research topic.
Longitudinal study	The study of a particular phenomenon over an extended period of time.
Matrix	Data supplied or displayed in the form of rows and columns.
Mean	The average value calculated by adding up the values of each case for a variable and dividing by the total number of cases.
Median	The middle value when all the values of a variable are arranged in order, sometimes known as the 50th percentile.
Method	The techniques and procedures used to obtain and analyse research data.
Methodology	The theory of how research should be undertaken; the philosophical framework within which research is conducted; the foundation upon which the research is based.
Mixed-method research	An approach to research that makes use of aspects of both positivism and interpretivism.
Mode	The most frequently occurring value of a variable.
Mono method	Use of a single data collection technique and corresponding analysis procedure or procedures.
Multiple bar chart	Diagram for comparing frequency distributions for categorical or grouped continuous data variables which highlights the highest and lowest values.
Multiple line graph	Diagram for comparing trends over time between numerical data variables.
Multiple methods	Use of more than one data collection technique and analysis procedure.
Negative correlation	Relationship between two variables for which, as the value of one variable increases, the value of the other variable decreases.

Negative skew	Distribution of numerical data for a variable in which the majority of the data are found bunched to the right with a long tail to the left.
Nominal data	Data that refers to descriptions.
Non-parametric statistic	Statistic designed to be used when data are not normally distributed. Often used with categorical data.
Non-probability sampling	Selection of sampling techniques in which the chance or probability of each case being selected is not known.
Non-response rate	The number of non-returned questionnaires as a percentage of the number distributed.
Normal distribution	Special form of the symmetric distribution in which the numerical data for a variable can be plotted as a bell-shaped curve.
Null hypothesis	Testable proposition stating that there is no significant difference or relationship between two or more variables.
Ordinal data	Data presented in an ordered fashion and the numbers assigned to the outcomes indicate the order of importance.
Parametric statistic	Statistic designed to be used when data are normally distributed. Used with numerical data.
Participant	The person from whom research data are gathered.
Participant researcher	Person who conducts research within an organisation for which they work.
Pie chart	Diagram frequently used for showing proportions for categorical data or a grouped continuous or discrete data variable.
Pilot test	Small-scale study to test a questionnaire, interview questions or observation schedule, to minimise the likelihood of respondents having problems in answering the questions and of data recording problems as well as to allow some assessment of the questions' validity and the reliability of the data that will be collected.
Population	The complete set of cases or group members.
Positive correlation	The relationship between two variables for which, as the value of one variable increases, the value of the other variable also increases.
Positive skew	Distribution of numerical data for a variable in which the majority of the data are found bunched to the left with a long tail to the right.
Positivism	An approach to research which usually attempts to establish cause-and-effect relationships.
Practitioner-researcher	Role occupied by a researcher when they are conducting research in an organisation, often their own, while fulfilling their normal working role.
Probability sampling	Selection of sampling techniques in which the chance of each case being selected from the population is known and is not zero.

Purposive sampling	Non-probability sampling procedure in which the judgement of the researcher is used to select the cases that make up the sample.
Qualitative data	Data in the form of words or meanings: non-numerical data or data that have not been quantified.
Quantitative data	Numerical data or data that represent the dimensions of what is being studied.
Random sampling	Probability sampling procedure that ensures that each case in the population has an equal chance of being included in the sample.
Range	The difference between the highest and the lowest values for a variable.
Ranking question	Closed question in which the respondent is offered a list of items and instructed to place them in rank order.
Rating question	Closed question in which a scaling device is used to record the respondent's response.
Ratio data	Numerical data for which the difference or 'interval' and relative difference between any two data values for a particular variable can be stated.
Raw data	Data for which little, if any, data processing has taken place.
Reflexive	The process of 'self-reference' where the researcher examines the interrelationship between their actions and the research context and outcomes.
Reliability	The extent to which data collection technique or techniques will yield consistent findings, similar observations would be made or conclusions reached by other researchers or there is transparency in how sense was made from the raw data.
Representative sample	Sample which represents exactly the population from which it is drawn.
Research	The systematic collection and interpretation of information with a clear purpose to find things out.
Research design	The framework that guides decisions about the collection and analysis of data.
Research ethics	The appropriateness of the researcher's behaviour in relation to the rights of those who become the subject of a research project or who are affected by it.
Research objectives	Clear, specific statements that identify what the researcher wishes to accomplish as a result of doing the research.
Research philosophy	Overarching term relating to the development of knowledge and the nature of that knowledge in relation to research.
Research population	Set of cases or group members that are being researched.
Research strategy	The general approach taken to answer research questions or achieve research objectives.
Respondent	The person who answers the questions, usually either in an interview or on a questionnaire (also referred to as a participant).

Response rate	The number of complete questionnaires returned as a proportion of the number distributed.
Sample	Sub-group or part of a larger population.
Sampling frame	The complete list of all cases in the population, from which a sample is drawn.
Scale	Measure of a concept, created by combining scores to a number of rating questions.
Scatter graph	Diagram for showing the relationship between two numerical or ranked variables.
Self-selection sampling	Non-probability sampling procedure in which the case (usually the individual) is allowed to identify their desire to be part of the sample.
Significance testing	Testing the probability of pattern such as a relationship between two variables occurring by chance alone.
Snowball sampling	Non-probability sampling procedure in which subsequent respondents are obtained from the information provided by initial respondents.
Stacked bar chart	Diagram for comparing totals and sub totals for all types of data variable.
Standard deviation	A measure of the average distance between all the values and the mean for a given variable. The smaller the standard deviation, the more similar are the values within the distribution.
Symmetric distribution	Description of the distribution of data for a variable in which the data are distributed equally either side of the highest frequency.
Systematic sampling	Probability sampling procedure in which the initial starting point is selected at random and then the cases are selected at regular intervals.
Table	Technique for summarising data from one or more variables so that specific values or instances can be read.
Theory	A logical model or framework of concepts that describes and explains how phenomena are related with each other and which would apply in a variety of circumstances.
Transcription	The written record of what a participant said in response to a question, or what participants said to each other in conversation, in their own words.
Triangulation	Data validation through cross-verification from more than two sources.
Validity	The extent to which a data collection method accurately measures what it was intended to do. Also the extent to which research findings are really about what they profess to be about.
Variable	Individual element or attribute upon which data have been collected.

| Variance | Statistic that measures the spread of data values; a measure of dispersion. The smaller the variance, the closer individual data variables are to the mean. The value of the variance is the square root of the standard deviation. |

Index